Credit Life
and
Disability Insurance

Credit Life and Disability Insurance

by

Gary Fagg
F.S.A., M.A.A.A.

Publisher:
CLICO Management, Inc.
Springfield, Ohio

Library of Congress Cataloging-in-Publication Data

Fagg, Gary, 1948–
Credit life and disability insurance.

Bibliography: p.
Includes index
1. Insurance, Credit life—United States.
2. Insurance, Credit disability—United States.
I.Title.
HG9977.F34 1986 368.3'2 86–21562
ISBN 0-9617162-0-7

TABLE OF CONTENTS

ACKNOWLEDGMENTS

This book began as a one-person project several years ago. So many people have contributed to the final result that I now have reservations about claiming authorship.

The work would not have succeeded without the support of the executive management of The Credit Life Insurance Company–Dwight Hollenbeck, Forrest J. Curtin, Lewis Boggs and the late Wesley Harrison. The combined experience of these men represents over 160 years in the credit insurance business. They were enthusiastic about the production of the book and were willing to see a significant amount of my time dedicated to its writing and publication.

An initial draft was completed in December, 1985 and a second draft was finished in April, 1986. Before the final draft was finished, over thirty people had made comments on parts of the text. These people expanded my knowledge of credit insurance and made the book more readable and accurate. While the time and effort of all these people is greatly appreciated, William F. Burfeind and David Bassindale provided extensive comments for which I am especially grateful.

The text as you read it is not precisely the way I wrote it. An actuary's version of the English language often differs somewhat from what most readers would expect. Preliminary editing was done by Pam Raikos and Nancy Prine, along with help from many technical reviewers. Formal editing was done by Dorothy Tegeler. The patience and assistance of these people is gratefully acknowledged.

Sam Booke, Sr., Charles M. Beardsley and Dr. Will Bagwell had a profound impact on my early personal and professional development. They instilled and nurtured in me a love of teaching and writing. More importantly, these three men, and the four executives of Credit Life, have set an example of how one should conduct oneself in business. They have all set high standards for honesty, integrity and quality of work product.

My wife, Mary Ann, and my assistant Mary Jane Tokosch, both provided support and assistance. Mary Jane maintained her cheerful disposition through numerous rewrites and drafts. Mary Ann had to put up with a strange work schedule and many nights alone while I sat at the office and worked.

Most of all, this book exists because of the people in the credit insurance industry. Very little of this text represents original thought on my part. It is simply a documentation of the products and procedures which have been developed by the people in the industry through the years. I hope the reader finds the book to be a worthy representation of our fine product and industry.

Gary Fagg
October, 1986

INTRODUCTION

"Neither a borrower, nor a lender be"
Hamlet

"Ah, take the cash, and let the credit go,"
The Rubaiyat of Omar Khayyam

Ignoring the advice of the poets, people have borrowed or lent money for thousands of years, but it has been in the last century that a major change has occurred in money brokering. Before, people borrowed primarily out of necessity to meet economic crises. Lenders were not always reputable and tended to prey on the financial stress of the borrower. Borrowing by consumers for goods they wanted, rather than just for items they had to have is a major economic distinction of twentieth century life. Financial institutions were established for the primary purpose of lending money to meet this growing demand.

In the first half of this century, the concept of borrowing money solely on an individual's earning power was introduced and accepted. Loans repaid in installments became the common standard. Initially, the installments were on a weekly basis, but gradually a monthly installment payment became the basis of most consumer goods lending. After World War II, the demand for consumer goods increased explosively. Consumers routinely borrowed to purchase automobiles and other goods. It became an acceptable and routine practice.

In the 1960s, consumer borrowing took a new direction with the widespread use of credit cards, which allowed the cardholder to borrow for any purpose, up to a preapproved limit. For today's consumer, borrowing is easy and convenient. We're surrounded by evidence as millions of consumers flex their "plastic borrowing muscle" each day.

The growth of financial institutions willing to lend has satisfied and, at the same time, fueled, the demand for borrowing. Credit unions, Morris Plan banks, finance companies, and acceptance corporations were the first to satisfy the demand. In the 1950s, commercial banks expanded into consumer lending and became a major force in consumer lending. Other lending organizations were formed to satisfy specialized needs, such as Production Credit Associations, which provide agricultural loans to farmers.

Consumer borrowing hinges on the central premise that the borrower can meet the debt obligations from his future wages and earning power. Future earnings serve as loan collateral. Since this premise was first introduced, lenders knew that the death or disability of the borrower could place the collateral of the loan in jeopardy. Insurance on the borrower's life and ability to work was introduced to protect the lender and cushion the borrower's loss.

Two specialty insurance products, *credit life insurance* and *credit disability insurance*, emerged to meet the specific needs associated with loan transactions. In general, credit life insurance pays off the loan obligation if the insured borrower or co-borrower dies. Credit disability insurance provides a monthly benefit equal to the loan's monthly payment if the primary borrower is disabled. Regulation of these products now requires that the insurance can only be sold in conjunction with a specific loan obligation. Because of this stipulation, the terms and conditions of a loan define the basic nature of coverage provided by a particular credit insurance policy.

Credit insurance products are a specialized subset of ordinary life and disability coverages. They share many of the characteristics of their ordinary insurance counterparts. Credit life insurance is simply term life insurance. Premiums are paid for life insurance protection for a specified term with specified amounts of insurance in force during the term of coverage. Most policy provisions are similar to their ordinary insurance counterparts. Credit disability insurance provides the same type of benefits as ordinary disability income policies. A monthly benefit is paid if the insured becomes disabled, once an initial waiting period of disability is satisfied. Policy provisions and the plans of benefit are similar to those found in the ordinary products.

However, the requirement that credit insurance products match a loan obligation and the marketing methods which evolved result in some characteristics which clearly set the coverages apart. Since the insurance product was tied to a specific debt, credit insurance pioneers developed a unique product structure when implementing the usual requirements for the insurance products. Loan balances are relatively small, so the amount of insurance sold has always been less than the average size of ordinary insurance policies. To meet the needs of the borrower, the insurance must be sold at the time the loan is extended. This resulted in a marketing approach where the products were offered to the borrower by the lender rather than by a fully trained insurance agent. To satisfy these criteria, policy forms, premium structures and underwriting conditions had to be simple. The following characteristics emerged to meet these conditions and apply to most credit insurance written today:

1. The average policy size is under $10,000, and the term of insurance is short, generally under sixty months.

2. The premium charged is a single premium paid at the inception of the policy. The premium is included in the amount advanced and financed along with the principal of the loan.

3. No underwriting conditions are imposed to qualify for the insurance except a maximum age limitation, generally

sixty-five. If a consumer qualifies for a loan, he qualifies for insurance if the loan is taken.

4. The same premium rate is charged to every consumer. There is just one rate for all ages and both sexes.

5. Coverage matches the loan obligation. Life insurance in force during the term of coverage is generally equal to the remaining payments due on the loan. The monthly disability benefit is equal to the loan's required monthly payment.

6. Insurance terminates when the loan obligation ceases. If the loan is repaid prior to the scheduled maturity date, a refund of the unearned single premium is paid to the borrower.

7. The first beneficiary of the policy proceeds is the lender, who uses the proceeds to extinguish the loan obligation. Any additional proceeds are paid to the second beneficiary or the estate of the insured.

8. Policy forms contain few exclusions.

The result is a product which can be easily explained and presented to the borrower. The borrower need only decide to accept or reject the insurance. If the insurance is accepted, the coverage takes effect immediately, along with the loan obligation.

Credit insurance provides advantages to both the borrower and the lender. The borrower has the security of knowing that a loan obligation will not be an added burden to the family in the event of death or disability. Medical bills or a reduction of income associated with death or disability usually creates additional financial strains on family resources.

Many borrowers are underinsured. They are aware of this fact, but choose to avoid the discussion and purchase of insurance. The ease of purchase of credit insurance, without inquiry as to the details of the insured's personal life or medical condition, is a definite plus in the minds of borrowers. Given the opportunity to meet a portion of their insurance needs quickly and easily, a high percentage of borrowers elect to purchase credit insurance.

The lender benefits by having added security concerning the borrower's ability to repay his obligation. The prospect of collecting the unpaid balance of a loan or of repossessing a consumer product from a widow or widower is not pleasant. Collecting from a disabled insured is just as taxing. Credit insurance provides a valuable social service, easing the burden on the lender and the borrower.

Lenders receive compensation from insurers for marketing the product to borrowers. This income can be a significant source of revenue. Some lenders even participate in the underwriting risk by forming subsidiary life insurance companies.

Benefits to borrowers and lenders, as well as a simplified product structure and marketing methods, account for widespread availability of credit insurance. For over sixty-five years, borrowers have purchased credit insurance in great numbers. The majority of consumer loans are insured with credit insurance.

The growth of three concepts–mass consumption of consumer goods, installment borrowing, and credit insurance–was interrelated, much like the chicken-and-the-egg quandary. Did mass consumption of consumer goods fuel the growth of installment borrowing, or did the availability of installment borrowing provide the basis for the mass consumption? Would installment borrowing have been available in vast quantities without the protection afforded by credit insurance products? All three concepts grew simultaneously and had a mutual cause and effect on each other. One thing is certain–these three concepts operating together have produced the highest standard of living in the history of the world and are firmly embedded in the fabric of our society. In the judgment of many people, our world has benefited greatly from the growth and acceptance of these concepts.

USE OF THE BOOK, TERMINOLOGY AND CAVEATS

This book is intended to serve the needs of a wide range of people in the credit insurance industry. In 1957, Dr. Daniel P. Kedzie published a rather complete description of the product and the industry in his book, *Consumer Credit Insurance*. Very little literature has been published since then, particularly in the last twelve years. This book attempts to fill this void. Since it may be thirty years before another book is written, this book is intended as a definitive treatment of all aspects of the product and the industry. For this reason, most readers will find a need for only portions of the book. Since the needs vary among readers, the book has been organized to provide general knowledge about each topic while also presenting the technical intricacies. Where the technical detail would not interest the general reader, the information has been assigned to an Appendix. Certain statistics and data which will be outdated soon after publication are also presented in Appendices.

The book covers *consumer credit insurance*, which is insurance written in conjunction with consumer goods lending. The underlying loans are made to purchase specific consumer goods or for day-to-day living expenses. Consumer lending excludes first mortgage lending, but does include second mortgage lending. Credit insurance has traditionally covered agricultural loans for farmers and educational loans for students. A small portion of consumer credit insurance now covers certain commercial loans.

"Credit life insurance" describes the life insurance products while "credit disability insurance" describes what is often called credit accident and health insurance in the published literature and industry usage. This disability income protection is one type of accident and health insurance, but the term "disability insurance" is more precise and more readable. The use of the term "credit insurance" is limited to those statements applicable to both products.

Credit insurance is generally sold covering installment loans, where the amount and term of the loan are fixed at the inception of the loan, which is repayable in equal monthly payments. Credit life insurance covers the life of the primary borrower and can also cover a co-borrower. The amount of insurance at any time during the loan is the sum of the remaining monthly payments.

Credit disability insurance provides a monthly benefit equal to the loan's monthly payment if the primary borrower is disabled any time during the term of the loan, once an initial qualifying period is met. Benefits continue as long as the insured is disabled, or until the scheduled maturity date of the loan, whichever comes first. The premium for the insurance is paid as a single premium. The single premium is added to the amount borrowed and financed.

Many variations on these standard plans exist in the marketplace and are described in this book. If a statement in the book does not appear in the context of one of the product variations, the reader can assume that the statement applies to the standard product. Many abbreviations are used in the book; each is shown in its expanded form the first time it is used. A glossary of terms and a list of abbreviations are contained in Appendix A for easy reference. An extensive bibliography documents most of the other published literature about the industry.

The term *lender* or *producer* refers to the corporate entity offering the product to the consumer. In most credit insurance transactions, the lender provides the funds. The terms *creditor, financial institution,* and *lending institution* are occasionally used and may be found in some of the cited literature. A significant amount of credit insurance is sold by automobile dealers and other retailers who do not lend money. The terms "lender" and "producer" are used in this book to encompass all sellers of credit insurance. The term *account* is also used to refer to a particular lender.

The terms *borrower* and *debtor* are used interchangeably to denote the consumer entering the debt obligation. The terms *loan* and *debt* are also used interchangeably and encompass installment sales contracts in addition to the usual connotation where cash is advanced to the borrower.

The word *policy* is used to represent the evidence of insurance, or the insurance itself on the individual insured borrower. Under *group insurance,* the actual insurance policy is between the insurance company and the lender. The individual is enrolled in the group and receives a certificate of insurance. Under *individual insurance*, the contract is between the insurance company and the insured. The insured buys insurance from the insurer and receives a policy directly. Since the text often refers to the insurance, constant use of a technically correct phrase like "individual policy or group certificate" would detract from the readability. When the discussion involves the actual group policy, the term "group policy" is used.

Lenders collect the premiums from the borrowers and send them to the insurance company. The premiums sent or remitted are *written premiums.* In this book, the term means the gross premiums collected from the insureds on new insurance issued less the premium refunds paid to those who terminate their coverage prior to maturity.

For the sake of convenience and readability, masculine pronouns are used throughout the book, as is common practice in technical books. No affront to women is intended.

A major difficulty in describing credit insurance products, insurer and lender practices, and administrative procedures is the wide diversity which exists in these areas. The reader will find extensive use of the words "usually," "some," "many," etc. The practice of using these qualifying words adds a degree of impreciseness to the book, but the practice is necessary to accurately reflect the diversity in the marketplace. It is difficult to make unqualified statements about a product marketed to millions of consumers by thousands of lenders and underwritten by hundreds of insurers, who are regulated by fifty different states. Readers will, undoubtedly, be able to find exceptions to the few remaining unqualified statements.

Samples of policy forms, reinsurance treaties, and other documents are included to illustrate the text. These documents are intended only as examples, not models of the way forms should be developed. Chapter Three describes common administrative practices, but there is no implication that this is the way things must be done, or even should be done. The same applies to Chapter Five in which several methods of reserving are described. These are not the only methods, and there is no implication that they are the best methods for any particular insurer.

Each section begins with basics before delving into the technical details and variations. A great deal of time was spent trying to simplify the Premium, Reserve, and Measurement of Profitability chapters. While still difficult, the reader should not ignore the chapters.

Except for Chapter Eleven, The Case for Credit Insurance, the main body of the book is intended as an objective treatment of the industry. The Case for Credit Insurance is intended as a positive statement of the merits of the products and the industry. No attempt is made to present the views of those critical of the product. Appendix B, Issues in Credit Insurance, presents opposing views, but reflects the author's opinions and biases.

CHAPTER ONE

CREDIT INSURANCE PRODUCTS

Credit insurance is designed to fulfill a borrower's loan obligation in the event the borrower dies or becomes disabled. The underlying loan, on which the need for the insurance derives, strongly influences the credit insurance product. The conditions and terms of the loan determine many of the characteristics of the credit insurance coverage.

Thirty years ago, the variety of products was limited. Loans were simple and fairly uniform in their provisions. Credit insurance was considered one of the simplest forms of insurance. With the evolution of lending practices, more complex credit insurance products were needed to fulfill a loan obligation in the event of a claim. The pace of evolution increased in the 1970s as the rapid fluctuation in interest rates forced even more radical changes in consumer lending practices. The credit insurance industry has adapted with new products and approaches to meet the changing lending environment. New products also evolved to reduce the total premium outlay, as the cost of the products rose due to longer term loans and higher loss experience under disability coverages.

As a result, many credit insurance products may be appropriate for a particular loan. However, selections must be made, a little like selecting the family dinner at a Chinese restaurant. Choose one selection from column A, one from column B, and so on. The lender, the borrower and the loan specifications each help determine the selections. The lender makes some selections based on the coverages it offers to its borrowers. Borrowers choose the type and extent of coverage desired.

CREDIT LIFE INSURANCE

A general definition of credit life insurance is:

Term life insurance purchased in conjunction with a consumer credit transaction, excluding first mortgage loans, which provides a death benefit sufficient to pay off the credit obligation in the event of an insured's death during the term of the coverage.

A *consumer credit transaction* includes cash loans, installment sales contracts, and credit card borrowing. These can be defined more specifically as:

- ***Cash loans.*** The borrower receives cash for the purchase of consumer goods or for other expenditures.

- ***Installment sales contract.*** The purchaser of a consumer product receives the product in return for entering into a debt obligation.

- ***Credit card borrowing.*** The borrower may receive cash, or act as a purchaser of a consumer product, by agreeing to repay the amount advanced by the lender.

In this book, the term "loan" is used to describe all of these debt obligations. The term "borrower" is used to describe the consumer entering into a loan by receiving cash or purchasing a consumer product.

There are exceptions to the general definition which are still considered credit life insurance. Some coverages do not insure the full amount of the debt, while others do not provide coverage for the full term of the loan. Some commercial loans are also insured with credit life insurance. The payments under certain automobile lease contracts may also be insured. These exceptions represent a small percentage of the total market.

Figure 1.1 describes options to consider when designing the credit life insurance product for a particular loan:

CHARACTERISTICS	OPTIONS
Type of Loan	Installment, Single payment, Combination, Open-end
Loan Conditions	Term, Amount, Payment pattern
Loan Interest Rate	Fixed, Variable
Number of Insureds	Single, Joint
Type of Policy	Group, Individual
Type of Coverage	Gross, Net payoff
Premium Mode	Single premium, Monthly outstanding balance
Coverage Period	Full, Limited
Eligibility Requirements and Exclusions	

Fig. 1.1 Credit life insurance characteristics and options.

TYPE OF LOAN

The type of loan determines the plan of insurance.

- ***Installment loans.*** Since installment lending is the cornerstone of consumer credit, installment loans account for the majority of loans insured by credit life insurance. The term *closed-end loan* is also used to describe these loans, which are for a fixed amount and term, repayable in equal monthly payments. The life insurance plan is decreasing term insurance.

- ***Level loans.*** Single payment loans are extended for short-term personal borrowing and for commercial loans. Since the only payment due from the borrower is at maturity, the term *level loan* is often used. These are also closed-end loans. The usual term is twelve months or less, and the loans are often renewed. If a loan is renewed, a new credit life policy is sold. Level term insurance is the plan of insurance.

- ***Balloon loans.*** Some loans require a combination of insurance plans. *Balloon loans* provide for monthly installment payments, plus a lump sum payment at maturity (the balloon). The installment portion is covered by decreasing term insurance, while the balloon portion is covered by level term insurance. This combination coverage may also be used for insuring certain types of automobile leases. Decreasing term insurance covers the monthly lease payments, while level term insurance covers the residual value of the automobile at the termination of the lease.

Figure 1.2 illustrates the combination of plans, showing an example of a gross coverage plan which is described more fully later in this chapter.

Details of loan: Twelve-month term with an 18% annual percentage rate.

Monthly payments of $100 plus an additional balloon payment of $400 due at the end of twelve months.

Balloon Note–Level and Decreasing Coverage

	Installment Portion of Loan	Balloon Portion of Loan	Total
Cash advanced	$1,084.75	$334.98	$1,419.73
Insurance premium	6.00	4.00	10.00
Finance charges	109.25	61.02	170.27
Total of payments	$1,200.00	$400.00	$1,600.00

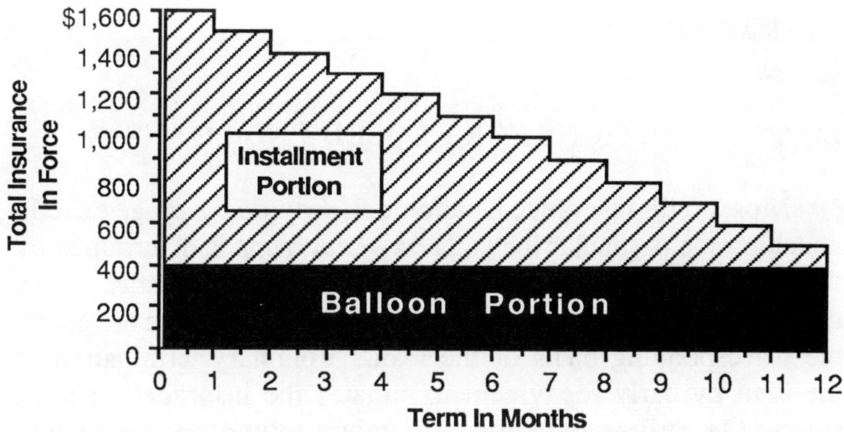

Fig. 1.2 A loan requiring a combination of insurance plans.

- ***Open-end Loan.*** The use of *open-end loans* in the consumer marketplace is growing. Credit card borrowing is one example of this type. If the card is valid, consumers can borrow cash or charge purchases up to their credit limit. Only a minimum monthly payment is required based on the outstanding balance of the account. Each month, the borrower may make a payment ranging from the minimum payment up to the outstanding balance of the account. The amount of debt can be increased at any time. Since the amount and term of the debt are not fixed, the loan is open-ended. The death benefit is equal to the outstanding balance of the account on the date of death. Banks offer credit life insurance on their credit card accounts. Some retail stores also make credit life insurance available on their revolving charge accounts. Most credit union loans are structured as open-end loans.

Although the insured's available credit is normally greater than the outstanding balance of the account, credit insurance laws and regulations do not permit the sale of insurance for the full line of credit. The insurance provided cannot exceed the outstanding balance. Exceptions to this rule are permitted for agricultural and educational loans in many states. For these loans, the amount insured can equal the loan commitment.

LOAN CONDITIONS FOR CLOSED-END LOANS

Most credit insurance is tailored to provide coverage exactly matching the particular loan. *Term of coverage* is determined by the term of the loan, normally expressed in months. The *effective date* and the *termination date* of the insurance are set by the corresponding dates of the loan. Voluntary termination of the loan by early repayment terminates the insurance in most states. On early termination, a premium refund, approximating the cost of insurance for the remaining term, is paid to the borrower.

The amount of the loan clearly affects the amount of insurance. The *principal* of the loan is the cash advanced, or the portion of the purchase price of the product which is financed. If a single premium is charged for the insurance, the *total amount advanced* usually includes the principal plus the insurance premium. Technically, the borrower has the option to pay the premium in cash, but the option is rarely exercised. Another term for the total amount advanced is *initial net indebtedness*. At the loan's inception, the *initial gross indebtedness* is also calculated. The interest charges over the scheduled term of the loan are determined. The initial gross indebtedness is the initial net indebtedness plus the *scheduled interest charges.*

If the loan is repayable in equal monthly installments, the monthly payment is equal to the initial gross indebtedness divided by the term of the loan. Each monthly payment provides for the payment of the interest charges for the current month based on the outstanding net indebtedness at the beginning of the month. The remainder of the monthly payment is applied to reduce the net indebtedness. The outstanding balance of the loan at any time is the remaining net indebtedness.

Details of loan: Twenty-four month term with an 18% annual interest rate compounded monthly.

Monthly payments of $50.

Cash advanced	$989.52
Insurance premium	12.00
Net indebtedness	1,001.52
Finance charges	198.48
Total of payments (Gross indebtedness)	$1,200.00

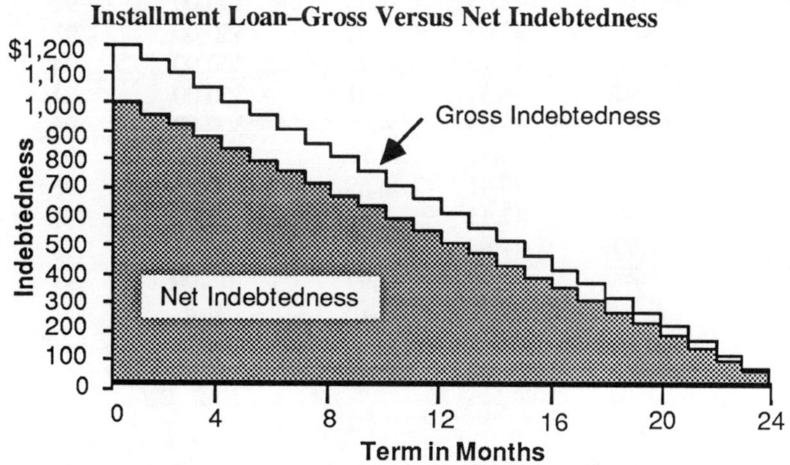

Fig. 1.3 Installment loan showing gross and net indebtedness.

The gross indebtedness declines in equal amounts on a monthly basis. The amount of monthly decrease is equal to the loan's monthly payment. The net indebtedness declines each month also, but the pattern of the decrease is not uniform, since interest charges consume more of the early payments. Figure 1.3 illustrates two types of indebtedness. Figure 1.4 shows the values by month for this loan.

End of Month	Net Indebtedness	Portion of Monthly Payment Applied: To Net Indebtedness	For Interest	Gross Indebtedness	Ratio of Net to Gross Indebtedness
0	$ 1,001.52	-	-	$ 1,200.00	.83
1	966.54	$ 34.98	$ 15.02	1,150.00	.84
2	931.04	35.50	14.50	1,100.00	.85
3	895.01	36.03	13.97	1,050.00	.85
4	858.44	36.57	13.43	1,000.00	.86
5	821.32	37.12	12.88	950.00	.86
6	783.64	37.68	12.32	900.00	.87
7	745.39	38.25	11.75	850.00	.88
8	706.57	38.82	11.18	800.00	.88
9	667.17	39.40	10.60	750.00	.89
10	627.18	39.99	10.01	700.00	.90
11	586.59	40.59	9.41	650.00	.90
12	545.39	41.20	8.80	600.00	.91
13	503.57	41.82	8.18	550.00	.92
14	461.12	42.45	7.55	500.00	.92
15	418.04	43.08	6.92	450.00	.93
16	374.31	43.73	6.27	400.00	.94
17	329.92	44.39	5.61	350.00	.94
18	284.87	45.05	4.95	300.00	.95
19	239.14	45.73	4.27	250.00	.96
20	192.73	46.41	3.59	200.00	.96
21	145.62	47.11	2.89	150.00	.97
22	97.80	47.82	2.18	100.00	.98
23	49.27	48.53	1.47	50.00	.99
24	-0-	49.27	.73	-0-	
Total		1,001.52	198.48		

Fig. 1.4 Dollar distribution of the installment loan shown in Figure 1.3.

Figure 1.3 is a simplification of the actual net indebtedness. During any loan month, the amount of the net indebtedness is affected by the lender's timing of interest charges. Interest for the month may be added to the net indebtedness at the beginning, middle, or end of the month; or interest may accrue continuously throughout the month. Net indebtedness declines in a series of irregular steps over the term of the loan, not on a curve, as it is sometimes described.

Single payment loans do not call for installment payments, but for a single payment at maturity. The initial net indebtedness is again equal to the principal plus the insurance premium. The scheduled interest charges plus the net indebtedness equal the initial gross indebtedness. The gross indebtedness remains level during the term of the loan. The net indebtedness increases during the term of the loan, since the interest accrues as time elapses. Figure 1.5 shows the gross and net indebtedness for a single payment loan. Figure 1.6 shows the values by month for this loan.

Details of loan: Twelve-month term with a 12% annual interest rate compounded monthly.

Single payment of $1,000 due at the end of twelve months.

Cash advanced	$ 877.45
Insurance premium	10.00
Initial net indebtedness	887.45
Finance charges	112.55
Total of payments (Gross indebtedness)	$1,000.00

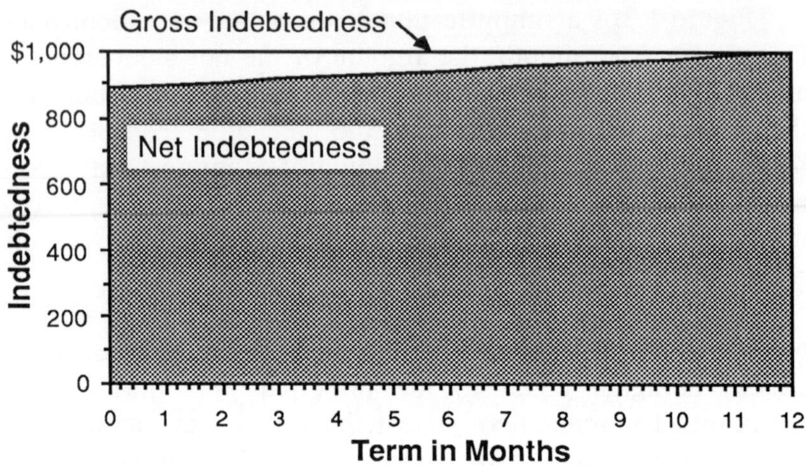

Fig. 1.5 Single payment loan showing gross and net indebtedness.

End of Month	Net Indebtedness	Gross Indebtedness	Ratio of Net to Gross
0	$ 887.45	$ 1,000.00	.89
1	896.32	1,000.00	.90
2	905.29	1,000.00	.91
3	914.34	1,000.00	.91
4	923.48	1,000.00	.92
5	932.72	1,000.00	.93
6	942.05	1,000.00	.94
7	951.47	1,000.00	.95
8	960.98	1,000.00	.96
9	970.59	1,000.00	.97
10	980.30	1,000.00	.98
11	990.10	1,000.00	.99
12	1,000.00	1,000.00	1.00

Fig. 1.6 Values by month for the single payment loan in Figure 1.5.

LOAN INTEREST RATE

Until recently, fixed interest rates characterized most consumer lending. Relatively stable interest rates and the short term of loans made *fixed-rate loans* possible. Fixed-rate loans continue to dominate installment lending. With fixed interest rates, the insurance can be clearly defined by term and amount at the inception of the loan.

When interest rates rose dramatically in the late 1970s, consumer loans up to forty-eight months were common. Faced with potential interest rate fluctuations, lenders began making *variable-rate* consumer loans. Although the administration is complex, improvements in computer power have made the process economically feasible.

These variable-rate loans provide for periodic recalculation of the loan conditions. For most loans, the monthly payment is held constant, and the loan term is made variable. If interest rates decline during the loan term, the loan is paid off prior to the scheduled maturity date. If interest rates rise, the term of the loan is extended or the amount of the final installment payment is increased. An alternative is to change the monthly payment when there is an adjustment in the interest rate.

NUMBER OF INSUREDS

If there is only one borrower, single life coverage is offered. When the loan has a co-borrower, joint life coverage is permitted in all states. A few states limit the coverage to a spouse. A joint policy terminates on the death of either insured. If both die simultaneously, the death benefit is only the stated amount of insurance on the primary insured. The cost of joint life insurance is generally much less expensive than single life coverage on each of the two lives.

GROUP OR INDIVIDUAL POLICY

Credit life insurance is available through group or individual policies. Under a *group policy*, the contractual relationship is between the insurance company and the lender. The lender is issued a group policy, where the group is defined as the consumers obtaining loans from the lender. When a borrower is insured, he is enrolled in the group and receives a certificate of insurance as evidence of the insurance. Under an *individual policy*, the contractual relationship is directly between the insurance company and the borrower. In this case, the borrower receives an individual policy as evidence of insurance.

Most credit insurance is sold under group policies. All states permit the borrowers from a particular lender to be considered an eligible group. An individual policy is generally used where an insurer desires to ask health questions. From the borrower's standpoint, there is little difference between the two types of policies. From the insurer's standpoint, there is a difference in the contractual relationship and certain administrative procedures, but there is little, if any, difference in the actual coverage provided or the premium rates charged.

The laws and regulations in many states contain *group maximum limits* which restrict the amount of insurance which can be provided by group insurance. There are several ways to compensate for this limitation. One option is to sell an individual policy, since no state limits the amount of insurance which can be written under an individual policy. Another option, available in some states, is to sell insurance with a death benefit equal to the maximum allowed, or the remaining indebtedness, whichever is less. For a loan which exceeds the state maximum, the amount of insurance is level until the indebtedness drops below the maximum. At that time, the amount of insurance begins to decrease in the normal pattern. While a standard name does not exist, the term *level-decreasing insurance* is appropriate. Figure 1.7 illustrates an example of a $120,000 loan with level-decreasing insurance.

A third option is to offer partial coverage of the loan by using the usual plans of insurance, but with insurance for less than the full amount of the loan. The coverage provided is proportionate to the full coverage throughout the term of insurance. For example, if the full coverage begins at $120,000, but the group maximum is $60,000, the partial coverage provided is equal to 50% of the insurance which would have been provided under the $120,000 policy. This partial coverage has little appeal, since the insurance is never sufficient to pay off the loan. The borrower must be told of the limitation on coverage, and the policy must contain clear and prominent disclosures.

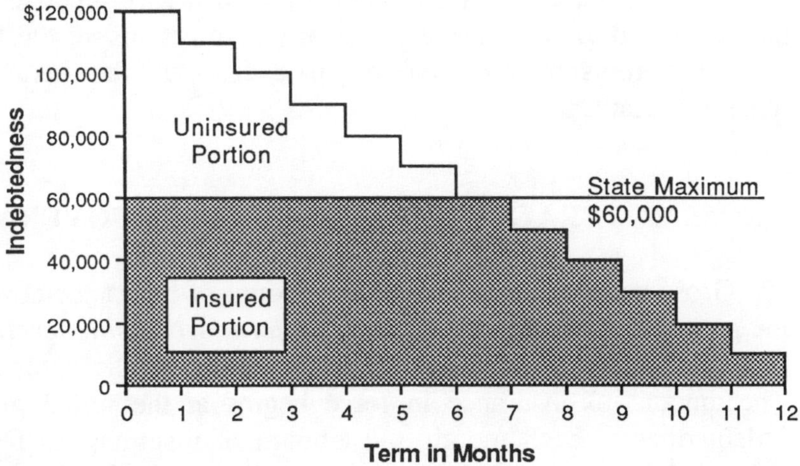

Fig. 1.7 Level-decreasing insurance.

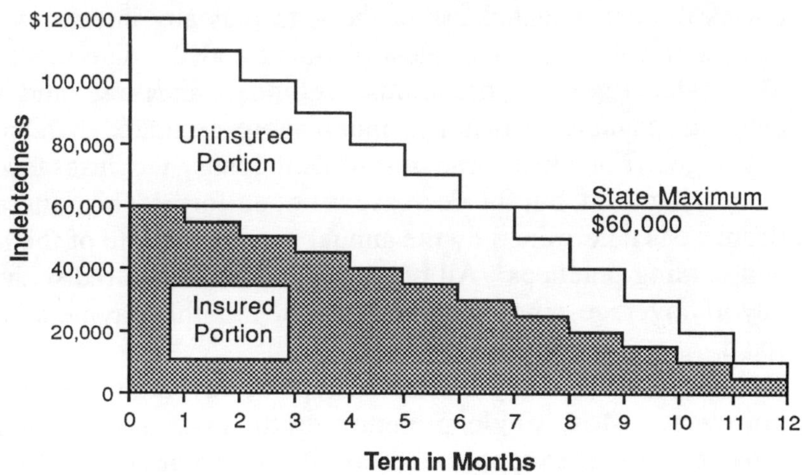

Fig. 1.8 Partial coverage insurance.

Insurance companies set a maximum limit on the amount of risk which will be accepted on any one life. This limit operates the same as a group maximum limit, but an insurer applies the maximum in all states and for both individual and group policies. If insurance is offered on loans exceeding the maximum, coverage can be provided with a level-decreasing plan or a partial coverage plan. Many insurers insure the full loan and reinsure the amount in excess of the insurer's maximum limit.

GROSS COVERAGE VERSUS NET PAYOFF COVERAGE

Gross coverage means that the amount of insurance covers the gross indebtedness of the loan. *Uniform decreasing term life insurance* is the resulting plan of insurance for installment loans. The amount of insurance in force begins at the initial gross indebtedness. Each month, the amount of insurance in force decreases by the amount of one monthly payment. In other words, the amount of insurance in force is the sum of the remaining monthly payments.

Net payoff coverage means that the amount of insurance covers the net indebtedness of the loan plus any interest which has accrued between the latest payment and the date of death. The calculation of premiums, refunds, reserves, and the amounts payable at death is much more complex than gross coverage. For closed-end installment loans, the insurance is decreasing term, but the decrease is not uniform. The pattern of decrease is determined by the annual percentage rate of the loan and lending practices. All open-end loans are insured with net payoff coverage, since the amount of the monthly payment is not fixed.

The lender usually selects the type of coverage offered to a borrower. Most single premium credit insurance offered is gross coverage, except in the credit union market. In recent years, some single premium credit insurance has been offered using net payoff coverage, particularly insurance covering large loans or loans with terms of over five years. A few states (including Maine and New York) require that all credit life insurance offered in those states be net payoff coverage. Other states require the use of net payoff coverage for loans exceeding specified terms, usually sixty months. Most credit union business is net payoff coverage.

Net payoff coverage is also used for variable interest rate loans. Most insurers cover the balance of the loan at death and extend the term of coverage if the loan term is extended. This extension of the amount of insurance is often limited to two monthly payments. The term extension is usually limited to two months.

Single payment loans are usually insured by level term life insurance for an amount equal to the initial gross indebtedness. A few loans are insured with net payoff coverage. Net payoff coverage results in increasing term insurance, since the net indebtedness increases as the interest accrues.

A variation, introduced in recent years, does not fit either description. It is a product named *critical period coverage*. To limit the total premium outlay, the amount of insurance offered is limited to a fixed number of monthly payments. The concept is to provide a benefit equal to enough loan payments so that the financial stability of the insured's household can be regained. The usual death benefit is equal to twelve monthly payments, or the remaining monthly payments, whichever is less. This is simply level term insurance, except for the last several months of the loan. Insurers may require the insured to sign a statement which clearly discloses that the insurance may not cover the entire debt. This product is not widely offered, although its disability counterpart is proving popular.

Details of loan:	Gross indebtedness:	$3,000
	Monthly payment:	$50
	Term of loan:	60 months
	Maximum benefit:	12 monthly payments

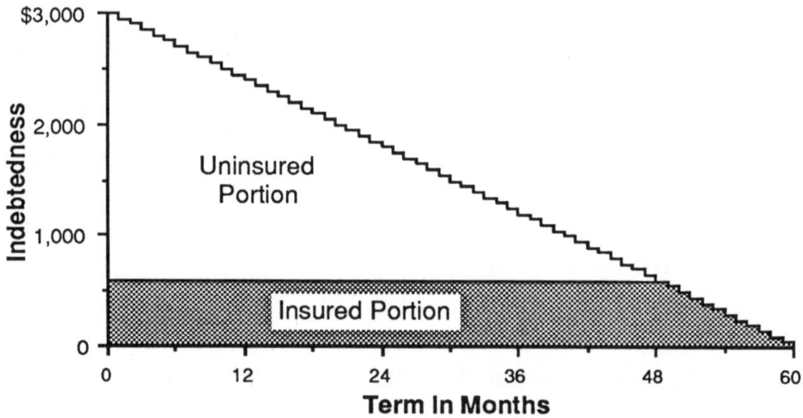

Fig. 1.9 Critical period coverage insurance.

Gross coverage has received criticism because the amount of insurance exceeds the net indebtedness. Net payoff coverage has been criticized because the insurance may not be sufficient to pay off the loan balance if the borrower has been delinquent in certain payments. A compromise approach, *net plus*, has been introduced recently. The concept is reasonable, but complicated.

Under net plus coverage, the amount of insurance has an initial value equal to the net indebtedness. Insurance remains level for a period of time and then begins to decrease. The period of level insurance is determined by the term of the loan. Insurance is level one month for each six months in the loan term. For example, on a loan of twenty-four months, the level period is four months. After the level period, the insurance decreases on a net indebtedness pattern using the loan's annual percentage rate, or an assumed rate for all loans. In addition, the term of the insurance coverage extends beyond the loan term for the number of months of level coverage. A premium refund is paid if the loan terminates on the scheduled maturity date.

Net plus is not permitted under most credit insurance regulations for two reasons:

1. The term of insurance extends beyond the loan term, and

2. The amount of insurance exceeds the gross indebtedness in certain months.

Acceptance of the concept of net plus will require a significant modification in the underlying concept of credit insurance regulation. No state has accepted the concept, but it has been introduced in Massachusetts.

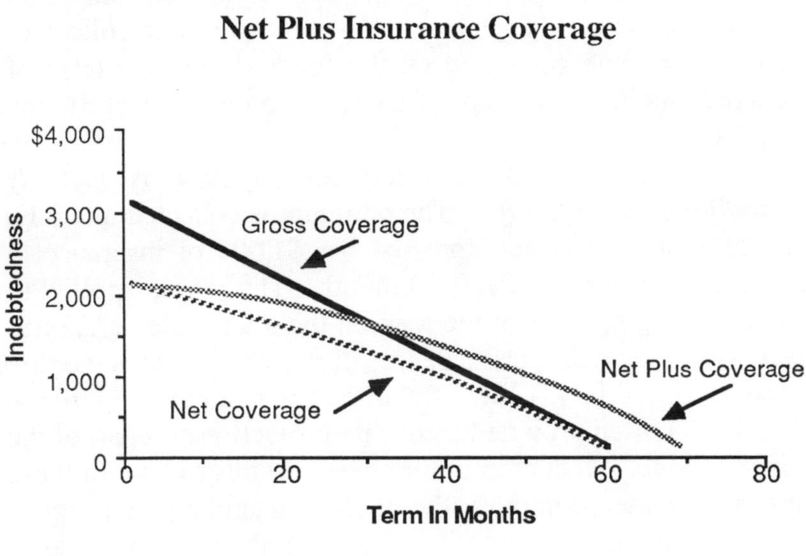

Fig. 1.10 Net plus insurance coverage.

PREMIUM MODE

Since the credit life policy provides a relatively small amount of insurance for a short term, the *single premium* payment mode has been traditional. A premium is calculated to pay for the full coverage provided, and is charged to the insured in one sum at the inception of the loan. The premium is usually added to the amount borrowed and financed along with the principal of the loan. Single premium rates are expressed in terms of the initial gross indebtedness, but the calculation reflects the actual coverage provided. Rates are expressed per $100 of initial gross indebtedness for each year of coverage; e.g., 50¢/100/year. The premium is 50¢ for each $100 of initial gross indebtedness, times the number of years of coverage.

This mode is important in maintaining administrative simplicity. Credit life insurance for a typical loan costs less than $200. Periodic premium billing and collection costs on individual loans would consume much of the premium collected. Investment income generated on the funds during the term of coverage is another advantage of the single premium mode to the insurer.

The alternative mode of premium payment is *monthly outstanding balance (MOB)*. The premium is collected monthly. MOB premium rates are expressed per $1,000 of insurance in force, often written as 80¢/1000/month. The rate is applied to the outstanding balance of the loan on the loan cycle date, or to an average of the daily loan balances during the previous month.

The MOB method is only used in certain situations. Until the 1960s, banks often provided credit life protection as a part of the lending service. Most credit unions still do this today. In these cases, the lender compiles the total outstanding balance of outstanding loans each month and applies the premium rate to the entire portfolio. The insurer books the premium as one payment. No individual insurance records or other detail information is maintained. This mode is also used in revolving charge credit transactions, with the premium again reported to the insurer in bulk.

When a lender provides the insurance without an identifiable charge to the borrower, the coverage is called *non-contributory*. Protection is provided to all borrowers, and the cost is absorbed by the lender. *Contributory coverage* occurs where the borrower has the option to purchase the protection and pays an identifiable charge. Except in the credit union market, almost all credit insurance is contributory. Since this is the common case, the reference to the contributory aspect is often omitted from the description.

COVERAGE PERIOD

Until recently, the coverage period of the insurance exactly matched the term of the loan. This situation still holds for most credit life policies.

As the term of some types of consumer loans grew longer (over sixty months), the cost of single premium credit insurance became prohibitive. As the dollar outlay rose, borrower resistance caused more consumers to decline the coverage. This resistance was addressed by selling less insurance. Net payoff coverage replaced gross coverage; however, more reduction was needed.

One alternative was to reduce the term of coverage. Because some states limit the scope of credit insurance policies to sixty months or less, this was a useful alternative. The common name for this product is *truncated life*. The amount of insurance is net payoff coverage for the full outstanding net indebtedness, but death must occur during the term of the insurance coverage. On loans of ten years or more, the coverage period offered is usually five years or less. One to three year coverage periods may be offered on shorter loans. Since many long-term loans are repaid prior to maturity, the coverage period is sufficient for most loans. Some insurers offer a renewal option at the expiration of the coverage if the loan is still in effect. Truncated life may be written with gross coverage, but the coverage provides more insurance and has a higher premium.

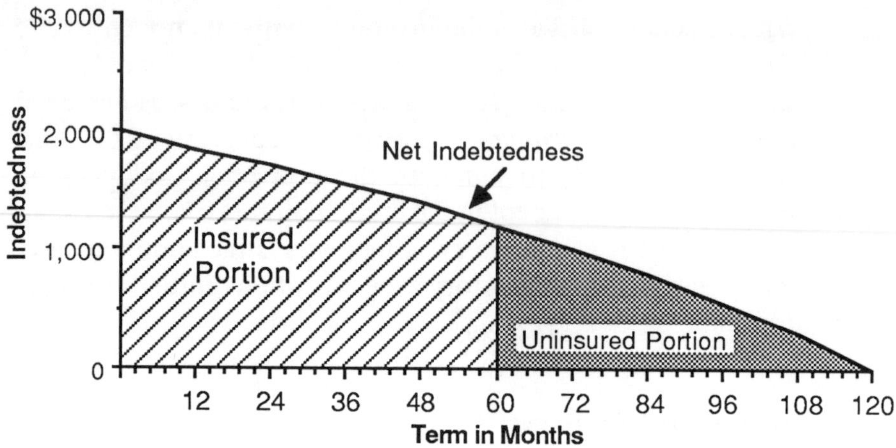

Fig. 1.11 Truncated life insurance coverage.

ELIGIBILITY REQUIREMENTS AND EXCLUSIONS

Age of the borrower is the only consideration affecting eligibility to purchase most credit life insurance policies. Generally, credit life insurance is available to borrowers under age sixty-five. The usual underwriting considerations–age, sex, health, and occupation of the borrower, are not a factor in determining whether insurance is offered, or the premium rate charged for the insurance.

A small number of policies require the borrower to sign a good health statement to obtain the insurance. A few policies, usually for larger amounts, require the borrower to provide medical information. Unacceptable risks are rejected.

Most credit life insurance is sold without any exclusions, except for suicide. If suicide is the cause of death and occurs within a specified time after issue (from six months to two years), the death benefit is limited to a return of the gross premium paid. Since the loan is not repaid, the survivor under a joint policy may be permitted to continue coverage. In that case, the refunded premium is the difference between the cost of joint life insurance and the cost of single life insurance.

CREDIT DISABILITY INSURANCE

A general definition of credit disability insurance is:

Disability insurance purchased in conjunction with a consumer credit transaction which provides a monthly benefit equal to the required monthly payment, while the insured is disabled, during the term of coverage.

The definition of a consumer credit transaction, and the exceptions to the general definition found in the previous section, also apply to disability. In addition, a few states permit other accident and health benefits to be sold in conjunction with credit insurance. Kentucky and West Virginia permit an extra charge if a *dismemberment benefit* is provided.

The selection process to describe a credit disability policy is similar to that of a credit life insurance policy. Several life options are not applicable, but a few additional options must be considered, due to the nature of the product and prevailing practice in the industry.

CHARACTERISTICS	OPTIONS
Type of Benefit	Monthly benefit, Lump sum benefit
Elimination or Waiting Period	Seven, Fourteen, Thirty, Ninety days
Elimination Period Benefit	Retroactive, Non-retroactive
Type of Loan	Installment, Single payment, Combination, Open-end
Loan Conditions	Term, Monthly payment
Loan Interest Rate	Fixed, Variable
Number of Insureds	Single, Joint
Benefit and Coverage Period	Full, Limited
Premium Mode	Single premium, Monthly outstanding balance
Preexisting Conditions	Covered, Excluded
Eligibility Requirements and Exclusions	

Fig. 1.12 Credit disability insurance characteristics and options.

TYPE OF BENEFIT

Most credit disability insurance sold covers closed-end installment loans with fixed monthly payments. This insurance provides a monthly benefit payable as long as the insured remains disabled, or until the scheduled maturity date of the loan, whichever occurs first. Since the benefit is the full monthly payment of the loan, including interest charges, the coverage is *gross coverage.* There is no disability counterpart to the net payoff life coverage. Benefits for a partial month of disablement are based on the pro rata portion of the month disabled; i.e., 1/30th of the monthly loan payment for each day of disability.

Disability policies distinguish between *his occupation* disabilities and *any occupation* disabilities. *His occupation* disability means that a person is unable to perform the essential tasks of his usual occupation. *Any occupation* disability means the person is unable to perform the duties of any occupation for which the person is reasonably suited by reason of education, training, or experience. Credit disability generally covers disabilities using an *any occupation* disability requirement. In certain states and certain markets, the *his occupation* definition is applied in the first twelve (or eighteen) months of disability. Thereafter, the *any occupation* test must be met for benefits to continue.

Single payment loans are repayable in a single sum, so monthly benefit disability coverage is not applicable. In some cases, a *lump sum*, total and permanent disability coverage is offered. This coverage provides for the full payment of the loan balance (the lump sum) if the insured is totally and permanently disabled. Lump sum benefits could be used for installment loans, but the product has rarely been offered for them in recent years.

There are two approaches used to determine whether the borrower is totally and permanently disabled. Except in the credit union market, the *presumptive test of disability* approach is used. If a borrower is disabled a specified number of continuous days, he is presumed to be totally and permanently disabled. A ninety-day requirement is standard, but other periods are possible.

The second approach is to pay the benefit whenever the insurer can determine that the disability is total and permanent. This approach is used in the credit union market, although a disability lasting six months is often accepted as being total and permanent.

ELIMINATION OR WAITING PERIOD

All credit disability policies require that the insured remain disabled for a certain number of days before any benefits are payable. This practice eliminates short-duration claims, which create as much administrative work as large claims. Eliminating the small claims significantly reduces the claim cost and the premium. The longer the elimination period is, the lower the premium.

Fourteen-day and thirty-day elimination periods are the industry standards. A fourteen-day elimination period means that the insured must remain disabled more than fourteen days before any benefit is payable for a particular disability. If the disability is not sustained over consecutive days, reference is made to the definition of disability in the policy. Normally, if the days disabled are separated by a short period of returning to work, all days of disability are counted. If the days disabled are separated by more than a few weeks, the disabilities are considered separate disabilities. The permitted period of work days is set by insurer practice, often 14 days. For each separate disability, the full elimination period must be satisfied. Once the elimination period is satisfied, it does not have any other impact on the benefits due under the policy.

In prior years, shorter elimination periods were used, notably three and seven days. Seven-day elimination periods are still permitted in some states, but the premium cost is rather high.

Lump sum coverage is for total and permanent disabilities. Under the presumptive approach, the specified number of days operates the same as an elimination period.

ELIMINATION PERIOD BENEFIT

There are two methods used to determine the benefit payable for the time disabled during the elimination period.

- ***Non-retroactive benefits*** means that no benefit is payable for the elimination period. Benefits begin to accrue only after the elimination period has elapsed. For a fourteen-day elimination period, the non-retroactive benefit begins with the fifteenth day of disability.

- ***Retroactive benefits*** provide for the payment of benefits from the first day of disability. Once a claimant has been disabled the required number of days in the elimination period, he receives benefits from the first day of disability.

If a claimant is covered under a fourteen-day non-retroactive benefit and remains disabled for forty days, he receives twenty-six days of benefit. Under a retroactive benefit, he receives benefits for the full forty days. No payment is made under either plan if the claimant is disabled fewer than fifteen days.

Technically, the determination of the elimination period and the elimination period benefit are separate. Common practice has resulted in a blending of the two terms. A non-retroactive benefit with a fourteen-day elimination period is often called *fourteen-day elimination coverage*, rather than *fourteen-day elimination, non-retroactive coverage*. A retroactive benefit with a fourteen-day elimination period is called *fourteen-day retroactive coverage*. In literature and data processing reports, the former benefit is often abbreviated 14NR or 14E, while the latter is designated 14R.

TYPE OF LOAN

- ***Installment loans***. The monthly payment defines the monthly disability benefit. The maximum potential benefit to the borrower at any time is the sum of the remaining monthly payments. A policy may contain a limit on the monthly benefit payable based on the maximum risk an insurer will accept on any one life.

- ***Single payment loans***. The only type of disability insurance offered is a lump sum benefit. If the insured is totally and permanently disabled, the outstanding balance of the loan on the date of disability is paid. More often than not, disability insurance is not offered on single payment loans.

- ***Open-end loans***. The borrower can increase the principal at any time by making additional purchases. Each month, lenders require a minimum payment which will pay off the current balance of the loan in about twenty-four months. A minimum dollar payment may be imposed; e.g., the smallest payment accepted may be ten dollars.

  The disability benefit may be a monthly benefit or a lump sum benefit. If a monthly benefit is provided, the benefit is the lender's required minimum monthly payment based on the account balance on the day of disability. If disability continues, benefit payments continue until this balance is repaid. Charges to the account after the date of disability are not covered. A lump sum benefit pays off the balance of the loan on the date of disability, once the determination is made that the disability is total and permanent.

  Open-end credit card and revolving charge account credit insurance is often sold with life and disability combined. The requirement of both coverages is necessary to produce a total premium sufficient to cover administrative costs. Since these balances are usually small, the total premium is small. Fixed overhead costs of processing are difficult to cover if only life insurance is sold. If the outstanding balance is less than $1,000, the monthly life premium may be one dollar or less.

LOAN CONDITIONS

The usual elements of a loan define the conditions of a credit disability policy on installment loans. In most cases, the term of coverage begins on the effective date of the loan and ends on the maturity date. Termination of the loan by early repayment terminates the insurance. A premium refund is paid to the insured on early termination.

LOAN INTEREST RATE

Fixed interest rate loans do not present any problems in disability insurance. Once the rate is set, the monthly payment is defined. If the loan has a variable interest rate, the monthly payment is usually fixed, based on the interest rate at the loan's inception. The term may be extended if the interest rates rise. Industry practice is to extend the term of the disability coverage if the term of the loan is extended. The extension is often limited to two months.

NUMBER OF INSUREDS

Joint disability coverage is prohibited in many states. Even in the few states where it is permitted, the coverage is rarely offered. One deterrent is the determination of disability. If the co-borrower is a non-wage earning spouse, evaluation of disability is far more subjective than for a wage earning individual. The industry practice and the legal restrictions are a carryover from the 1950s when the typical family had only one wage earner. While this is not the case today, many of the second incomes are from part-time work or avocations. The legal prohibitions have not been seriously fought by the industry, as the cost of single life disability insurance is already high.

COVERAGE PERIOD

The customary credit disability policy provides coverage for the full term of the loan. Benefit payments continue until the scheduled maturity date of the loan if the claimant remains disabled. In many policies, benefits may continue for two months after the maturity date, if the insured is disabled on the maturity date, and the loan is not paid off due to delinquent payments.

Loans in excess of sixty months are common in second mortgage lending. The exposure to long-term claims concerns insurers. The single premium mode also produces large premiums which deter some borrowers from purchasing the insurance. The percentage of borrowers electing disability coverage on long-term loans is low. Low penetration percentages tend to result in poor loss experience, because bad risks tend to elect to buy the insurance, while few of the good risks purchase the product. In insurance terminology, this tendency is called *anti-selection*. The borrower is selecting against the insurer based on his knowledge of his health condition.

One solution to the problem is to offer coverage for the full term of the loan, but limit the number of monthly benefit payments to a specific number of months, (or the remaining term if less). Since the period immediately after a disability begins is the most crucial financially, the product is called *critical period coverage*. The advantages are a reasonable total dollar outlay and essential protection for the borrower.

For example, a two-year benefit period may be sold on a ten-year loan. A disability is covered if it occurs any time during the ten years. The maximum number of benefit payments is twenty-four, regardless of the duration of the disability. If the disability occurs during the last two policy years, the maximum benefit is limited to the remaining number of months.

Critical period policies are usually offered for loans of sixty months or more. Initially, the benefit period offered was thirty-six months. The trend in recent years has been toward twelve-month and twenty-four-month benefit periods. These shorter benefit periods reduce the total premium charge compared to standard plans.

A small volume of disability insurance sold is truncated coverage, which requires the disability to occur during the term covered by the life insurance. Monthly benefit payments continue only until the end of the term of insurance.

PREMIUM MODE

The mode of premium for disability is generally the same as for life coverage. If the life premium mode is single premium, the disability premium mode is single premium. On most open-end credit card and revolving charge accounts, both life and disability are on an MOB basis. A premium rate is calculated which can be applied to the outstanding indebtedness.

Where the lender provides credit life insurance free of charge, the life premium mode is MOB. Except in the credit union market, a lender rarely provides disability insurance free of charge. Disability insurance is not offered or contributory coverage is offered on a single premium mode. Credit unions often provide the life insurance and lump sum, total and permanent disability insurance. However, some credit unions offer disability insurance as an option to the borrower. These contributory policies may be either single premium or MOB.

PREEXISTING CONDITIONS

Credit life insurance is generally offered to all borrowers without regard to any existing health problems. To obtain the loan, the applicant is presumably in good health and possesses the ability to repay the loan. For most credit insurance policies, medical questions are not asked, so the insured is not required to disclose prior health problems. The cost of underwriting and the delays in accepting coverage are not acceptable given the size of the credit insurance premium and the amount of coverage. Still, the borrower may have existing impairments which may cause future disabilities. A *preexisting condition* is an impairment for which the insured has been treated prior to the effective date of the insurance.

Insurers have the option of covering preexisting conditions or excluding them. If preexisting conditions are excluded, the standard exclusion is a *six and six exclusion*. This means that a disability is not covered if the insured becomes disabled from a preexisting condition within six months after the effective date, if any treatment for that preexisting condition occurred within the six months prior to the effective date. No benefits are payable even if the disability extends beyond six months after the effective date. If the last treatment of a preexisting condition occurred more than six months prior to the effective date, the disability is covered. If the disability starts more than six months after the effective date, the disability is covered, even if the treatment was within six months prior to the effective date. Figures 1.13 and 1.14 show how this works.

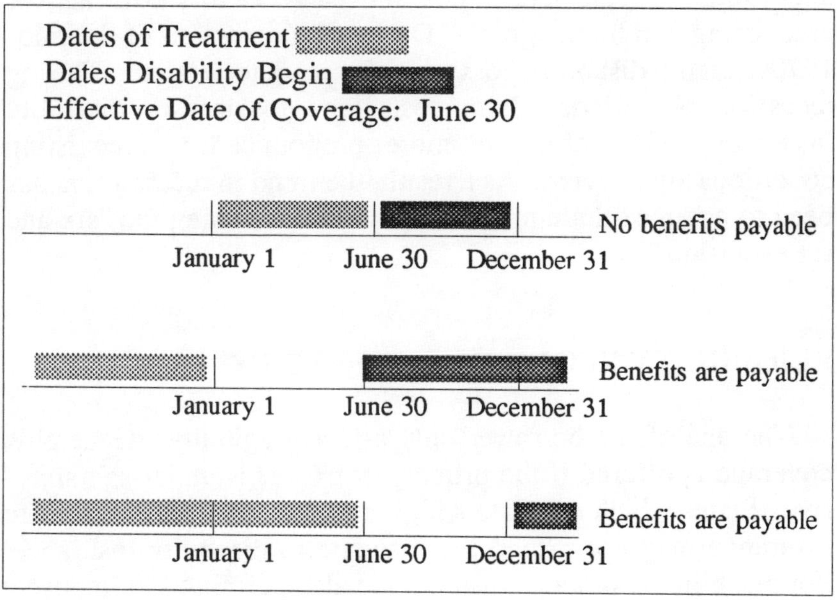

Fig. 1.13 Description of a six and six exclusion.

Effective Date of Coverage	Date of Last Treatment	Date Disability Began	Benefits Payable
6-30-85	3-15-85	9-15-85	None
6-30-85	3-15-85	3-15-86	Covered
6-30-85	9-15-84	9-15-85	Covered
6-30-85	9-15-84	3-15-86	Covered

Fig. 1.14 Examples of the application of a six and six exclusion.

States specify maximum premium rates for credit insurance. Insurers using a "six and six exclusion" are permitted to charge the standard rate. An additional 10% is often permitted if the insurer covers preexisting conditions.

Preexisting conditions were not commonly covered until the late 1960s. In the late 1960s and early 1970s, coverage of preexisting conditions grew. During the recession of the mid-1970s, credit disability loss experience deteriorated. During recessionary periods, claim costs tend to rise for disability insurance. The effect is more pronounced if preexisting conditions are covered. As a result, the trend in recent years has been to again exclude preexisting conditions using the "six and six exclusion."

ELIGIBILITY REQUIREMENTS AND EXCLUSIONS

The age of the borrower only affects eligibility. Generally, coverage is offered if the primary borrower is under age sixty-five. States which mandate a higher maximum age limit for life insurance may not extend the mandate to disability insurance. For disability insurance, insurers are also permitted to impose a second underwriting restriction in many states. The insurer may require that the borrower be *actively-at-work* on the effective date of the insurance. The borrower is not eligible for coverage unless he is working thirty or more hours per week. Other disability policy underwriting criteria, such as occupation and amount of income, are not considered.

Exclusions are few. Disability from normal pregnancy and self-inflicted injuries are the only common exclusions. Other exclusions occasionally used are for disabilities resulting from non-prescription drug use, acts of war, or aviation in non-scheduled flights.

SUMMARY OF LIFE INSURANCE PLANS

The following is a **general** description of the typical characteristics of today's credit life products. All plans may provide single life or joint life coverage and may be issued under a group or an individual policy. Coverage begins on the effective date of the loan and terminates on the maturity date of the loan, except as noted. If the loan is repaid prior to the expiration of the insurance term, the insurance terminates.

SINGLE PREMIUM DECREASING GROSS COVERAGE

The insurance provided is uniform decreasing term insurance with an initial amount equal to the initial gross indebtedness. Insurance decreases each month by the amount of one monthly payment. During the loan term, the amount of insurance is equal to the sum of the remaining monthly payments. This is the most common form of credit life insurance, since it is used for most closed-end installment loans.

SINGLE PREMIUM LEVEL GROSS COVERAGE

Term coverage is provided with an amount of insurance equal to the initial gross indebtedness. The amount of insurance is level throughout the term of the loan. This plan is used for single payment loans.

SINGLE PREMIUM DECREASING NET PAYOFF COVERAGE

Decreasing term insurance is provided with an amount of insurance which begins at the initial net indebtedness. During the loan term, the insurance is equal to the scheduled outstanding net indebtedness of the loan, possibly with some additional provision for delinquent payments or changes of loan conditions on variable interest rate loans. Net payoff coverage is used for some closed-end installment loans and most long-term loans.

MONTHLY OUTSTANDING BALANCE COVERAGE

Insurance is provided which pays off the outstanding balance of the loan on the date of death. Coverage is purchased monthly with a premium based on the loan balance on the monthly billing date. While the coverage may be used for closed-end installment loans, its use has generally been limited to open-end borrowing. This coverage is used for non-contributory plans, and for credit card and revolving charge account business.

TRUNCATED LIFE COVERAGE

Coverage is identical to single premium decreasing net payoff coverage, except that the term of the insurance coverage is shorter than the term of the loan. Insurance is provided for the full net indebtedness during the term of the insurance coverage. A renewal option may be offered when the insurance expires. Truncated life is offered on long-term loans.

CRITICAL PERIOD LIFE COVERAGE

Insurance is provided for the full term of the loan, but the amount of insurance is not tied to the loan balance. The death benefit is equal to a stated number of monthly payments, or the remaining monthly payments, whichever is less. Single premium plans are usual, but MOB plans are possible. The coverage is offered in situations where the objective is to offer some insurance protection with a minimum premium dollar outlay.

SUMMARY OF DISABILITY PLANS

The following is a **general** description of the common plans of disability insurance. For monthly benefit plans, any elimination (or waiting) period may be selected, and the elimination period benefit may be retroactive or non-retroactive. Insurance covers only the primary borrower. Coverage begins on the effective date of the loan and terminates on the expiration of the loan. Insurance terminates if the loan is repaid prior to maturity. Disability insurance is usually not offered unless the borrower purchases the life insurance, or the life insurance is provided by the lender.

MONTHLY BENEFIT GROSS COVERAGE

If the conditions of disability are met, a monthly benefit is paid equal to the monthly loan payment on closed-end loans or the minimum payment due on open-end loans. The borrower must remain disabled for the minimum number of days specified in the policy's elimination period. Benefit payments continue until disability ceases, or the maturity date of the loan, whichever occurs first. Proportionate benefits are paid for a partial month of disability. The premium mode is single premium on most closed-end loans and MOB on open-end loans.

LUMP SUM COVERAGE

The coverage pays the outstanding balance of the loan on the date of disability once the claimant satisfies the policy's definition of total and permanent disability. The premium mode is usually MOB.

CRITICAL PERIOD DISABILITY COVERAGE

A monthly benefit is payable if disability occurs any time during the term of the loan once the elimination period is satisfied. However, the maximum number of benefits is limited to a stated number of payments, or the remaining payments, whichever is less.

CHAPTER TWO

DIRECT WRITERS, CAPTIVES, AND PRODUCERS

The credit insurance market is a mature industry. A wide range of insurance companies offer the product to consumers in practically every situation where consumer credit is extended to a borrower. The only exceptions are first mortgage loans, which are insured using individual ordinary or group insurance products due to the long-term nature of the loan transaction, and many commercial loans. Producers of credit insurance span a cross section of American corporations–banks, automobile dealers, credit unions, retail outlets, savings and loan associations, and many others. Often the producers participate in the underwriting risk through the formation of direct-writing insurance companies or reinsurance companies which are owned by the producer.

TYPES OF INSURANCE COMPANIES

The *direct writer* is the insurance company issuing the policy; its name is on the policy. The direct writer has the contractual relationship with the insured. Regardless of any reinsurance arrangement, the direct writer must meet the obligations guaranteed by the policy.

Reinsurance is the transfer of risk from one insurance company, the direct writer, to a second insurance company, the *reinsurer.* The direct writer is said to *cede* the risk to the reinsurer who *assumes* the risk. Consequently, the terms *ceding company* and *assuming company* are used to reference the two parties. The reinsurer may transfer part or all of the risk to a third insurance company. The first reinsurer is said to *retrocede* the business. The second reinsurer again assumes the business and is called the *retrocessionaire.*

A specialized subset of both direct writers and reinsurers is *captive insurance companies.* In the credit insurance market, a captive is an insurer or reinsurer owned or controlled by the producer of the credit insurance. In most cases, the insurance business of a captive is solely the credit insurance sold by the producer.

Insurance companies are formed under two types of ownership. Stockholders form a *stock life insurance company.* Stockholders provide the capital to start the company, which they own and control. Policyholders own a *mutual life insurance company.* Since the policyholders are a large group in widely dispersed locations, real control of the company is in the hands of management or the board of directors. Profits from the operations belong to the owners. The profits are paid to stockholders as common stock dividends. In a mutual company, profits are returned to the policyholders as policyholder dividends.

Many of the largest life insurers are mutual companies organized in the 1800s, but new mutual insurance companies have not been organized in recent years. About 80% of the life insurers are stock companies, but measured by size of assets, mutual companies are about equal to stock companies. Most direct writers of credit insurance and all captives are stock companies.

DIRECT WRITERS

Of the approximately 1,800 life insurance companies in the United States, over one-third are involved in credit insurance in one form or another. Direct writers come in all sizes. Some of the smallest direct writers are credit insurers. On the other hand, several of the largest life insurance companies are actively involved in the industry. Direct writers of credit insurance can be classified as:

- Full-Line Ordinary Insurance Companies
- Credit Insurance Specialty Companies
- Direct-Writing Captives

- ***Full-Line Ordinary Companies*** offer the entire gamut of insurance products including ordinary life, annuities, accident and health, and group insurance. Credit insurance is simply one line of business. Its importance to these insurers varies widely, although the line is often a sideline. Credit insurance may be just one area of the group insurance department.

- ***Credit Insurance Specialty Companies*** are direct writers, independent of a particular producer, whose primary line of business is credit insurance. Specialty companies played a dominant role in the development of the industry. These companies began by specializing in one market segment of the credit insurance market; e.g., bank business. Many expanded into other market segments, and then into other insurance lines.

- ***Direct-Writing Captives*** often began as reinsurance companies. As the volume of the producer's business grew, it became advantageous to develop the underwriting and administrative capacity in-house. Finance companies have evolved as the most significant insurers in this category, but some banks have developed direct-writing capability. General agents have occasionally formed captives which began as reinsurers, grew to direct-writing captives, and then progressed to full-line companies.

The formation of a direct-writing insurance company requires substantial time and significant capitalization. A direct writer is incorporated in one state, its state of domicile. Requirements for formation vary from state to state. A direct writer can be formed in Arizona in about six months with only $600,000 in capital and surplus. By contrast, Ohio requires $2,500,000 of capital and surplus, and the process may take several years.

A direct writer can issue policies only in states where it is licensed. Once the insurer is formed in its domiciliary state, it may proceed to obtain licenses in other states. To become licensed, the insurer must meet the capital and surplus requirements of the state in question. Other requirements may be imposed, and the process is often slow. To obtain licenses in all 50 states could take many years, even with sufficient capitalization. A direct writer is a *domestic* insurer in its domiciliary state. In other states where it is licensed, a direct writer is a *foreign* insurer. If licensed in another country, it is an *alien* insurer.

Direct writers are primarily governed by the regulations of their state of domicile. The domiciliary state assumes most of the regulatory burden of its domestic companies. The direct writer, however, must comply with the regulations of each particular state where a policy is issued. Some states, notably New York, have *extraterritorial regulations.* To be licensed in New York, one must be willing to abide by certain regulations wherever the company writes business. If a company is licensed in 49 states, the missing state is usually New York.

Direct writers usually perform the following administrative functions:

- Premium Receipt and Reconciliation
- Agent Licensing
- Policy Form Preparation, Filing and Issuance
- Claims Administration and Payment
- Financial Accounting

CAPTIVES

Producers of credit insurance control the business and decide which direct writer to use. For the sale, premium collection, and policy delivery, the producer is paid a front commission or service fee by the direct writer. As the size of a producer's book of business grows, the producer may wish to participate in the underwriting risk. The sale of credit insurance is a sideline to a primary line of business, such as automobile sales or lending. Therefore, the producer may not want to divert resources to the formation and operation of a direct-writing insurance company. The functions of a direct writer require expertise, and adherence to rather stringent regulations.

Initially, a producer may negotiate *retrospective compensation.* The past experience of the producer's business is evaluated periodically, considering all elements of income and expense. If the business has been profitable, the direct writer shares part of the underwriting profit with the producer. This could be called *one-sided reinsurance.* The producer has the potential for additional compensation but no downside risk. The retrospective compensation cannot be less than zero. None of the regulatory complications of operating an insurance company are present.

As the producer's volume continues to grow, the loss experience becomes more predictable. The producer may want all of the underwriting profit and investment income. When the producer is ready to accept the downside underwriting risk and certain regulations, a captive reinsurer is formed.

In return for an administration fee, often called the *retention,* the direct writer agrees to reinsure the producer's business into the producer's captive reinsurance company. Part of the direct writer's administration may include management of the captive. In theory, the direct writer becomes a service company, and the risk is ceded to the captive. Unfortunately, more than one direct writer has learned the hard way that it is responsible to the insured. The direct writer, not the claimant, has the problem of receiving reimbursement from a reinsurer. A direct writer must never forget whose name is on the policy.

The formation of a reinsurance company offers the simplest method of assuming the underwriting risk. The direct writer retains the necessity of compliance with policy form regulations, agents' licensing requirements, and statistical reporting. As a part of its usual administrative functions, the direct writer must prepare premium, compensation, claim information, and *monthly cessions* (accounting reports). The reinsurer simply receives a monthly accounting of all financial items relating to its business. The reinsurer must only account for its investment portfolio and the monthly accounting reports.

A reinsurance captive can be formed and licensed in only one state. Certain states have encouraged the formation of captives with low capital requirements and streamlined formation procedures. This is particularly advantageous to a producer operating its primary business on a multi-state basis. A producer operating on a multi-state basis would need to have a direct-writing insurance company licensed in each state. Compliance with the regulations of each state requires time, effort, and expense.

Arizona dominates as the state of domicile for reinsurance captives. A domestic Arizona life **reinsurance** company can be formed with $100,000 capital and $50,000 surplus. An Arizona reinsurance company can only assume business from other insurers. It cannot issue policies directly without meeting the higher capital and surplus requirements specified for an Arizona direct writer. The Arizona Department is well-organized for formation and supervision of credit insurance reinsurance captives. The formation process can be accomplished in about four months. Several lawyers and actuaries in the Phoenix area are proficient in aiding producers in the formation process. Formation costs are usually under $4,000. Annual filing fees are under $5,000. The administrative offices of the reinsurer can be located outside of Arizona. As a result, about one-fourth of the insurance companies in the United States are domiciled in Arizona. Texas, Louisiana, and Delaware are other likely sites for captives.

Arizona and most other states limit the risk that an insurer or reinsurer can accept on any one life to 10% of its capital and surplus. If the company has $150,000 of capital and surplus, it can accept up to $15,000 of risk on any one life. Since most credit insurance policies are for amounts under $15,000, the limitation does not usually pose any problem for credit insurers or reinsurers.

Prior to 1977, Arizona required only $25,000 of capital and $12,500 of surplus. In 1977, a regulation was passed requiring the current limits. Any reinsurer not meeting the new requirements was classified as a *limited capital company* and was required to increase capital by $10,000 per year until the new requirements were met. A limited capital company could accept only $3,000 of risk on any one life. This classification was eliminated by 1986.

Sites for captive reinsurers are not limited to the fifty states. Offshore captives are popular in the automobile dealer market. Offshore captives are subject to far less regulation and have the potential for a more favorable tax situation.

Bermuda and the Cayman Islands are the more substantial offshore sites for captives, since the capital requirements are not trivial–$350,000 and $240,000 respectively. Regulation is achieved by the requirement of an annual independent CPA audit. Offshore regulation is based on generally accepted accounting principles (GAAP). These principles do not reflect the conservatism of United States statutory accounting practices. In contrast to Bermuda and Cayman are the Turks and Caicos Islands. For about $4,000 in formation costs, one can be the proud owner of an insurance company. Regulation is practically non-existent.

Favorable tax status can be obtained if the reinsurer qualifies as a *non-controlled foreign corporation*. If certain conditions are met, the reinsurer is not subject to United States taxation until the profits are brought back into the United States. Since these sites are tax-free sites, any income grows tax-free until repatriated. Qualifying for this tax-favored status is not easy. While the laws are complex, the general requirement for qualifying is met if:

1. More than 25% of the voting stock is owned by a non-U.S. resident or another non-controlled foreign corporation, or

2. The owners are U.S. residents, but no individual owns 10% or more of the stock and all operations are conducted offshore.

An offshore reinsurer failing to qualify is a *controlled foreign corporation*, subject to the U.S. tax laws, as is any domestic insurer. Given the favorable tax treatment of small life insurance companies under the 1984 Tax Act, there are now few reasons to form offshore captives.

The ownership of a captive is vested in the producer. For a bank or other financial institution, the reinsurer will usually be a wholly-owned subsidiary. Occasionally, a group of producers will band together to form an *exotic reinsurance company*. An exotic is a reinsurance company with more than one class of stock. Automobile dealers form most exotics. Each automobile dealer agrees to use the same direct writer. Each dealer's business is ceded to the exotic, but separate monthly accountings are done for each dealer. The profit on each dealer's business inures to that dealer's class of stock. Investment income is apportioned among the different classes of stock. This form of ownership provides a method of spreading the overhead operating costs of the captive. In addition, the combined volume may qualify for a lower administrative fee from the direct writer. Direct writers charge lower fees for large producers, reflecting economies of scale in administrative operations. On the negative side, participating in an exotic can result in bickering among the owners. Serious problems arise when one class has bad loss experience. Even worse problems occur when one dealer goes bankrupt, and the captive fails to receive premiums.

In some cases, a direct writer will form, own, and operate the exotic. The direct writer owns the common stock, and each producer is sold a class of preferred stock. The direct writer cedes the business to the exotic. The profits on a producer's business inure to its class of preferred stock. This type of exotic is used for small banks, savings and loan groups, and credit unions in addition to automobile dealers. Exotics are also called "condominium companies" and "rent-a-captive."

WRITTEN AND EARNED COINSURANCE TO CAPTIVES

Credit insurance is normally ceded to a captive on a *coinsurance* basis. Coinsurance means that the direct writer and the reinsurer split the premiums, claims, producer compensation, and premium taxes in proportion to the coinsurance percentage. If the coinsurance percentage is 50%, the two parties split each income and expense element 50-50, except the direct writer's administrative fee. In captive reinsurance, the coinsurance percentage is often 100%, transferring all of the underwriting risk to the captive.

Coinsurance in the credit insurance market has two forms–written and earned. Coinsurance on a *written reinsurance* basis means that the transaction passes from the direct writer directly and immediately to the reinsurer. As premiums are collected by the direct writer, the proportionate share is paid to the reinsurer by the direct writer. Claims are charged each month to the reinsurer as paid by the direct writer. Cash is transferred each month to or from the reinsurer, reflecting the income and expense elements. In other words, the reinsurer replaces the direct writer from a financial standpoint.

Earned reinsurance is like retrospective compensation, except that the compensation can be negative. The direct writer holds the money and accounts for the transaction on its books as if the business were not reinsured. The past experience is reviewed monthly or quarterly to determine if the business has resulted in profits or losses to the direct writer. Since the determination is based on actual past experience, these are *earned profits or losses*. Earned profits are paid to the reinsurer. If the result is a loss, however, the reinsurer must reimburse the direct writer.

A simplified example may help in understanding this difficult concept. The example considers only the cash transactions, ignoring the reserve aspects.

Consider four single premium policies sold on January 1, each with a policy term of three months, with a combined premium of $100. In the second month, one policy has a claim for $40. The lender deducts 30% of premium as its compensation. The coinsurance percentage is 100% of the risk. The direct writer charges an administration fee equal to 10% of premiums, which is reflected as a negative expense item by the direct writer.

CASH TRANSACTIONS OF THE DIRECT WRITER

	January	February	March	Total
Premiums Collected	$100	$ -0-	$-0-	$100
Compensation Paid	30	-0-	-0-	30
Claims Paid	-0-	40	-0-	40

If coinsurance is on a written basis with monthly settlements, the cash flow by month is:

	Direct Writer's Cash			Reinsurer's Cash
	Written	Ceded	Net	Assumed
January Premiums	100	100	-0-	100
Compensation	(30)	(30)	-0-	(30)
Claims	-0-	-0-	-0-	-0-
Administration Fee	-0-	(10)	10	(10)
Net Cash Flow	70	60	10	60
February Premiums	-0-	-0-	-0-	-0-
Compensation	-0-	-0-	-0-	-0-
Claims	(40)	(40)	-0-	(40)
Administration Fee	-0-	-0-	-0-	-0-
Net Cash Flow	(40)	(40)	-0-	(40)
March Premiums	-0-	-0-	-0-	-0-
Compensation	-0-	-0-	-0-	-0-
Claims	-0-	-0-	-0-	-0-
Administration Fee	-0-	-0-	-0-	-0-
Net Cash Flow	-0-	-0-	-0-	-0-

For the direct writer, "net" is equal to written minus ceded amounts. The reinsurer would have a cash profit of $60 in January, a cash loss of $40 in February, and no gain or loss in March. All of the premiums are earned when the policies expire at the end of March. The direct writer has a net cash income of $10. This is not all profit, as the direct writer must pay its cost of administration and premium taxes.

By contrast, if the coinsurance is on an earned basis with quarterly settlements, the direct writer does not make any ceded entries in its financial reports for January or February. At the end of March, the direct writer would send the reinsurer the net profit of $20, ($100-$30-$40-$10).

The reinsurer takes as much risk as possible on a written basis. Whoever holds the money gets the investment income. Since the reinsurer has the risk, it is better to have the investment income.

Two non-underwriting considerations may preclude a reinsurer from accepting all business on a written basis. First, to be a life insurance company under current tax law, more than 50% of a company's reserves must be life insurance reserves. To maintain this percentage, a credit reinsurer may have to limit the amount of disability business reinsured on a written basis, (see page 342). Second, establishing reserves may create an artificial loss in the statutory financial statement, *surplus drain*. The insurer establishing the reserves must be able to absorb this temporary financial loss by having sufficient capital and surplus. Disability insurance creates the most surplus drain. By reinsuring on an earned basis, the surplus drain is absorbed by the direct writer, (see page 320).

Most captives accept 100% of the risk where permitted, but some states frown on a direct writer simply being an administrator and not retaining any risk. For example, New York does not permit 100% coinsurance of New York business. Maryland, Florida and Connecticut do not permit reinsurance of business produced in their state unless the ultimate reinsurer is licensed in the state. An Ohio direct writer cannot reinsure except to a reinsurer licensed in Ohio. However, if the reinsurer is licensed but not domiciled in Ohio, it may assume the business and retrocede it to a company not licensed in Ohio. Several states prohibit or severely limit offshore reinsurance.

The process of reinsuring business is governed by a *reinsurance treaty* between the ceding company and the assuming company. The treaty is a contract specifying the details of the risk transferred, the flow of money, each party's responsibilities, the blocks of business reinsured, the percentage of risk reinsured, and the type of reinsurance. Administrative clauses detail the reporting requirements and any expense charges. Disputes between the parties are usually settled by arbitration, following procedures in the arbitration clause.

An *insolvency clause* is required by many states. It generally specifies that the reinsurer will continue to meet its obligations to the direct writer, or its statutory successor, even if the direct writer becomes insolvent. A *termination clause* defines the procedure to be followed if one party decides to terminate the treaty, and the disposition of the business which is in force when the treaty is terminated. In most cases, the reinsurance continues until the business in force expires. Some treaties permit the direct writer to *recapture* the business in force; i.e., the risk is transferred back to the direct writer and all liability of the reinsurer ceases.

Under written reinsurance, the funds are transferred to the reinsurer, including the funds the direct writer must recover as claims are paid. In addition, the direct writer may be licensed in states which impose conditions on the reserve credit the direct writer takes on the business ceded. For these reasons, the direct writer usually requires that funds be maintained in trust equal to the statutory reserves on the business reinsured. These funds are placed in a bank and are held for the security of the direct writer under the terms of a *custodial trust agreement.* Under earned reinsurance, the funds are retained by the direct writer, who establishes the statutory reserves, until the profits or losses emerge. Therefore, a custodial trust agreement is not required.

A sample written reinsurance treaty, sample custodial trust agreement, and a sample earned reinsurance treaty follow at the end of the chapter. These are only samples, as there is little consistency among insurers and reinsurers on contract wording.

There are several differences between a written and earned treaty, primarily relating to the difference in the flow of funds. The typical differences are:

	Written Reinsurance	**Earned Reinsurance**
Definition of premium ceded	Net written premiums	Net earned premiums
Definition of claims ceded	Paid claims	Incurred claims
Definition of expenses ceded	Percentage of net written premiums	Percentage of net earned premiums
Accounting period	Monthly	Monthly or quarterly

The terms are defined in the treaties. In addition, there may be a difference in the termination provision. Most written treaties and many earned treaties can be terminated for new business on thirty days' notice, but the reinsurance on the business in force continues until the business matures unless both parties agree to a recapture of the business. If the captive is switching to a new direct writer, the new direct writer may negotiate to take over the existing business from the prior direct writer. Under earned reinsurance ceded to an Arizona captive, the direct writer usually gives the captive the right to terminate all business on thirty days' notice, as specified in the sample treaty. Chapter Eight includes historical information regarding this practice.

OTHER FORMS OF CREDIT REINSURANCE

Due to conservatism or state limitations, some captives place a dollar limit on the maximum risk they will retain on any one life, say \$25,000. This may be done with *excess of loss reinsurance* or coinsurance. Using excess of loss reinsurance, the captive would only be responsible for the first \$25,000 of any claim. Once the amount in force drops below $25,000, the captive has the full risk. From the captive standpoint, this works the same as the level-decreasing coverage described in Chapter One.

Using coinsurance, the coinsurance percentage is set at issue for each policy and is maintained during the term of the policy. For a policy in excess of $25,000, the coinsurance percentage is $25,000 divided by the initial amount of insurance. If the policy is for $50,000, the coinsurance percentage is 50%. The captive would retain only 50% of the risk, even after the amount in force drops below $25,000.

These limitations can be implemented by limiting the amount ceded to the captive by the direct writer. Alternatively, the captive may accept 100% of the risk and retrocede the excess risk to a third-party reinsurer.

EXAMPLES OF EXCESS OF LOSS AND COINSURANCE

Excess of Loss Arrangement: The captive is responsible for the first $25,000 on any claim.

Coinsurance Arrangement: For any policy with an initial amount of insurance over $25,000, the excess is reinsured on a coinsurance basis for the duration of the policy.

Excess of loss examples:

Date of Policy	Initial Amount of Insurance	Date of Death	In force on Date of Death	Captive's Share
1-1-85	$50,000	2-5-86	$40,000	$25,000
3-1-85	30,000	2-5-86	20,000	20,000

Coinsurance examples:

Date of Policy	Initial Amount of Insurance	Captive's Percentage	Date of Death	In force on Date of Death	Captive's Share
1-1-85	$50,000	50.0%	2-5-86	$40,000	$20,000
3-1-85	40,000	62.5%	2-5-86	24,000	15,000
6-1-85	20,000	100.0%	2-5-86	18,000	18,000

Stop-loss reinsurance can be used to protect the captive if the losses exceed a specified overall limit. In credit insurance, the limit is expressed as a loss ratio percentage, say 70%. If losses exceed 70% of premium, the stop-loss reinsurer would be responsible for the losses in excess of 70%. In a captive arrangement, the direct writer cedes to the captive on a coinsurance basis. The captive may then turn and buy stop-loss reinsurance from the direct writer or a third-party reinsurer.

Another type of reinsurance used in credit insurance is the *unknown accumulation cover*. A borrower may obtain several loans from one producer, or even from different producers insured by the same direct writer. The insurer can accumulate a substantial amount of insurance on one life. Many insurers do not maintain individual in force files, or do not check for concurrent policies. This reinsurance coverage protects the insurer if losses exceed a specified limit on any one life, provided the excess insurance resulted from a claimant's having two or more policies with the insurer.

PRODUCERS OF CREDIT INSURANCE

Credit insurance is offered to the borrower at the place where the loan is extended. Thus, the primary producers are lending institutions. Practically all lending institutions offer or provide credit insurance. These institutions include:

- Banks
- Savings and Loan Associations
- Credit Unions
- Finance Companies
- Production Credit Associations

Credit insurance is also offered in conjunction with installment sales contracts where the thrust of the business is the sale of consumer goods or services. These businesses include:

- Acceptance Corporations
- Automobile, Mobile Home and Recreational Vehicle Dealers
- Retail Outlets
- Other Situations

From the insurer's viewpoint, the producer's primary function is to offer the insurance product to the borrower. The percentage of the borrowers electing the insurance is directly related to the enthusiasm of the producer. The *penetration rate* is the percentage of borrowers electing to purchase coverage, compared to the number of loans extended where the borrower qualifies for insurance. Penetration rates vary dramatically by producer. On life insurance, a penetration rate of over 60% is considered excellent. On disability insurance, the higher cost results in a range of 40% to 60% being acceptable. Higher penetration rates almost always result in better loss experience.

Management's commitment to the product directly impacts the attitude of the person presenting the product to the borrower. Many producers maintain penetration rates by salesperson or loan officer. In some cases, compensation is indirectly tied to the penetration rate. This compensation is usually some form of incentive compensation. The mere calculation and distribution of a penetration report may favorably impact the penetration rate.

To assist in the sale, insurers provide training and sales literature to the producer. Two promotional sales brochures, one recent and one from twenty years ago, are shown in Figures 2.1 and 2.2. The thrust is the same, but the two styles reflect the changes in our society over twenty years. Training is provided by the home office sales staff or the insurer's general agent. In larger lending institutions, a lender may have someone whose function is to encourage, train, and monitor lending officers. Large automobile dealerships often assign one person the responsibility of completing the sale by offering a financing package. These finance and insurance specialists (F&I men) are trained in the completion of the paperwork of the transaction. If the sale is financed, credit insurance is offered. Compensation of F&I people is often related to performance and penetration rates.

Easy To Acquire

There's no application to fill out, no medical exam to take.

You are eligible no matter what your occupation or how hazardous it is.

Easy To Pay

Your premiums will be automatically included in your regular loan payment. There's no separate check to write or lump sum payment required.

Your insurance goes into effect the moment you sign up for your loan.

How Benefits Are Paid

Benefits are paid directly to the financial institution should you die or become disabled.

To qualify for disability payments, you need not be confined to a hospital bed – but you must be totally disabled and under a doctor's care.

The information in this folder is only an overview of the insurance coverage. The certificate of insurance summarizes the provisions contained in the policy.

Life Insurance

Protects Your Family While Your Loan Is Outstanding

If you were to die before your loan is paid off, this insurance pays it for you.

As long as your payments are up to date, your loan papers will be marked "paid in full" and sent to your family.

Accident And Health Insurance

Makes Your Loan Payments If You're Disabled And Can't Work

If you become ill or are injured in an accident, this insurance pays your installment loan.

Payments begin after the required waiting period and continue as long as you are disabled for the term of your insurance or until your loan is paid, whichever occurs first.

The amount paid each month is based on 1/30th of your monthly payment for each day of your disability.

Why This Insurance Is Good Insurance To Have

You And Your Family Will Be Protected

This insurance assures you and your family that your loan will not present a heavy financial burden because of your death or disability.

You'll Enjoy Peace Of Mind Knowing You Are Protected

You won't have to worry whether or not you or your family will be able to meet your obligation if something happens to you.

What You Should Know About This Insurance

Affordable Premiums

Your coverage will decrease with each loan payment, so you'll pay for just the insurance you need to cover your loan. And no more.

Fig. 2.1 Recent promotional sales brochure.

WHY Credit Life and Disability Insurance?

BECAUSE . . . it protects your family when they need protection most.

It brings you security and peace-of-mind.

It can provide the means of making payments while you are disabled.

It can wipe out your debts at your death.

It lets your family keep collateral used as security for the loan.

It relieves friends and relatives of responsibility for your obligations.

It is low-cost, short-term protection tailored to your debt transaction.

It is easy to get. No medical required. We handle all the details.

As long as you are there, your family's world is safe. All their problems can be settled at the throne of Dad's chair.

But if Dad's chair were left empty because of his—

—sickness
—an accident
—or his death

would they have to shoulder the burden of making the regular payments on family obligations?

Credit Disability Insurance can assist you in making installment payments during periods of disability; Credit Life Insurance can pay off the debt balance remaining at your death.

It means better living, today, for you and your family. You can now use your credit safely.

Credit Life and Disability Insurance is—

—easy to get
—necessary
—economical.

Fig. 2.2 Promotional sales brochure from twenty years ago.

The producer will select one form of coverage to offer consumers for a particular type of loan. Single premium, full benefit programs are widely used. For disability insurance, one plan will be offered, such as fourteen-day retroactive coverage. Offering only one plan simplifies the sale. The consumer is only faced with a purchase/refuse decision. If a consumer does not want insurance, he is often asked to sign a form stating that coverage is not desired. This procedure reminds the salesperson to discuss the product and protects the producer in situations where the consumer claims coverage was not offered.

BANKS

Since banks extend the widest range of loan products, they offer a variety of credit products. The principal categories of lending are:

- Consumer Goods Lending
- Credit Card Lending
- Second Mortgage Lending
- Commercial Lending

- ***Consumer Goods Lending.*** Automobile sales generate most of the consumer goods lending at a bank, since many consumers obtain automobile loans at their bank. Banks have the widest range of penetration rates. Prior to 1960, many banks provided non-contributory credit life insurance as a part of the loan package, or did not offer the product at all. Bankers were reluctant to sell insurance, but their attitude gradually changed. Today, nearly all banks offer the product as an option to the borrower.

  For installment loans, credit insurance is usually offered on the single premium plan for full coverage benefits. Banks use a variety of disability plans. Fourteen-day retroactive and thirty-day non-retroactive disability coverages are the most frequently selected plans.

- ***Credit Card Lending.*** Individual banks offer their own VISA and MasterCard credit cards. In addition, banks offer customers *lines-of-credit.* A line-of-credit may be provided by allowing a high limit on a credit card or by a pre-authorized loan that can be exercised by writing a check. Credit insurance is offered at the time these accounts are established or by subsequent mail solicitation. The consumer signs a statement that permits the bank to include a charge for credit insurance. A monthly outstanding balance premium is charged on the loan cycle date. The premium is based on the average daily balance in the account for the prior month or the balance on the loan cycle date. Proceeds of the insurance are based on the balance of the account on the date of death or disability. Life insurance is usually for the full unpaid balance, while disability insurance is usually a ninety-day lump sum disability benefit.

- ***Second Mortgage Lending.*** While second mortgage lending is similar to consumer goods lending, the term of second mortgage loans tends to be longer and the amounts higher. Home remodeling or major purchases, such as swimming pools, recreational vehicles, and vacation homes, generate the demand for second mortgage loans, also called home equity loans. The collateral is the borrower's equity in his home; a second mortgage lien is placed on the home. The term of the loan is usually seven to ten years, but many loans are repaid prior to maturity. Sale of the collateral, in addition to the normal percentage of consumers who repay loans early or refinance loans, produces early terminations. The high amounts and long terms produce high single premiums and exposure to long-term disability claims. To counteract these characteristics, net payoff life, truncated life, or critical period disability may be offered instead of the standard plans.

- ***Commercial Lending.*** Credit insurance for commercial loans is relatively new and not widespread. Where commercial loans are made to small businesses, the owners of the business are often asked to personally guarantee the loan. An insurable interest exists, and insurance may be written on the lives of the owners guaranteeing the loan. Commercial loans are usually single payment loans for durations of three, six, or twelve months. They are often renewed at a reduced amount.

  Since these loans are for amounts in excess of the usual consumer loans, some underwriting may take place. These underwritten policies match the regular credit policy, except that an application is taken. Short form, *non-medical underwriting* is applied in most cases. The height, weight, and occupation of the borrower, and two or three general health questions are asked. For example:

  1. Have you seen a doctor for any reason in the last three years?

  2. Do you have, or have you been told you have high blood pressure, cancer, heart disease, or diabetes?

  3. To the best of your knowledge, are you in good health?

  Field underwriting by the producer will take place if the borrower's height and weight are within certain ranges, and the answers to the questions do not indicate health problems. Where these conditions are not met, the application is sent to the insurer for approval. Applications are accepted or rejected; substandard rating is not used. On underwritten policies, some states require the premium rates to be lower than the maximum rates permitted for standard plans without underwriting.

Insurance coverage for large loans may be offered using non-credit policy forms. The coverage and premium structure is the same as a credit policy, but the policy must comply with ordinary insurance regulations. Lending officers or sales personnel must have a regular insurance license. In California for example, the credit insurance regulations limit the scope of credit insurance to loans of ten years or less. If the term of the loan exceeds 120 months, the policy is outside the credit regulation. A non-credit policy is often used for long-term commercial loans and second mortgage lending.

SAVINGS AND LOAN ASSOCIATIONS

Credit insurance produced by savings and loan associations is new. Prior to 1982, a federally-chartered savings and loan could not write consumer loans. This changed with deregulation of financial institutions permitting them to write consumer loans and offer credit insurance, but growth of credit insurance sales has been slow.

Some state-chartered savings and loan associations were permitted to write some loans other than first mortgage loans, mostly second mortgage loans. Credit insurance products mirrored the marketplace for the banks.

A few states have hybrid, state-chartered institutions which are neither banks nor savings and loan associations. In Washington state, there are mutual savings banks. Governed by special sections of state law, the mutual savings banks are free to pursue any insurance activity. Savings banks in Connecticut, New York, and Massachusetts are permitted to sell a limited set of ordinary plans.

CREDIT UNIONS

The growth of credit unions in the 1970s led to increased opportunities for insurers to write credit insurance. Credit unions usually provide non-contributory life insurance protection as a part of the loan package. In many cases, a total and permanent disability benefit is also included as a *rider* (or additional benefit) to the life insurance policy. Total and permanent disability coverage is used because the coverage is considerably cheaper than the standard plans of disability insurance. These non-contributory coverages are purchased from insurers with monthly outstanding balance premiums.

Some credit unions have begun to charge for the life insurance. Also, many credit unions do not provide the disability insurance, but offer disability insurance on a contributory basis. The premium mode is usually monthly outstanding balance, since open-end lending is far more prevalent in credit unions than other financial institutions. A few credit unions provide total and permanent coverage and offer the optional contributory coverage at the same time. Thirty-day non-retroactive coverage is prevalent.

CUNA Mutual Life Insurance Society has specialized in credit unions from its inception and remains the dominant insurer in this market. As the credit unions began to offer contributory disability insurance, other insurers entered the credit union market. One insurer may provide the non-contributory life product, while another insurer writes the contributory disability product. This is one of the few situations where a producer uses different insurers for the two product lines.

FINANCE COMPANIES

Finance companies began as small cash loan lenders. Their marketing focus remains on the small borrower, but thrusts have been made into upscale lending markets. Previously, there were many independent finance companies, but the industry has consolidated. Today the industry is dominated by large nationwide and international corporations. These corporations own widely-licensed direct writers. Some finance company captives now write credit business for other producers, and a few have entered ordinary lines of business. Some of the finance companies and their insurers are:

FINANCE COMPANY	INSURER
Associates Corporation of North America	Associates Financial Life Insurance Company
Avco Financial Services	Provident Alliance Life Insurance Company
Beneficial Corporation	The Central National Life Insurance Company of Omaha
Household International	Alexander Hamilton Life Insurance Company of America

Customers of finance companies often have a long, continuous borrowing relationship. Lending in the small loan market is often for day-to-day expenses or financial problems rather than specific consumer purchases. Loans are often refinanced. While each loan is a separate transaction, a loan relationship may continue for many years.

Finance companies offer standard credit insurance products. Their penetration rates are the highest in the credit industry, probably because loan officers are encouraged to offer credit insurance in connection with the loan transaction. This practice is not to the consumer's detriment, since small loan borrowers are the most underinsured segment of the borrowing population.

Finance companies have moved actively into home equity lending. They have led in the development of new credit insurance products to cover the long-term, high-limit loans.

PRODUCTION CREDIT ASSOCIATIONS (PCA)

PCAs are a unique form of lending institution, designed to provide credit to farmers. The Prudential Insurance Company of America and Old Republic Life Insurance Company have been the leaders in this market. Prior to planting time, the farmer gets a loan commitment for the year. During the year, the commitment is exercised to pay the expenses of the farm year. At the end of the year, the income from the harvest is used to repay the loan. At the same time, a new loan commitment is made for the next season. Interest is charged on the amount of credit used. Banks extend agricultural loans on the same basis.

This market is an exception to the rule that one cannot sell credit insurance in excess of the outstanding indebtedness. Level term credit life is sold for the full amount of the loan commitment. The logic is that the full commitment will be needed to produce the year's crop.

ACCEPTANCE CORPORATIONS

Manufacturers of vehicles and other costly consumer goods have formed financing corporations, called acceptance corporations, to facilitate the financing of the purchase of their products. Automobile acceptance corporations are the largest and include:

- Chrysler Credit Corporation
- Ford Motor Credit Corporation
- General Motors Acceptance Corporation

Manufacturers of trucks, farm implements and other durable goods provide similar financing through subsidiaries. In a typical arrangement, the dealer or retailer sells the product under an installment sales contract and finances the purchase himself. Prior to delivery of the product, the borrower's application for credit is forwarded to the acceptance corporation for approval. If approved, the acceptance corporation buys the loan from the dealer by paying the dealer the discounted value of the loan payments. The interest rate used to discount the loan payments generally produces a profit to the dealer for arranging the financing. If the loan application is not approved, the dealer has three options:

1. Offer the loan to a local lending institution,

2. Carry the loan himself, or

3. Cancel the sale of the product.

Previously, the parent corporation or the acceptance corporation arranged with an independent insurance company to offer credit insurance along with the financing assistance. A widely licensed direct writer was needed, since most of the manufactured goods were sold nationwide. The group credit policy issued to General Motors Acceptance Corporation was the largest group policy in the world for many years. Now, most acceptance corporations are affiliated with a widely licensed direct writer which is owned by the acceptance corporation or the parent corporation.

AUTOMOBILE, MOBILE HOME, AND RECREATIONAL VEHICLE DEALERS

Automobile dealers are clearly the most colorful producers of credit insurance. The product is sold wherever cars are sold from the smallest used car lot to the largest new car dealerships. Some dealerships produce $500,000 or more of credit insurance premiums annually. Standard single premium, full benefit plans are sold. Most disability coverage is sold on the fourteen-day retroactive plan.

While some dealers sell credit insurance offered by an affiliate of their acceptance corporation, many use an independent insurer. Since most dealerships are independently owned and geographically diverse, the business is spread among many direct writers of credit insurance. Dealer business requires attention and personal contact, yet the majority of dealerships do not write the volume of premium needed to justify the involvement of home office sales personnel or the development of widespread regional sales offices. Therefore, insurers often solicit automobile dealer business through general agents.

Sales of mobile homes and recreation vehicles require loans for large amounts and for long terms. The term and amount of these loans dictate that only credit life insurance is offered, although critical period disability coverage is now being introduced. Foremost Life Insurance Company has specialized in the mobile home business and is the leading insurer. The pricing is difficult since mobile home buyers are often young people starting a home or older people looking for smaller accommodations after the children have left the home. The result is an unusual age distribution as compared to a typical block of credit insurance business.

RETAIL OUTLETS

Wherever consumer goods are financed, a market opportunity for credit insurance exists. Large nationwide retailers often have revolving charge accounts for consumers' purchases. The insurance coverage parallels the bank credit card market.

Furniture and appliance stores generate installment sales contracts similar to automobile dealers. Credit insurance is offered, but the volume in this market is small, since many purchases are for small amounts.

OTHER SITUATIONS

Limited opportunities exist in other lending environments. One example is stockbrokers' margin accounts for common stock purchases. Several credit insurers have tried to write this market without much success. Balances tend to be for large amounts and the average age is high.

SAMPLE WRITTEN REINSURANCE TREATY

CREDIT LIFE AND DISABILITY
COINSURANCE CONTRACT OF REINSURANCE

ISSUED TO

SOUND AND SECURE LIFE INSURANCE COMPANY
ANYTOWN, USA
(hereinafter referred to as the "Company")

by

ABC LIFE INSURANCE COMPANY
PHOENIX, ARIZONA
(hereinafter referred to as the "Reinsurer")

ARTICLE I - REINSURANCE COVERAGE

A. By this Contract, the Company obligates itself to cede to the Reinsurer, and the Reinsurer obligates itself to accept as reinsurance of the Company, the coinsurance percentage of the Company's liability under the credit life and disability insurance risks specified in Exhibit "A" attached hereto (hereinafter referred to as the "Reinsured Policies").

B. The liability of the Reinsurer shall begin simultaneously with that of the Company. In no event shall the reinsurance be in force and binding unless the Reinsured Policies are in force and unless the issuance and delivery of the Reinsured Policies constituted the doing of business in a state in which the Company was properly licensed.

C. Reinsurance under this Contract shall be on a coinsurance basis and shall follow the original forms of the Company.

D. The amount of reinsurance under this Contract shall be maintained in force without reduction so long as the amount of insurance carried by the Company on the Reinsured Policies remains in force without reduction, except as provided in Article XIII.

ARTICLE II - COMPUTATION OF REINSURANCE PREMIUMS

The reinsurance premiums to be paid by the Company to the Reinsurer shall be the Reinsurer's pro rata share of the net written premiums collected by the Company during the accounting period under each Reinsured Policy. Net written premiums are the gross premiums charged the insureds less any refunded premiums paid to the insureds.

ARTICLE III - CLAIMS

The Reinsurer shall be liable hereunder for its pro rata share of all claims paid by the Company on the Reinsured Policies.

ARTICLE IV - COMMISSIONS AND EXPENSE ALLOWANCE

The Reinsurer shall pay the Company its pro rata share of all commissions paid by the Company on the Reinsured Policies at the rates specified in Exhibit "A." In addition, the Reinsurer shall pay the Company the expense allowance specified in Exhibit "A."

ARTICLE V - REPORTS AND REMITTANCES

A. Within twenty (20) days after the end of each calendar month during the currency of this Contract, the Company shall provide a report to the Reinsurer, on forms mutually acceptable to both parties, setting forth for the month just completed:

1. Ceded net written premium;
2. Ceded paid claims;
3. Ceded commissions and expense allowances;

4. Ceded mortality reserves and unearned premiums as of the end of the calendar month;

5. Ceded outstanding claims as of the end of the calendar month (including reported claims and reserves for incurred but not reported claims).

B. The balance, if positive, of (1) less (2) less (3) shall be remitted by the Company to the Reinsurer with each monthly report. Any balance due the Company shall be remitted by the Reinsurer within twenty (20) days following receipt and verification of the Company's report.

C. The Reinsurer agrees to maintain funds in trust equal to the Company's statutory reserves on the Reinsured Policies in accordance with the Custodial Trust Agreement between the Company, the Reinsurer, and XYZ Bank of Arizona, N.A., dated concurrently herewith.

ARTICLE VI - OVERSIGHTS

If failure to comply with any terms of this Contract is shown to be unintentional and the result of misunderstanding or oversight on the part of either the Company or the Reinsurer, both the Company and the Reinsurer shall be restored to the positions they would have occupied had no such misunderstanding or oversight occurred.

ARTICLE VII - POLICY CHANGES

If a change is made in the Reinsured Policies which affects reinsurance hereunder, the Company shall immediately notify the Reinsurer of such change.

ARTICLE VIII - TAXES, ASSESSMENTS AND EXPENSES

Neither party hereto shall be liable to the other for taxes, assessments or any expenses, except as specified in Article IV, resulting from reinsurance hereunder. The Company shall furnish the Reinsurer with all necessary information so that the Reinsurer will not be required to perform any office work other than the regular bookkeeping entries made in connection with reinsurance accounting.

ARTICLE IX - INSPECTION OF RECORDS

The Reinsurer shall have the right at any reasonable time to inspect, at the office of the Company, all books and documents relating to the reinsurance under this Contract.

ARTICLE X - INSOLVENCY

A. In the event of the insolvency of the Company, this reinsurance shall be payable directly to the Company or to its liquidator, receiver, conservator, or statutory successor on the basis of the liability of the Company without diminution because of the insolvency of the Company or because the liquidator, receiver, conservator, or statutory successor of the Company has failed to pay all or a portion of any claim. It is agreed, however, that the liquidator, receiver, conservator or statutory successor of the Company shall give written notice to the Reinsurer of the pendency of a claim against the Company, indicating the Reinsured Policy for which the claim would involve a possible liability on the part of the Reinsurer, within a reasonable time after such claim is filed in the conservation or liquidation proceeding or in the receivership, and that during the pendency of such claim, the Reinsurer may investigate such claim and interpose, at its own expense, in the proceeding where such claim is to be adjudicated, any defense or defenses that it may deem available to the Company.

B. It is further understood and agreed that, in the event of insolvency of the Company, the reinsurance under this Contract shall be payable directly by the Reinsurer to the Company or to its liquidator, receiver, conservator or statutory successor, except (a) where the Contract specifically provides another payee of such reinsurance in the event of the insolvency of the Company and (b) where the Reinsurer, with the consent of the direct insured or insureds, has assumed such policy obligations of the Company as direct obligations of the Reinsurer to the payees under such policies and in substitution for the obligations of the Company to such payees.

ARTICLE XI - ARBITRATION

A. In the event of any dispute or difference of opinion hereafter arising with respect to this Contract, it is hereby mutually agreed that such dispute or difference of opinion shall be submitted to arbitration. One Arbiter shall be chosen by the Company, the other by the Reinsurer, and an Umpire shall be chosen by the two Arbiters before they enter upon arbitration, all of whom shall be active or retired disinterested executive officers of insurance companies. In the event that either party should fail to choose an Arbiter within thirty (30) days following a written request by the other party to do so, the requesting party may choose two Arbiters who shall, in turn, choose an Umpire before entering upon arbitration. If the two Arbiters fail to agree upon the selection of an Umpire within thirty (30) days following their appointment, each Arbiter shall name three nominees of whom the other shall decline two, and the decision shall be made by drawing lots.

B. Each party shall present its case to the Arbiters within thirty (30) days following the date of appointment of the Umpire. The Arbiters shall consider this Contract as an honorable agreement rather than merely as a legal obligation, and they are relieved of all judicial formalities and may abstain from following the strict rules of law. The decision of the Arbiters shall be final and binding on both parties.

C. If more than one reinsurer is involved in the same dispute, all such reinsurers shall constitute and act as one part for purposes of this Article and communications shall be made by the Company to each of the reinsurers constituting one party;

provided, however, that nothing herein shall impair the rights of such reinsurers to assert several, rather than joint, defenses or claims, nor be construed as changing the liability of the reinsurers participating under the terms of this Contract from several to joint.

D. Each party shall bear the expense of its own Arbiter, and shall jointly and equally bear with the other the expense of the Umpire and of the arbitration. In the event that the two Arbiters are chosen by one party, as above provided, the expense of the Arbiters, the Umpire and the arbitration shall be equally divided between the two parties.

E. Any arbitration proceeding shall take place in Anytown, USA.

ARTICLE XII - PARTIES TO CONTRACT

This is a contract for indemnity reinsurance solely between the Company and the Reinsurer. The acceptance of reinsurance hereunder shall not create any right or legal relation whatever between the Reinsurer and the insured or the beneficiary under any Reinsured Policy.

ARTICLE XIII - DURATION OF THE CONTRACT

A. This Contract shall become effective at 12:01 A.M. on December 31, 1985, and shall continue in force until terminated pursuant to Paragraph B below.

B. This Contract may be terminated for new business by either party giving thirty (30) days written notice by certified mail to the other party. Reinsurance of the Reinsured Policies in force on the date of termination shall continue until the natural expiration of the Reinsured Policies.

C. This Contract may be amended by mutual consent, in writing, of both parties.

IN WITNESS WHEREOF, the parties hereto, by their respective duly authorized officers, have executed this Contract in duplicate.

ATTEST:

SOUND AND SECURE LIFE INSURANCE COMPANY

____

By:____________________________

Title:__________________________

ATTEST:

ABC LIFE INSURANCE COMPANY

____

By:____________________________

Title:__________________________

Dated: _________________________

EXHIBIT A

ATTACHED AND MADE A PART OF THE REINSURANCE CONTRACT EFFECTIVE DECEMBER 31, 1985, BETWEEN SOUND AND SECURE LIFE INSURANCE COMPANY AND ABC LIFE INSURANCE COMPANY.

RISKS REINSURED:

All certificates of credit life and disability insurance issued after December 31, 1985 under the group policy issued by the Company to ABC National Bank designated by the Company's internal control number A001.

COINSURANCE PERCENTAGE:

Credit life insurance: 100%
Credit disability insurance: 60%

COMMISSIONS:

Credit life insurance:	25% of net written reinsured premiums
Credit disability insurance:	25% of net written reinsured premiums

EXPENSE ALLOWANCE:

Credit life insurance:	10% of net written reinsured premium
Credit disability insurance:	10% of net written reinsured premiums

SAMPLE TRUST AGREEMENT

CUSTODIAL TRUST AGREEMENT
Effective: December 31, 1985
entered into by and between

SOUND AND SECURE LIFE INSURANCE COMPANY
Anytown, USA
(hereinafter referred to as the "Company")

and

ABC LIFE INSURANCE COMPANY
Phoenix, Arizona
(hereinafter referred to as the "Reinsurer")

and

XYZ BANK OF ARIZONA, N.A.
Phoenix, Arizona
(hereinafter referred to as the "Bank")

SECTION 1 - PURPOSE OF AGREEMENT

1.1 Pursuant to the terms hereof, the Reinsurer obligates itself to deliver to and deposit with the Bank "securities" (as defined in 3.1) which shall be held by the Bank as collateral for the payment of amounts due the Company thereafter under the Coinsurance Contract of Reinsurance, effective December 31, 1985, between the Company and the Reinsurer (hereinafter referred to as the "Reinsurance Contract.") The securities thus held by the Bank are hereinafter referred to as the "Fund."

1.2 During the term of this Agreement and for the purposes expressed herein, the Reinsurer hereby pledges with and grants to the Company a security interest in the Fund held by the Bank as agent and bailee for the Company.

SECTION 2 - DEPOSITS TO AND WITHDRAWALS FROM FUND

2.1 Within 10 days after this Agreement is executed by the Reinsurer, the Reinsurer shall deliver to the Bank securities with market value (determined as in 3.2) at least equal to all statutory reserves applicable to the risk ceded to the Reinsurer under the Reinsurance Contract. Such reserves shall include, but not be limited to, mortality reserves on life insurance policies, unearned premium reserves on disability policies, and claim reserves for claims incurred but not reported, claims in course of settlement, and continuing disability claims.

2.2 Within 10 days after the end of each calendar quarter, commencing with the calendar quarter ending March 31, 1986, the Reinsurer shall deposit with the Bank such additional securities as may be necessary to increase the aggregate market value of the Fund to an amount at least equal to the said statutory reserves on the last day of the quarter.

2.3 However, should the aggregate market value of the Fund at the end of any calendar quarter be greater than the amount required in 2.2, the Reinsurer may withdraw securities from the Fund so as to reduce the aggregate market value of the Fund to an amount not less than the amount required in 2.2.

2.4 The Reinsurer may at any time withdraw securities from the Fund provided that concurrently therewith securities of equal or greater market value are deposited in the Fund, and the Bank is authorized to permit such substitution of securities without notice to the Company and without the Bank making any determination of the value. The Reinsurer shall give the Company written notice of each and every withdrawal or substitution, setting forth all details relating thereto, on or before 10 days after each such transaction.

2.5 All securities, other than cash, deposited by the Reinsurer with the Bank pursuant to 2.1, 2.2, or 2.4 shall be accompanied by executed assignments, endorsements in blank or stock powers, as appropriate, to enable the Company to transfer title to such securities pursuant to the Company's right and authority under Section 4. The Bank shall have no obligation to determine the enforceability of such instruments. Any such instruments, which are not part of the security, shall be held and safeguarded by the Bank and delivered to the Company, if the Company is entitled under Section 4 to take possession of the securities applicable thereto, or returned to the Reinsurer with any withdrawals of the applicable securities by the Reinsurer pursuant to 2.3, 2.4 or Section 8.

SECTION 3 - SECURITIES

3.1 The term "securities" as used herein is defined as any combination of (a) cash, (b) certificates of deposits issued by any national or state chartered bank or savings and loan association, (c) United States Government issued or guaranteed bonds, bill or notes, (d) any other bonds with a Standard & Poor's quality rating of "A" or better, or (e) money market funds up to $100,000 provided that the amount invested is fully insured by the FDIC or FSLIC.

3.2 For the purposes of this Agreement, the market value of securities shall be determined as follows: (a) at the time any securities are deposited initially with the Bank, and with respect to securities on deposit at the end of each calendar quarter, the Reinsurer shall in good faith place a tentative market value on said securities and shall notify the Company of such valuation by supplement to the Bank's quarterly activities report; (b) if the Company disagrees with such tentative market valuation, it may so notify the Reinsurer within 30 days after the date it receives the Bank's quarterly activities report and the Reinsurer's supplement thereto; and (c) in the event the parties cannot resolve any difference with respect to the market value of the securities, the market value of the security in dispute shall be determined by using the definition of "value" set forth by the

Valuation Committee of the National Association of Insurance Commissioners.

SECTION 4 - COMPANY'S CLAIM ON FUND

4.1 In the event the Reinsurer defaults upon its obligation to pay any balance due the Company under the Reinsurance Contract, or in the event the Reinsurer is in default with respect to required deposits under this Agreement, the Company may take possession of the securities represented by the Fund and sell the same at public or private sale or exercise such other rights as may be permitted by applicable statute; provided, however, that the Company first complies with 4.2.

4.2 The Company may demand possession of the Fund, and the Bank is authorized to deliver the Fund to the Company, upon receipt by the Bank of the Company's affidavit stating that (a) 10 days' notice (as provided in 4.3) has been given to the Reinsurer, and (b) the Reinsurer is in default (as provided in 4.1), which default has not been cured by the Reinsurer within the 10 days since notice was given; and (c) the Company is entitled to receive from the Bank the securities currently in the Fund.

4.3 Notice of default must be given in writing to the Reinsurer, and shall set forth the fact of the default and that the Company will take action to claim the securities currently in the Fund at the end of 10 days following delivery of notice to the Reinsurer. The Reinsurer may cure such default within the 10-day period.

4.4 The Company shall return to the Reinsurer any amount by which the proceeds of the sale (after reimbursement for reasonable and necessary legal and other expenses incurred in connection therewith) of such securities pursuant hereto exceeds the balance due the Company under the Reinsurance Contract. The Reinsurer shall continue to be liable for any amount by which balances due the Company exceed the said net proceeds of the sale.

SECTION 5 - INTEREST, DIVIDENDS AND EXPENSES

5.1 Any interest or dividends from securities deposited in the Fund shall be payable by the Bank to the Reinsurer; provided, however that no such amount shall be withdrawn by the Reinsurer unless after such withdrawal the value of the Fund shall be at least equal to the value required at all times in accordance with this agreement.

5.2 All fees and expenses charged by the Bank for its services under the terms of this Agreement shall be paid by the Reinsurer.

SECTION 6 - BANK

6.1 The Bank agrees to provide copies of quarterly activities reports to the Reinsurer and the Company as soon as possible following the end of each calendar quarter. Said reports shall show all deposits, withdrawals, substitutions and a listing of securities in the Fund as of the end of the quarter.

6.2 The Bank shall in no way be responsible for determining (a) market value or rating of the initial deposit of securities by the Reinsurer, (b) market value or rating of any securities as may from time to time be substituted by the Reinsurer, or (c) the amount of securities required to be deposited by the Reinsurer.

6.3 The Bank is not a party to, and is not bound by, or charged with notice of, any contract or agreement out of which this Agreement may arise.

6.4 The Bank is not responsible or liable in any manner whatever for the sufficiency, correctness, genuineness or validity of the subject matter of this Agreement or any part thereof, or for the form or execution thereof, or for the identity or authority of any person executing or depositing it.

6.5 The Bank's capacity as agent and bailee is strictly limited to the act of holding the funds subject hereto for and on behalf of the Company to create a valid and perfected pledge pursuant to the applicable statutes, and the Bank assumes no greater or further responsibility to the Company than is required for this purpose.

6.6 The Bank shall be protected in acting upon any written notice, request, waiver, consent, certificate, receipt, authorization, power of attorney or other paper or document which the Bank in good faith believes to be genuine and what it purports to be.

6.7 The Bank shall not be liable for anything which it may do or refrain from doing in connection herewith, except its own negligence or willful misconduct.

6.8 The Bank hereby waives any right of set-off and all other rights and remedies against or affecting the Fund.

6.9 The Bank may at any time resign from, and terminate its capacity hereunder by written notice to both the Company and the Reinsurer effective in the manner and at the time described herein. The Reinsurer, upon receipt of such notice, shall undertake to obtain the agreement of a successor depository to act in accordance with all agreements of the Bank hereunder, including its acting in the capacity of bailee and agent for the Company pursuant hereto. The choice of depository is subject to approval by the Company, which approval shall not be unreasonably withheld if the depository so chosen is chartered as a national or state bank and has capital and surplus of at least $10,000,000.00. In the event the Reinsurer is unable to obtain such an approved successor depository within 30 days from its receipt of notice from the Bank, the Bank is authorized to turn over the Fund to the Company, as pledgee in possession of the collateral. In such event, the Company shall, until an approved successor depository is found, hold the Fund pursuant to the Terms hereof, being fully substituted for the Bank except that

Section 6 hereof shall not apply. Upon the Bank's delivery of the Fund to the successor depository or, if none is approved, to the Company, along with a closing statement showing all activities (as contemplated in 6.1 hereof) from the last quarterly report, the Bank shall be discharged of further responsibilities hereunder.

SECTION 7 - ACCESS TO RECORDS

7.1 The Company by its duly appointed representative, shall have the right at any reasonable time to examine all papers in the possession of the Reinsurer and the Bank applicable to this Agreement, and the Fund deposited and maintained hereunder.

SECTION 8 - TERMINATION

8.1 This Agreement shall terminate and the Bank shall release and deliver to the Reinsurer all securities held in the Fund pursuant to this Agreement upon termination of the Reinsurance Contract, but only if Company notifies Bank in writing of such termination. Upon receipt by the Bank of written notice from the Reinsurer stating that all of the Reinsurer's obligations to the Company under the Reinsurance Contract have been discharged, this agreement shall terminate; provided, however, that no such securities will be released to the Reinsurer unless written notice of the proposed termination and release is first given to the Company and the Company shall not have objected to the same in writing within 10 days after receipt of such written notice and Company shall notify Bank in writing of such termination.

SECTION 9 - CONSTRUCTION AND EFFECT

9.1 This Agreement and all proceedings pursuant hereto shall be governed by the laws of the state of Arizona.

9.2 This Agreement shall be binding upon and shall inure to the benefit of the parties hereto, their successors and assigns.

9.3 This Agreement may be executed in any number of counterparts or by attached documents, all of which shall constitute one and the same original.

IN WITNESS WHEREOF, the parties hereto by their respective duly authorized representatives have executed this Agreement as of the dates undermentioned:

For the Reinsurer:

This ________ day of ____________________, 198___.

____
ABC LIFE INSURANCE COMPANY

For the Bank:

This ________ day of ____________________, 198___.

____
XYZ BANK OF ARIZONA, N.A.

For the Company:

This ________ day of ____________________, 198___.

____
SOUND AND SECURE LIFE
INSURANCE COMPANY

SAMPLE EARNED REINSURANCE TREATY

CREDIT DISABILITY
COINSURANCE CONTRACT OF REINSURANCE

ISSUED TO

SOUND AND SECURE LIFE INSURANCE COMPANY
ANYTOWN, USA
(hereinafter referred to as the "Company")

by

ABC LIFE INSURANCE COMPANY
PHOENIX, ARIZONA
(hereinafter referred to as the "Reinsurer")

ARTICLE I - REINSURANCE COVERAGE

A. By this Contract, the Company obligates itself to cede to the Reinsurer, and the Reinsurer obligates itself to accept as reinsurance of the Company, the coinsurance percentage of the Company's liability under the credit disability insurance risks specified in Exhibit "A" attached hereto (hereinafter referred to as the "Reinsured Policies").

B. The liability of the Reinsurer shall begin simultaneously with that of the Company. In no event shall the reinsurance be in force and binding unless the Reinsured Policies are in force and unless the issuance and delivery of the Reinsured Policies constituted the doing of business in a state in which the Company was properly licensed.

C. Reinsurance under this Contract shall be on a coinsurance basis and shall follow the original forms of the Company.

D. The amount of reinsurance under this Contract shall be maintained in force without reduction so long as the amount of insurance carried by the Company on the Reinsured Policies remains in force without reduction, except as provided in Article XIII.

ARTICLE II- COMPUTATION OF REINSURANCE PREMIUMS

The reinsurance premiums to be paid by the Company to the Reinsurer shall be the Reinsurer's pro rata share of the net earned premiums during the accounting period under the Reinsured Policies. Net earned premiums are the gross written premiums charged the insureds less any refunded premiums paid to the insureds for the accounting period; plus the unearned premiums on the Reinsured Policies at the beginning of the accounting period; less the unearned premiums on the Reinsured Policies at the end of the accounting period.

ARTICLE III - CLAIMS

The Reinsurer shall be liable hereunder for its pro rata share of all claims incurred by the Company on the Reinsured Policies during the accounting period. Incurred claims are equal to the claims paid during the accounting period; less the claim reserves at the beginning of the accounting period; plus the claim reserves at the end of the accounting period. Claim reserves include reserves for claims incurred but not reported, claims in course of settlement, and continuing claims.

ARTICLE IV - COMMISSIONS AND EXPENSE ALLOWANCE

The Reinsurer shall pay the Company its pro rata share of all commissions incurred by the Company on the Reinsured Policies at the rates specified in Exhibit "A." In addition, the Reinsurer shall pay the Company the expense allowance specified in Exhibit "A."

ARTICLE V - REPORTS AND REMITTANCES

A. Within twenty (20) days after the end of each calendar month during the currency of this Contract, the Company shall provide a report to the Reinsurer, on forms mutually acceptable to both parties, setting forth for the month just completed:

1. Ceded net earned premium;

2. Ceded incurred claims;

3. Ceded incurred commissions and expense allowances;

4. Ceded unearned premiums as of the end of the calendar month;

5. Ceded outstanding claims as of the end of the calendar month (including reported claims and reserves for incurred but not reported claims).

B. The balance, if positive, of (1) less (2) less (3) shall be remitted by the Company to the Reinsurer with each monthly report. Any balance due the Company shall be remitted by the Reinsurer within twenty (20) days following receipt and verification of the Company's report.

ARTICLE VI - OVERSIGHTS

If failure to comply with any terms of this Contract is shown to be unintentional and the result of misunderstanding or oversight on the part of either the Company or the Reinsurer, both the Company and the Reinsurer shall be restored to the positions they would have occupied had no such misunderstanding or oversight occurred.

ARTICLE VII - POLICY CHANGES

If a change is made in the Reinsured Policies which affects reinsurance hereunder, the Company shall immediately notify the Reinsurer of such change.

ARTICLE VIII - TAXES, ASSESSMENTS AND EXPENSES

Neither party hereto shall be liable to the other for taxes, assessments or any expenses, except as specified in Article IV, resulting from reinsurance hereunder. The Company shall furnish the Reinsurer with all necessary information so that the Reinsurer will not be required to perform any office work other than the regular bookkeeping entries made in connection with reinsurance accounting.

ARTICLE IX - INSPECTION OF RECORDS

The Reinsurer shall have the right at any reasonable time to inspect, at the office of the Company, all books and documents relating to the reinsurance under this Contract.

ARTICLE X - INSOLVENCY

A. In the event of the insolvency of the Company, this reinsurance shall be payable directly to the Company or to its liquidator, receiver, conservator, or statutory successor on the basis of the liability of the Company without diminution because of the insolvency of the Company or because the liquidator, receiver, conservator, or statutory successor of the Company has failed to pay all or a portion of any claim. It is agreed, however, that the liquidator, receiver, conservator or statutory successor of the Company shall give written notice to the Reinsurer of the pendency of a claim against the Company, indicating the Reinsured Policy for which the claim would involve a possible liability on the part of the Reinsurer, within a reasonable time after such claim is filed in the conservation or liquidation proceeding or in the receivership, and that during the pendency of such claim, the Reinsurer may investigate such claim and interpose, at its own expense, in the proceeding where such claim is to be adjudicated, any defense or defenses that it may deem available to the Company.

B. It is further understood and agreed that, in the event of insolvency of the Company, the reinsurance under this Contract shall be payable directly by the Reinsurer to the Company or to its liquidator, receiver, conservator or statutory successor, except (a) where the Contract specifically provides another payee of such reinsurance in the event of the insolvency of the Company and (b) where the Reinsurer, with the consent of the direct insured or insureds, has assumed such policy obligations of the Company as direct obligations of the Reinsurer to the payees under such policies and in substitution for the obligations of the Company to such payees.

ARTICLE XI - ARBITRATION

A. In the event of any dispute or difference of opinion hereafter arising with respect to this Contract, it is hereby mutually agreed that such dispute or difference of opinion shall be submitted to arbitration. One Arbiter shall be chosen by the Company, the other by the Reinsurer, and an Umpire shall be chosen by the two Arbiters before they enter upon arbitration, all of whom shall be active or retired disinterested executive officers of insurance companies. In the event that either party should fail to choose an Arbiter within thirty (30) days following a written request by the other party to do so, the requesting party may choose two Arbiters who shall, in turn, choose an Umpire before entering upon arbitration. If the two Arbiters fail to agree upon the selection of an Umpire within thirty (30) days following their appointment, each Arbiter shall name three nominees of whom the other shall decline two, and the decision shall be made by drawing lots.

B. Each party shall present its case to the Arbiters within thirty (30) days following the date of appointment of the Umpire. The

Arbiters shall consider this Contract as an honorable agreement rather than merely as a legal obligation, and they are relieved of all judicial formalities and may abstain from following the strict rules of law. The decision of the Arbiters shall be final and binding on both parties.

C. If more than one reinsurer is involved in the same dispute, all such reinsurers shall constitute and act as one part for purposes of this Article and communications shall be made by the Company to each of the reinsurers constituting one party; provided, however, that nothing herein shall impair the rights of such reinsurers to assert several, rather than joint, defenses or claims, nor be construed as changing the liability of the reinsurers participating under the terms of this Contract from several to joint.

D. Each party shall bear the expense of its own Arbiter, and shall jointly and equally bear with the other the expense of the Umpire and of the arbitration. In the event that the two Arbiters are chosen by one party, as above provided, the expense of the Arbiters, the Umpire and the arbitration shall be equally divided between the two parties.

E. Any arbitration proceeding shall take place in Anytown, USA.

ARTICLE XII - PARTIES TO CONTRACT

This is a contract for indemnity reinsurance solely between the Company and the Reinsurer. The acceptance of reinsurance hereunder shall not create any right or legal relation whatever between the Reinsurer and the insured or the beneficiary under any Reinsured Policy.

ARTICLE XIII - DURATION OF THE CONTRACT

A. This Contract shall become effective at 12:01 A.M. on December 31, 1985, and shall continue in force until terminated pursuant to Paragraph B or C below.

B. This Contract may be terminated for new business by the Company giving thirty (30) days written notice by certified mail to the Reinsurer. Reinsurance of the Reinsured Policies in force on the date of termination shall continue until the natural expiration of the Reinsured Policies.

C. This Contract may be terminated by the Reinsurer giving thirty (30) days written notice by certified mail to the Company. Termination by the Reinsurer may be for new business only, or, at the option of the Reinsurer, may be for both new business and business in force on the date of termination.

D. This Contract may be amended by mutual consent, in writing, of both parties.

IN WITNESS WHEREOF, the parties hereto, by their respective duly authorized officers, have executed this Contract in duplicate.

ATTEST:	SOUND AND SECURE LIFE INSURANCE COMPANY
______________________	By: ______________________
	Title: ______________________
Dated: ______________________	

ATTEST:	ABC LIFE INSURANCE COMPANY
______________________	By: ______________________
	Title: ______________________
Dated: ______________________	

EXHIBIT A

ATTACHED AND MADE A PART OF THE REINSURANCE CONTRACT EFFECTIVE DECEMBER 31, 1985, BETWEEN SOUND AND SECURE LIFE INSURANCE COMPANY AND ABC LIFE INSURANCE COMPANY.

RISKS REINSURED:

All certificates of credit disability insurance issued after December 31, 1985 under the group policy issued by the Company to ABC National Bank designated by the Company's internal control number A001.

COINSURANCE PERCENTAGE:

Credit disability insurance:	40%

COMMISSIONS:

Credit disability insurance:	25% of net earned reinsurance premiums

EXPENSE ALLOWANCE:

Credit disability insurance:	10% of net earned reinsurance premiums

CHAPTER THREE

HOME OFFICE OPERATIONS

This chapter describes the home office operations of credit insurance companies in marketing and administering the products. The common industry practices, methods of operation, and procedures are presented to give a general picture of the operations. There is no implication that these practices are the way things must be done, or even that they are the way things should be done. Common variations are discussed, but many other variations are possible. The diversity of products, lender practices, and insurer practices results in a wide range of valid approaches.

SALES AND SALES ADMINISTRATION

In a credit insurance company, the sales area plays a critical role, often extending beyond the usual responsibilities found in other lines of insurance. In addition to soliciting new accounts, the sales force performs many service functions. Salespeople often train the producers' personnel, work as liaisons with the producers when problems arise, and implement rate changes and product modifications. The sales force frequently monitors the financial experience of the producers and initiates corrective action. A separate sales administration area often handles day-to-day administrative details.

For a credit insurer, the sales effort is directed at the producer of the business, rather than the ultimate insured. Since each market segment requires a different approach, insurers tend to direct their efforts toward one or two primary markets, while individual salespeople often market to just one particular segment. Given the vast number of producers and their wide geographical spread, many insurers augment the home office sales staff with independent general agents.

The primary responsibilities of the home office sales staff include soliciting new producers and servicing existing accounts. Credit insurance is a mature marketplace. Virtually all of the potential producers of the product already have a credit insurance program in place. In most situations, compensation to producers has risen to the point where further increases of any magnitude are difficult to offer. Therefore, the sales effort generally promotes the insurer's range of products and service abilities.

The need for an insurer to distinguish itself from the competition creates pressure to find distinctive features in products which are fundamentally similar. One approach has been to liberalize underwriting restrictions. Insurers have gradually increased the *guaranteed issue limit*; i.e., the amount of insurance which will be accepted by the insurer without any medical questions or examinations. Another approach has been to introduce underwritten policies with issue limits up to $250,000. A third approach has been to develop alternative coverages, such as truncated life and critical period disability. Neither the high issue limits nor the alternative products are likely to generate significant amounts of business, but they give the sales staff something to discuss with the producers, rather than just the promise of better service.

Many insurers offer promotional material and training to the producer's staff. This helps the insurer secure new producers and achieve more sales from existing producers. Consumer literature is usually limited to generic brochures extolling the value of credit insurance. The brochure usually describes what the insurance covers and emphasizes the security of knowing the loan is insured. A wider range of material is available aimed at the individual presenting the product to the consumer. Sample sales presentations, slide and movie shows, and motivational meetings are designed to convince the solicitor that the product has value for the consumer and the producer.

In the automobile dealer market, insurers have developed and promoted the concept of a specialist within the dealership to handle the finance and insurance elements of the automobile sale. Most dealerships now have one or more individuals whose primary function is to prepare the paperwork of the sale, to explain the financing options, and to offer credit insurance. If the consumer wants to finance the purchase and buy the insurance, all of the paperwork can be done at the dealership. Insurers and general agents conduct finance and insurance schools to train the "F & I" people. Some insurers even help the dealership find qualified personnel for the job.

Successful promotion of the product at the producer level depends on management commitment. If the producer's top management does not take an active role in stressing the importance of the product's sale, the attitude filters down through the organization. One tool for management review is a penetration report. The penetration rate is the percentage of eligible borrowers who purchase the insurance. It is useful to analyze penetration rates based on both number and size of loans. Statistics are maintained by individual lending officer and summarized by branch or location. The mere compilation and publication of a penetration report improves the awareness of the importance of the product. Since the data required to produce the report includes information on all loans, penetration reports are usually prepared by the producer. Insurers assist in designing and evaluating the report. Some insurers have computer programs available. In a few cases, the producers supply the loan information, and the insurer produces the report.

Many credit insurers are regional companies operating within a limited geographical area. For these insurers, the internal sales staff may be adequate to meet the desired production goals. Insurers operating on a wider scale may have regional sales offices; however, a widely licensed insurer usually receives a portion of its business through independent general agents who operate within a limited geographical area.

The role of the general agent is to provide local sales and service functions. The independent agent is particularly valuable in the automobile dealer and credit union market segments, which consist of thousands of relatively small accounts. Travel and overhead costs prevent an insurer from using company personnel unless the insurer commits to a large staff with many locations. General agents usually only offer the products of one credit insurer. Insurers may offer the general agent a geographical exclusive, although many do not. Home office staff may be available to assist the general agent in the solicitation of large accounts.

Service functions of the sales staff and general agents include the responsibility of maintaining contact with existing accounts. Each account should be contacted at least once a year to insure that operations are running smoothly. A new product or sales material available from the insurer provides the salesperson an opportunity to meet with the producers. The meeting can also serve as a forum to determine changes in a producer's products and markets. A new loan product or a new lending area can mean additional credit insurance sales.

The sales force is also responsible for discussing and implementing program changes. Several states require periodic rate deviations. In other situations, the loss experience of an account may require the implementation of an upward or downward rate deviation. In any case, the reason for the change must be explained to the account. Old rate charts must be replaced by the new material and a common implementation date coordinated. Where rate deviations are not feasible, bad loss experience may require a switch to a more restrictive policy form or a different plan of insurance; e.g., changing from a 14-day retroactive disability plan which covers preexisting conditions to a 30-day non-retroactive plan which excludes preexisting conditions. A review of the account's lending practices may determine the source of the adverse experience or the commission rate may require adjustment. The sales force must convey the need for the changes and attempt to retain the account while correcting the profitability situation. As a last resort, the account may be canceled.

Unlike ordinary insurers, credit insurers often depend on the sales staff to monitor the profitability of the producers and general agents. Actuarial involvement tends to be limited. Until recent years, there were few actuaries involved in credit insurance. While the measurement of profitability requires technical knowledge, a well-constructed data processing report can supply all of the necessary information. A loss ratio analysis is possible, since the claim and expense elements can be expressed as a percentage of premiums. It does not take an actuary to recognize that a loss and expense ratio over 100% is bad.

Experience reports are usually produced quarterly for each account. If an account has branch locations, reports are often prepared for each branch and recapped in total for all branches. Accounts may want to know their experience by location to pinpoint problem areas. The experience of a general agent is maintained by account and summarized in total. Generally, insurers evaluate the general agent on his overall book of business. Accounts with bad experience are reviewed with the general agent, but the agent often determines the action to be taken if his overall business is acceptable.

The quarterly accounting usually displays year-to-date experience and inception-to-date experience. The displayed data follows the items discussed in Chapter Six, Measurement of Profitability. A sample accounting is shown in Figure 3.1.

PERIOD COVERED LAST REPORT

CURRENT YEAR

	LIFE	DISABILITY	TOTALS	PER CENT
1. NET WRITTEN PREMIUM				
2. PLUS BEGINNING RESERVE				
3. LESS ENDING RESERVE				
4. EARNED PREMIUM DURING PERIOD				
5. PER CENT OF EARNED PREMIUM				
LIFE DISABILITY				
6. TOTAL PER CENT OF EARNED PREMIUM				
7. EXPENSES				
A. LOSSES				
1. PAID				
2. LESS BEGINNING CONTINGENT RESERVE				
3. PLUS ENDING CONTINGENT RESERVE				
4. LESS BEGINNING IBNR RESERVE				
5. PLUS ENDING IBNR RESERVE				
6. TOTAL				
B. COMMISSIONS				
1. AGENT				
2. OVERRIDE AGENT				
3. TOTAL				
C. CONTINGENT PAYMENTS				
D. OTHER EXPENSE				
8. TOTAL EXPENSES				
9. BALANCE END OF PERIOD (L6-L8)				
10. BALANCE PREVIOUS PERIOD				
11. NET BALANCE				
EARNED - INCURRED LOSS RATIO				

Fig. 3.1 Quarterly experience report.

SALES ADMINISTRATION

A separate section of the sales department may be dedicated to handling the administrative functions and maintaining contact with the accounts on day-to-day operational matters. This permits the sales force to concentrate on personal contact and new sales. It also recognizes certain facets of human nature. Good salespeople often do not care for detail administrative work. Technical, detail-oriented people rarely make good salespeople. There are exceptions, but a functional separation usually makes sense.

A primary sales administration function is the initial setup work for a new account. Insurers usually have a master file of account information, which contains information needed to process all administrative and operational aspects of an account's business. A useful internal restriction is to withhold shipment of any policy forms or supplies until all of the master file information is complete. The data may be entered into a computer file to provide automated editing of premium reports. Sales administration is responsible for keeping the information in the file up-to-date.

Each new account must be supplied with reporting procedures and forms, policy forms, and rate calculation material. Reporting procedures detail the reporting requirements, including the timing of reports and the materials which must be submitted. Reporting forms with instructions for their use and procedures for claim handling are also sent.

Policy forms are supplied by the insurer. A group policy must be prepared and certificates supplied to accounts which sell credit insurance through a group plan. If the account is writing individual policies, the individual policy forms are supplied along with policy applications, if applicable. Certificates and individual policies are usually sequentially numbered for control purposes and a record is maintained of the numbers supplied to each account. Accounts are required to return unused certificates or policies if the relationship with the insurer is terminated.

Insurers also provide the account with the material for rate calculation. The majority of accounts still use rate charts, but the trend is definitely towards the use of factor cards and programmable calculators. New charts must be printed if none of the insurer's existing charts fit the new account. In some cases, the material provided by the previous insurer is used.

Sales administration has on-going service requirements. Changes in procedures, policy forms, rates, and compensation must be implemented and documented. Information files must also be updated to retain their usefulness. This area also works with the accounts on operational problems. Follow-up calls are made where accounts are late in reporting. Sales administration also responds to procedural questions from the accounts.

Compliance with agent licensing requirements may be a part of the sales administration's responsibilities. Although the actual licensing process is usually handled by a separate department, sales administration oversees the process to insure that all necessary licenses are in place. This includes the licensing of general agents and appropriate licensing at the account level.

COMPENSATION TO HOME OFFICE SALES STAFF, GENERAL AGENTS, AND PRODUCERS

One difference between home office sales staff and general agents is in compensation. Home office personnel are salaried. Their volume of production and the insurer's profitability of business produced influence continued employment, raises, and promotions, but the majority of their compensation is a base salary. In part, this recognizes that much of the sales staff's effort is directed towards service work. In addition, the production from an account, and even its retention as an account, is often beyond the control of the salesperson. For example, the economic downturn of 1980-82 caused a dramatic reduction in credit insurance production, which was unrelated to the performance of the sales staff. Banking industry mergers may result in the loss of an account by one insurer. Compensation based primarily on salary promotes the acquisition of better quality business with more emphasis on service. Offsetting these benefits may be a reduction in the drive to acquire new business; therefore, some form of incentive compensation plan is generally used to reward new production. Striking a happy medium between new sales and service is difficult.

Compensation to general agents depends on the volume of business produced and, possibly, the profitability of the business. The compensation is paid in either or both of the following forms:

- ***Override commission.*** An override commission is the percentage of premium paid to the general agent on the business he produces. The term "override" is a carry over from ordinary insurance where the general agent's commission was over and above the commission paid to the soliciting agent. In credit insurance, it is the difference between the total compensation paid by the insurer and the amount received by the account.

  In some cases, the insurer provides the general agent a total compensation percentage applicable to a particular state and market segment. The general agent has flexibility in the amount of compensation offered to each account. However, in many cases, the override commission is the same percentage for all business of the general agent, and the insurer determines the account's compensation. Override commissions are guaranteed and paid without regard to profitability. This creates a real incentive to produce business. The insurer must monitor profitability and be prepared to take corrective action.

Override commissions are normally paid as *front commissions*. A front commission means the entire amount is deducted from the premium as the premium is collected. A *return commission* is paid by the general agent to the insurer on any premium refunds. The usual procedure is to apply the override percentage to the gross premium collected minus the refunds paid for the month.

- ***Retroactive or contingent commissions.*** In an effort to encourage a general agent to produce profitable business, the insurer may make a portion or all of the general agent's compensation contingent on his business being profitable. The insurer will set an expense charge representing the insurer's general expenses and taxes. Each quarter (or annually) the experience of the general agent is evaluated. The amount eligible for profit sharing is:

Earned premiums

less Incurred claims

less Paid compensation to accounts and override commissions

less Incurred insurer expense charges.

The remainder is the profit on the business. The insurer shares part or all of the profit with the general agent. The general agent cannot lose from this arrangement; i.e., he is not responsible if the result is a loss. The insurer, however, may recover prior contingent commissions paid to the general agent if the experience becomes unprofitable as time passes. This chargeback on prior payments is not included in all retroactive commission agreements. Some arrangements are on a "pure earned" basis. The accounting deducts incurred compensation to accounts and incurred override commissions, rather than the paid amounts. The details of the calculation are usually a part of the general agent's written agency contract with the insurer.

ACCOUNT COMPENSATION

Compensation to an account includes at least one of the following forms:

- ***Front Commission.*** Similar to the override commission, a front commission is guaranteed compensation paid to an account based on net written premium (gross minus refund premiums). The amount of compensation is usually expressed as a percentage of premium. This is the usual form of compensation in most market segments, except credit unions and some bank business. The percentage varies with the level of gross premiums charged, but typical commission rates are 30% to 40%. Many states place a maximum limit on the percentage which may be paid on business written in the state. See Appendix D.

- ***Service Fees.*** Some state and federal regulations do not permit the payment of commissions to financial institutions. These same regulations usually permit service fees which are designed to allow reimbursement of the actual cost of offering the products. In some cases, the fees are expressed in dollars based on number of insureds or other unit expense factors. In most cases, the fee is converted to a percentage of premium for ease of calculation and administration. Service fees usually are only 5% to 10% of premium.

Producers may receive additional income from experience refunds or policyholder dividends. An example is the combination of insurance and banking regulations in Ohio. Banks can receive only a front service fee of 10% or less, but can receive an experience refund.

- ***Experience refund or retroactive commission.*** A portion of the compensation to a producer may be contingent on the profitability of the producer's business. Insurers generally require that the producer generates a minimum volume of credit insurance business before he can qualify for an experience refund. The experience of the producer is evaluated periodically. Some or all of the profits remaining after the insurer's expense charge are paid to the producer. The insurer can usually recover prior experience refunds if experience turns bad. If the sum of all experience refunds is negative, the producer is not responsible for the loss, but the negative refund is carried forward to future accounting periods.

  Figure 3.2 contains hypothetical experience of a producer showing how the experience refund formula works. This producer has an "85/15 retro" arrangement. This means the insurer's expense charge is 15%. The producer receives all of the profit remaining after the insurer deducts the expense charge, claims, and front commissions. The insurer's expense charge includes provision for general expenses, premium taxes, risk charge, and insurer's profit. Traditionally, insurers do not include investment income in the calculation; only underwriting profit is shared with the producer. Experience on life and disability is combined in the calculations to avoid paying experience refunds on a profitable line while absorbing a loss on an unprofitable line.

  Even for large accounts, loss experience does have significant fluctuation, particularly from quarter to quarter and even from year to year. Insurers have adopted several practices which have the effect of deferring the underwriting profits, thus avoiding the need to recover current losses from prior payments. A typical approach is to calculate the experience quarterly, but only make a cumulative payment annually. Many insurers calculate pro rata unearned premiums on disability insurance. Some insurers simply include a claim fluctuation reserve, either explicitly or as part of the claim reserve. These approaches smooth the pattern of the payment of the experience refunds.

DETERMINATION OF EXPERIENCE REFUND PAID TO A PRODUCER
ALL AMOUNTS BASED ON EXPERIENCE FROM INCEPTION
THROUGH THE OUARTER SHOWN

	3-31-86	6-30-86	9-30-86	12-31-86
1. GROSS MINUS REFUND PREMIUMS	100,000	200,000	300,000	400,000
2. UNEARNED PREMIUMS, END OF QUARTER"	70,000	130,000	180,000	240,000
3. EARNED PREMIUMS, INCEPTION TO DATE [(1) - (2)]	30,000	70,000	120,000	160,000
4. INSURER'S EXPENSE CHARGE [.15 x (1)]	15,000	30,000	45,000	60,000
5. FRONT COMMISSIONS PAID [.10 x (1)]	10,000	20,000	30,000	40,000
6. PAID CLAIMS	2,000	13,500	38,500	45,000
7. CLAIM RESERVES, END OF QUARTER	2,000	5,000	9,000	12,000
8. INCURRED CLAIMS, INCEPTION TO DATE [(6) + (7)]	4,000	18,500	47,500	57,000
9. UNDERWRITING PROFIT DUE PRODUCER [(3) - (4) - (5) - (8)]	1,000	1,500	(2,500)	3,000
10. PRIOR EXPERIENCE REFUNDS PAID	0	1,000	1,500	0
11. AMOUNT DUE PRODUCER, OR DUE INSURER IF NEGATIVE [(9) - (10)]	1,000	500	(1,500)*	3,000

* CANNOT BE GREATER THAN PRIOR REFUNDS PAID TO PRODUCER

Fig. 3.2 Sample experience refund calculation

- ***Policyholder dividends.*** Mutual insurance companies are owned by the policyholders and the profits of the company belong to them. Profits are returned to the policyholder through annual dividends. For credit insurance, the producer is the group policyholder. Mutual insurers devote substantial resources to ensure an equitable distribution of profits among their policyholders.

For group credit business, the allocation by policyholder generally follows the calculation procedure of experience refunds, except that the insurer expenses are an allocation of the actual expenses to process the producer's business. All policyholders are eligible for a dividend, regardless of size, although unprofitable accounts usually do not receive a dividend. The allocation among the profitable accounts may not be an exact reflection of the individual producer's experience. This reflects the practice of retaining a small portion of the profits as a permanent contribution to the surplus of the insurer and the practice of pooling the loss experience on small producers.

LIMITATIONS ON COMPENSATION

Over the years, states have imposed limitations on the maximum compensation paid by insurers to general agents and producers in order to protect insurer solvency and to impose some controls on product pricing. Appendix D lists states with limitations and the maximum percentage permitted in each state. These limitations are commonly called *commission caps*.

Some states limit only front compensation (commissions and service fees), while others attempt to place a maximum limit on all forms of compensation by defining compensation as any form of financial benefit to the producer. Some regulations specify separate percentages for general agents and producers.

COMPENSATING BALANCES

In the competition for the credit insurance business of financial institutions, insurers may offer to maintain deposits in the institution. One common practice is to maintain deposits equal to one year of credit insurance premiums written by the financial institution. When interest paid on these deposits is less than market rates, the deposits are considered *compensating balances* and provide a financial advantage to the lending institution. Many states now prohibit compensating balances or include them in the definition of compensation in a commission cap regulation.

If a state does not prohibit compensating balances, the deposits are often maintained in non-interest-bearing checking accounts. Deposits in passbook savings accounts, interest-bearing checking accounts, or certificates of deposit paying the financial institution's usual rates of interest are not considered compensating balances.

REINSURANCE

The willingness of a direct writer to reinsure the business into the producer's captive insurance company may be considered a form of compensation. A few commission cap regulations include reinsurance profits. These provisions have not been enforced or tested in court. Many industry personnel believe the regulations would not be considered valid. A basic problem exists in determining the underwriting profit before the business matures. When the producer accepts reinsurance, the profits are no longer guaranteed and could even produce a loss. This changes the nature of the profits from compensation to underwriting profits in a risk-bearing enterprise.

AGENT LICENSING

State laws and regulations require that only licensed agents may solicit insurance in the state. Each state specifies the requirements for the licensing of agents and the scope of their activity. As with most aspects of state regulation, uniform provisions have not been adopted. Some states have specific provisions relating to credit insurance which simplify or eliminate licensing requirements for those agents writing only credit insurance. In addition, an insurer must *appoint* the licensed agents who represent it.

An agent must be licensed in his state of residency. In his home state, he is a *resident agent*. Many states permit an out-of-state resident to solicit insurance in the state if the agent obtains a non-resident license. The *non-resident agent* only needs to provide proof of home state licensing, complete an application, and pay the fee.

A first-time agent must complete an application for licensing in his home state. Each state specifies general requirements concerning the moral character of a potential agent. References, fingerprints, and/or a photograph may be required. A sample application displaying the typical requirements is shown in Figure 3.3. Insurers are often required to attest to the character of the agent. To fulfill this requirement, insurers may order an inspection report using investigative services such as Equifax.

Having completed the application, a first-time agent must also pass a written examination. Some states require pre-examination schooling. The agent's desired line of business determines which examinations are needed. A full-line, life and disability insurance examination is comprehensive; however, examinations for a limited credit insurance license, where permitted, are less demanding. In many states, an examination is not required for a limited credit insurance license.

After an agent obtains a license, he is appointed to represent specific insurers. An agent must be appointed by each insurer he represents. After the appointment is complete, the agent can solicit or place insurance for that insurer.

Agents must maintain their licenses, which require renewal every one or two years, depending on the state requirement. Renewal is the responsibility of the agent, not the insurer. An insurer, however, must determine that all of its agents have properly renewed their licenses. The renewal process is simple–a simplified renewal application or a portion of the first-time application is completed. The insurer must also renew the appointment of its agents.

A growing trend is a continuing education requirement. Agents must complete a certain number of hours of course work or other specified endeavors to fulfill the requirement. Requirements may vary by the number of years the agent has been a licensed agent. Some states also impose the requirement on non-resident agents. Credit insurance licenses are usually exempt from the continuing education requirement.

Modest fees are charged by the states for each step in the process. Examination fees are under $50. Licensing fees, first-time or renewal, are generally $25 or less. Separate fees are charged for each line of business. Higher fees may be charged for non-resident licenses. Agent licensing fees are paid by the agent, who pays one fee to be licensed regardless of the number of insurers he represents. Insurers are charged a fee to appoint an agent, generally under $25. A few states require that the agent be bonded.

Any person or corporation receiving commissions for the sale of insurance must be licensed. Credit insurance commissions can be paid directly to a corporation in most states; however, non-insurance regulations may prohibit a financial institution from receiving commissions. The corporation must obtain a license. At least one employee of the corporation must fulfill all of the agent requirements and be the active agent for the corporation. Two or more employees are usually licensed to avoid delays if an employee-agent terminates his position with the corporation.

For credit insurance, many states simplify the process, recognizing both the limited scope of the lending officer in offering insurance and the simplified nature of the product being sold. The lending institution or automobile dealer is licensed whenever a state permits corporation licensing. An individual must be licensed in states without corporation licenses. These states generally permit an *assignment of commission.* Here the agent agrees to assign the commissions to the corporation employing him. In these situations, he is acting in the same manner as the active agent under a corporation license. Form 1099, reporting the annual amount of commission to the IRS by the insurer, designates the assignee as the recipient of the income.

Wherever possible, credit insurers use the group exemption permitted by many states. An individual does not need to be licensed to enroll insureds under a group policy. Group credit insurance policies are issued to the lenders. Employees of the lender may enroll borrowers under the group policy provided the employee is not directly compensated for the enrollment.

In states with a group exemption, even the corporation does not have to be licensed if no commissions are paid. Service fees for specific administrative activities are not considered commissions. Credit unions usually fall into this category.

Credit insurers often use independent general agents to solicit accounts. Override commissions are paid to the general agent for the acquisition and service of accounts. Independent general agents must fulfill the same requirements as soliciting agents. Salaried home office employees do not need a license to solicit accounts, since commissions are not paid.

FORM 20 ALABAMA RESIDENT APPLICATION FOR LIFE/DISABILITY LICENSE REV-11-84

INSURER complete SECTION I TYPE ONLY DATE________________

The________________________ of________________________
Name of Insurance Company City State

NAIC COMPANY CODE

requests that a license be issued to applicant for the lines checked.

FULL NAME________________________________
Last First Middle

AGENT NUMBER

____
City of Residence

(CLASS I)
License Fee $5.00

LIFE____DISABILITY____CREDIT LIFE____CREDIT DISABILITY____OTHER____

COMPANY NAME
AND ADDRESS

The Company has investigated and hereby endorses the applicant as an individual of good business standing and character This report will be furnished to the Commissioner of Insuranc upon request. The Company understands that all Alabama licenses must be mailed to the same address. Mail the licens to the address shown here.

____
Signature of Authorized Company Officia]

____
Typed Name Title

APPLICANT complete SECTION II Answer every question IN FULL or this application will be returned to the Company for correction. TYPE OR PRINT IN INK.

FULL NAME________________________AGE____DATE OF BIRTH____________
Last First Middle

RESIDENT ADDRESS________________________________
Number & Street City Zip Code County

BUSINESS ADDRESS________________________________
Number & Street City Zip Code

TELEPHONE NUMBER (RESIDENCE)____________ TELEPHONE NUMBER (BUSINESS)____________

PLACE OF BIRTH____________________ ARE YOU A UNITED STATES CITIZEN?____________

1. Are you a bona fide resident of Alabama?______ How long have you lived here?__________
   Give your resident address for the past five years. (City and State Only)

   ____
   City State City State City State City State

2. Are you presently licensed for the lines of insurance checked above?______________
   If yes, name the company you represent.________________________
   If no, have you been licensed during the past two years for these lines?__________
   If so, during what calendar year?________________________
   Have you ever held a resident license in another state?______If yes, name the state_____
   and the date you held the license_______. Has this license been cancelled?__________
3. Are you engaged in any other business?______ If so, describe____________________
4. Will you devote only part of your time to the insurance business?______________
5. Check your highest educational achievement. GRADE SCHOOL___HIGH SCHOOL___COLLEGE_____
6. If this application is for a license to sell Credit insurance, are you a full-time employee of the institution granting the credit?______If so, give the name of the lending institution.________________________________
   NAME OF BUSINESS

   ____
   Number & Street City Zip Code

Fig. 3.3 Sample insurance license application.

SKIP THIS QUESTION IF YOU ARE PRESENTLY LICENSED FOR THE LINES REQUESTED

7. FIVE-YEAR EMPLOYMENT RECORD: Begin with present employment. If you are self-employed, describe what you do and give address and phone number.

PRESENT EMPLOYMENT: ______________________ ______________________
Name of Employer Street Address City

(a) ______________________
Position-Previous employ. Name of Employer - City State Zip Phone Number
Why did you leave this position?______________________

(b) Position-Previous employ. Name of Employer - City State Zip Phone Number
Why did you leave this position?______________________

(c) Position-Previous employ. Name of Employer - City State Zip Phone Number
Why did you leave this position?______________________

USE SEPARATE SHEETS FOR EMPLOYMENT IF NECESSARY.

8. Has your application for license ever been declined by any insurance department? ________
9. Has your license ever been suspended or revoked? . . . . ________
10. If married, has your husband or wife ever applied for or held a license to solicit insurance in any state? . . . . ________
(a) Has such license been refused, suspended, or revoked? . . . . ________
11. Have you ever been charged with or convicted of a felony or of any crime involving moral turpitude? . . . . ________
12. Are there any outstanding judgements against you? . . . . ________
13. Does any insurer or general agent claim any indebtedness in default by you under any agency contract or otherwise? . . . . ________
14. Have you ever had an agency contract cancelled involuntarily? . . . . ________
15. Do you intend to use this license principally for the purpose of procuring insurance on your own risks or interests or those of your relatives or the officers, directors, stockholders, partners, or employees of any partnership, association, or corporation of which you or a member of your family is an officer, director, substantial stockholder, partner, or employee? . . . . ________
16. Is this license to be used principally for procuring insurance on the lives of customers of a retail merchandise establishment or department store? . . . . . . ________
(a) If so, does the retail establishment or store maintain at least one place of business in this state which is used by the customer for the payment of premium? . . . . ________
Give the name and location of business______________________

NOTE: A "Yes" answer to any question 8 - 16 requires an explanation on separate sheets attached to this application.

"I, ______________________, under penalty of perjury, as set out in the Criminal Chapter of the Code of Alabama 1975, hereby swear or affirm that all answers and responses to questions or inquiries contained in this application are true and correct and complete answers and responses and that all answers and responses herein are to be considered by the Commissioner of Insurance as material to the execution of his duties under the Alabama Insurance Code in his decision upon this application and that I have read and am familiar with the sections of the Alabama Insurance Code setting forth the qualifications for the license for which I am making this application and that I am withholding no information which would affect my qualifications for this license for which I am making application."

SWORN TO and subscribed before me this ____ day of ________, 19____.

____
Signature of Applicant

____
Notary Public Commission Expires

THE COMPANY SHOULD MAIL THIS FORM WITH ALL FEES DUE TO:

ALABAMA INSURANCE DEPARTMENT
Agents' License Division
135 South Union Street
Montgomery, AL 36130-3401

Fig. 3.3 Sample insurance license application (continued).

PREMIUM BOOKING

Each account submits monthly reports regarding the business processed for the month. The typical reporting arrangement is known as *report and remittance.* An account summarizes the business issued and the refunds made. Remittance for the gross premium minus refund premium, less any deducted compensation, is sent to the insurer along with the supporting documentation. For single premium business, supporting documentation consists of a copy of the group certificate or individual policy. Documentation may not be required for monthly outstanding balance business.

The insurer receives and date-stamps the mail. The account is assigned a booking identification number which is coded on all correspondence the insurer receives. Account identification numbers are verified, then the remittance is separated and sent to the escrow area for deposit. Reports and supporting documentation are routed to the premium report processing area.

Remittance can take several forms, but payment by check is most common. Where depository arrangements are negotiated, the lender may deposit the amount directly into the appropriate account. In the financial institution market segment, premiums are often deposited in a checking, savings, or money market account. The deposit slip is sent to the insurer.

Supporting documentation must be keyed into a format suitable for computer entry into the in force system. The format may be punch cards, but most insurers now have on-line systems. Data is keyed during the day using CRTs and processed overnight on a batch basis.

The policy data and the report summary pass through an edit system. The edit system addresses a master file containing information about the account. These account master records contain information concerning policy limits, approved plans of insurance, and premium rates. These parameters are applied to the policies submitted. Policy data is checked for accuracy of the calculations and compliance with policy provisions. An exceptions listing is produced.

Submitted certificates, reports, and the computer listings are sent to a booking clerk for review. Reports received are not always perfect, as this list of common errors and the general range of tolerance permitted by insurers shows.

Error	**Tolerance**
Policy amount greater than maximum	Up to 20%
Term greater than maximum term	Up to 12 months
Calculated gross premium incorrect	A difference of up to $10
Age greater than maximum age	Up to 3 years
Report total incorrect	A difference of $25 to $100 depending on the size of the remittance.

Similar tolerances are accepted on refund calculations. These tolerances are representative of an occasional error in reporting by an account. Frequent errors or continued violation of policy limits by an account must be addressed by the sales department. If an error results in a violation of state regulations, a correction is required. For example, in Ohio a loan in excess of 60 months must be on the net payoff plan. If such a policy is issued as gross coverage, the insurer will insist that the policy be rewritten as required.

Verification of gross premiums on net payoff coverage requires that the loan's annual percentage rate (APR) be coded. The master file must contain a notation about the premium formula used by the lender. Insurers often assume a representative APR and select one formula as the basis of their edit calculations. Since the edit calculations may not reflect the actual premium calculation, a wider tolerance range is permitted before an error condition is flagged.

Most insurers book the business as received. An account is sent a correction notice and adjustments are made in subsequent reports. If a policy is unacceptable, the account will be notified to cancel the insurance. If age or term is missing, an assumed age or term is coded, but a request is sent to obtain the correct information.

Monthly outstanding balance business is much simpler. There are few items to audit. The account supplies the amount in force, usually without detail on individual insureds except for certain information which may be required for auditing purposes. The group premium rate is applied and the compensation deducted. Any errors found are corrected in a subsequent report.

Some reports are received without money, so insurers maintain listings of amounts due from accounts. Aged account receivable reports are monitored for delinquent accounts. The policies have been issued, and the premium collected from the insured. The insurer must honor the policies, but collection from the account is the insurer's problem. A second system is needed to verify that all active accounts provide reports. When an account changes insurers, they may not notify the old insurer.

A different reporting method is used by some insurers–the billing method. The method is used mostly for individual policies with an application. An application for insurance is completed by the proposed insured. At the end of the month, the applications are forwarded to the insurer. Applications are keyed into the data processing system and a billing prepared which is sent to the account. The net amount due the insurer must be remitted by the account within a specified time, usually 30 days.

CLAIMS ADMINISTRATION

The claim procedures and administrative systems accommodate the specialized nature of the products. As with other operating departments, the claims department must be organized to handle a relatively high volume of transactions. Standardized procedures and forms, generally simpler than comparable ordinary life and disability insurance items, are necessary. Standardization is a goal, but it is often difficult to achieve in light of the varied lending practices and administrative procedures of lenders. Consistency of claim handling, timeliness of processing, and adherence to policy provisions are the guiding principles.

Credit life insurance claims usually do not require an investigation. Few life claims are denied, because of the limited amount of contestable information supplied by the insured at issue and the limited number of eligibility requirements and exclusions. Preexisting condition exclusions result in a greater number of investigations and subsequent denials in disability insurance.

Even some of the largest insurers use a manual system for life claims. Most insurers have the payment of disability claims automated to some extent. On-line systems are common. Records are entered and updated on CRTs during the day and batch processed overnight. Within the department, individual claim folders are maintained for each claim.

Claim departments usually have an administrative unit and an examination unit. The principal goal of this separation is to ease the paperwork on examiners, so they can concentrate on the adjudication of the claim itself. Administrative unit personnel open the mail, do basic data entry, and assemble the claim files and supporting documentation. After examination of the claim, these personnel will assemble form letters and payments for mailing, and file the material.

Examiners are classified by level of experience and training. Examiners often have a maximum payment they may authorize without approval, especially on life claims. Life claims may be paid by a separate set of examiners, but the number of life claim examiners is small compared to the number of disability claim examiners. In a department, about 90% of the time and resources is dedicated to disability claims. Examiners often pay claims from all lenders. Claims are assigned by an alphabetic allocation, using the insured's last name. In larger departments, some allocation may be made based on the level of difficulty of the claim and the examiner's level of experience. Special lenders or unusual policy forms may have designated examiners. Each examiner is provided a set of policy forms, or a digest of the provisions and exclusions of each form. Supervisory personnel oversee the process for consistency of treatment and approval of large claims.

DEATH CLAIMS

Claims processing on credit life policies is relatively simple, so payments are usually made within a week after receipt. The usual requirements are: a completed claim form (Figure 3.4), a certified copy of the death certificate, and a copy of the evidence of insurance. A copy from the lender of the note and the loan's payment history may be required.

Claim forms are normally obtained from, and returned to, the lender. Some lenders do preliminary screening for accuracy of information and completeness of data. In most cases, claims are sent by the lender to the insurer for processing, although some lenders have draft authority up to specified limits. A general agent may perform the preliminary screening in some market segments, primarily automobile dealer business. Claim forms can be obtained from, and filed directly with, the insurer.

The claim form is straightforward. Basic data on the insured is requested along with the specification of any secondary beneficiary. The loan balance is completed by the lender. If an application was taken which contained underwriting questions, answers to certain questions concerning the cause of death may be required if the death occurred during the *contestable period*–two years in most states. An authorization to release medical information is common on the claim form used for an underwritten policy.

A certified copy of the death certificate is required, but a newspaper obituary or other proof may be accepted in unusual circumstances. In addition, a copy of the individual policy, group certificate, or group enrollment card is needed. Where missing, verification from the insurer's in force files or the lender's files is made.

When a claim package is received, it is date-stamped and assigned an internal claim number, and a claim folder is prepared. Existing claim folders are reviewed to see if the insured has filed a disability claim or if a duplicate life claim folder has been set up. The forms submitted and any existing files on the insured are passed to an examiner.

The examiner must verify that the deceased is the insured. The death certificate is verified for its seal of certification and absence of irregularities. The name and age of the deceased are compared to the evidence of insurance to avoid father/son, mother/daughter confusion. The effective date and expiration date of the insurance are compared with the date of death.

Policy provisions are reviewed. Age on the death certificate is compared with the attained age calculated from the evidence of insurance. The claim may be denied if the insured misstated his age at issue, and his actual age exceeded the maximum issue age of the policy.

If suicide is the cause of death, the benefit may be limited to a return of premium. The limited benefit only applies if the claim occurs during the time specified in the suicide provision, usually one year from the issue date of the insured's coverage. Investigation may be needed if suicide is suspected, but not listed, as the cause of death.

Some policies contain a simple *good health statement.* An insured is required to sign a statement that he is in good health, to the best of his knowledge and belief. These are not always useful at claim time. After all, the statement is an opinion by the insured of his good health. A person who spends every night in a bar may consider it perfectly normal to consume a pint of liquor a day. As one insured said, "Everybody is dying of something."

Some health statements and individual policy applications require disclosure of certain conditions or treatment by a physician in recent years. When death occurs within the contestable period, the examiner may request an *Attending Physician Statement*, if the cause of death indicates possible misrepresentation.

After all necessary facts have been gathered, the claim will be approved or denied by the examiner. Supervisory personnel will review large claims and all denials. If approved, checks will be issued. One check is usually sent to the lender, who sends any excess over the loan balance to the second beneficiary. Where required by state law, insurers draw two checks and mail them separately, one to the lender to extinguish the unpaid balance and one to the second beneficiary for any excess.

DISABILITY CLAIMS

The review process for disability claims is more complicated and time-consuming. New claims require research for compliance with policy forms, which contain more exclusions than credit life forms. Disability claims are more subjective. An examiner must judge the validity and severity of a claim. Since claims usually continue for more than one payment, ongoing review and processing is necessary.

Claim files are segregated between open and closed files. Open claims are classified as continuing claims in the payment status or pending claims still under development and investigation. Open claim files are maintained within easy access of the examiners and the administrative units. Closed claims are claims for which the final payment has been made because of termination of disability, expiration of the coverage, or denial. Notice of termination is not received on some claims;

PROOFS OF DEATH
Submitted to

CLAIMANT'S STATEMENT

(Instructions for completing proof forms are on reverse side)

1. a. Deceased's name in full ____

   b. Residence ____

2. a. Date and place of Deceased's BIRTH.
   b. Source from which date of BIRTH obtained. (Family record or other record or certificate of birth should be referred to.)
   a. Date ____ Place ____
   b. ____

3. a. Policy Number   b. Effective date of insurance

4. Beneficiary to the extent of the Deceased's indebtedness: (Financial Institution)   a. **Balance at date of death $**

5. a. Beneficiary for any balance remaining: b. Relationship to Deceased

6. a. Date and place of DEATH.   a. Date ____ Place ____
   b. Cause of death.   b. ____

NOTE: IF THE POLICY HAS BEEN IN FORCE FOR MORE THAN TWO YEARS AT THE INSURED'S DEATH, ANSWERS TO QUESTIONS 7, 8, 9 AND 10 MAY BE OMITTED.

7. a. When did Deceased first complain or give other indications of his last illness?   a. Date ____
   b. When did Deceased first consult a physician for his last illness?   b. Date ____

8. a. On what date did Deceased last attend to his usual work?   a. Date ____
   b. Occupation at date of death.   b. ____

9. Names and addresses of all physicians who attended Deceased during his last illness and during five years prior thereto:

Name	Address	Date of Attendance	Disease or Condition

10. What other Life, Health or Accident insurance was carried on the life of the Deceased?

Name of Company	Policy Dated	Amount of Insurance

The undersigned hereby make claim to said insurance in ____ and agree that the written statements and affidavits of all the physicians who attended or treated the Insured, and all other papers called for by the instructions hereon, shall constitute and they are hereby made a part of these Proofs of Death, and further agree that the furnishing of this form, or of any other forms supplemental thereto, by said Company shall not constitute nor be considered an admission by it that there was any insurance in force on the life in question, nor a waiver of any of its rights or defenses.

Dated at ____, this ____ day of ____, 19____

Financial Institution ____

By ____ Title

Beneficiary for balance ____

K94 (REV. 3-83)   ITEM#LK0094-V001

AUTHORIZATION TO OBTAIN INFORMATION

I authorize any physician who has examined or treated the deceased; any hospital or medical or medically related facility where the deceased has been confined, treated or examined; or any other individual or organization which has provided the deceased with health care services to release information concerning the deceased's medical history, mental or physical condition, or treatment which may be requested by ____ or its duly authorized representative for the purpose of determining eligibility for the benefits requested.

I also authorize any employer, insurer or other organization or person having any non-medical records or information concerning the deceased to release the information to ____ or its duly authorized representative for the purpose of determining eligibility for the benefits requested.

I understand that a photocopy of this authorization shall be as valid as the original, and that I, or my authorized representative, may receive a copy of this authorization if I request it.

This authorization shall remain valid for the duration of the claim.

Date: ____ **Signature** ____

Relationship to Insured: ____

Fig. 3.4 Sample claim form for life insurance.

INSTRUCTIONS FOR COMPLETING PROOFS OF DEATH

CLAIMANT'S STATEMENT

The statement should be completed by the Financial Institution and the person or persons to whom the balance of any insurance in excess of the indebtedness is payable. The order of priority for any balance is: (1) Wife or husband; (2) Child or children, in equal shares if more than one; (3) Father or mother, in equal shares if both are living. If none of the aforesaid beneficiaries are living at the death of the Insured, any such balance shall be paid to the executors or administrators of the estate of the Insured.

If any balance is payable to a minor or a mentally incompetent person, the statement should be completed by the legally appointed guardian, an official certificate of whose appointment and qualification must be furnished.

If any balance is payable to the estate or executors or administrators of the insured, the statement should be completed by the executor or administrator, a certificate of whose appointment and qualification must be furnished.

If any balance is payable to "children" or others of a class, an affidavit should be furnished, giving the name and birthdate of each. If any have died, the affidavit should give the date and place of death, and should also state whether he or she died unmarried, intestate, and without issue.
The settlement check will be made payable jointly to the Financial Institution and the person to receive any balance.

A certified copy of the death certificate should be submitted for any deceased beneficiary.

PHYSICIAN'S STATEMENT

In most cases a certified copy of the insured's death certificate will be acceptable. However, if the policy is within the contestable period, statements should be obtained from all physicians who treated the insured during the five year period preceding death.

Fig. 3.4 Sample claim form for life insurance (continued).

the claimant just stops sending in Continuance of Disability forms (Figure 3.6). A procedure is established to close these open files after a period of inactivity, usually two to six months. Closed files are maintained in central records and warehoused after a few years.

The lender usually supplies the form used for the initial filing of a disability claim (Figure 3.5). Sections are completed by the insured, the lender, and the insured's physician. An employer's statement may be required or may only be required on a case-by-case basis, depending on the insurer's practices. Questions are directed at establishing the existence of a disability and verification that the claimant's condition prevents gainful employment. An authorization to release medical records and information is required.

When a new claim form is received, it is date-stamped and assigned a claim number. A search of disability files is made to determine whether the claimant has had a prior claim or has a duplicate file in process. Insurers may maintain a separate file, in alphabetic order by name, showing only the name of the insured and his claim number to speed up the search process.

Verification of the policy's in force status is normally made by the lender. When the lender information is complete and evidence of insurance is submitted, further verification is unlikely, but insurers with individual in force files may check the status on the company's records. When verification is necessary, backup files of policies issued, often on microfilm or computer files, will be researched. If the lender reports a zero loan balance, the loan may have been repaid and the insurance policy canceled. The date of cancellation is obtained to determine if the policy was in force on the date of disability. All forms and prior claim files are gathered and assigned to an examiner.

The examiner has four choices: pay, deny, investigate, or develop the file. Development of the file involves securing all of the basic information to adjudicate (settle) the claim. Once development is complete, the examiner must decide whether to investigate the claim, deny the claim, or authorize the payment.

Four questions are uppermost in the examiner's mind:

1. Is the claimant disabled?

2. Has the disability occurred during the policy term?

3. Have all policy conditions been met?

4. Are any policy exclusions applicable?

The statements of the insured and the physician are reviewed to determine the diagnosis. Standard medical reference publications may be reviewed to judge the reasonableness of the statements made. Then the inability to work is determined. An employer's statement, if obtained, is reviewed to verify that the claimant has been out of work.

Some claim forms ask supplementary questions about other disability benefits to assist in the evaluation. If the claimant is receiving worker's compensation payments, disability pension payments, or social security disability payments, these payments support the existence of disability. Inquiry may be made to determine the duration of these payments, as the payments may indicate the existence of a preexisting condition. If a claimant is receiving unemployment compensation, the examiner may require further information. Except in a few states, a disabled person is not normally eligible for unemployment compensation.

The date disability was incurred is compared to the effective date and the expiration date of the insured's coverage. If a refund has been paid, the date incurred must precede the cancellation date. Age of the insured on the evidence of insurance is compared to the claim forms to verify that the insured is the claimant.

An examiner reviews the evidence of insurance and the policy forms to determine the conditions and exclusions of the claimant's coverage. The most demanding aspect of claims examination is the determination of preexisting conditions. The standard clause excludes preexisting conditions if:

Treatment was received within six months prior to the effective date and disability for the treated condition commenced within six months after the effective date.

Variations abound. Other possibilities include:

1. *Treatment was received within six months prior to the effective date and treatment was received within six months after the effective date (regardless of the date of disability).*

2. *Treatment was received within twelve months prior to the effective date and disability occurred within twelve months after the effective date.*

3. *Disability occurred during the policy term (or within the first two policy years) if treatment was received within the six months prior to the effective date.*

Under the standard provision, a preexisting condition is covered if the disability occurs more than six months after the effective date. If disability occurs during the first six months, no payments are made for that disability even if the disability extends beyond six months.

Most states restrict the preexisting condition exclusion on renewed or refinanced loans. Here an insured cancels an old loan and obtains a new loan for an increased amount; e.g., the ever popular bill-consolidation loan. If both loans are insured under the same group master policy, the insurer cannot start a new exclusion period. The "six and six" periods apply to the effective date of the original loan. Insurers are usually permitted, however, to apply a new "six and six" period on the portion of the new loan which exceeds the prior loan. Under line-of-credit coverage or credit card business, each new advance has its own "six and six" period. Some insurers forego this procedure and ignore the exclusion once the original period is satisfied.

The other policy exclusions are checked for compliance. Disability caused by normal pregnancy is the only frequently used exclusion. Other exclusions include intentionally self-inflicted injury, and disability resulting from aviation on non-scheduled flights. Many conditions excluded in other health and disability coverages are covered by credit disability products. Examples of these covered conditions include elective surgery and mental and nervous conditions.

If the insured's application contained medical questions, the insured's responses are reviewed. The claim diagnosis is compared to the conditions addressed in the insured's statements to see if misrepresentation has occurred. Inaccurate answers are not cause for denial if the date of disability is beyond the contestable period. Inaccurate answers unrelated to the cause of the claimed disability are not a valid basis for denial of the claim.

The final question is one of eligibility for coverage in the first place. Disability policies often contain an *actively-at-work* clause. In order for the insurance to be effective, the insured must have been working for a certain period of time prior to the effective date. Even if preexisting conditions are covered, the insured cannot be disabled on the effective date. Compliance with maximum age provisions is also checked.

Investigation takes many forms. Forms and form letters are available to cover practically all variations of inquiry. Phone inquiry may be used when written documentation is not required. This method has gained popularity due to delays in mail time and the cost of sending a letter. Examiners are required to keep a phone record of each call, except for minor questions. Investigations may be ordered from inspection companies, such as Equifax or Hooper Holmes. These are primarily used to determine the claimants' activity–whether they are working at other jobs, doing strenuous work or play, etc.

Only a small number of claims are investigated beyond simple inquiry for information. Estimates of investigated claims range from 2%-5%. Overall, typical denial rates are 4%-7% of all new claims. This would include denials where the dates of disability are outside the coverage dates, and where other conditions and exclusions are clearly not met and an investigation is not required.

All denials are reviewed by senior personnel in claims. In rare instances, legal staff may be asked for an interpretation of policy wording, but the claims department makes the final decision. One must recognize that lenders and sales personnel do have an occasional influence that would not be tolerated in ordinary insurance. Their involvement is always in the claimant's favor–to pay a claim that might otherwise be denied. As a result, there is little litigation over claims.

Closer scrutiny may be needed for claims reported long after the date of disability. In many cases, the claimant was just unaware of his coverage, and the claim is usually valid. Policies often contain a clause requiring the timely filing of a claim. In general, a claim must be filed within one year after disability ends. Although the clause permits an insurer to deny a late reported claim, the clause is rarely invoked except where there are questions concerning the validity of the claim itself.

Some insurers have the examiner estimate a *case reserve*–the expected months of disability times the monthly benefit. Although many insurers now use other methods to determine disability claim reserves for financial statement purposes, the process has been retained by some claim departments, since it serves as a good training tool for examiners.

Once a claim is approved, the examiner will specify the date the next medical examination is required. The completed, approved file is sent to the administrative unit for claim payment and refiling.

Disability claims may involve more than one payment, with some claims extending several years. Approximately one-third of the claims are *first and final*. The initial claim represents the total claim. Other claims require a periodic certification of continued disability by the insured and his physician. When a payment is authorized, a check is sent to the lender. A form is often sent to the claimant notifying him of the payment made to the lender. If the payment is not a final payment, the claimant will receive a form to submit with further claims if disability continues. A date on the form specifies when the form is to be completed. This Continuance of Disability form must be completed every 30-90 days, depending on insurer practice, diagnosis, and physician comments. The claimant is told to wait the required time before completing the form unless disability ends before the specified period is completed.

When the Continuance of Disability form is received, it is date-stamped and forwarded with the claim file to an examiner. The examiner's job is straightforward–to determine if the disability has continued. A review is made of the expiration date of the coverage and the expected duration of the claim. Continuing claims can be processed and approved quickly. Approved files are sent to the administrative unit for payment.

Simplified procedures are used for obvious long-term disability claims. Automatic pay systems are designed for the convenience of the claimants and for administrative efficiency. The claimant must certify his continued disability periodically, but a Physician's Statement is only required every three to six months.

Insurers sometimes receive a request to pay off the loan rather than continue the monthly benefit payments. On severe claims, this may be to the insurer's advantage from an economic standpoint. If an insurer makes the monthly payment until expiration, the total claim will include the interest on the loan. Prepayment forgoes the cost of interest, since only the principal balance is repaid. While insurers do not encourage this practice, they are usually willing to consider a request.

Proper handling of claims and fair treatment of claimants is a concern for the insurer and state regulators. The work of the examiners and the claim department is closely reviewed by corporate management, internal and external auditors, and state regulators. Time of service and quality of work are measured and reviewed.

Audits and standards of performance begin internally within the claims department. Time of service is measured and tracked. Daily or weekly tabulations of output for each examiner are maintained. Examiners generally segregate their day between new and continuing claims. An examiner is expected to *handle* about 5-30 new claims a day and handle about 40-70 continuing claims. A handle may involve inquiry or investigation. Total handles are the number of files an examiner processes in a day. The number of actual payments will be somewhat less. Department records are maintained on pending claims and turnaround times. The usual goal is to process new claims not involving investigation within five working days. On continuing claims, a common goal is three working days. Supervisory personnel monitor these reports closely to insure timeliness of processing. Output of the department is a factor in the performance evaluation of the individual examiners and of the supervisory personnel.

Individual claims are also reviewed. A random sampling of approved claims and all denials are reviewed by senior claims personnel. A corporate claims audit committee may also be in place to audit individual claims and department performance. The results of the audits are incorporated into the ongoing training program.

Complaints from insureds regarding the handling of claims may be received directly from the insureds or referred to the insurer by a state insurance department. They are usually received and processed by the legal department with assistance from claims. Periodic reports may be prepared summarizing the complaints received, their status, and their resolution. Senior management and claims department management consider complaints seriously and review the report carefully.

Audits are also performed by the corporate internal audit staff. A section of the internal audit team may be dedicated to claims. External CPA audits also involve claims. These audits concentrate more on the timeliness, accounting, and conformance with corporate policy than on a qualitative audit of the handling of claims.

On triennial examination, state examiners sample claim files for consistency, fairness, and accuracy. The sampling can be extensive at times. Policyholder complaint files are reviewed for the nature of complaints and their resolution.

The training of claim personnel is continuous, both from feedback of audits, and from outside seminars on medical terminology, letter writing skills, and time management. A formal training program is available through the International Claims Association, which gives five professional examinations. Topics include: Fundamentals of Life and Health Insurance, Medical Terminology, Legal Aspects of Claim Handling, and Claims Administration. Successful completion of the examinations confers the status of Diplomate.

DISABILITY CLAIM FORM

Instructions to Claimant: Please have the following statements completed.
1. Employer's Statement (have your employer complete this first)
2. Attending Physician's Statement (have your doctor complete)
3. Claimant's Statement (you complete)
4. When completed in full return this form to the Creditor or Agent from whom it was obtained.

CREDITOR OR AGENT'S STATEMENT *(if available) ATTACH COPY OF CERTIFICATE OF INSURANCE*

Date__________19_____Loan or Finance Account No.__________Original amount of indebtedness $__________

Payable in________Monthly installments of $__________ each. Present unpaid balance of indebtedness $__________

Certificate or policy of insurance number__________

Date issued:__________19_____Monthly benefit shown in certificate or policy $__________Form No.__________

Life Insurance Premium $__________Accident and health insurance premium $__________

Agency (if any)__________Address__________

Name of Dealer (if any)__________Name of Creditor__________

Address:__________ (street) (city, state) (zip code) Address:__________ (street) (city, state) (zip code)

Completed by:__________Phone No.__________ (area code and number)

CLAIMANT'S STATEMENT (please print clearly)

The undersigned, insured under the above numbered policy issued by represents to the Company that he is now or has been totally disabled during the term of the policy and for the purpose of applying for benefits under said policy answers the following questions and represents and warrants that said answers are true, complete and correct.

1. Full Name__________Social Security #__________
2. Mailing Address__________ (street) (city & state) (zip code) Phone No.__________ (area code & number)
3. Street Address (if different)__________ (street) (city & state) (zip code) Age__________
4. Occupation__________Are you self employed?__________
5. Duties performed in job__________
6. Name and complete address of employer__________
7. Attending physician__________Complete address__________
8. Dates you were totally disabled and prevented from performing any task pertaining to your occupation?
   From__________To__________
9. Describe the nature and details of your disability__________
10. When did symptoms appear or accident happen?__________
11. If accident, where?__________
12. Have you ever had the same or similar condition? YES__________ NO__________ If yes, state when and describe and give doctor's name who treated you for the condition__________
13. What doctors have treated you for any sickness or accident in the last three years?
   (A) Name and complete address of doctor (B) Why were you treated? (C) Dates you were treated
14. Are you receiving disability pension or compensation? YES__________ NO__________ For what?__________
   Date of first payment__________19__________
15. Are you receiving workman's compensation? YES__________ NO__________ If yes, give dates__________
16. Are you receiving unemployment compensation? YES__________ NO__________ If yes, give dates__________

ASSIGNMENT

I hereby assign to__________ (Name of Creditor)

__________ (Address)

to the extent of its interest as creditor, any indemnity payable under this claim.

I further agree that by furnishing this blank and investigating the above claim, shall not be held to admit the validity of any claim or to waive the breach of any condition contained in the policy.

Date:__________Claimant's Signature__________

K87 (REV 2-82) ITEM #LKØØ87-VØØ3

AUTHORIZATION TO OBTAIN INFORMATION

I authorize any physician who has examined or treated me, any hospital or medical or medically related facility where I have been confined, treated or examined, or any other individual or organization which has provided me with health care services to give any and all information about my medical history, mental or physical condition, or treatment to or its authorized representative, upon its request, for the purpose of determining my eligibility for the benefits I have requested.

I also authorize any employer, insurer or other organization or person having any non-medical records or information about me to give any and all such information to the or its authorized representative, upon its request, for the purpose of determining my eligibility for the benefits I have requested.

I understand that a photocopy of this authorization shall be as valid as the original. I know that I, or my authorized representative, may receive a copy of this authorization upon request.

This authorization shall remain valid for the duration of my claim.

Date:__________ Claimant's Signature__________

Fig. 3.5 Form for filing an initial disability claim.

ATTENDING PHYSICIAN'S STATEMENT

1. Patient's name and address

2. Date of birth

3. Primary diagnosis:

4. What other disease(s) are secondary to, complicated with, or a sequence of this condition:

5. Is this condition due to injury or sickness arising out of patient's employment? YES ( ) NO ( ) If yes, give date:

6. Is condition due to Pregnancy? YES ( ) NO ( ) Please describe any complications:

7. (A) Nature of surgical or obstetrical procedure, if any (describe fully):

(B) Date performed_____________, 19_____

inpatient ( ) outpatient ( )

8. Give dates of all other medical (non surgical) treatment, if any:

Office_____________
Other_____________
If hospital, from_____________To_____________
Name of hospital_____________
Complete address_____________

9. Date symptoms first appeared or accident happened:

10. Date patient first consulted you for this condition:

11. Patient ever had same or similar condition? YES ( ) NO ( ) If yes state when and describe:

Referred by: Dr._____________Address_____________

12. Patient still under your care for this condition? YES ( ) NO ( ) If no, give date released

13. Dates patient was continuously totally disabled (unable to work):
From_____________To_____________

14. Dates patient was partially disabled:
From_____________To_____________

15. If still disabled, date patient should be able to return to work:

16. Date Physician's Name (print) Degree

Physician's Signature Telephone Number (area code + number)

Street address City State Zip Code

EMPLOYER'S STATEMENT (Not part of Physician's Statement)

Employee's Name Date Hired Name of Company

On what date did he first stop work entirely because of this sickness or injury? , 19

On what date did he resume any part of his work, supervisory or otherwise? , 19

Was injury or disease covered under Workmen's Compensation? YES_____________ NO_____________

(If YES give name and address of your compensation carrier)

Date injury?

Date_____________19_____ Signature of Employer_____________ (Title)

Phone No._____________ Address_____________ (Street and No.) (City, State) (Zip Code)

Fig. 3.5 Form for filing an initial disability claim (continued).

(REVERSE SIDE IS FOR ATTENDING PHYSICIANS REPORT) WHEN BOTH SIDES ARE COMPLETED, FOLD, INSERT IN RETURN ENVELOPE, STAMP AND MAIL.

CONTINUANCE OF DISABILITY REPORT (SUPPLEMENTAL REPORT)

THE FURNISHING OF THIS BLANK IS FOR THE CONVENIENCE OF THE CLAIMANT AND IS NOT AN ACKNOWLEDGEMENT OF LIABILITY OR WAIVER OF ANY RIGHT.

CLAIM NUMBER	ACCOUNT NUMBER	DO NOT COMPLETE THIS REPORT UNTIL →	COMPLETION DATE	UNLESS TOTAL DISABILITY ENDS BEFORE SUCH DATE	NOTIFY US IMMEDIATELY OF ANY ADDRESS CHANGE

CLAIMANT'S STATEMENT

1 DATE OF BIRTH	2 AGE	3 HEIGHT	4 WEIGHT	5 PHONE NUMBER
				AREA CODE ( )

6 GIVE DATES PHYSICIANS HAVE TREATED YOU SINCE LAST REPORT

OFFICE	HOME	HOSPITAL	OTHER (SPECIFY)

7 NAMES AND ADDRESSES OF OTHER PHYSICIANS TREATING YOU SINCE LAST REPORT

NAME	STREET	CITY, STATE, ZIP

8 WERE YOU CONFINED TO A HOSPITAL SINCE LAST REPORT ☐ NO ☐ YES

FROM	TO	HOSPITAL NAME / STREET / CITY

9 WHAT ARE YOUR ACTIVITIES AND HOW DO YOU SPEND YOUR TIME?

10 DESCRIBE ANY CHANGE IN YOUR CONDITION

11 HAVE YOU RESUMED WORK? ☐ YES ☐ NO

DATE RESUMED WORK

12 HAS YOUR ADDRESS CHANGED SINCE YOUR LAST REPORT? (TEMPORARILY OR PERMANENTLY) USE SPACE BELOW FOR CORRECTION

STREET ______

CITY ______

SIGN HERE X ______
CLAIMANT'S SIGNATURE

______ SOCIAL SECURITY NUMBER ______ DATE OF REPORT

NAME AND ADDRESS OF CLAIMANT

AUTHORIZATION TO OBTAIN INFORMATION

I authorize any physician who has examined or treated me, any hospital or medical or medically related facility where I have been confined, treated or examined, or any other individual or organization which has provided me with health care services to give any and all information about my medical history, mental or physical condition, or treatment to ______ or its authorized representative, upon its request, for the purpose of determining my eligibility for the benefits I have requested.

I also authorize any employer, insurer or other organization or person having any non-medical records or information about me to give any and all such information to ______ or its authorized representative, upon its request, for the purpose of determining my eligibility for the benefits I have requested.

I understand that a photocopy of this authorization shall be as valid as the original. I know that I, or my authorized representative, may receive a copy of this authorization upon request.

This authorization shall remain valid for the duration of my claim.

Date ______ Claimant's Signature ______

Fig. 3.6 Continuance of Disability claim form.

ATTENDING PHYSICIAN'S STATEMENT HEALTH OR ACCIDENT INSURANCE CLAIM (SUPPLEMENTAL REPORT)

ATTENDING PHYSICIANS STATEMENT (REGARDING PATIENT NAMED ON REVERSE SIDE IN CLAIMANT STATEMENT)

1. DIAGNOSIS AND CONCURRENT CONDITIONS CAUSING TOTAL DISABILITY

2. SURGICAL OR OBSTETRICAL PROCEDURE, IF ANY, DESCRIBE FULLY.

DATE PERFORMED ______ ☐ INPATIENT ☐ OUTPATIENT

HOSPITAL NAME ______

CITY, STATE, ZIP ______

3. GIVE DATES OF OTHER MEDICAL (NON-SURGICAL) TREATMENTS, IF ANY SINCE LAST REPORT

OFFICE	HOME	HOSPITAL	OTHER (SPECIFY)

4. WHAT DATE IS SCHEDULED FOR YOU TO SEE PATIENT AGAIN? IF NONE, PLEASE EXPLAIN.

REMARKS:

5. PROGRESS

☐ RECOVERED ☐ IMPROVED ☐ UNIMPROVED

6. IS PATIENT STILL UNDER YOUR CARE? ☐ YES ☐ NO — IF NO. SPECIFY DATE SERVICES TERMINATED

7. PATIENT WAS CONTINUOUSLY TOTALLY DISABLED (UNABLE TO WORK?)

FROM TO

8. PATIENT WAS PARTIALLY DISABLED

FROM TO

9. IF STILL TOTALLY DISABLED, WHAT DATE SHOULD PATIENT BE ABLE TO RETURN TO WORK, IF SPECIFIC DATE IS NOT KNOWN, PLEASE ESTIMATE.

NAME OF PHYSICIAN **PLEASE PRINT** DEGREE

STREET ADDRESS AREA CODE ( ) PHONE NUMBER

CITY STATE ZIP CODE

PHYSICIAN SIGNS HERE X ______ ATTENDING PHYSICIAN'S SIGNATURE

DATE OF STATEMENT ______

Fig. 3.6 Continuance of Disability claim form (continued).

CAPTIVE REINSURANCE ADMINISTRATION

Insurers active in the captive reinsurance business must prepare an array of information to cede the business to the captive. Insurers provide monthly or quarterly accountings on the business processed. Additional information is provided at year-end to assist the captive in the preparation of its annual statement. Some insurers prepare the annual statement and tax return for the captive.

REINSURANCE CEDED ON A WRITTEN BASIS

If the business is ceded to the captive on a written reinsurance basis, the business passes from the direct writer directly to the captive. The details of the flow of business are governed by the reinsurance treaty. The typical arrangement provides for a monthly transmittal of the transactions.

A *reinsurance cession*, or *ceding statement*, is prepared each month listing the cash transactions. Cession statements are provided about 15-20 days after the end of the month. The balance, if positive, of the gross premiums minus refund premiums, less paid claims, paid compensation, and the ceding fee, is remitted to the captive reinsurer along with the cession.

The *ceding fee* is the percentage of gross premiums minus refund premiums charged by the insurer for general expenses, premium taxes, and direct writer profit. Premium taxes are only paid on direct written business and are the responsibility of the direct writer. States do not tax reinsurance premiums paid by the direct writer to the reinsurer, although a federal excise tax is charged on premiums ceded to offshore reinsurers. Ceding fees range from 6% to 20%, with the lower range reflecting an exceptionally large producer. Some direct writers charge on a sliding scale, such as 12% for the first $500,000 of annual premium, 10% on the next $500,000, and 8% thereafter. The ceding fee may reflect aspects of the reporting arrangements and direct expenses. A producer reporting business by computer tape may have a lower ceding fee than one reporting on individual certificates. A producer willing to use factor cards instead of rate charts may have a lower ceding fee. A few direct writers charge a portion of the ceding fee based on a percentage of premium plus the direct cost of certain expense items; e.g., rate charts.

Included with the monthly cession is a report of the required reserves at the end of the period. This usually covers statutory active life reserves and claim reserves. Unearned premium reserves for life insurance and disability reserves on the Rule of 78 and pro rata may be provided in order for the captive to prepare GAAP financial statements.

Captives are usually licensed in only one state, which is usually different from the direct writer's state of domicile. The direct writer may be widely licensed and may face restrictions from other states. In order for the direct writer to take reserve credit in its statutory financial statement for business ceded to a non-admitted reinsurer, a custodial trust (also called a *security fund*) must be established. (See the sample Trust Agreement at the end of Chapter Two). Even without regulatory requirements, the establishment of a trust is good business practice.

When the reinsurance treaty is executed between the direct writer and a captive reinsurer, a separate trust agreement is drawn between the two parties and a bank. The bank agrees to hold securities in trust for the direct writer in the event the captive defaults on its obligations under the reinsurance treaty. Ownership of the assets and the investment income remains with the captive. The trust is simply a pledge of the securities. The bank does not have any obligations except to hold the funds. The bank charges an annual fee from $1,000 to $10,000 depending on the size of the trust and the number of transactions.

In theory, the trust can be funded with any admitted assets permitted an insurance company. In practice, the permissible assets are usually limited to cash, certificates of deposit, U.S. government bonds, and high quality corporate bonds. Most insurers require that the market value of the assets in the trust equals or exceeds the required statutory reserves. If the producer of the business receives front compensation, the statutory reserves may exceed the actual cash received by the captive reinsurer.

If business is reinsured to an offshore captive reinsurer, state regulations governing the direct writer usually require that an *irrevocable evergreen letter of credit* be used instead of a trust account. The letter of credit must be issued by a U.S. bank. The adjectives "irrevocable" and "evergreen" describe a letter of credit which is an unqualified promise by the bank to pay the funds to the direct writer on demand. State insurance regulations require the letters of credit to be valid for a period of one year or more. The captive is required by the bank to maintain assets or deposits at the bank to secure its promise to pay. Banks charge an annual fee of 1/2%-1% of the amount of the letter of credit.

At year-end, the direct writer generally supplies all of the information the captive needs to complete its statutory annual statement and federal income tax return. Cash transactions for the year are summarized. The December reserve statement provides the year-end reserves. A policy exhibit showing the transactions based on number of insureds and amount in force is provided. Some insurers provide an actuarial certification of the reserves and the data for Page 6 (Analysis of Increase of Reserves) of the statutory annual statement. Insurers may provide a separate set of reserves for tax calculations.

A few direct writers include preparation of the statutory statement and tax return as a part of the services provided in the ceding fee. Others offer the services on an hourly consulting basis, recognizing that the degree of difficulty varies widely. Many captives prepare their own financial statements or rely on independent actuarial or accounting firms. Monthly or quarterly GAAP financial statements are often prepared.

REINSURANCE CEDED ON AN EARNED BASIS

The accounting for earned reinsurance is different, and primarily follows the description of retroactive commissions and experience refunds. Cessions are prepared monthly or quarterly in accordance with the reinsurance treaty. Underwriting profit is determined after the deduction of the ceding fee (which replaces the insurer's expense charge in the retroactive commission calculation). The fundamental difference is that any negative balance must be paid to the direct writer. A trust account is not required because the direct writer holds all funds until the profits or losses actually emerge.

INVESTMENTS

The investment department of a credit insurer has a few specialized activities relating to the methods of marketing credit insurance. The investment philosophy tends to reflect the nature of the product and industry practices.

Investment departments attempt to match the terms of the invested funds with the terms of the underlying liabilities. The short-term nature of credit insurance products dictates a commitment of a large portion of the invested assets to short-term and medium-term investments. Even without the necessity for compensating balances and deposits, credit insurers often invest heavily in certificates of deposit and short-term bonds. If an insurer is active in the financial institution market segment, the number of checking accounts, savings accounts, and certificates of deposit is large. Automated systems are needed to keep records updated. Bank statement reconciliation requires a significant amount of time.

If the insurer is active in captive reinsurance, the investment department must monitor the activity in the trust accounts. The financial institution holding the funds in trust provides a quarterly report of the assets in the trust. The captive reinsurer or the investment department must determine the market value of the funds as of the end of the quarter. The total market value is compared to the required balance in the trust to test for compliance with the trust agreement. Follow-up is necessary to insure that the trust account is maintained at the proper level.

If the arrangement with the captive involves offshore reinsurance, an irrevocable letter of credit is usually required in lieu of a custodial trust. The investment department must compare the amount of the letters of credit posted to the required balance.

POLICY FORMS

State laws and regulations contain rather detailed and specific requirements about the contents and appearance of policy forms. As with other aspects of state regulation, a diversity of requirements exists. Policy forms must be filed by the insurer in all states where the form is used. In most states, insurance department approval is required before the forms can be used.

Credit insurance can be issued as group insurance or as individual insurance. The group concept is prevalent. Group insurance is the only plan used for non-contributory business generated by credit unions and a few banks. In other market segments, both approaches are used, almost interchangeably. The insurance provided, premium charged, coverage provisions, and policy administration have few, if any, differences–only the policy form is materially different. Many of these differences are a matter of form and not substance.

GROUP POLICY FORMS

The basic concept of group insurance is that the contractual relationship is between the insurance company and the group policyholder (the lender). A group policyholder has a financial relationship with potential insureds which creates an *insurable interest*. An insurable interest is present in the lender-borrower relationship, as the lender may suffer financial loss if the borrower is disabled or dies.

Early group statutes were written before lender groups were envisioned. The lack of permissive state regulations concerning the definitions of eligible groups hindered early use of the group concept in credit insurance. In all states, lender groups are now eligible for group insurance protection.

A group master policy is issued to the lender by the direct-writing insurance company. The policy specifies eligibility conditions. Borrowers of the group policyholder may be enrolled under the group policy if they meet the eligibility standards.

The following material describes the common provisions of group policies. Representative policy wording is shown in italics. See Figures 3.7 and 3.8 for examples of an actual group policy application and group certificate.

INSURING CLAUSE

The insuring clause describes the benefits paid under the various life and disability plans of insurance offered by the lender. Plans are described in broad terms. For life insurance, the description includes level and decreasing plans, and may cover either single or joint lives. Disability clauses permit various elimination periods with retroactive or non-retroactive options and generally insure only the primary insured. In this manner, a lender may add to or change its desired life and disability plans without amending the policy. An individual's certificate will specify the particular options selected by the insured if more than one plan is offered by the lender. The certificate contains the possible options, and the desired benefits are selected by marking the appropriate benefit box.

The suicide provision is often contained in the insuring clause. A benefit is paid when the cause of death is suicide, but the benefit is limited to a return of premium for a certain period following issue. The limited benefits are paid if suicide occurs during the first policy year in most states. Some states limit the period to six months, while others permit periods of up to two years. Missouri permits a limited benefit only if the insurer can prove that the insured contemplated suicide when the policy was purchased. This effectively covers suicide for the full benefit.

For truncated life coverage, the insuring clause is often identical to the standard wording for a net payoff plan. In the schedule of benefits on the certificate of insurance, both a loan term and a term of insurance will be specified. The truncated life coverage is effected by entering an insurance term which is less than the loan term. Somewhere on the certificate will be a prominent disclosure that the insurance may not cover the full term of the loan.

LIFE INSURANCE - *GROSS COVERAGE - DEATH BENEFIT - Upon receipt at the Home Office of due proof of death of any Debtor while he is insured under this Policy, we will pay to you the amount of insurance then in force. If Decreasing Life insurance is selected, the amount of insurance in force is the Original Amount of Insurance shown on the Debtor's certificate until the first payment due date. After that, the amount of insurance declines each month by an equal amount. That amount is the Original Amount of Insurance divided by the number of months of the term of insurance. The initial amount of insurance shall not exceed the initial amount of the debt. In no event will the amount of insurance per life exceed the maximum life insurance benefit shown on the Insured's certificate. In no event will life insurance be issued for a term in excess of the term stated in your application. If Level Life insurance is selected on the Debtor's certificate, the amount in force shall be equal to the Amount of Insurance shown in his certificate and shall remain constant for the entire term of insurance.*

If Joint Life insurance is elected, the amount of insurance shall be that as described above, whichever is applicable, in the event of death of either the Debtor or the Co-Debtor. Only one benefit will be paid under the Joint Life provision. If both of the Debtors die at the same time, only one benefit shall be paid under the Certificate. The method of payment shall be determined as though the Debtor had died first, and the Co-Debtor survived. After such payment all insurance under the Policy shall cease.

The maximum amount of life insurance under this Policy shall not exceed the amount stated in your application. The amount of insurance shall not exceed the amount of debt at the time insurance under this Policy becomes effective. If the Debtor (or Co-Debtor if Joint Life coverage is selected) commits suicide within 1 year of his Effective Date, our liability shall be limited to an amount equal to the premium paid for the insurance.

NET PAYOFF WORDING - AMOUNT OF DECREASING LIFE INSURANCE. The amount of Decreasing Life insurance in force is the unpaid principal balance due on the loan on the date of death. It does not include more than 2 delinquent monthly payments or any unearned interest. We will not pay more than the original amount of debt or the Maximum Life Insurance Benefit in the Schedule.

DISABILITY INSURANCE *Monthly Disability Benefit -When we receive at our Home Office proof in writing from a legally qualified physician other than the Debtor, that he has, while insured, become totally disabled as defined herein, and continues to be disabled for more than the waiting period marked on the Debtor's Certificate, we will pay to you the Monthly Disability Benefit shown on the Debtor's Certificate. Payment will begin with the day of such disability shown on his Certificate. We will pay for the number of days of said disability at 1/30th of the rate of the Monthly Disability Benefit. The Maximum Monthly Disability Benefit shall not exceed the amount stated in your application. Payments will stop when the Debtor is not totally disabled any more, when benefits are paid to the end of his stated term of insurance, or when the debt is paid off. We reserve the right to require written proof of continuing total disability from time to time.*

CRITICAL PERIOD WORDING - Payments will stop when you are not totally disabled anymore or when benefits are paid to the end of the Term of Insurance or the end of the Maximum Disability Benefit Period, whichever comes first.

ELIGIBILITY CLAUSE

The eligibility clause specifies the requirements a borrower must meet to be eligible for coverage. A maximum age will be specified. Each state requires insurance to be accepted on all borrowers up to a specified maximum if *prima facie rates* are used. (Prima facie rates are the maximum rates an insurer may charge without demonstrating a need for a higher rate.) The most common provision requires a borrower to be under age 65 at issue, or for the debt to terminate prior to age 66. A few states require coverage up to age 70. New York requires rate reductions if age 65 or age 70 limits are used (10% and 5% respectively), since the prima facie rates assume that a maximum age limitation is not imposed.

Eligibility for disability insurance usually requires the insured to meet an *actively-at-work* test–the insured must have worked 30 hours a week for the period of from one to two months prior to the effective date. State regulations will specify eligibility limits for the business issued in the state. A few states permit an insurer to require the actively-at-work test for life insurance, while others do not permit any actively-at-work test for life or disability. A few states require acceptance of insureds who are unemployed due to layoff if they are subject to job recall.

Eligibility - All natural persons who are your Debtors (including a Co-Debtor, if Joint Life coverage is selected and extra premium is paid) are eligible for coverage under this Policy except: (1) persons who have attained the eligibility age stated in your application subject to the MISSTATEMENT OF AGE provision; or (2) persons who are not obligated to repay the debt at and from the date of the debt; and (3) persons specified in the application as ineligible.

Eligibility - To be eligible for total disability insurance, the Debtor must be employed for wage or profit at least 30 hours a week for the period of not less than one month prior to the Effective Date stated in his Certificate or be unemployed due solely to layoff, subject to recall.

COVERAGE CLAUSE

The coverage clause specifies when insurance begins and ends for an insured. An insured must be alive for coverage to be effective. The maximum amount of insurance on any one life and the maximum term permitted is defined, possibly by reference to the group policy application.

The bold portion of the following sample shows the language some states require when referring to the effective date if a loan is renewed or refinanced and both loans are insured under the same group policy. The purpose of the clause is to measure the effective date from the date of the first loan, at least to the extent of the outstanding balance of the old loan at the time of refinancing. This affects the effective date of the suicide clause, the incontestable period, and any preexisting condition clause on disability. Amounts loaned in excess of the old balance are subject to the new effective date. This approach is also used on credit card and line-of-credit coverages. Each new advance has a different effective date for the measurement of the clauses mentioned above.

Coverage - All eligible Debtors may, after the effective date hereof, be insured against loss of life for the amount necessary to discharge their debt to the Creditor on the date of death, provided required premium is remitted to the Company. All insurance shall terminate: (1) upon the discharge or release of such debt; (2) if the property upon which the debt is based is legally repossessed; (3) if a judgment is entered in any court as to the debt; or (4) by the transfer of such debt to another debtor not insured hereunder. Insurance as to any one Debtor shall not take effect until the effective date of this Policy and until the later of: (1) the date the Debtor becomes obligated to the Creditor; or (2) when a Certificate is issued, its stated effective date; and unless on said date said Debtor is alive. ***In any renewal or refinancing of a debt insured hereunder, the effective date as to any policy provision shall be deemed to be the first date on which the Debtor became insured under the Policy at least to the extent of the amount and term of such debt outstanding at the time of such renewal or refinancing.*** *Such insurance shall in no case exceed: (1) the maximum amount of insurance; or (2) the maximum term stated in the application. If there is more than one Debtor on the same loan, only the Debtor first signing the instrument evidencing the debt shall be insured, unless the Creditor, at the time the insurance becomes effective: (1) notifies the Company by designating one of the other persons signing such instrument as the Debtor insured under the Policy; or (2) issues Joint Life coverage as provided herein on a Co-Debtor. An application for coverage may be required from eligible Debtors. If so, said application will be attached to and made part of any Certificate which may be issued to the Debtor.*

CONSIDERATION AND PREMIUMS

A consideration clause is necessary for legal purposes since the policy is a legal contract. The premium rates are defined for the plans of insurance, usually by reference to a schedule or the group application.

Consideration - This Policy is issued in consideration of: (1) your application, a copy of which is attached to and made a part of this Policy; (2) payment by you of all premiums on their due date, as later provided; and (3) your furnishing the report of coverage to us with each premium remittance.

Premiums - Premiums under this Policy are payable as stated in the application. You shall pay them to us, sending them with the reports and information required. All premiums are payable directly to us at our Home Office. Except as herein provided, the payment of a premium shall not maintain this Policy in force beyond the date the next premium is due.

REPORTS

Lenders are required to maintain records of insureds covered under the group policy. Reports are provided to the insurance company of the new business issued and certificates refunded during the month.

Reports - You shall maintain a record of the facts of the insurance as they pertain to each debtor. You shall furnish us with such information concerning the insurance as we, or the laws, rules or regulations of the state in which this Policy is issued may from time to time require. This includes: (1) the names and ages of Debtors insured; (2) the amounts and terms of the respective debt; (3) copies of certificate, cancellations, changes and additions.

GRACE PERIOD

A 30-day or 31-day grace period is permitted for the remittance of premium by the lender to the insurer.

Grace Period - We will allow a 31-day grace period for any premium due, except the first. If a premium payment is not paid within the grace period, this Policy and all insurance on lives of Debtors for which premiums have not been paid shall stop at the end of the 31 days. This Policy may stop at an earlier date, not prior to the end of the period for which premiums have been paid, should you give us written notice of cancellation.

ENTIRE CONTRACT, INDIVIDUAL CERTIFICATES

This clause contains several general statements required of all group policies. An insurer can use only statements made by the insured which are contained in the written application, if any. For most credit insurance, no application is taken, so an insurer does not have any defense for a claim. The suicide provision, the preexisting condition clause, and the exclusions, however, may limit or deny a benefit for a specific coverage. Conceptually, the insurer accepts the claim, but the benefits under the claim are limited or zero.

If an application is taken, the insured may sign a good health statement and answer a few health questions. To be used as a defense for a claim, the application must be signed, and a copy attached to the certificate of insurance provided to the insured. Statements made are representations, not warranties. By signing a good health statement, the insured is not guaranteeing that he is in good health, only that he thinks so, to the best of his knowledge and belief.

Each insured must be given a certificate which provides evidence of insurance. The certificate describes the specific plans of insurance selected and the associated premium. Benefits and coverage are summarized. Eligibility requirements are stated along with any limitations or exclusions. For the most part, the certificate is a concise version of the group policy provisions as they relate to the insured. In the event of a discrepancy between the group policy and the certificate, the group policy governs. Insurers sometimes lose in court, however, trying to enforce the group policy when the certificate has an error.

Entire Contract - This Policy, including any attached supplemental agreements and riders, your application and any applications of Debtors are the complete contract of insurance. Statements made by you or Debtors in an application shall, in the absence of fraud, be deemed representations and not warranties. No statement made by you or a Debtor shall be used in any contest unless contained in a written application which is or has been furnished to you, the Debtor, or his estate.

Individual Certificates - We will furnish to you individual certificates which you will deliver to each insured Debtor at the time the debt is incurred. The information in the certificate will describe the insured Debtor's coverage under the Policy.

TERMINATION OF INSURANCE

Clauses will specify the conditions of termination of the group policy and the individual borrower's coverage. Group policies can be terminated by either the lender or the insurer, usually on 30 days' notice. Coverage on individual insureds continues until natural expiration on single premium business. Monthly outstanding balance business terminates on the date the policy terminates.

Insurers will rarely flat cancel a lender's policy. A lender is often offered reduced compensation, which is incentive for the lender to search for a new insurer. Lenders do change insurers. Notice of termination is given to the old insurer by the lender, and a new group policy is issued by the new insurer beginning on the date of termination of the old policy. For group single premium business, the new insurer may negotiate with the old insurer to assume the business in force . On MOB business, the new insurer takes over the entire block on the effective date of the new policy.

Individual coverages stop when the term expires. Prior to expiration, coverage is stopped if the insured requests cancellation or if the loan is terminated. Credit insurance must be canceled when the loan is discharged in most states. Neither the insured nor the insurer has an option to continue coverage.

Some states require that joint insurance be permitted to continue if coverage on one insured stops because of suicide or misstatement of age.

Refunds equal to the unearned premium are paid on single premium plans if insurance terminates prior to expiration of the term of insurance. In most states, a refund is not paid on life insurance coverage if a death benefit is paid. Refunds are not required if less than $1.00 (higher limits are permitted in some states).

When This Policy Stops - This Policy may be stopped by either party giving the other 30 days' written notice. If the Policy stops, insurance on the lives of Debtors already insured will remain in effect. After the Policy stops, no new insurance will become effective.

When Individual Insurance Stops - The insurance on the life of any individual Debtor shall not extend beyond the maturity date of his debt. Insurance stops when: (1) the term of insurance in the Debtor's certificate of insurance expires; (2) when the debt is paid in full, renewed or refinanced, or otherwise stops; or (3) the date we receive the Debtor's written request to stop insurance, whichever happens first. Joint Life coverage must be stopped as to both insureds and not individually on either person. When we receive notice from you that a Debtor's insurance is canceled before the term of insurance shown in his certificate expires, we will refund to you the unearned premium for the remaining term. This includes any unearned disability premium if the Debtor dies. You will pay or credit the refund to the Debtor. The refund will be computed in accordance with the appropriate refund formula approved by the Insurance Commissioner of the state in which the Policy is delivered. No refund or credit need be made if the amount to be refunded does not exceed $1.00.

INCONTESTABILITY

This is a standard clause in life and disability insurance policies. It means that misrepresentations made in the application cannot be used as a defense for a claim if the death or disability occurs after the contestable period. A two-year contestable period is prevalent. After coverage has been in force for two years, a claim is incontestable except for fraud. The application of fraud is usually limited to identity of the insured; e.g., a son takes out the insurance but names his father as the insured.

Incontestability - This Policy shall be incontestable, except for non-payment of premiums, after it has been in force for 2 years from its date of issue. No statement made by any insured Debtor with regard to his insurability shall be used to contest the insurance or deny a claim for a period of 2 years during his lifetime, unless the statement was made fraudulently.

MISSTATEMENT OF AGE

If insurance is issued on a borrower who misstates his age, and his true age is over the maximum age of eligibility, the insurer will return the original premium. The error is usually discovered at the time of claim. The claim is denied on the basis that the insurance was never in force.

Misstatement of Age - If any one Debtor has stated that he is under the eligibility age but he is not, we will return the premium when we discover this and will not pay any benefits.

A different situation arises when the insured states his true age, and it is beyond the eligibility limit. If the insurance is issued by the lender, the insurer must discover the error and rescind the certificate. States often limit the time an insurer may rescind the certificate to 60 or 90 days from the effective date of the certificate. If the insurer does not discover the error at issue, the coverage is in force and the insurer is liable for any claim.

CLAIM CLAUSE

Several clauses define the process of claim filing and the beneficiaries under the policy. The insurer must be notified of a claim, and a claim form completed. Proof of loss should be submitted within a reasonable time, but insurers are liberal in the acceptance of claims even if the reporting is significantly delayed.

The first beneficiary of a group credit insurance policy is the lender, to the extent of the unpaid indebtedness. For gross coverage life insurance, the claim payment will usually exceed the outstanding indebtedness because the indebtedness includes the unearned finance charges. Any excess is payable to the insured's estate or to a named second beneficiary.

Notice of Claim - We must receive written notice within 30 days after any loss covered by the Debtor's Certificate occurs or begins, or as soon as is reasonably possible. Notice given by or on behalf of the Debtor or the Beneficiary to us at the Home Office, or to any of our authorized Agents, with enough information to identify the Debtor, shall be deemed notice to us.

Payment of Claims - All proceeds of this Policy, including any supplemental agreement or riders attached, are payable to you to the extent of your interest to reduce or pay off the unpaid debt of the Debtor. Your interest shall be the amount of the debt owed to you by the Debtor on the date we pay a claim. The balance, if any, is payable to the Debtor, if living, otherwise to the Second Beneficiary, if living, otherwise to the insured's estate. If proceeds are payable to an insured's estate or to a beneficiary who cannot execute a valid release, we can pay proceeds up to $1,000 to someone related to the insured or to a beneficiary by blood or marriage whom we consider to be entitled to the proceeds. We will be discharged to the extent of any payment made in good faith.

DISABILITY - *Claim Forms - A claim form will be sent to the Debtor within 15 days after his notice has been given. If the claimant does not receive the forms within 15 days, he may send the proof of loss on any type form. Such proof must: (1) show the date and cause of the total disability; (2) show that the Debtor requires and is receiving regular treatment from a licensed physician other than himself; and (3) be signed by the Physician.*

DISABILITY - *Proof of Loss - The proof of loss forms must be returned to us within 90 days after the end of the period of total disability. If the claimant cannot send the proof within the 90 days, it must be sent as soon as possible. The additional time cannot exceed 1 year unless he is legally incapable.*

DISABILITY - *Time of Payment of Claims - We will pay any benefit due on a monthly basis, after we receive the proof of loss, while the total disability of the Debtor and our liability continue. Any benefit unpaid when our liability has ended will be paid immediately after we receive final written proof of loss.*

EXCLUSIONS CLAUSE

Life policies often do not contain any exclusions, although some policies exclude war or non-scheduled aviation. Pregnancy is usually excluded in disability insurance, but the primary exclusion is preexisting conditions.

If preexisting conditions are totally excluded, the date of the initial onset of the disability must be after the effective date of coverage for any benefits to be payable. The standard "six and six" clause specifies that benefits are not payable if disability begins within six months after the effective date for an accident or sickness treated within six months prior to the effective date. Policies are issued which cover preexisting conditions, but the insured must not be disabled on the effective date.

Exclusions - No disability benefit shall be payable if the disability of the Debtor: (1) is a result of normal pregnancy; (2) occurs while the Debtor is in the armed services of any country (upon notice to us of entry into an armed service, a pro-rata refund of all premium will be made); or (3) is due to aviation, except as a fare-paying passenger.

SAMPLE PREEXISTING CONDITION EXCLUSIONS - (1) Total Disabilities Not Covered. We will not pay a claim or refund the premium if your disability results from a preexisting condition for which you received medical advice, diagnosis or treatment within 6 months before the Effective Date, and which caused loss within 6 months following the Effective Date. (2)

Total Disabilities Not Covered. We will not pay the claim or refund the premium if your disability begins within 2 years after the Effective Date as a result of a preexisting medical condition. A preexisting medical condition is one for which you saw, or were under treatment by, a physician or a chiropractor both within the 6 months before and the 6 months after the Effective Date shown in the Schedule. (3) Total Disabilities Not Covered. We will not pay the claim or refund the premium if your disability begins within 2 years after the Effective Date of this Certificate as the result of a preexisting condition for which you received medical advice, diagnosis or treatment before the Effective Date of this Certificate. After 2 years, disability resulting from such condition is covered. (4) Exclusions From Total Disability Benefit. No disability benefits shall be payable hereunder for any disability caused by or resulting from any sickness contracted or injury sustained prior to the Effective Date of the Debtor's insurance hereunder and as a result of which the Debtor was totally disabled at any time during the six months preceding said Effective Date.

DEFINITIONS CLAUSE

A variety of terms used in the policy may be defined. Significant are the definitions of accident, sickness, and disability.

Two definitions of disability are in use:

1. *His occupation*–the claimant need only prove that he is prevented from performing the tasks of his regular occupation.

2. *Any occupation*–the claimant must prove he is unable to perform the tasks of any job for which he is qualified by reason of his education, training, or experience.

The definition of "any occupation" disability is applied in most credit disability policies . This is more restrictive than a "his occupation" definition. Some states require the use of the "his occupation" definition at least for a certain period, usually 12 months. Under this scenario, the insurer must apply the "his occupation" test for the first twelve months of disability. After 12 months, the more restrictive definition must be met for benefits to continue.

Definitions - "Debtor" means the primary obligor or first signer on the instrument evidencing the debt unless you, at the time insurance becomes effective, notify us by designating one of the other persons signing such instruments as the insured. No joint disability insurance on any one debt is available under this Agreement. "Injury" means bodily injury caused by an accident occurring after the Effective Date of the Debtor's insurance which results directly and independently of all other causes in loss covered by the Policy. "Sickness" means sickness or disease causing disability to begin on or after the Effective Date of the Debtor's insurance which results in loss covered under the Policy. "Total Disability" means that during the first 12 consecutive months of disability, the Debtor is unable to perform the duties of his occupation for wage or profit because of sickness or accidental injury. After the first 12 consecutive months of total disability, the definition changes and requires that the Debtor not be able to perform the duties of any occupation for which he is reasonably qualified by education, training or experience. He must require and be receiving regular treatments from a licensed physician other than himself.

GENERAL CLAUSES

The following clauses are representative of a variety of general provisions. Several of the clauses are required by state regulation. Others are optional and serve to cover minor items of the contract.

Legal Actions - No legal action may be started until 60 days after we have received the due proof of loss. No legal action may be started 3 years after the proof is required to be given.

Changes in Policy - No changes in this Policy shall be valid unless: (1) approved by 2 of our executive officers; and (2) endorsed on this Policy. No agent has the authority to change this Policy or to waive any of its provisions.

Gender Usage - When a personal pronoun is used in this Policy in the male gender (he, his, him) it should be understood to include the female gender, unless the context clearly indicates otherwise.

General Provisions - A. Clerical Error: The insurance shall not be void if you fail due to clerical error to furnish the information necessary with regard to insurance under the Policy. The insurance of any insured Debtor shall not stop if, due to clerical error, you: (1) fail to make the required premium payments; or (2) report in error that a Debtor's insurance is to be canceled. B. Nonparticipating: This policy shall not be entitled to share in our surplus earnings. C. Examination of Records: All of your records with information pertinent to the insurance under the Policy shall be open to our examination during the Policy term and within 1 year after the Policy stops.

Assignment - The insurance provided under this Policy is non-assignable.

Conformity with State Statutes - Any provision of this Agreement which, on its Effective Date, is in conflict with the statutes of the state in which the Debtor resides on such date is amended to conform to the minimum requirements of such statutes.

Physical Examination - While a claim is pending we have the right at our expense to have the claimant examined by a physician when and as often as we feel is necessary.

When This Agreement Stops - This Agreement shall automatically stop if any of the following events occur: (1) a premium for this Agreement is not paid when due or within the Grace Period provided in the Policy; or (2) the Policy is stopped. The insurance on the lives of any Debtor already insured will remain in effect for the period the premium has been paid if the Agreement is stopped.

APPLICATION
is Hereby Made to

by

____

____
(herein called the Creditor)

for a group policy to provide insurance with regards to certain persons who are or who become indebted to the Creditor. The type of coverages to be offered under said group policy are those coverages checked below:

- ☐ A. Creditors Group Life Insurance
- ☐ B. Creditors Group Life Insurance and Total Disability Benefits
- ☐ C. Creditors Group Life Insurance and Optional Total Disability Benefits

WAITING PERIOD FOR TOTAL DISABILITY

If a disability coverage shall be offered under the Group Policy the following waiting period for disability shall apply: Elimination Period: ________ days. Retroactive: Yes ☐ No ☐ *Special ☐

*Special refers to a special full monthly benefit plan after satisfaction of Elimination Period.

CLASSES OF INDEBTEDNESS

The classes of indebtedness to be covered are as follows:

BENEFITS AND LIMITATIONS OF LIFE INSURANCE

Age	Maximum Amount	Maximum Term	Premium Rate	Special Qualifications

BENEFITS AND LIMITATIONS OF TOTAL DISABILITY INSURANCE

Age	Maximum Amount	Maximum Term	Premium Rate	Special Qualifications

COLLECTION OF PREMIUMS

Premiums are to be collected by the Creditor from the Debtors on the following basis:

- ☐ A. Single Premium collected in advance for the full term of the indebtedness.
- ☐ B. Monthly Premiums collected on the insured outstanding balance.

REMITTING OF PREMIUMS

The Creditor shall remit premiums collected from the Debtors to the Company on the following basis:

- ☐ A. Single Premium for the full term of the indebtedness.
- ☐ B. Monthly Premiums on the insured outstanding balance.

ELIGIBILITY AGE

No Debtor who has attained the age of ________ shall be eligible for insurance under the group policy.

TERMINATION AGE — (if monthly premium plan)

The insurance of any Debtor insured under the group policy shall terminate upon attaining age ________ .

SPECIAL PROVISIONS

EFFECTIVE DATE

If this application is accepted by the Company, the policy shall be effective from 12:01 A.M., Standard Time, at the Creditor's address on the ____________ day of ________________ , 19 ____, for the term of one year and unless discontinued as provided therein, said policy shall be automatically renewed from year to year.

Dated at ____________________ this day of __________________, 19 ____.

____________________ Witness   ____________________ Creditor

____________________ Agent   by: ____________________ Title

Fig. 3.7 Sample group policy application.

CERTIFICATE OF INSURANCE

6906

SCHEDULE Account No.

Name of Debtor (called you)________	Name of Co-Debtor (also called you)________ (Complete only for Joint Life)	AGE Debtor Co-Debtor (65 Maximum)

Address ________ (Street) (City) (State) (Zip)

Creditor ________ Second Beneficiary ________

Effective Date Month Day Year	Term of Insurance (Months)	Scheduled Expiration Date Month Day Year	Monthly Loan Payment	Maximum Monthly Disability Benefit	Maximum Amount of Life Insurance
			$	$1,000.00	$75,000.00

COVERAGES	LIMITS OF LIABILITY		PREMIUM
☐ SINGLE DECREASING LIFE	ORIGINAL AMOUNT OF LIFE INSURANCE	$	$
☐ JOINT DECREASING LIFE	ORIGINAL AMOUNT OF LIFE INSURANCE	$	$
☐ SINGLE LEVEL LIFE	AMOUNT OF LIFE INSURANCE	$	$
☐ JOINT LEVEL LIFE	AMOUNT OF LIFE INSURANCE	$	$
☐ DISABILITY BEGINNING ____ DAY AFTER A ____ DAY WAITING PERIOD	MONTHLY TOTAL DISABILITY BENEFIT	$	$
		TOTAL PREMIUM	$

THIS CERTIFICATE MAY AT ANY TIME WITHIN 10 DAYS AFTER ITS RECEIPT BY THE INSURED, BE RETURNED BY DELIVERING IT OR MAILING IT TO THE COMPANY OR TO THE CREDITOR THROUGH WHOM IT WAS PURCHASED. IMMEDIATELY UPON SUCH DELIVERY OR MAILING, THE CERTIFICATE WILL BE DEEMED VOID, AND ANY PREMIUM PAID ON IT WILL BE REFUNDED.

WHAT YOU GET

We certify that if we have been paid the premium shown in the Schedule you are insured for the coverage shown in the Schedule, subject to the terms of the Group Policy issued to the Creditor.

WHO GETS PAID

Claim payments are made to the Creditor named in the Schedule to pay off or reduce your debt. If claim payments are more than the balance of your debt, the difference will be paid to you or to the Second Beneficiary named in the Schedule, if any, or to your estate.

WHAT WE WILL PAY

Single Decreasing Life Insurance Benefit. If you die while you are insured for single decreasing life coverage, we will pay the amount of insurance in force at the time of your death after we receive proof of your death.

Amount of Decreasing Life Insurance. The amount of decreasing life insurance is the Original Amount of Life Insurance shown in the Schedule until the first payment due date. After that, your insurance declines each month by an equal amount. That amount is the Original Amount of Life Insurance divided by the number of months in the Term in the Schedule.

Single Level Life Insurance Benefit. If you die while you are insured for single level life coverage, we will pay the Original Amount of Life Insurance shown in the Schedule after we receive proof of your death.

Joint Life. If you selected joint life coverage, we will pay the amount of insurance provided under the applicable provision above on the death of either you or your co-borrower. Only one death benefit will be paid under this certificate. If you and the co-borrower die at the same time, we will pay as though you had died and the co-borrower survived.

Total Disbility Insurance Benefit. (This coverage applies only to the first person named in the Schedule and only if a disability charge is indicated in the Schedule.) If you are insured for total disability insurance, we will pay a benefit if you file written proof that you became totally disabled while insured and continue to be totally disabled for more than ____ days. Payment will be calculated from the ____ day of disability. The benefit will be equal to 1/30th of your regular payment shown in the Schedule for each day of disability to be compensated. Payments will stop when you are not totally disabled any more or when benefits are paid to the scheduled maturity date, whichever comes first.

INSURED'S CERTIFICATE

Fig. 3.8 Sample group certificate.

Definition of Total Disability. During the first 12 consecutive months of total disability, total disability means that you are not able to perform the important duties of your occupation because of sickness or accidental injury. After the first 12 consecutive months of total disability, the definition changes and requires that you not be able to perform the duties of any occupation for which you are reasonably qualified by education, training or experience. You will be required to give us written proof of your continuing total disability from time to time.

WHAT WE WON'T PAY

Misstated Age. If you stated you are under 66, but you are not, we will return your premium when we discover this and will not pay any benefits. If you are insured for joint life coverage, we will refund 40% of the life premium paid and the survivor will still be covered.

Suicide. We won't pay any claim if you commit suicide within one year of the Effective Date shown in the Schedule, but we will refund the insurance premiums. This also applies to your co-borrower, if you applied for joint life coverage.

Total Disabilities Not Covered. We won't pay the claim or refund the premium if your disability is the result of:

1. normal pregnancy;
2. declared or undeclared war;
3. flight in non-scheduled aircraft; or
4. intentional self-inflicted injury.

WHEN INSURANCE STOPS — REFUNDS

This insurance stops on the Scheduled Expiration Date, or when your loan is paid off, renewed, refinanced or otherwise stops, whichever happens first. If your insurance stops before the Scheduled Expiration Date in the Schedule, you will be given a refund or a credit on your account of unearned premium. This refund or credit will be calculated using a formula approved by the Insurance Commissioner, but refunds or credits of less than a dollar won't be made.

WHAT THE CONTRACT IS AND HOW YOUR STATEMENTS AFFECT IT

The Group Policy, the Application for the Group Policy, and the Application of Borrower, if any, are the complete contract of insurance. All statements made by you in your Application are considered to have been made to the best of your knowledge and belief. No statement can be used to void this insurance or deny a claim unless the statement is in your signed Application. After 2 years from the Effective Date in the Application no statement made by you in your Application can be used to void this insurance or deny a claim.

LIMITATIONS

Once the life insurance benefit has been paid, all other insurance under this Certificate stops.

RULES FOR FILING A TOTAL DISABILITY CLAIM

You must write us or our agent about your total disability claim within 30 days after the beginning of your total disability or as soon after that as you can. We will send you claims forms within 15 days after you tell us about the claim. If we don't send the forms in 15 days, you can simply send us written proof of your disability. The proof must show the date and the cause of the total disability and how serious it is and it must be signed by a physician or a chiropractor. The proof of total disability must be sent to us no later than 90 days after your total disability ends. If it is impossible to file within 90 days, you must file as soon as you can. Unless you have been legally incapable of filing the proof of total disability, we won't accept it if it is filed after one year from the time it should have been filed. You can't start any legal action until 60 days after you send us the proof of your total disability. You can't start any legal action more than 3 years after the proof is filed.

RULES FOR FILING A LIFE CLAIM

We must be given a certified copy of the death certificate as proof of a life claim.

CONFORMITY WITH STATE STATUTES

Any part of the Group Policy which, on the Effective Date of the Group Policy, conflicts with the statutes of the state where the Group Policy was delivered is changed to conform to the minimum standards of those statutes.

PHYSICAL EXAMINATION AND AUTOPSY

We at our own expense have the right, and you must allow us the opportunity, to examine your person as ofter as is reasonably required while a claim is pending and to make an autopsy in case of death, if it is not forbidden by law.

Secretary President

Fig. 3.8 Sample group certificate (continued).

INDIVIDUAL POLICIES

Under an individual policy, the contractual relationship is directly between the insured borrower and the insurer. Individual policies are used for several reasons:

1. Group statutes may contain a maximum amount limit which is lower than the limit desired by the lender, or

2. An application is taken requiring health questions, or

3. It is a company practice of the insurer to issue individual policies.

Policy forms are a blend of the group policy and the group certificate. Since the form is the insurance contract, it must be more extensive than a certificate.

Other than the wording applicable to the group policyholder/insurer relationship, the clauses of the individual policy generally follow the description of the group policy.

SINGLE PREMIUM CREDIT LIFE AND/OR CREDIT DISABILITY INSURANCE APPLICATION

SCHEDULE Account No.

Name of Proposed Insured Debtor (called you)	Name of Proposed Insured Co-Debtor (also called you) (Complete only for Joint Life)	Debtor	Co-Debtor AGE (65 MAXIMUM)
Address (Street) (City)	(State) (Zip)		
Creditor	Second Beneficiary	Annual Percentage Rate %	

EFFECTIVE DATE Month Day Year	TERM OF INSURANCE Months	MAXIMUM LIFE INSURANCE BENEFIT $ 75,000.00	MAXIMUM MONTHLY DISABILITY BENEFIT $ 500.00

COVERAGE		LIMIT OF LIABILITY	PREMIUM
☐ SINGLE DECREASING LIFE	☐ JOINT DECREASING LIFE	ORIGINAL AMOUNT OF INSURANCE $	$
☐ SINGLE LEVEL LIFE	☐ JOINT LEVEL LIFE	ORIGINAL AMOUNT OF INSURANCE $	$
☐ DISABILITY – Benefits Commence ☐ 1st Day ☐ 15th Day ☐ 31st Day After waiting period of ☐ 14 days ☐ 30 days		MONTHLY DISABILITY BENEFIT $	$
			TOTAL PREMIUM $

287167

TO BE ELIGIBLE FOR TOTAL DISABILITY INSURANCE, YOU MUST BE EMPLOYED FOR WAGE OR PROFIT AT LEAST 30 HOURS PER WEEK FOR A PERIOD OF NOT LESS THAN 1 MONTH PRIOR TO THE EFFECTIVE DATE OR UNEMPLOYED DUE SOLELY TO LAYOFF SUBJECT TO RECALL.

You are applying for insurance in the amount and for the term as shown above and agree to pay the premium shown above. Where insurance is required by the Creditor, you have the option of furnishing existing or new insurance.

Give the name and address of your regular physician on the lines below, then answer the following questions.

Physician's Name and Address (Debtor) ______________ Physician's Name and Address (Co-Debtor) ______________

(1) Proposed Insured Debtor Ht.__ft. __in. Wt.__lbs. Proposed Insured Co-Debtor Ht. __ft. __in. Wt. ____lbs.

(2) During the past five years, have you received any medical care or treatment for cancer, heart, lungs, diabetes, high blood pressure, circulatory system, kidney or the liver?

Proposed Insured Debtor Yes ☐ No ☐ Proposed Insured Co-Debtor Yes ☐ No ☐

(3) Have you within the past five years been confined in any hospital or sanitarium for treatment or observation?

Proposed Insured Debtor Yes ☐ No ☐ Proposed Insured Co-Debtor Yes ☐ No ☐

If you answered yes to either question, give details on the lines below. Include the names and addresses of any additional physicians or hospitals involved other than your regular physician listed above.

Proposed Insured Debtor ______________ Proposed Insured Co-Debtor______________

You have read the questions and answers above and they are true and complete, to the best of your knowledge and belief. You understand that no insurance will take effect until this Application is approved by the Company. If the insurance is not approved, any premium paid will be refunded.

This insurance covers only the person(s) signing the request for this insurance. Subject to approval by the Company, there will be an Individual Policy delivered within __30__ days which will more fully describe the insurance. The term of insurance will start as of the date the debt is incurred. It will stop at the end of the Term of Insurance shown above. You are not eligible for insurance if you have reached your 66th birthday.

You authorize any licensed physician, medical practitioner, hospital, clinic, or other medically related facility, insurance company, the Medical Information Bureau or other organization, institution, or person that has any records or knowledge of you or your health to give or its reinsurer(s) any such information. A photocopy of this authorization shall be as valid as the original.

You acknowledge receiving a copy of the Consumer Report Notification.

______________, 19____ ______________ ______________

Date — Signature of Proposed Insured Debtor — Signature of Proposed Insured Co-Debtor

APPLICANT'S COPY

Fig. 3.9 Sample individual policy application.

CONSUMER REPORT NOTIFICATION

Information regarding your insurability will be treated as confidential. The or its reinsurer(s), may, however, make a brief report hereon to the Medical Information Bureau, a non-profit membership organizatic. of life insurance companies, which operates an information exchange on behalf of its members. If you apply to another Bureau member company for life or health insurance coverage, or a claim for benefits is submitted to such company, the Bureau, upon request, will supply such company with the information in its file.

Upon receipt of a request from you, the Bureau will arrange disclosure of any information it may have in your file. (Medical information will be disclosed only to your attending physician.) If you question the accuracy of information in the Bureau's file, you may contact the Bureau and seek a correction in accordance with the procedures set forth in the Federal Fair Credit Reporting Act. The address of the Bureau's information office is Post Office Box 105, Essex Station, Boston, Massachusetts 02112, telephone number (617) 426-3660. or its reinsurer(s), may also release information in its file to other life insurance companies with whom you may apply for life or health insurance, or to whom a claim for benefits may be submitted.

Federal law requires that notice of investigation be given to persons applying for insurance.

In making this application for insurance to it is understood that an investigative consumer report may be prepared whereby information is obtained through personal interviews with your neighbors, friends, or others with whom you are acquainted. This inquiry includes information as to your character, general reputation, personal characteristics and mode of living. You have the right to make a written request within a reasonable period of time to receive additional, detailed information about the nature and scope of this investigation.

THIS NOTIFICATION **MUST** BE RETAINED BY THE PROPOSED INSURED.

Fig. 3.9 Sample individual policy application (continued).

SINGLE PREMIUM CREDIT LIFE AND/OR CREDIT DISABILITY INSURANCE POLICY

SCHEDULE Account No.

Name of Proposed Insured Debtor (called you)	Name of Proposed Insured (Complete only for Joint Life) Co-Debtor (also called you)	Debtor | Co-Debtor AGE
Address (Street) (City)	(State) (Zip)	(65 MAXIMUM)
Creditor	Second Beneficiary	Annual Percentage Rate %

EFFECTIVE DATE Month Day Year	TERM OF INSURANCE Months	MAXIMUM LIFE INSURANCE BENEFIT $ 75,000.00	MAXIMUM MONTHLY DISABILITY BENEFIT $500.00

COVERAGE		LIMIT OF LIABILITY	PREMIUM
☐ SINGLE DECREASING LIFE	☐ JOINT DECREASING LIFE	ORIGINAL AMOUNT OF INSURANCE $	$
☐ SINGLE LEVEL LIFE	☐ JOINT LEVEL LIFE	ORIGINAL AMOUNT OF INSURANCE $	$
☐ DISABILITY – Benefits Commence ☐ 1st Day ☐ 15th Day ☐ 31st Day After waiting period of ☐ 14 days ☐ 30 days		MONTHLY DISABILITY BENEFIT $	$
			TOTAL PREMIUM $

287167

WHAT YOU GET
We certify that if we have been paid the premium shown in the Schedule you are insured for the coverage shown in the Schedule, subject to the terms of this Policy.

WHO GETS PAID
Claim payments are made to the Creditor named in the Schedule to pay off or reduce your debt. If claim payments are more than the balance of your debt, the difference will be paid to you or to the Second Beneficiary named in the Schedule, if any, or to your estate. If proceeds are payable to your estate or a beneficiary who cannot execute a valid release, we can pay proceeds up to $1,000 to someone related to you or the beneficiary by blood or marriage whom we consider to be entitled to the proceeds. We will be discharged to the extent of any payment made in good faith.

WHAT WE WILL PAY
Single Decreasing Life Insurance Benefit. If you die while you are insured for Single Decreasing Life coverage, we will pay the amount of insurance after we receive proof of your death.

Amount of Decreasing Life Insurance. The amount of decreasing life insurance in force is the unpaid principal balance due on the loan on the date of death. It does not include more than 2 delinquent monthly payments or any unearned interest. The initial amount of insurance shall not exceed the initial amount of principal debt. In no event will the amount of insurance per life exceed the Maximum Life Insurance Benefit stated in the Schedule.

Single Level Life Insurance Benefit. If you die while you are insured for Single Level Life coverage, we will pay the Amount of Insurance shown in the Schedule after we receive proof of your death. The initial amount of insurance shall not exceed the initial amount of principal debt. In no event will the amount of insurance per life exceed the Maximum Amount of Life Insurance Benefit shown in the Schedule.

Joint Life. If you selected Joint Life coverage we will pay the amount of insurance provided under the applicable provision above at the death of either you or your co-debtor. Only one death benefit is payable under this provision. If you and your co-debtor die at the same time, we will pay as though you had died and your co-debtor survived.

Total Disability Insurance Benefit. To be eligible for total disability insurance, you must be employed for wage or profit at least 30 hours a week for a period of not less than 1 month prior to the Effective Date or unemployed due solely to layoff subject to recall. If you are insured for total disability insurance, we will pay a benefit if you file written proof that you became totally disabled while insured and continue to be totally disabled for more than the waiting period marked in the Schedule. Payment will be calculated from the day benefits commence as marked in the Schedule. The amount of total disability benefits paid will never be more than the amount owing on your loan. The benefit will be equal to 1/30th of your Monthly Disability Benefit in the Schedule for each day of disability to be compensated, but not more than the Maximum Monthly Disability Benefit in the Schedule per month. Payments will stop when you are not totally disabled any more or when benefits are paid to the end of the Term of Insurance, whichever comes first. Your co-debtor is not eligible for total disability insurance.

Definition of Total Disability. Total disability means that you are not able to perform the duties of any occupation for wage or profit for which you are reasonably qualified by education, training or experience because of sickness or accidental injury for which you require and receive regular treatments from a licensed physician other than yourself.

INSURED'S POLICY

Fig. 3.10 Sample individual policy.

WHAT WE WON'T PAY

Misstated age. If you stated you are under age 66, but you are not, we will return your premium when we discover this and will not pay any benefits. If you stated you are age 66 or older and we do not return your premium within 60 days of the Effective Date, you are insured. This also applies to your co-debtor, if you elected joint life coverage.

Suicide. We won't pay any claim if you commit suicide within 6 months from the Effective Date shown in the Schedule, but we will refund the insurance premiums. This also applies to your co-debtor, if you elected joint life coverage.

Total Disabilities Not Covered. We won't pay the claim or refund the premium if your disability:
(1) is a result of normal pregnancy; or
(2) is the result of an intentionally self-inflicted injury.

WHEN INSURANCE STOPS — REFUNDS

This insurance stops when the Term of Insurance in the Schedule expires, or when your loan is paid off, renewed, refinanced or otherwise stops, whichever happens first. If your insurance stops before the Term of Insurance in the Schedule expires, you will be given a refund or a credit on your account of unearned premium. This refund or credit will be calculated using the appropriate formula approved by the Insurance Commissioner in the state in which this Policy is delivered. No refund or credit of less than $1.00 need be made. If you die, we will refund any unearned disability premium to the person entitled to it.

WHAT THE CONTRACT IS AND HOW YOUR STATEMENTS AFFECT IT

This Policy and your Application, if any, are the complete contract of insurance. All statements made by you in your Application are considered to have been made to the best of your knowledge and belief. After 2 years from the Effective Date, no statement can be used to void this insurance or deny a claim unless that statement is in your signed Application.

RULES FOR FILING A TOTAL DISABILITY CLAIM

Written notice of your total disability claim must be furnished within 20 days after the beginning of your total disability or as soon after that as you can. You will be sent a claim form within 15 days after your notice is given. If you are not sent the form in 15 days, you can send us written proof of your total disability. Such proof must: (1) show the date and the cause of the total disability; (2) show that you require and receive regular treatment from a licensed physician other than yourself; and (3) must be signed by the physician. The proof of total disability must be sent to us no later than 90 days after your total disability ends. If it is impossible to file within 90 days, you must file as soon as you can. Unless you have been legally incapable of filing the proof of total disability, we won't accept it if it is filed after one year from the time it should have been filed.

RULES FOR FILING A LIFE CLAIM

We must be furnished with: (1) a certified copy of the death certificate; and (2) a claim form completed by the Creditor.

LEGAL ACTIONS

You can't start any legal action until 60 days after you send us the proof of loss as required by this Policy. You can't start any legal action more than 5 years after the proof is required to be given.

PHYSICAL EXAMINATION AND AUTOPSY

While a claim is pending, we have the right at our own expense to have you examined by a physician when and as often as we feel is necessary. We may also have an autopsy made in case of death unless it is forbidden by law.

CONFORMITY WITH STATE STATUTES

Any part of this Policy which on its Effective Date conflicts with the statutes of the state where this Policy was delivered is changed to conform to the minimum standards of those statutes.

Secretary | **President**

Fig. 3.10 Sample individual policy (continued).

POLICY FILING

The process of developing a policy form and obtaining insurance department approval is a long and tedious one. Forms must meet the credit insurance regulations of each state where approval is desired. While different forms are not required for each state, minor variations in state regulations make it difficult for a form to be widely used without amendments.

A draft form of a proposed policy is prepared. For credit insurance, this is generally a variation of an existing form. Insurers will have a bank of standard worded clauses from which the appropriate clauses are selected and assembled. Today's word processing capabilities simplify the process, replacing the cut and paste approach.

An initial review is made for compliance with state regulations where the policy is to be filed. A master policy filing manual is referenced. Certain filing requirements, such as filing fees, are compiled by various insurance company trade associations. Insurers add comments based on experience from prior filings.

A growing compliance concern is the requirement of *readable forms*. The majority of states now require credit insurance forms to comply with readability standards. The *Flesch scoring method* is used to assess the readability of forms. This method judges the document's comprehension difficulty by counting the syllables in the words used, and number of words in a sentence. The method is not perfect, but it produces an objective standard of readability.

States require Flesch scores of 40-50. The higher the score, the easier it is to understand the document. A score of 50 indicates the material is comprehensible to a person with a 9th-grade education. Widely licensed insurers often prepare new forms to a readable standard to meet the highest score required in any of their states of license.

Rates must be filed. If the rates do not exceed the maximum rate permitted in the state, actuarial assistance is often unnecessary. Non-standard rates must be proven to be in compliance with maximum rate standards. Actuarial justification is needed for age-rated policies, critical period coverage, and monthly outstanding balance disability plans. In most states, maximum rates are not specified for these plans–there is just a general requirement that the rates are actuarially equivalent to the maximum rates. Virginia requires an actuarial certification that the rates are expected to produce a 50% loss ratio.

The policy form is typeset, and a printer's proof is pulled. States specify a minimum size print to eliminate the fine print used in earlier days. A 10-point type is acceptable to all states. The proof is reviewed by legal staff and policy filing staff for final approval, then a limited number of copies are printed.

A package is assembled for submission to each state where approval is desired. Two copies of the form are completed using "John Doe" information. A cover letter describes the submission. Approval is quicker if the form represents only a few changes to an existing approved form. Flesch score results and certification, along with any additional certifications, are included. If required, a check for the filing fees must be enclosed. Most states charge a filing fee of about $10.00.

Long delays while waiting for a response from insurance departments sometimes occur during the approval process. Most states are able to respond to the initial filing in 30-45 days, but 90 days is possible. If the department has an objection to particular language or clauses, the approval time can be drawn out. Each written response can take another 60-90 days. Many states have a *deemer* provision in their laws and regulations which provide that a filing is deemed approved unless the department objects within a specified period of time. The period is usually 30 days, but departments are changing their regulations to provide for longer periods. If the department submits an objection within the deemer period, the deemer provision does not apply.

Average time from the draft stage to final approval is six months. This is the average, but it may take 12-18 months for unusual filings. Once approved, forms can be printed and put into use quickly. Insurers maintain a file of all approved policies, or a summary, for use by the sales, underwriting, policy issue and claims departments.

Several trends are clear. Many states now require that a form be submitted and approved by the insurer's domiciliary state before they will consider the form. Submission of solicitation and advertising material is now requested by some states, particularly for credit card coverages. The filing may be informational, but acceptability of the promotional material may impact the approval of the form. A few states are beginning to require approval of promotional material.

Insurers have adjusted procedures to overcome the long lead time. Drafts are now prepared using CRTs and micro-computers, and software is available to automatically calculate the Flesch score. Internal typesetting capabilities can cut delays and allow flexible scheduling.

Wherever possible, certain policy form information is filed on a *variable reference basis*. Variable references are items which are left blank in the filing, although the insurer may specify in a cover letter any absolute limits. This material includes maximum terms, amounts, and ages. The insurer may also specify that the layout of the insurance information (name, age, etc.) may be varied somewhat to fit the requirements of the lender's data processing system. This helps in reducing repeat submissions caused by minor revisions.

CHAPTER FOUR

PREMIUMS

In the early days of credit insurance, the calculation of the premium charged to the consumer was simple, just as loans were. There were few state regulations governing the premium charged. The intervening years have produced an environment where the rate calculations are complex, often requiring a computer. Loans now vary widely in their repayment pattern. Insurance coverage may be net payoff coverage or some other unusual coverage pattern. All states now indirectly regulate the premium charged, often introducing unique factors into the calculation.

This discussion of premiums begins with a specific loan example which represents the typical credit insurance transaction. From the specific case, the formulas will be displayed representing some of the variations found in today's marketplace.

Insurance on installment loans for the purchase of automobiles constitutes the typical credit insurance transaction. In this instance, the consumer borrows a gross amount of $9,600 for a term of 48 months and purchases single premium decreasing gross coverage. The gross note includes the portion of the purchase price financed, the scheduled interest charges over the term of the loan, and the insurance premium. The monthly loan payment is the gross note divided by the loan term:

$$\frac{\$9{,}600}{48} = \$200$$

The gross note depends on the insurance premium, which is a function of the gross note. This circular relationship can be solved with straightforward algebra. Certain firms specialize in doing these calculations. These specialty firms produce *rate charts* or *factor cards* used by the lending officer when doing the actual premium calculations. Other lenders use programmable, hand-held calculators or microcomputers for the calculations. The calculations which produce this result will be reviewed in a later section of this chapter.

State regulations specify the maximum single premium which may be charged for single life decreasing gross coverage. One state has a life insurance rate of 65¢ per hundred dollars of initial gross indebtedness, per year of coverage. This is abbreviated 65¢/100/year. The rates are linear, which means the consumer is charged 65¢ for each $100 of coverage and for each year of coverage. For the example, the credit life single premium is:

(65¢/100/year) x (number of $100s of coverage)
x (number of years of coverage) =

$$.65 \times \frac{9{,}600}{100} \times \frac{48}{12} = \$249.60$$

This premium provides uniform decreasing term life insurance for 48 months. The amount in force in any month is the sum of the remaining scheduled monthly payments. Loan payments are due at the end of the month measured from the effective date of the loan, unless the loan has an odd number of days to first payment.

Credit disability rates are not linear; i.e., the rate for two years of coverage is not twice the rate for one year of coverage. Most state regulations specify a table, by term, of maximum single premiums per $100 of initial gross indebtedness. Typical rates for 14-day retroactive coverage are:

Term of Loan	Gross Premium Per $100 of Initial Gross Indebtedness
12	$2.20
24	3.00
36	3.80
48	4.30
60	4.70

For the example, the cost of credit disability coverage on the 14R plan is:

(Rate per $100 for a 48 month loan)
x (number of $100s of coverage) =

$$4.30 \times \frac{9{,}600}{100} = \$412.80$$

This plan provides a benefit of $200 for each month that the insured is disabled until the scheduled maturity date of the loan. A proportionate daily benefit is paid for any partial month of disablement. The insured must remain disabled at least 14 days to receive any payment. If the insured is disabled in the first month, the maximum number of benefit payments is 48. In the 48th month, only one benefit payment is possible.

If the loan has a co-borrower, joint life insurance is offered. The insurance in force is paid if either of the co-borrowers dies. Premiums for joint life are expressed as a multiple of the single life rate. A multiple of 1.6 is common. For the example, the joint life premium is $249.60 x 1.6 = $399.36. Joint disability coverage is rarely sold.

STATE REGULATIONS AFFECTING RATES

State life insurance laws and regulations do not permit an insurance commissioner to regulate rates. Credit insurance regulations, however, permit the commissioner to disapprove policy forms if the benefits provided are not reasonable in relation to the premium charged. For credit insurance, the practical result is the establishment of *prima facie rates,* which are the maximum rates an insurer may charge without demonstrating a need for higher rates.

The underlying assumption of prima facie rates is that an insurer charging a rate less than or equal to the prima facie rate is presumed to have provided reasonable benefits for the premium charged. In theory, the prima facie rates are determined by measuring the actual claim costs and dividing them by the benchmark loss ratio. The *benchmark loss ratio* is the ratio of the benefits to premium, expressed as a percentage, which is deemed reasonable to provide a fair return to the borrower. Most states specify a benchmark loss ratio in regulation or law. A 50% benchmark is common. See Appendix D for the benchmark loss ratios for each state. If the benefits paid are 50% or more of the premiums charged, the benefits provided are judged reasonable. If a state studies the claim costs and finds them to be 32.5¢/100/year, the prima facie rate would be (.325)/(.50) = 65¢/100/year. In practice, prima facie rates are set in the political arena and may reflect the art of negotiation more than the art of actuarial science.

Prima facie rates are not an absolute maximum rate. If an insurer can demonstrate that a portion or all of its business is producing a loss ratio in excess of the benchmark loss ratio, the insurer may request an *upward deviation.* The insurer files the loss experience and requests permission to charge a *deviated rate* in excess of the prima facie rate. Many states accept deviations with proper actuarial justification. Deviated rates are primarily found in credit disability rating, particularly credit union business.

Insurers are permitted to charge less than the prima facie rates; however, most credit insurance is sold at the prescribed prima facie rate. Non-contributory credit union life business is a specific market segment where the prevailing rates charged are below prima facie rates. For this reason, non-contributory business is often exempt from prima facie rate regulation. A few states require insurers to periodically file experience and make adjustments in the rates charged to produce a loss ratio equal to or greater than the benchmark loss ratio. If a reduction is required, the adjustment is called a *mandatory downward deviation.* If an upward adjustment is indicated, the insurer usually has the option of whether or not to implement the rate increase.

Appendix D also includes a general guide to the prima facie rates permitted by the various states. These rates should only be used as a general guide. States are prone to change prima facie rates periodically. Several states have complex rating structures which are not completely reflected in the appendix. Note the wide variation of rates permitted across the country for essentially the same coverage. Chapter Nine provides details about the evolution of prima facie rating.

The most glaring omission in the premium calculations above is the lack of data about the specific insured. In charging prima facie rates, an insurer must accept certain conditions. In most states, an insurer must accept all persons who qualify for a loan except:

1. Persons who are over age 65 at the time of loan, or whose loan does not expire before age 66, and

2. For disability insurance, persons who are not gainfully employed or actively-at-work for at least 30 hours per week.

Claims may only be denied if:

1. Death is caused by suicide within a specified time (from six months to two years), or

2. Disability occurs within six months after the effective date relating to a condition for which the insured was treated within six months prior to the effective date

(commonly referred to as the "six and six exclusion"). Insurers are permitted to charge an additional 10% of prima facie rates in several states if the policy covers preexisting conditions.

Rates are unisex and uni-age for single life coverage–one rate for all ages and both sexes. Joint life multiples reflect that one of the insureds is usually a female with lower expected mortality costs. Underwriting is usually not permitted, but a simple statement by the insured that he is in good health may be required by the insurer in many states, (a *good health statement*). The rate calculations do not reflect that the age of the insured increases during the term of the loan. Since the term of credit insurance policies is short, the yearly increment in the mortality or morbidity costs is usually not material.

Prima facie rates in certain states reflect variations in claim costs and expenses among market segments. Prima facie rates may vary by class of lender, volume of credit insurance sold by a lender, and/or average policy size. The rates may also reflect an interest or mortality discount.

Claim costs vary by the type (class) of lender reflecting the characteristics of the borrowers of the lenders. In life insurance, the variation is small, however, material variation is found in disability insurance.

Although the definition of the classes varies by state, the following list represents the major classes:

- Automobile Dealer
- Bank
- Credit Union
- Finance Company

For life insurance, claim costs are usually highest for finance company business and lowest for non-contributory credit union business. Finance companies and small loan operations have more clientele from a lower socio-economic group than the other classes. The overall claim costs are 10%-20% higher. Non-contributory credit union business has lower claim costs, since coverage is provided to all borrowers, providing a better spread of risk. Since all borrowers are insured, there is no anti-selection against the insurer. Only a few states vary life rates by class, but many permit class experience and class rating in deviation filings.

For disability insurance, finance companies and credit unions have materially higher claim costs. Most credit union disability coverage is offered on a voluntary (or contributory) basis. Some credit unions are sponsored by larger employers who have attractive fringe benefits. In some situations, the combination of credit insurance and fringe benefits can give a few insureds a backache just thinking about the possibilities. Claim costs vary by the employer's industry. Clerical and professional group experience is often comparable to bank business. Light and heavy industries have claim costs 30% to 100% over the other classes of business. These variations are reflected in some states which have prima facie rates by class. The industry distinctions are commonly used in deviation filings.

Several states require prima facie rates to be discounted for lenders producing larger volumes of credit insurance. The rationale behind the reduction is that the large lenders have lower expense margins from economies of scale. The requirements are designed to produce a lower profit margin for large lenders, many of whom own captives. Prima facie rates are specified depending on the premium produced by a lender annually, or the average amount in force during a year for the business from one lender. The reductions are a percentage reduction or a separate set of specified rates. An example is the New Jersey decremental scale:

11:2-3.12 NEW JERSEY ADMIN. REGULATIONS

f. Standards for premium rates for credit life insurance shall be as follows:

1. If premiums are paid monthly on outstanding balances:

Average Amount of Insurance In Force on All Debtors Of A Creditor	Monthly Premium Rates For $1,000 of Insurance In Force
Less than $250,000	$1.00
250,000 to 1,000,000	0.85
1,000,000 to 5,000,000	0.77
5,000,000 and over	0.69

2. If premiums are paid in one sum for the entire duration of the indebtedness:

Average Amount of Insurance In Force on All Debtors of a Creditor	Single Premium Rates (Discounted for Interest and Mortality) Per $100 of Initial Insured Indebtedness Repayable in Indicated Number of Equal Monthly Installments			
	6	12	24	36
Less than $250,000	$0.35	$0.64	$1.21	$1.76
250,000 to 1,000,000	0.29	0.54	1.03	1.49
1,000,000 to 5,000,000	0.27	0.49	0.93	1.35
5,000,000 and over	0.24	0.44	0.83	1.21

Fig. 4.1 New Jersey decremental scale.

In addition to a discount for lender volume, New York requires a discount for lenders whose average policy size is larger. The rationale is that the per policy unit costs are spread over more insurance in force, resulting in lower unit expense levels, although no studies have been presented which substantiate the rationale.

Several states permit higher rates for insurance sold on loans governed by small loan laws. These laws govern cash loans of $500 or less. Prima facie rates are higher than standard due to the higher unit costs and higher claim costs for this group of insureds.

Single premiums are standard in the industry. Short-term policies for low amounts of insurance dictate the need for a single premium charge. An insurer obviously receives cash up front, which is invested. Investment income is a source of profit just as premium income is. Eight states require insurers to introduce an interest discount in their premium calculation. Instead of a flat rate per year of coverage, the rate per year is discounted with interest depending on the term of the loan. For terms under 60 months, the discount has only a small effect on the premium charged the consumer, but adds complexity to the rate calculation.

For credit life insurance, the premium is earned at death in most states. When an insurer pays a death claim, a refund of the life insurance unearned premium is not paid. A few states require a small mortality discount to prima facie rates if the insurer does not refund the unearned premium at death.

LIFE INSURANCE PREMIUM FORMULAS

Prima facie rates are stated as a single premium rate per $100 per year (as the example) or as a monthly outstanding balance rate per $1,000 of insurance in force for the month, abbreviated MOB. The two rates are related by the general formula:

$$SP_n = \frac{1}{10} \times (MOB)_n \times \sum_{t=1}^{n} (\text{In force})_t$$

where n = the term of the loan

$(MOB)_n$ = the MOB rate per \$1,000 in force at term n

$(\text{In force})_t$ = the amount of insurance in force, in \$100s during month t

SP_n = the single premium per \$100 of initial insured indebtedness for a loan of n months

$\sum_{t=1}^{n}$ = summation of the $(\text{in force})_t$ for t = 1 to t = n

$= (\text{In force})_1 + (\text{In force})_2 + ... + (\text{In force})_n$

= [(the amount of insurance in force in the first month) + (the amount of insurance in force in the second month), and so on for n months]

This formula does not include any interest or mortality discount. In other words, the single premium is the undiscounted sum of the monthly premiums. The factor (1/10) converts the MOB rate per \$1,000 to a single premium rate per \$100. If a state specifies its prima facie rate as a single premium per \$100 per year, the MOB rate will vary by term. If a state specifies the MOB rate as the same for all terms, the single premium per \$100 per year will not be linear. An example may help.

For decreasing gross coverage, the summation of the amounts in force can be solved by the Rule of 78 so the formula reduces to:

$$SP_n = \frac{(n+1)}{20} \times (MOB)_n$$

Consider two states--one specifies that the prima facie rate is 65¢/100/year while the second specifies the prima facie rate as an MOB rate of \$1.00/1000/month.

Loan Term	State With Single Premium: Single Premium Per $100 per year	State With Single Premium: MOB Rate	State With MOB Rate: Single Premium Per $100 per year	State With MOB Rate: MOB Rate
12	$ .65	$ 1.000	$ .650	$ 1.00
24	.65	1.040	.625	1.00
36	.65	1.054	.617	1.00
48	.65	1.061	.613	1.00

Fig. 4.2 Comparison of single premiums and MOB premiums.

For example, consider a $100 loan with a term of 24 months. For a state specifying the single premium rate, the rate is 65¢ for each year of coverage so:

$$SP_{24} = (24/12) \times .65$$

$$= 1.30$$

$(MOB)_{24}$ is calculated from the formula:

$$(MOB)_{24} = SP_{24} \times (20/25)$$

$$= 1.30 \times (20/25)$$

$$= 1.04$$

For the state specifying the MOB rate, the single premium for a 24-month loan is:

$$SP_{24} = (25/20) \times 1.00$$

$$= 1.25$$

The single premium per year of coverage is:

$$\text{SP per year for a 24-month loan} = SP_{24} \,/\, (\text{number of years of coverage})$$

$$= 1.25 \,/\, (24/12)$$

$$= .625$$

Most states specify the single premium rate. Stating the MOB rate has more theoretical appeal and is gaining in popularity. Some states specify both, but the two rates specified may not be actuarially equivalent. In these states, the single premium rate specified is used for single premium business, and the MOB is used for MOB business. In discussions concerning prima facie rates, the single premium rate is often referenced per $100 for a term of 12 months. The phrase "Indiana is a 65¢ rate state" indicates that the single premium per $100 for a 12-month loan in Indiana is 65¢.

For level coverage, the general formula reduces to:

$$SP_n = \frac{n}{10} \times (MOB)$$

For level insurance, the rates are always linear and the MOB rate is constant for all terms unless the state has an interest discount in the formula. To calculate a single premium for level insurance given the single premium for decreasing insurance, the formula is:

$$^{l}SP_n = {}^{d}SP_n \times \frac{2n}{n+1}$$

where $^{l}SP_n$ = single premium for level coverage for a term of n months

$^{d}SP_n$ = single premium for decreasing gross coverage for a term of n months

Substituting n = 12 in these formulas produces the following results, which provide a quick conversion among the various plans given an MOB rate.

$^{d}SP/100/year = .65 \times (MOB\ Rate)$	decreasing gross coverage
$^{l}SP/100/year = 1.2 \times (MOB\ Rate)$	level coverage
$^{l}SP/100/year = 1.846 \times {}^{d}SP/100/year$	decreasing to level

NET PAYOFF COVERAGE

These simplified formulas for decreasing gross coverage are possible because the coverage decreases by a uniform amount each month. Such simplifications are not possible for net payoff coverage. In almost all net payoff regulations, the MOB rate is specified as level for all loan terms. The single premium for each term must be calculated by computer using the generalized formula:

$$SP_n = \frac{1}{10} \times (MOB) \times \sum_{t=1}^{n} (\text{In force})_t$$

The coverage in force by month must be calculated separately for each loan term. The pattern of decrease is not uniform and varies by loan term, the annual percentage rate of the loan, and lending practices.

The interest rate of the loan clearly affects the pattern of decrease. The higher the interest rate, the slower the insurance in force decreases. The method by which the lender earns interest is another factor. Does the lender earn interest on the *Rule of 78* or the actuarial method? (See Chapter Six for more information on the Rule of 78). Finally, the timing of the interest charges matters. In some states, a lender may charge a month's interest if any portion of a month elapses (one day equals one month), while other states require that interest charges be added on the 15th day of the loan month. In other situations, interest is not charged until the end of the month, or interest accrues continuously throughout the month.

One reason for gross coverage is that the insurance in force during the loan exceeds the net indebtedness. In the event a borrower has been delinquent on certain payments, the insurance in force is normally sufficient to cover delinquencies also. Net payoff policies often insure the scheduled unpaid indebtedness plus a certain number of delinquencies, often two payments. In most states, the insurer is permitted to assume that a certain number of delinquencies will occur during the loan. This assumption increases the amounts in force over the scheduled amounts in force and results in additional premium to the insurer to cover the cost of insuring the delinquent payments.

In short, the calculations of net payoff rates for actual use are not for the faint of heart. Rate calculations require a computer, a knowledge of the lending practices of the lender, and an obsession for calculations with six-decimal accuracy.

INTEREST AND MORTALITY DISCOUNTS

States requiring discounts use one of two approaches. Most states use an *add-on interest rate* in the formula:

$$^{d}SP_{n} = (MOB) \times \frac{n+1}{20 \times [1+(n \times i / 24)]} \quad \text{decreasing gross coverage}$$

$$^{l}SP_{n} = (MOB) \times \frac{n}{10 \times [1+(n \times i / 24)]} \quad \text{level coverage}$$

where i = the add-on interest rate as a decimal

Add-on rates of 3.5% for decreasing coverage and 5.3% for level coverage are common in the state regulations. As with all add-on rates, the effective rate of interest is higher and varies by term. For example:

Term	Add-on Interest Rate	True Effective Interest Rate
12	3.5%	5.7%
24	3.5%	5.5%
36	3.5%	5.4%
48	3.5%	5.3%
60	3.5%	5.3%
120	3.5%	5.1%

Fig. 4.3 Comparison of add-on and effective interest rates.

A second method of discounting is to introduce a factor into the general formula:

$$SP_n = \frac{1}{10} \text{ x } (MOB)_n \text{ x } \sum_{t=1}^{n} (\text{In force})_t \,/\, (1+i)^{t-1}$$

where i = the nominal monthly interest rate

In two states, a *mortality discount* is added by increasing the discount rate by one-half of one percent (.5%).

MINOR CONSIDERATIONS

Premiums for critical period life coverage, truncated life, net plus coverage, or any other special pattern are calculated directly using the general formula. Some loans provide an odd number of days to first payment; i.e., 45 days to first payment. Single premiums in the rate charts will reflect the additional in force at the beginning of the loan and the additional number of days in the term of coverage.

Premiums for balloon loans can be calculated by separating the level and decreasing portions and performing the standard calculations. The alternative is to use the general formula and the combined amount in force each month. The two approaches may produce different results if a state has MOB rates, decreasing single premium rates, and level single premium rates which are not actuarially equivalent.

JOINT LIFE MULTIPLES

Joint life rates are a multiple of single life rates. The multiple varies by state from a low of 1.40 to a high of 2.00. A multiple of less than 2.00 reflects the rationale that one of the insureds is female with lower mortality costs and/or that certain expense savings result from two insureds on a single sale.

MOB COVERAGES

Credit unions often provide credit life insurance to all borrowers, absorbing the cost in the finance charges. They contract with an insurer to cover all outstanding loans. Premiums are paid monthly based on the average outstanding loans during the previous month or the outstanding loans at the end of the month. The MOB rate is applied to the total loans outstanding to produce the premium remitted to the insurer. Increasingly, credit unions are switching to a contributory basis using an MOB premium charge. The members electing coverage have the premium added to their loan balance at the end of the month.

Credit card coverages use the same procedure. The MOB rate is applied to the loan balance on the loan cycle date to determine the premium charged the insured. In the event the state specifies only a single premium per $100 per year, the equivalent MOB rate for a twelve or twenty-four month term is generally used.

DISABILITY PREMIUM FORMULAS

Disability premium calculations are much simpler than those for life insurance. They are usually single premiums as specified in the prima facie rates for the state. Rates are specified for each plan permitted in the state. Disability coverage is rarely sold with level loans, nor is joint disability coverage generally available. Since disability coverage insures the entire monthly payment, the concept of net payoff does not apply. Lender-size discounts do apply in the same manner as life insurance. Interest discounts, if any, are reflected in the specified table of single premiums. The comparable concept of mortality discounts does not apply since the policy does not terminate in the event of a claim.

Some states specify the single premium rate for each loan term, but most states specify the prima facie rate at certain terms. Rates for intervening terms are usually calculated by *straight-line interpolation*, but ten states have *banded rates* by terms–a single rate applies for terms under 12 months, a second rate for terms of 13-24 months, etc.

Figure 4.4 shows the single premium rates per $100 for loans of 12 to 24 months. Arizona specifies a rate for each term. Colorado specifies a rate for each six-month interval and the rates in italics are calculated by straight-line interpolation. Florida has the same rate for terms of 6 months or less, for terms of 7-12 months, etc.

TERM	ARIZONA	COLORADO	FLORIDA
12	1.82	**2.49**	2.20
13	1.89	*2.53*	2.60
14	1.96	*2.58*	2.60
15	2.02	*2.62*	2.60
16	2.09	*2.66*	2.60
17	2.15	*2.71*	2.60
18	2.21	**2.75**	2.60
19	2.27	*2.78*	3.00
20	2.33	*2.82*	3.00
21	2.39	*2.85*	3.00
22	2.45	*2.89*	3.00
23	2.51	*2.92*	3.00
24	2.57	**2.96**	3.00

Fig. 4.4 Comparison of disability rates

The values for Colorado are rounded to the nearest cent. For the terms of 13 to 17 months, the straight-line method of interpolation uses the monthly increment, which is the same for each month. The total difference between the 12-month rate and the 18-month rate is:

$2.75 - 2.49 = $.26

The monthly increment is:

$.26 / 6 = $.0433 per month.

The rate for 13 months is:

$2.49 + .0433 = $2.5333

The rate for 14 months is:

$2.5333 + .0433 = $2.5766

CRITICAL PERIOD COVERAGES

Benefit payments for critical period coverages are limited to a stated number or the expiration of the policy, whichever involves fewer payments. Maximum benefit periods are not standardized throughout the industry and vary from six months to five years. Most states have not issued prima facie rates, since the coverage is new and loss experience is limited. As with most non-standard coverages, one must develop a reasonable approach and submit the method to the individual insurance departments for approval. Florida requires the use of critical period coverage for policies with terms over 60 months and has adopted a table of prima facie rates.

To develop rates, a set of basic claim costs for disability insurance is needed. Only two studies of credit disability experience have produced basic claim costs–the 1968 NAIC Disability Study and 1974 NAIC Disability Study (see Chapter Ten). Both studies are outdated and do not reflect current claim costs. A third table, the 1964 Commissioners Disability Table or its subsequent modifications, is occasionally used even though it represents ordinary disability claim costs. The assumption made is that the internal relationship between plans is valid even though the level of experience no longer applies.

For example, to price a two-year critical period benefit with 14-day retroactive coverage, one of the previously mentioned tables would be selected. Using the table, the claim cost ratio of the two-year benefit to a full-term benefit would be calculated for each term. The ratios would then be applied to 14R full-term benefit prima facie rates for the state. This results in a rate which contains the same expense margin (expressed as a percentage of the gross premium), as the margin contained in the prima facie rates.

MOB premiums are charged on credit card business, revolving charge accounts, and most credit union business. Credit cards and revolving charge accounts are open-end loans. The consumer may borrow additional amounts and make flexible monthly payments, subject to a minimum specified amount. One approach is to provide a standard plan (14R, 14E, 30R, 30E) which pays a benefit equal to the minimum monthly payment due on the account. Most of these accounts have a minimum payment required which will extinguish the current indebtedness in about 24 months. An MOB disability premium is calculated, assuming a 24-month term using the usual conversion formula:

$$MOB_{24} = \frac{20}{25} \times SP_{24}$$

This MOB premium is applied to the outstanding balance on the monthly processing date for each account. The same procedure is used in credit union business, but the term may be longer. The insurer must file the method used with the state, except for the few states which specify an MOB rate for disability insurance.

A second approach is to sell 90-day lump sum coverage. Single premiums are calculated in the same manner as critical period coverages. Relationships between the 90-day coverage and a standard plan are determined by using a published table. The ratio is applied to the standard plan prima facie rate, then a conversion is made to an MOB rate.

Most credit unions charge an MOB premium on both open-end and closed-end loans. When the term is known, the MOB/SP formula can be used for the appropriate term. For simplicity of administration, an average MOB rate may be developed. Periodically, the loan portfolio is analyzed, a weighted average term is determined, and the MOB equivalent calculated for that term. This rate is used for all loans, subject to state insurance department approval.

DEVIATED RATES AND CASE FILINGS

As stated before, an insurer may file for upward rate deviations. In addition, some states require mandatory downward deviations from prima facie rates if experience is more favorable than the benchmark loss ratio.

The following discussion summarizes the deviation process applicable to most states; however, state regulations are diverse and sometimes ambiguous. An actual filing for a deviation requires knowledge of the particular state regulation as well as its interpretation by the state's insurance department.

Deviations are usually filed on a *case basis*. A case is the experience of one or more accounts. An account is the basic level of experience, representing the experience of a single lender writing in one class of business, on one plan of insurance. Life and disability are always separate. For life insurance, all coverages are usually combined–single and joint, level and decreasing. Disability filings segregate the experience by plan (14R, 30E, etc.).

Experience is generally filed on a one-state basis. Most regulations permit the filing of multi-state experience where a lender has multi-state operations, but this option is rarely used.

Selection of the accounts to comprise a case varies by state. Most states do not require mandatory deviations. For these states, insurers can define a case in any reasonable manner, subject to regulatory approval. An example was the credit union market in the 1970s. As credit unions began to offer disability insurance as an optional coverage in the early 1970s, credit insurers moved into the marketplace. Initially, the coverages were sold at prima facie rates. By 1975, insurers were realizing that credit union claim costs were significantly higher than the other classes of business. To correct substantial underwriting losses, insurers began to file for upward deviations.

Three groupings of accounts were used by various insurers. The variations were:

1. Large credit unions were rated by themselves.

2. A class deviation was filed for all credit union business of an insurer in a state.

3. A separate deviation was filed for all credit unions of a particular type of industry–clerical and professional, light industry, heavy industry.

States were reasonable in considering the rate deviation requests and a few ultimately adopted separate prima facie rates for credit unions.

Deviations are rarely found in bank or automobile dealer business. In a voluntary deviation state, the insurer will face closer scrutiny of its definition of a case. Suppose a large automobile dealer has a high disability loss ratio. An insurer will have difficulty getting a deviation unless the other automobile dealers are also deviated. The life experience also may be reviewed. The general argument is that an insurer is not permitted to deviate bad business while writing good business at prima facie rates.

The 1979-80 NAIC Model Regulation provides for mandatory downward deviations. Several states, notably Pennsylvania and New York, currently require mandatory rerating. Where deviations are required, the method of grouping accounts into cases will be specified by regulation, although some latitude is permitted. A regulation will usually specify one set of rules, but an insurer may file its own set of rules for approval.

Several concepts and definitions are needed before proceeding. Regulations will specify levels of *credibility*. Credibility is the weight assigned to past experience as a predictor of the true experience. This concept is discussed in more detail in Chapter Six, Measurement of Profitability. Generally, the larger the volume of business produced by an account, the more credible the experience. Large accounts are fully credible; i.e., their actual experience is presumed to be the true experience, and a rate deviation is based solely on their experience. Medium-sized accounts are partially credible. Their deviated rate is based partially on their actual experience and partially on the prima facie rate. Small accounts are not credible. Their actual experience is considered an unreliable predictor of the true experience. Non-credible accounts must be written at prima facie rates or pooled with other small accounts to obtain a credible case for rating purposes.

Most deviation procedures define credibility in terms of earned premium. This was a practical compromise because of the lack of available data when the regulations were first written. Earned premium does have some relevance, but a given level of earned premium results in more exposure on life insurance than on disability, reflecting the difference in premium levels. The alternatives are to use *life years exposed* or number of claims. Small credit insurers did not maintain number of claims or life years exposed, so the earned premium was the easiest available base. The 1979-80 NAIC Model Regulation allows an insurer the option of choosing either life years exposed or number of claims as the basis for measuring credibility.

Deviations are filed based on an *experience period*. The standard experience period is three years. If a case is fully credible within a shorter time, the experience period is the minimum number of years needed to meet the volume requirements of a fully credible case. If a case is fully credible each year, the deviation is based on only the latest year of experience; however, the period cannot be less than one year. A deviated rate remains in effect for the time covered by the experience period. If a filing is based on three years of experience, the new rate is charged for three years in the future. At the end of three years, a new deviation filing is required. Cases reaching full credibility in one year must be refiled annually.

Since the implementation of new rates involves the cost of new rate charts and personnel time, a *no-action corridor* is provided. A "nickel corridor" is common. If the indicated deviated rate for a term of twelve months is within 5¢ of the current rate, no change in rate is required or permitted. The 1979-80 NAIC Model Regulation uses 5% as the corridor. If the indicated deviated rate is within 5% of the current rate, no change in rate is required or permitted. This narrows the life corridor, but expands the disability corridor as compared to the nickel corridor. On voluntary upward deviations, there may be a loss ratio corridor in some states. Although the benchmark loss ratio may be 50%, an insurer cannot deviate rates unless the loss ratio is over 60%.

One major problem with deviated rates is *portability.* The general concept embodied in the 1979-80 NAIC Model Regulation and most state regulations is that a deviated rate for a lender remains in effect for the experience period regardless of a change of insurers. A filing based on three years of experience remains in effect for three years, even if the lender changes insurers. The problem occurs on both upward and downward deviations. If a lender is notified that rates will be increased, the management may be upset and find an insurer willing to write the business at the old rate. On downward deviations in a state using the straight loss ratio approach to pricing, the lender's compensation is reduced. Another insurer may be willing to charge higher rates and pay the old level of compensation. Often the problem arises where the lender is part of a pooled case and does not feel its experience is homogeneous with the rest of the pool.

The regulations are usually clear, but the enforcement of them is sometimes lax. Only New York and Pennsylvania seriously enforce the portability provisions of their regulations. Insurers may be unwilling to follow deviation regulations when the state is not willing to enforce portability requirements. As a result, several states have mandatory deviation regulations which are not operative.

PREMIUM REFUNDS

Many consumer loans are terminated before the scheduled maturity date. Consumer goods may be sold to another party thereby terminating the loan. For automobile loans, the car may be voluntarily sold after a few years or involuntarily sold as a result of an accident or repossession. General borrowing for vacations or temporary economic pressures is often refinanced or rolled over into new loans. Finance company clientele may carry debt for many years by periodically refinancing the indebtedness. Many loans are simply repaid early.

If credit insurance was purchased with a single premium charge, the unearned portion of the single premium applicable to the unused policy term on early termination is refunded to the consumer. A refund equal to the gross unearned premium is rebated to the consumer. In practice, the refund is a part of the loan closing calculation and is used to reduce the loan payoff amount. Where the loan obligation has been sold to another financial institution, *third party paper*, the refund may be paid directly by the insurer to the borrower.

Until recently, refunds for decreasing life insurance and disability insurance were the Rule of 78 gross unearned premiums. If a loan is paid off in the first 15 days of a loan month, no credit is taken for that month. After 15 days, the calculation assumes the full month has expired. A Rule of 78 factor is calculated using the general formula:

$$\frac{t \times (t+1)}{n \times (n+1)}$$

where t = the number of remaining months
n = the original loan term in months

This factor is multiplied times the original gross single premium to produce the premium refund.

For single premium level life coverage, the benefits provided each month are equal, so a pro rata unearned premium is theoretically correct and is used in practice. The refund equals:

$$\frac{t}{n} \times \text{(original gross single premium)}$$

where t = the number of remaining months
n = original loan term in months

Refunds are not generally paid on monthly outstanding balance business. In the situations where refunds are paid, they are equal to one-half of the latest monthly premium paid.

In recent years, a few states have adopted refund methods other than the Rule of 78. One method used for net payoff life coverage and disability coverage is the *Single Premium Method*, occasionally called the *Rule of Anticipation.* The refund is the gross single premium for a policy having the same benefits and term as the unexpired coverage. A more complete title would be "the single premium for the remaining term and benefits." A major drawback on net payoff coverage is that the remaining single premium must be calculated at the same interest rate as the original loan. This means a vast array of rate chart tables or stored computer data to cover the range of interest rates charged over a period of five or more years.

With disability insurance, a few states require a refund which is the mean, or average, of the unearned premium calculated on the Rule of 78 and the pro rata method. The refund produced by this method is close to the Single Premium Method and is much easier to apply in practice.

State regulations provide a minimum refund threshold. In previous years, a refund did not have to be paid if it was less than $1.00. Higher dollar limits are now permitted in some states.

USE OF RATE CHARTS AND FACTOR CARDS

The actual premium calculation for a loan with credit insurance must conform to exacting standards. Loan conditions, details of financing rules, and insurance regulations must be applied to produce a rate calculation. These calculations must be done by literally thousands of lending officers. As a result, a specialized industry has evolved to produce charts which reduce the calculation to a simplified process. Preparation of these charts is a major cost in writing credit insurance, as they are customarily supplied by the insurer. With varying interest rates, loan practices, insurance plans, and possibly deviated rates, the insurer almost needs a separate rate chart for every lender.

Until the late 1960s, rate calculations were simpler, so insurers provided rate charts. An insurer could often get by with only a few different charts for a particular state. Because charts could be printed in quantity, the expense was reasonable. A rate chart book included rates similar to Figure 4.5 for a range of interest rates, stepping through the range in .25% increments. The rate chart book needed sections for all terms and plan combinations (life only, life and disability, joint life only, joint life and disability, no insurance). Consequently, the publication was often several hundred pages long. Rate charts were the industry standard for fifty years.

RATE CHART

12 Monthly Payments - 12% Interest
Loan with Single Life Insurance and
14 Day Retroactive Disability Insurance

Unpaid Balance	Monthly Payment	Life Premium	Disability Premium	Finance Charge	Total of Payment
1	0.09	0.01	0.03	0.04	1.08
2	0.18	0.01	0.06	0.09	2.16
3	0.27	0.02	0.09	0.13	3.24
4	0.36	0.02	0.12	0.18	4.32
5	0.46	0.03	0.15	0.34	5.52
6	0.55	0.03	0.18	0.39	6.60
7	0.64	0.04	0.21	0.43	7.68
8	0.73	0.05	0.24	0.47	8.76
9	0.82	0.05	0.27	0.52	9.84
10	0.92	0.06	0.30	0.68	11.04
20	1.84	0.11	0.60	1.37	22.08
25	2.30	0.14	0.75	1.71	27.60
30	2.76	0.17	0.90	2.05	33.12
40	3.68	0.23	1.20	2.73	44.16
50	4.60	0.29	1.50	3.41	55.20
60	5.52	0.34	1.80	4.10	66.24
70	6.44	0.40	2.10	4.78	77.28
75	6.90	0.43	2.25	5.12	82.80
80	7.36	0.46	2.40	5.46	88.32
90	8.28	0.52	2.70	6.14	99.36
100	9.20	0.57	3.00	6.83	110.40
200	18.40	1.15	6.01	13.64	220.80
300	27.60	1.72	9.01	20.47	331.20
400	36.81	2.30	12.01	27.41	441.72
500	46.01	2.87	15.02	34.23	552.12
600	55.21	3.45	18.02	41.05	662.52
700	64.41	4.02	21.02	47.88	772.92
800	73.62	4.59	24.03	54.82	883.44
900	82.82	5.17	27.03	61.64	993.84
1000	92.02	5.74	30.04	68.46	1104.24

Fig. 4.5 Ohio rate chart for gross coverage life and 14R disability insurance.

As the expense mounted and variations proliferated, alternatives were developed. Factor cards were introduced. Use of factors can reduce the number of pages to ten or fewer significantly reducing costs. While the actual rate calculation is not difficult, it appears more complex. While lenders have resisted the change, the bottom-line costs have gradually overcome the resistance.

Examples follow for calculating an Ohio loan using a rate chart and a factor card. The consumer borrows $1,000 for a 12-month term. Single life decreasing credit life insurance and disability on the 14R plan are selected. The loan's annual percentage rate is 12%.

First, the calculation is performed for gross coverage using a rate chart and a factor card. Then, the calculation is done for net payoff coverage to show the difference in the two coverages.

EXAMPLE FOR GROSS COVERAGE USING A RATE CHART

Rate charts are so easy to use that detailed instructions are not needed. Using Figure 4.5, the applicable amounts are on the left side of the page for a loan with life and disability insurance.

Across the line for an unpaid balance of $1,000, the displayed components are:

Monthly payment	$ 92.02
Life insurance premium	5.74
Disability insurance premium	30.04
Finance charges	68.46
Gross note (total of payments)	1,104.24

The consumer borrows $1,000.00 to be repaid in monthly installments of $92.02 for 12 months. Over the 12 months, a total of $1,104.24 will be repaid. This is the gross note. If the insured dies in the first month, the death benefit is $1,104.24.

Rates for an odd dollar amount of gross indebtedness are obtained by adding the appropriate lines. If the initial gross indebtedness had been $945, the amounts on lines 5, 40, and 900 would be added to produce the total result.

As a cross check, the 1985 Ohio life insurance rate for gross coverage at 12 months is 52¢/100/year. Applying this rate, the gross premium is:

$$.52 \times \frac{(1{,}104.24)}{100} \times \frac{(12)}{12}$$
$$= 5.74$$

The 1985 Ohio disability rate per $100 at 12 months for the 14R plan is $2.72. The plan illustrated here covers preexisting conditions. A 10% surcharge is permitted over the usual rates for 14R with a six and six exclusion. To cross check the rate chart:

$$2.72 \times \frac{1{,}104.24}{100} = 30.04$$

EXAMPLE OF GROSS COVERAGE USING A FACTOR CARD

Instructions for the use of a factor card and the page needed for this calculation are shown in Figure 4.6.

INSTRUCTIONS

1. LOCATE PAYMENT FACTOR FOR RATE OF INTEREST AND TERM.
2. MULTIPLY UNPAID BALANCE BY PAYMENT FACTOR TO GET MONTHLY PAYMENT.
3. MULTIPLY RESULT BY NUMBER OF MONTHS IN TERM TO GET TOTAL OF PAYMENTS.
4. MULTIPLY TOTAL OF PAYMENTS BY INSURANCE PREMIUM(S) VERIFICATION FACTOR TO GET PREMIUM(S).
5. SUBTRACT UNPAID BALANCE AND PREMIUM(S) FROM TOTAL OF PAYMENTS TO GET FINANCE CHARGE.
6. MULTIPLY UNPAID BALANCE BY OAI FACTOR TO GET ORIGINAL AMOUNT OF INSURANCE.
7. PREMIUM AMOUNT(S) AND OAI SHOULD BE ROUNDED OFF (NEAR CENT), HOWEVER, DO NOT ROUND OFF PAYMENT AMOUNT (TRUNCATE).

SINGLE LIFE & 14 DAY RETRO + PE

INT	MONTHS									
RATE	6	12	18	24	30	36	42	48	54	60
10.25	.176036	.091152	.062818	.048653	.040181	.034560	.030575	.027606	.025322	.023520
10.50	.176166	.091276	.062944	.048781	.040312	.034694	.030713	.027748	.025467	.023670
10.75	.176295	.091401	.063070	.048909	.040443	.034829	.030851	.027890	.025613	.023820
11.00	.176425	.091526	.063196	.049037	.040575	.034963	.030990	.028033	.025760	.023972
11.25	.176555	.091651	.063322	.049166	.040706	.035099	.031129	.028176	.025908	.024124
11.50	.176685	.091777	.063448	.049295	.040838	.035234	.031268	.028319	.026056	.024276
11.75	.176815	.091902	.063575	.049424	.040971	.035370	.031408	.028463	.026204	.024429
12.00	.176944	.092027	.063702	.049553	.041103	.035506	.031548	.028608	.026353	.024583
12.25	.177074	.092153	.063828	.049683	.041236	.035643	.031689	.028753	.026503	.024738
12.50	.177204	.092278	.063955	.049812	.041369	.035780	.031830	.028899	.026653	.024893
12.75	.177334	.092404	.064082	.049942	.041503	.035917	.031972	.029045	.026804	.025049
13.00	.177464	.092530	.064210	.050072	.041636	.036055	.032114	.029191	.026956	.025206
13.25	.177595	.092656	.064337	.050203	.041770	.036193	.032256	.029339	.027108	.025364
13.50	.177725	.092782	.064465	.050333	.041905	.036332	.032399	.029486	.027261	.025522
13.75	.177855	.092908	.064593	.050464	.042039	.036470	.032543	.029635	.027414	.025680
14.00	.177985	.093034	.064721	.050595	.042174	.036610	.032687	.029783	.027568	.025840
14.25	.178116	.093161	.064849	.050726	.042309	.036749	.032831	.029932	.027722	.026000
14.50	.178246	.093287	.064977	.050858	.042445	.036889	.032976	.030082	.027878	.026161
14.75	.178376	.093414	.065105	.050990	.042580	.037029	.033121	.030233	.028033	.026323
15.00	.178507	.093540	.065234	.051122	.042716	.037170	.033266	.030383	.028190	.026485
15.25	.178637	.093667	.065363	.051254	.042853	.037311	.033412	.030535	.028347	.026648
15.50	.178768	.093794	.065491	.051386	.042989	.037452	.033559	.030686	.028504	.026812
15.75	.178899	.093921	.065621	.051519	.043126	.037594	.033705	.030839	.028662	.026976
16.00	.179029	.094048	.065750	.051651	.043263	.037736	.033853	.030992	.028821	.027141
16.25	.179160	.094175	.065879	.051785	.043401	.037878	.034000	.031145	.028981	.027307
16.50	.179291	.094302	.066009	.051918	.043539	.038021	.034149	.031299	.029141	.027474
16.75	.179422	.094430	.066138	.052051	.043677	.038164	.034297	.031453	.029301	.027641
17.00	.179552	.094557	.066268	.052185	.043815	.038307	.034446	.031608	.029462	.027809
17.25	.179683	.094685	.066398	.052319	.043954	.038451	.034596	.031764	.029624	.027977
17.50	.179814	.094813	.066528	.052453	.044093	.038595	.034746	.031920	.029787	.028147
17.75	.179945	.094940	.066659	.052587	.044232	.038740	.034896	.032076	.029950	.028317
18.00	.180076	.095068	.066789	.052722	.044371	.038885	.035047	.032233	.030114	.028488
18.25	.180207	.095196	.066920	.052857	.044511	.039030	.035198	.032391	.030278	.028659
18.50	.180339	.095324	.067051	.052992	.044651	.039176	.035350	.032549	.030443	.028831
18.75	.180470	.095453	.067182	.053127	.044792	.039322	.035502	.032708	.030608	.029004
19.00	.180601	.095581	.067313	.053263	.044932	.039468	.035654	.032867	.030774	.029178
19.25	.180732	.095709	.067444	.053398	.045073	.039615	.035807	.033026	.030941	.029353
19.50	.180864	.095838	.067576	.053534	.045214	.039762	.035961	.033187	.031109	.029528
19.75	.180995	.095966	.067707	.053671	.045356	.039909	.036115	.033347	.031277	.029703
20.00	.181126	.096095	.067839	.053807	.045498	.040057	.036269	.033509	.031445	.029880
20.25	.181258	.096224	.067971	.053944	.045640	.040205	.036424	.033670	.031615	.030057
20.50	.181389	.096353	.068103	.054080	.045782	.040354	.036579	.033833	.031784	.030235
20.75	.181521	.096482	.068235	.054217	.045925	.040503	.036735	.033995	.031955	.030414
21.00	.181653	.096611	.068368	.054355	.046068	.040652	.036891	.034159	.032126	.030594
21.25	.181784	.096740	.068500	.054492	.046211	.040802	.037047	.034323	.032298	.030774
21.50	.181916	.096869	.068633	.054630	.046355	.040952	.037204	.034487	.032470	.030955
21.75	.182048	.096999	.068766	.054768	.046499	.041102	.037362	.034652	.032643	.031137
22.00	.182180	.097128	.068899	.054906	.046643	.041253	.037520	.034818	.032817	.031319
22.25	.182311	.097258	.069032	.055045	.046787	.041404	.037678	.034984	.032991	.031502
22.50	.182443	.097388	.069166	.055183	.046932	.041555	.037837	.035150	.033166	.031686
22.75	.182575	.097518	.069299	.055322	.047077	.041707	.037996	.035317	.033342	.031871
23.00	.182707	.097647	.069433	.055461	.047222	.041859	.038156	.035485	.033518	.032056
23.25	.182839	.097778	.069567	.055600	.047368	.042012	.038316	.035653	.033694	.032242
23.50	.182972	.097908	.069701	.055740	.047514	.042165	.038476	.035822	.033872	.032429
23.75	.183104	.098038	.069835	.055880	.047660	.042318	.038637	.035991	.034050	.032616
24.00	.183236	.098168	.069970	.056020	.047806	.042472	.038799	.036161	.034229	.032805
24.25	.183368	.098299	.070104	.056160	.047953	.042626	.038961	.036331	.034408	.032994
24.50	.183500	.098429	.070239	.056300	.048100	.042780	.039123	.036502	.034588	.033184
24.75	.183633	.098560	.070374	.056441	.048248	.042935	.039286	.036673	.034768	.033374
25.00	.183765	.098691	.070509	.056582	.048395	.043090	.039449	.036845	.034950	.033566
LIFE FACTOR	.002800	.005200	.007600	.010000	.012400	.014800	.017200	.019600	.022000	.024400
A&H FACTOR	.021200	.027200	.031300	.034300	.036900	.039200	.041400	.043300	.045100	.046900

PREPARED BY CARLETON FINANCIAL, 1801 COMMERCE DRIVE, SOUTH BEND, IN 46624

M-7356-52L-OH-272AH14R+PE

Fig. 4.6 Ohio factor card for gross coverage life and 14R disability insurance.

Following the card's instructions, the results are:

1. Payment factor	=	.092027
2. Payment	=	1,000.00 x .092027
	=	92.027 truncated to 92.02
3. Total of payments	=	12 x 92.02
	=	1,104.24
4. Life premium	=	.005200 x 1,104.24
	=	5.742 rounded to 5.74
Disability premium	=	.027200 x 1,104.24
	=	30.035 rounded to 30.04
5. Finance charge	=	1,104.24 - 1,000.00 - 5.74 - 30.04
	=	68.46

Note: Financing laws require the payment calculation to be truncated instead of rounded. A few lenders apply the truncation in the calculation of the monthly payment, but adjust the final payment to correct for the understatement.

EXAMPLE OF NET PAYOFF COVERAGE USING A FACTOR CARD

If the lender sells net payoff coverage, a different rate chart or factor card is necessary. A net payoff factor card is used for the next example.

INSTRUCTIONS

1. LOCATE PAYMENT FACTOR FOR RATE OF INTEREST AND TERM.
2. MULTIPLY UNPAID BALANCE BY PAYMENT FACTOR TO GET PAYMENT.
3. MULTIPLY RESULT BY NUMBER OF PAYMENTS IN TERM TO GET TOTAL OF PAYMENTS.
4. MULTIPLY TOTAL OF PAYMENTS BY INSURANCE PREMIUM(S) VERIFICATION FACTOR TO GET PREMIUM(S).
5. SUBTRACT UNPAID BALANCE AND PREMIUM(S) FROM TOTAL OF PAYMENTS TO GET FINANCE CHARGE.
6. THE PREMIUM AMOUNT(S) SHOULD BE ROUNDED (NEAR CENT) HOWEVER, DO NOT ROUND PAYMENT AMOUNT (TRUNCATE).

SINGLE LIFE & 14 DAY RETRO + PE PAYMENT FACTORS

INT RATE	FAC-TORS	MONTHS								
		6	12	18	24	30	36	42	48	60
10.25	PMT	.176029	.091136	.062793	.048618	.040135	.034501	.030503	.027520	.023401
	LIFE	.002761	.005042	.007247	.009380	.011442	.013437	.015367	.017234	.020790
	A&H	.021200	.027200	.031300	.034300	.036900	.039200	.041400	.043300	.046900
	OAI	1.034065	1.044104	1.052483	1.059945	1.067246	1.074478	1.081889	1.089188	1.104395
10.50	PMT	.176158	.091260	.062918	.048745	.040264	.034634	.030639	.027659	.023547
	LIFE	.002760	.005038	.007239	.009366	.011421	.013407	.015327	.017183	.020713
	A&H	.021200	.027200	.031300	.034300	.036900	.039200	.041400	.043300	.046900
	OAI	1.034297	1.044364	1.052779	1.060281	1.067629	1.074916	1.082388	1.089752	1.105111
10.75	PMT	.176288	.091385	.063044	.048872	.040394	.034767	.030775	.027798	.023693
	LIFE	.002759	.005034	.007231	.009351	.011399	.013376	.015286	.017131	.020637
	A&H	.021200	.027200	.031300	.034300	.036900	.039200	.041400	.043300	.046900
	OAI	1.034528	1.044624	1.053075	1.060617	1.068013	1.075353	1.082885	1.090314	1.105828
11.00	PMT	.176417	.091509	.063169	.048999	.040524	.034900	.030911	.027938	.023840
	LIFE	.002758	.005031	.007223	.009337	.011377	.013346	.015246	.017080	.020561
	A&H	.021200	.027200	.031300	.034300	.036900	.039200	.041400	.043300	.046900
	OAI	1.034759	1.044885	1.053371	1.060954	1.068396	1.075791	1.083383	1.090880	1.106548
11.25	PMT	.176547	.091634	.063294	.049127	.040655	.035033	.031048	.028078	.023988
	LIFE	.002757	.005027	.007214	.009323	.011356	.013316	.015206	.017029	.020485
	A&H	.021200	.027200	.031300	.034300	.036900	.039200	.041400	.043300	.046900
	OAI	1.034991	1.045145	1.053666	1.061291	1.068783	1.076229	1.083883	1.091446	1.107271
11.50	PMT	.176676	.091759	.063420	.049254	.040785	.035167	.031185	.028219	.024136
	LIFE	.002756	.005023	.007206	.009309	.011334	.013285	.015166	.016978	.020410
	A&H	.021200	.027200	.031300	.034300	.036900	.039200	.041400	.043300	.046900
	OAI	1.035222	1.045405	1.053962	1.061628	1.069166	1.076667	1.084382	1.092014	1.107994
11.75	PMT	.176806	.091884	.063546	.049382	.040916	.035301	.031322	.028360	.024285
	LIFE	.002755	.005020	.007198	.009295	.011313	.013255	.015126	.016927	.020335
	A&H	.021200	.027200	.031300	.034300	.036900	.039200	.041400	.043300	.046900
	OAI	1.035453	1.045666	1.054258	1.061965	1.069552	1.077107	1.084882	1.092581	1.108720
12.00	PMT	.176936	.092009	.063672	.049511	.041047	.035435	.031460	.028501	.024434
	LIFE	.002754	.005016	.007190	.009281	.011291	.013225	.015086	.016877	.020261
	A&H	.021200	.027200	.031300	.034300	.036900	.039200	.041400	.043300	.046900
	OAI	1.035685	1.045926	1.054555	1.062304	1.069937	1.077546	1.085383	1.093149	1.109446
12.25	PMT	.177066	.092134	.063798	.049639	.041178	.035570	.031599	.028643	.024584
	LIFE	.002753	.005012	.007182	.009267	.011270	.013196	.015047	.016827	.020187
	A&H	.021200	.027200	.031300	.034300	.036900	.039200	.041400	.043300	.046900
	OAI	1.035916	1.046186	1.054851	1.062642	1.070323	1.077988	1.085888	1.093719	1.110175
12.50	PMT	.177195	.092259	.063924	.049768	.041310	.035705	.031737	.028786	.024735
	LIFE	.002752	.005008	.007174	.009253	.011249	.013166	.015008	.016777	.020113
	A&H	.021200	.027200	.031300	.034300	.036900	.039200	.041400	.043300	.046900
	OAI	1.036147	1.046446	1.055148	1.062980	1.070710	1.078429	1.086390	1.094292	1.110907
12.75	PMT	.177325	.092384	.064050	.049897	.041442	.035840	.031876	.028929	.024886
	LIFE	.002751	.005005	.007166	.009239	.011228	.013136	.014969	.016728	.020040
	A&H	.021200	.027200	.031300	.034300	.036900	.039200	.041400	.043300	.046900
	OAI	1.036379	1.046708	1.055444	1.063319	1.071097	1.078869	1.086894	1.094866	1.111640
13.00	PMT	.177455	.092510	.064177	.050026	.041574	.035976	.032016	.029072	.025038
	LIFE	.002751	.005001	.007158	.009225	.011206	.013107	.014930	.016678	.019968
	A&H	.021200	.027200	.031300	.034300	.036900	.039200	.041400	.043300	.046900
	OAI	1.036611	1.046968	1.055741	1.063657	1.071483	1.079312	1.087400	1.095437	1.112377

PREPARED BY- CARLETON FINANCIAL, 1801 COMMERCE DRIVE, SOUTH BEND, IN 46624

M-7357-52L-NPO(04)AH14R + PE-OH

Fig. 4.7 Ohio Factor card for net payoff life and 14R disability insurance.

Following the card's instructions, the results are:

1. Payment factor	= .092009
2. Payment	= 1,000.00 x .092009 = 92.009 truncated to 92.00
3. Total of payments	= 12 x 92.00 = 1,104.00
4. Life premium	= .005016 x 1,104.00 = 5.538 rounded to 5.54
Disability premium	= .027200 x 1,104.00 = 30.028 rounded to 30.03
5. Finance charge	= 1,104.00 - 1,000.00 - 5.54 - 30.03 = 68.43
6. Original amount of insurance	= 1,000.00 x 1.045926 = 1,045.93

The example illustrates several aspects of net payoff coverage. The total amount borrowed is the unpaid balance plus the insurance premiums (1,000.00 + 5.54 + 30.03 = 1,035.57). In Ohio, lenders are permitted to charge a full month of interest if the loan is in force for any portion of the month. If the insured dies within the first month, he is liable for one month of interest on the loan. This is a simple interest loan, so the interest in the first month is:

$$1{,}035.57 \times (.12/12) = 10.36$$

Therefore, the amount of insurance provided is sufficient to pay off the balance plus one month of interest,

$$1{,}035.57 + 10.36 = 1{,}045.93$$

Unlike gross coverage, the amount of insurance will not decline uniformly each month. A monthly payment is used to pay the interest charge for the month and the remainder of the payment applied to reduce the unpaid indebtedness. In the second month,

$$\text{Unpaid indebtedness} = 1{,}035.57 - (92.00 - 10.36) = 953.93$$

$$\text{Amount of insurance} = 953.93 + [953.93 \times (.12/12)] = 963.47$$

Note that the life and disability premium factors shown on this net payoff factor card are expressed as a function of the gross note, not the unpaid indebtedness.

Factors for the disability coverage are the same in Figures 4.6 and 4.7. Since the disability coverage applies to the monthly payment, all coverage is gross coverage. If an insured is disabled, the loan continues and interest charges must be paid. The concept of net payoff coverages does not apply to disability insurance.

CHAPTER FIVE

RESERVES

Before investigating the measurement of profitability, the preparation of financial statements, or the preparation of any loss experience, an understanding of the concept of reserves is needed. An insurance company collects premiums to place insurance in force. When single premiums are charged for credit insurance protection, the insured's full premium is collected at the time the policy is issued. Therefore, the insurance company receives money which must be used to pay claims in the future. Since the insurer must honor any claim which occurs during the policy term, monies must be on hand to pay the actual claims. A *reserve* is an estimate of the amount of money an insurer must hold back for the future claim payments.

The following hypothetical example applies to a group of policies sold on January 1, 1986 with a total premium of \$1,000, all with a 24-month policy term. The commission is 30%, so the insurer receives \$700 on January 1. Everything is rosy on January 1–the insurer has \$700 in its pocket. However, the insurer has not made \$700 in profits. Claims will occur which must be funded out of these premiums. Assume \$600 of claims are paid in 1986 and 1987, \$300 each year.

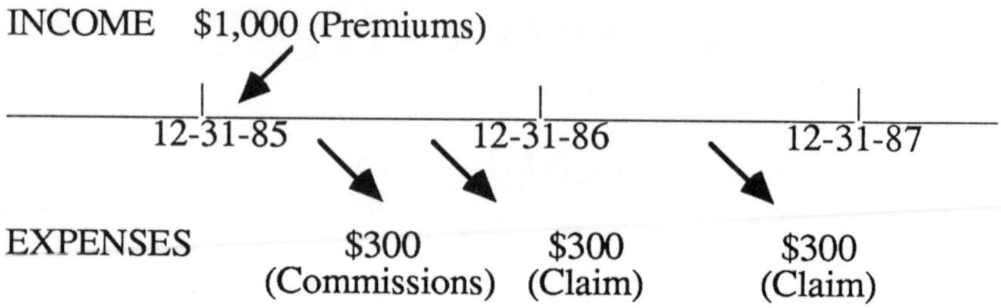

Although reserves are calculated on a policy-by-policy basis, only the aggregate amount is important. Reserves are not cash or other assets, but rather a liability of the insurer which must be supported by assets. All corporate assets are available to support the total reserves. An insurer must maintain assets greater than its reserves, but the cash is not stored away in a vault. The $700 is invested in any prudent manner management chooses.

In the long run, reserves do not matter. When all policies have expired, actual profit is income less claims and expenses–reserves are zero. The measurement of profit reduces to counting the cash amounts. On December 31, 1987, the policies have expired and no further risk remains. Profit is $100, plus investment income, less general expenses and taxes. Assume these latter items are zero for this discussion.

Insurers cannot stop their operations and let all of the business expire to judge how well they are performing financially. Instead, day-to-day operations require a judgment about whether the business being written is profitable. Periodically, insurers must prepare financial statements. Dramatic financial amounts are at stake in accurately measuring interim financial results.

Reserves are an *accounting timing mechanism.* They are needed only to properly present accounting statements before all of the business expires. Since reserves serve to allocate profits between accounting periods, they are a timing mechanism. They affect the timing of the emergence of profits. Still, they have no effect on the amount of ultimate profits.

A financial statement must be prepared on December 31, 1986. At this time, $700 has been collected and $300 has been paid in claims. Although the insurer has $400 in cash, the insurer did not earn $400 in 1986. The claims to be paid in 1987 must be estimated and held in reserve. The reserve will determine how much profit is allocated between 1986 and 1987, but it will not affect the ultimate amount of profit. For example, if the December 31, 1986 reserves are set at $400, 1986 profits will be zero and 1987 profits will be $100. On the other hand, reserves of $350 will result in $50 of earnings in 1986 and $50 in 1987. Reserves clearly affect the timing of emerging profits.

In practice, reserves are constantly changing. New premiums are flowing in, claim payments are flowing out, and the remaining terms of policies in force decrease each day. Theoretically, reserves change every day, but as a practical matter, reserves are only calculated for specific accounting dates–end of month, end of quarter, and end of year. Reserve calculations apply to a specific point in time, such as the accounting date, December 31, 1986 in the example.

Before proceeding, consider the uses of financial accountings. Accountings are prepared for four primary purposes:

1. Determination of the profitability of an account to evaluate whether to continue writing new business produced by the account,

2. Determination of the profitability of an account to calculate experience refunds, contingent commissions, or policyholder dividends,

3. Presentation of statutory financial statements, for submission to state insurance departments and with the federal income tax return,

4. Presentation of financial statements to stockholders or policyholders.

Since the purposes and the audiences of accountings vary, the method used to calculate reserves may be different for each type of accountings. Reserves are always an estimate. The methods of preparing the estimate may differ, or the degree of conservatism in the estimate may vary. Reserves for all accountings, however, are based on the same principles and comprised of the same components.

BASIC RESERVE PRINCIPLE FOR SINGLE PREMIUM CREDIT INSURANCE

Reserves must be established which provide for all claim payments to be made after the accounting date for all business in force on the accounting date.

For single premium business, since all of the premiums have been collected at issue, enough money must be set aside to pay all future claims.

A second principle is that the reserves are an aggregate amount. The total reserves will be calculated in several components. While the goal is to calculate each component accurately, reserves are judged by whether the aggregate reserves exceed aggregate future claims. Reserves are not earmarked for particular policies or claims, although the reserves may be calculated on a policy-by-policy basis.

CATEGORIES OF RESERVES

There are two categories of reserves. The first category applies to claims which will happen in the future (after the accounting date). On the accounting date, most of the insureds are alive and in good health; however, some of these insureds will die or become disabled after the accounting date but before their policy expires. The reserves for this group of insureds are *active life reserves.* The term "active life" refers to the insured; i.e., active life reserves are calculated on life and disability business. Common terms for active life reserves are: unearned premium reserve, policy reserve, and mortality reserve (for life insurance only).

The second category applies to the future payments to be made after the accounting date on those claims which occurred prior to the accounting date. There are some insureds who have died or become disabled prior to the accounting date but have not received total payment for their claim. Reserves for this group are called *claim reserves.* The rule is:

> ***A claim reserve must be established for all claim payments to be made after the accounting date, where the insured died or was disabled prior to the accounting date.***

Claim reserves are further subdivided depending on certain factors. The three subdivisions are:

- ***Incurred But Not Reported (IBNR).*** A claim which occurred prior to the accounting date, but which was not reported to the insurance company before the accounting date.

- ***Claim In Course of Settlement (CCS or ICOS).*** A claim which occurred and was reported to the insurance company prior to the accounting date, but on which the claim payment was not issued as of the accounting date.

- ***Continuing Claim.*** In disability insurance, a claimant may receive additional benefits after the accounting date if the claimant remains disabled. A continuing claim reserve is an estimate of the benefits which will be earned and paid after the accounting date for disabilities which occurred prior to the accounting date. These reserves do not have a standard name but may be called contingent reserves, present value reserves, or the present value of future unaccrued benefits.

Only IBNR and CCS claims apply to life insurance, since a claim involves only one payment. For disability insurance, the IBNR reserve and the CCS reserve is technically the portion earned between the date of disablement and the accounting date. The continuing claim reserve includes an element for the post-accounting date benefits on IBNR and CCS claims.

For example, if an insured died on December 31, and the accounting date was also December 31 the claim would be an IBNR. The claim would have occurred, but the insurance company would not have been notified before the accounting date. A claim which was received by the insurer on December 31 is a CCS claim. The claim would have occurred and been reported, but the payment would not go out until after December 31.

Graphically,

ACTIVE LIFE RESERVES

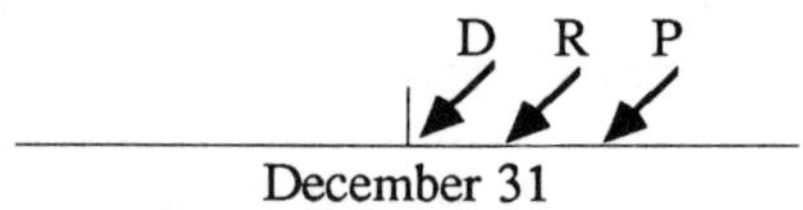

IBNR RESERVES

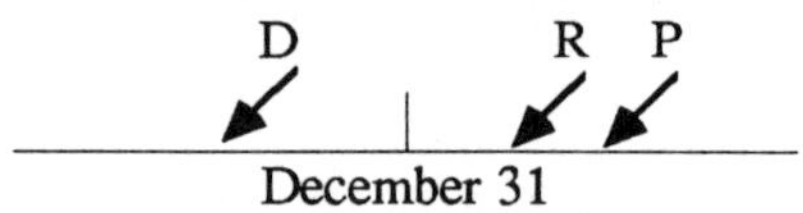

CCS RESERVES

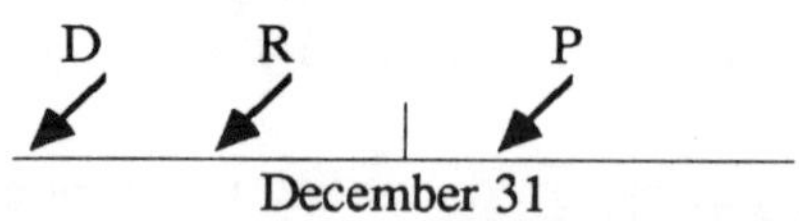

CONTINUING RESERVES (DISABILITY ONLY)

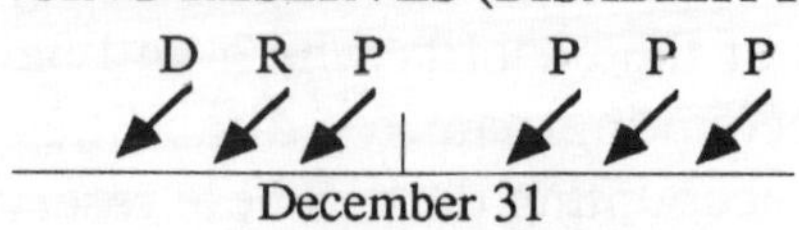

where D = date of death or disablement
R = date reported to the insurance company
P = date of actual claim payment

Clearly the combination of the active life reserves and claim reserves covers all possible future claim payments. The calculation of active life reserves is prescribed by law, regulation, or traditional formulas. Claim reserve methods are not prescribed anywhere, so significant variation is found within the industry.

CALCULATION OF ACTIVE LIFE RESERVES FOR SINGLE PREMIUM BUSINESS

For life insurance, active life reserves are either unearned premium reserves or mortality reserves. The generic term "policy reserve" may be used for either type, although it normally applies to mortality reserves. Both types attempt to estimate the future claims; only the method of estimation is different.

Unearned premium reserves are based on the assumption that the portion of the original premium applicable to the remaining term and amount of insurance will be adequate to pay future claims. Gross premiums are used, so the method includes both the portion of the premium to be used for claims and the portion to be used for expenses. If the business is profitable, the estimate contains an element of conservatism equal to the expense element.

The reserve is calculated by multiplying the original gross premium times an unearned premium factor. Factors are developed which represent the proportion of the remaining coverage compared to the total coverage provided over the entire loan term. This is the same concept as the calculation of refunds in Chapter Four. The standard methods used to calculate the factors are:

Single premium decreasing gross coverage:	Rule of 78
Single premium level coverage:	Pro rata
Single premium decreasing net payoff coverage:	Rule of 78 or Single Premium Method

In preparing factors for both bases, insurers generally make an assumption that all policies are issued on the 15th of the month. Since most valuations are as of the end of a month, this results in a half-month correction factor. Factors for Rule of 78 and pro rata unearned premiums are:

$$\text{Rule of 78 unearned premium factor} = \frac{(t - .5) \times (t + .5)}{n \times (n+1)}$$

$$= \frac{t^2 - .25}{n \times (n+1)}$$

$$\text{Pro rata unearned premium factor} = \frac{t - .5}{n}$$

where n = the original term in months
t = the number of full or partial months remaining from the valuation date to the expiration of the policy
= n - [12 x (valuation year - issue year) + (valuation month - issue month)]

An alternative formula for making the half-month correction in the Rule of 78 unearned premiums is to calculate the numerator as the average of the Rule of 78 factor for (t-1) months to run and t months to run. This produces a slightly different formula:

$$\text{Rule of 78 unearned premium factor} = \frac{t^2}{n \times (n+1)}$$

The difference in the factors between the two formulas is small, and either formula is acceptable in practice.

For net payoff coverage, the Rule of 78 understates the reserves, although the understatement is not dramatic. If the Single Premium Method is used, an average APR may be assumed for all loans to reduce the number of factors.

A separate procedure is not needed for joint life policies. The gross premium charged reflects the additional risk from insuring two lives. The joint life gross premium is used in the calculation of the gross unearned premiums using the usual formulas.

Mortality reserves approach the problem from another standpoint. A mortality table is a set of probabilities. For each age, the probability of death within the next year is determined. These probabilities are applied to each policy based on the age of the insured, the amount of insurance in force, the plan of insurance, and the remaining term. Reserve factors are calculated which reduce the actual reserve calculation to a simple process much as rate charts are used to calculate premiums. Reserve factors for net payoff are different from gross coverage due to the difference in the amount of coverage provided over the loan term.

Mortality tables are produced from industry inter-company studies of actual claim experience. An age-rated study of credit life mortality rates has not been done, so a mortality table of credit insurance experience is not available. Instead, prior studies of ordinary life or group life claim experience are used. The most widely used table is the 1958 Commissioners Extended Term table (1958 CET). This is a study of mortality experience under an ordinary life non-forfeiture option called extended term insurance. If a whole life policy is surrendered, the cash value may be applied to buy term insurance. This was a study of 1950-54 experience. What does this have to do with credit insurance today? Nothing. However, the table is judged to be a conservative estimate of credit insurance experience. Other tables used are the 1958 Commissioners Standard Ordinary table (1958 CSO), 130% of 1958 CSO, the 1960 Commissioners Standard Group table (1960 CSG), or 130% of 1960 CSG. For ages relevant to credit insurance, the 1958 CET table is equal to 130% of the 1958 CSO table. A 1980 CSO and a 1980 CET table have been developed. The 1980 CET has been accepted by several states, but has not been adopted as the reserve standard in any state.

Since claims are to be paid in the future, the expected payments are discounted for interest. Interest rates used in the calculation of the reserve factors are determined by the insurer's actuary. For statutory reserves, states specify a maximum rate, usually 4.5%. Insurers may use any rate less than or equal to the state maximum. A separate set of interest rates and factors may be used for federal income tax reserves. The short policy terms make the choice of an interest rate of little significance. A change of 1% in the interest assumption results in approximately 1.5% change in the reserves. It is an inverse relationship; increasing the interest rate 1% decreases the reserves 1.5%.

For joint life insurance, the reserve factors are often a multiple of the single life factors. A few insurers simply double the in force amount, resulting in a multiple of two. Most insurers use a multiple of the single life reserve factors, generally from 1.60 to 2.00. Alternatively, an age setback may be used. Although the actual age of the joint insured is rarely used, an assumption is made that the second insured is three to six years younger than the primary insured.

Actual reserve valuations may be on a policy-by-policy (i.e., seriatim) basis or a group basis. Many insurers maintain an individual in force file and apply reserve factors policy-by-policy. Some larger companies use grouped in force files which do not retain policy data on an individual basis. For example, policies may be grouped by five-year (quinquennial) age bands. Reserve factors are developed which are appropriate to the valuation method used.

Since unearned premiums are based on the original gross premiums, otherwise identical policies will have different reserves depending on the gross premium charged. Mortality reserves will be the same for identical policies. One cannot easily predict which basis will produce the larger reserves. In states where the gross premium rates are low, mortality reserves will exceed the unearned premium reserves. In high-rate states, the reverse is true. Overall, 1950 CET mortality reserves will approximately equal the unearned premium reserves if the gross premium rate is 45¢/100/year. The actual relationship will depend on the particular mix of ages, terms, and proportion of joint business.

Mortality reserves are normally used for statutory financial statements and federal income tax returns. Unearned premiums are used for all other accounting purposes.

Data on four single life, gross coverage policies and a demonstration of the calculation of unearned premium reserves and mortality reserves using the 1958 CET table at 3% valued at December 31, 1986 follows.

POLICY DATA

Policy Number	Date of Issue	Policy Term	Original In Force	In Force on 12-31-86	Original Gross Premium	Policy Type	Age of Insured
1	1-01-86	24	24,000	24,000	576	Level	33
2	6-30-86	36	18,000	15,000	324	Decr	28
3	6-30-86	48	12,000	10,500	192	Decr	48
4	9-15-86	48	12,000	11,250	192	Decr	58

The remaining in force was calculated based on exact duration at 12-31-86. Premium rates used to calculate the gross premiums, per $100 per year, are $1.20, .60, .40, and .40 respectively. In the following formulas, n = original term and t = remaining term.

The following calculations use the mid-month issue assumption, but an exact calculation based on actual days is equally valid. For the purposes of reserve calculations, valuations generally assume all policies are issued on the 15th of the month. Final amounts are rounded to the nearest dollar.

POLICY NUMBER 1

12-31-86 unearned premium, mid-month assumption, pro rata unearned premiums

$$= \text{(original gross premium)} \times \frac{t - .5}{n}$$

where n = 24
t = 24 - [12 x (86 - 86) + (12 - 1)]
= 13

= 576 x (13 - .5) / 24
= 300

POLICY NUMBER 2

12-31-86 unearned premium, mid-month assumption, Rule of 78 unearned premiums

$$= \text{(original gross premium)} \times \frac{(t - .5)\,(t + .5)}{n \times (n+1)}$$

where n = 36
t = 36 - [12 x (86 - 86) + (12 - 6)]
= 30

= 324 x (29.5 x 30.5) / (36 x 37)

= 219

Here are sample mortality reserve factors per $1,000 of insurance in force for these policies (mid-month issue assumption).

Policy Number	Age	Months Remaining	Decreasing Reserve Factor	Level Reserve Factor
1	33	12.5	$ 1.46	$ 2.80
2	28	29.5	3.16	6.15
3	43	41.5	12.04	24.47
4	58	44.5	30.65	62.18

POLICY NUMBER 1

12-31-86 Mortality reserve

= (Remaining in force in 1,000s) x (Reserve factor per $1,000)

= (24,000 / 1,000) x 2.80

= 67

POLICY NUMBER 2

12-31-86 Mortality reserve

= (Remaining in force in 1,000s) x (Reserve factor per $1,000)

= (15,000 / 1,000) x 3.16

= 47

The results for all four policies are:

Policy Number	Mortality Reserve	Unearned Premium Reserve	Ratio of Mortality Reserve to Unearned Premium
1	67	300	.22
2	47	219	.21
3	126	144	.88
4	345	165	2.09

ACTIVE LIFE RESERVES FOR SINGLE PREMIUM DISABILITY BUSINESS

Disability active life reserves are held on a gross unearned premium basis. Again, the concept is to hold back the remaining proportion of the original risk on the accounting date.

Unfortunately, there has not been a definitive study to establish the proper basis to earn disability premiums. Investigation of this matter has led to much debate, but no resolution.

It is possible to prepare a morbidity table, which is the disability counterpart to a mortality table. A morbidity table is a set of probabilities estimating the number of insureds who will become disabled in the following year. Attempts were made in the 1968 NAIC Disability Study and 1974 NAIC Disability Study to produce morbidity rates for credit disability insurance, but both studies had serious technical flaws. Credit disability data processing systems just do not maintain the level of detail necessary to do a world class morbidity study. The 1968 Study was adopted by the NAIC and served as the basis of the prima facie rates in many states, but it is completely outdated at this time. In life insurance, old mortality tables can remain in use, since declining death rates make them conservative. Rates of disability have increased significantly since 1968, so the table is useless in estimating the current level of claim costs. The 1974 Study was never adopted by the NAIC.

In life insurance, the expected claim cost declines as the amount of insurance in force declines. Since the rate of mortality is approximately level over the short term, the ratio of the remaining exposure to the original exposure represents the proportion of original risk remaining. Disability is different. The maximum amount of a claim can be affected by the remaining term. Under a 48-month term policy, the insured can earn from 1 to 48 benefit payments depending on the timing and duration of the disability. Most claims do not last for the full remaining term. Claimants who recover may have subsequent disabilities.

For single premium credit disability, Rule of 78 unearned premium reserves understate the proportion of remaining risk to the original risk. Pro rata unearned premiums overstate the remaining proportion. In recent years, a move to use the arithmetic mean, or average, of the two bases has gained wide acceptance. It is possible to prove that the Rule of 78 is too liberal and pro rata too conservative. Highly trained experts approached the problem and just decided to split the difference.

Thus the "proper" reserve is judged by many to be the mean, or average, of the Rule of 78 and pro rata unearned premiums.

Another recent approach is the Single Premium Method, also called the Rule of Anticipation. The unearned premium is the gross single premium for the remaining term and remaining benefits. These unearned premiums are close to the mean of Rule of 78 and pro rata.

Comparison Of Unearned Premium Factors For Various Methods

	— Unearned Premium Factors —				— Ratio Of Various Factors —		
Remaining Term	Rule of 78	Pro Rata	Mean	Single Premium Method	Rule of 78/ Pro Rata	Rule of 78/ Mean	Mean/ S. Premium
24	1.00	1.00	1.00	1.00	1.00	1.00	1.00
23	.92	.96	.94	.94	.96	.98	.99
22	.84	.92	.88	.89	.92	.96	.99
21	.77	.88	.82	.84	.88	.94	.98
20	.70	.83	.77	.78	.84	.91	.98
19	.63	.79	.71	.73	.80	.89	.97
18	.57	.75	.66	.68	.76	.86	.97
17	.51	.71	.61	.63	.72	.84	.96
16	.45	.67	.56	.58	.68	.81	.96
15	.40	.63	.51	.54	.64	.78	.96
14	.35	.58	.47	.49	.60	.75	.96
13	.30	.54	.42	.44	.56	.72	.96
12	.26	.50	.38	.40	.52	.68	.96
11	.22	.46	.34	.35	.48	.65	.96
10	.18	.42	.30	.31	.44	.61	.96
9	.15	.38	.26	.27	.40	.57	.97
8	.12	.33	.23	.23	.36	.53	.98
7	.09	.29	.19	.19	.32	.48	1.01
6	.07	.25	.16	.15	.28	.44	1.03
5	.05	.21	.13	.11	.24	.39	1.15
4	.03	.17	.10	.07	.20	.33	1.38
3	.02	.13	.07	.04	.16	.28	1.79
2	.01	.08	.05	.02	.12	.21	2.62
1	.00*	.04	.02	.00*	.08	.15	5.23

*Less than .01

Fig. 5.1 Comparison of unearned premium factors.

These Rule of 78 and pro rata factors are based on exact months remaining using the standard formulas:

$$\text{Rule of 78 factor} = \frac{t \times (t+1)}{n \times (n+1)}$$

$$\text{Pro rata factor} = t / n$$

where t = remaining term

The mean is the average of the Rule of 78 factor and the pro rata factor. The factors are rounded to two decimals, but the ratios are calculated using the exact factors.

Factors for the single premium method are based on the Texas rates for 14-day retroactive coverage for a 24-month original term. Single Premium Method factors will vary by plan and by state depending on the slope of the gross premium scale.

ACTIVE LIFE RESERVES FOR MOB BUSINESS

For MOB business, the active life reserve may be zero if all premiums are due on the first of the month. At the end of a month, the coverage has expired. Even when the premiums are due on the first of the month, many insurers hold a half-month reserve. The reserve held is one-half of the premium reported in the prior month. This practice stems from the traditional assumption that all policies are issued in the middle of the month and that premiums are due on the first day of the policy month.

CLAIM RESERVE CALCULATION METHODS IN GENERAL

Active life reserves are calculated on a policy-by-policy basis using specified tables or formulas. Using this method, the calculation seems to be a precise number, but in reality the answer is still an estimate.

An actuary rarely gets the feeling of preciseness when working with claim reserves. Indeed, it is sometimes difficult to feel secure that the answer is even in the ballpark. All methods of claim reserving involve the application of prior experience and subjective judgment. Conditions change, so methods which worked in the past may no longer give good results. Both art and science are used to arrive at the final result.

The remainder of this chapter discusses methods of claim reserving which are used in practice. No method is perfect. There is no implication that the methods discussed are the best methods or that they are always appropriate in the situations described. Setting of claim reserves is difficult and requires good professional judgment and a knowledge of the business being evaluated. Even the most sophisticated methods may fail to produce adequate reserves when changes are occurring in the underlying business or in the conditions affecting the duration or reporting of claims. To demonstrate the methods, examples with a small number of claims are used. Development of reliable factors depends on the availability of credible past experience which can be expected to apply to the business being evaluated. A few sections contain factors which have been found in studies of actual experience of typical blocks of credit business. They are included as general guidelines and should not be applied without verification of their applicability to the business in question. Although actuarial knowledge is useful in many aspects of credit insurance, this is one area where qualified actuarial expertise and judgment are required.

Five general methods are used by insurers to set claim reserves:

- Factor method
- Lag or completion method
- Case method
- Direct tabulation
- Loss ratio method

The *factor method* is widely used. Prior claim payment experience is studied to determine the actual experience during some time period in the past. The experience is related to a quantity which will be available on the accounting date in question.

The *lag method* is often used for disability insurance. Prior experience is studied to estimate the average remaining period of disability after the accounting date. Factors are developed based on the time the insured has been disabled on the accounting date.

Under the factor and the lag methods, more than one prior accounting date is studied. Generally, studies are made of each prior year using a December 31 accounting date. For example, factors would be developed by tracking the experience of open disability claims on December 31, 1980. Then separate factors are developed by tracking the open claims on December 31, 1981, and so on. The experience of the different accounting dates is reviewed for consistency and trends. The final factors are a blend of the studies from several different accounting dates. Examples of the two methods are demonstrated in the following section.

The *case reserve method* is the easiest to understand and apply but can only be used for known disability claims. A knowledgeable claims person reviews each reported claim and estimates the remaining time of disability. The reserve is the product of the remaining months of disability times the claimant's monthly benefit.

A senior claims person can review each claim and set the reserve. Smaller companies may find this method appropriate, but the method becomes impractical as the volume of claims grows. Problems arise when different claims personnel set the reserves on their claims. Consistency is lost, and the level of expertise will vary. One problem facing all claims personnel is the quality of data provided to judge the severity of a claim. A noticeable deterioration in the time spent by doctors or their staff in completing claim forms has been evident in recent years. Ultimately, an insurer must resort to the factor or lag method. Case reserves must be tested by the type of study used for the factor or lag method. The runoff from prior years is studied to judge whether prior years' reserves were adequate.

A subset of the case method is the *armchair method.* A qualified person goes into a deep trance and comes out with an estimate! This method is more widely used than one would expect.

The *direct method* can only be used in a few situations. The most common use is for calculating life claims in course of settlement. On the accounting date, the claims department totals the benefits payable on claims which have been received but not paid.

The *loss ratio method* is occasionally used where the data is not present to apply the other methods. If the incurred claim-earned premium loss ratio is known, the incurred claims can be calculated as the product of the loss ratio times the earned premium. Subtracting paid claims from incurred claims gives the claim reserves in total. However, the loss ratio cannot be calculated without a proper determination of the claim reserves, so the relationship is circular. This method is implemented in practice by assuming a loss ratio. The results are only as good as the assumption.

For example, the loss ratio is assumed to be 70% and is applied to the following data:

Paid claims in 1986:	\$ 60,000
Claim reserve 12-31-85:	\$ 15,000
Written premium in 1986:	\$100,000
Unearned premium 12-31-85:	\$ 60,000
Unearned premium 12-31-86:	\$ 70,000

Calculation of claim reserves at 12-31-86:

Earned premium for 1986

= (Premium written in 1986) + (12-31-85 Unearned premium) - (12-31-86 Unearned premium)

= 100,000 + 60,000 - 70,000

= 90,000

Incurred claims for 1986
= (Assumed loss ratio) x (Earned premium for 1986)

= .70 x 90,000

= 63,000

In addition, Incurred claims for 1986
= (Paid claims for 1986) - (Claim reserve at 12-31-85)
+ (Claim reserve at 12-31-86)

63,000 = 60,000 - 15,000 + (Claim reserve at 12-31-86)

18,000 = Claim reserve at 12-31-86

For each of these methods, a life insurer has the option of discounting the future payments with interest. The short term nature of the future payout reduces the necessity for such discounting. For the life insurance reserves, the effect would be negligible. Using an interest discount for disability reserves can reduce the reserves 5%-8% depending on the interest rate selected. An estimate of these claim reserves may have a margin of error of 5%-10%. Many insurers forego discounting for interest and just consider the omission as an element of conservatism. Casualty insurers are not permitted to discount claim reserves for interest.

LIFE CLAIM RESERVE METHODS

The factor method is widely used. Life claims are reported quickly, so a study of the previous year's experience is usually sufficient.

For example, the life IBNR is normally calculated on the factor method by relating the reserve to the insurance in force. One approach to prepare an accounting on December 31, 1986, is to review the experience of 1986. A tabulation is made of all claims paid in 1986 where the date of death was before January 1, 1986, but where the claim was reported in 1986. These claims are divided by the insurance in force on December 31, 1985 to produce a factor, as 80¢ per $1000. If 1987 experience is comparable, there will be 80¢ of IBNR claims for each $1,000 of insurance in force. This factor is multiplied by the insurance in force on December 31, 1986 to produce the IBNR reserve. Any known reporting problems affecting the number of claims or policies in force, and any other trends, should be taken into account.

The direct method is used by smaller insurers. Since the reserve is not needed until 30 to 45 days after the accounting date, the IBNR claims received in the interim can be counted. An estimate is made for any future claims. Some small insurers with stable volumes of business have set their IBNR reserve conservatively and held the same reserve for years.

Claims in course of settlement are customarily set by the direct method, although insurers using the factor method for IBNR claims may also use the factor method for CCS. When studying the prior year claims under the factor method, all claims paid in the year, incurred prior to the accounting date are included, regardless of the date reported.

EXAMPLE OF FACTOR METHOD TO CALCULATE IBNR AND CCS RESERVE

Month	Paid Claims in 1985	Percentage of Claims in Month to Total	Cumulative Percent
January	2,413,618	47.5	47.5
February	1,221,817	24.0	71.5
March	628,263	12.4	83.9
April	310,067	6.1	90.0
May	134,131	2.6	92.6
June	165,780	3.3	95.9
July	83,393	1.6	97.5
August	22,274	.4	97.9
September	52,442	1.0	98.9
October	35,852	.7	99.6
November	9,915	.2	99.8
December	7,529	.2	100.0
Total	5,085,081	100.0	

Paid Claims represent claim payments in the month which had a date of death prior to 1-1-85 (IBNR and CCS).

Life insurance in force on 12-31-84: $5,844,387,000

IBNR and CCS Factor

= (Total IBNR and CCS claims) / (In force on 12-31-84)
= (5,085,081) / (5,844,387,000)
= .00087
= $.87 per $1,000

In force on 12-31-85: $7,758,319,000

IBNR and CCS Reserve on 12-31-85

= (Factor) x (In force on 12-31-85)
= (.00087) x (7,758,319,000)
= 6,749,738

This is the actual experience of a large credit insurance company for the dates shown. The factor represents a fairly typical block of credit insurance business, but the experience is predominantly bank business. This factor should not be used indiscriminately, as other insurers will have different experience.

DISABILITY CLAIM RESERVE METHODS

Various methods, or combination of methods, are used to set disability claim reserves. Since disability claim reserves are more subjective and tend to fluctuate more widely from year to year, some insurers use several methods and select the final reserves from the range of results produced.

An insurer using the lag method or the case reserve method for known claims must use a separate method for IBNR claims, generally a factor method based on claims paid or unearned premiums. A *total factor method* may be used to estimate the total of all three subdivisions at once. Many combinations of methods are possible. Each method has its advantages and disadvantages, so the final choice of the appropriate method for any particular insurer is best left to the actuary setting the reserves for that insurer.

LAG OR COMPLETION METHOD

A prior accounting date is selected. The open claims on this date are tracked until completion of all claims. The claims are tracked separately for each claim duration on the accounting date. A study is done of all claimants who had been disabled for one month or less at the accounting date, those disabled for between one and two months at the accounting date, etc. Studies are done for each month up to two years, then for annual durations. The average future payout for each duration is calculated. For example, the result may be:

Months Disabled On Accounting Date	Average Months of Disability After Accounting Date
0 - 1	4.0
1 - 2	3.7
2 - 3	3.5

This result means a claimant disabled for less than one month prior to the accounting date is expected to remain disabled for an additional four months after the accounting date. The claim reserve for the current accounting date is calculated by summing the monthly benefits on all open claims for claimants disabled for one month or less, and multiplying the sum by four. The method can only be used on known claims, so a separate approach is needed for IBNR reserves.

It is clear to see that the factors do not apply to individual claims. Some claimants will recover within the next month while some may be disabled for several years. An actuary may assume that the average is appropriate and has not changed from the prior history, or may introduce trend factors into the calculation.

The data can be viewed from a different perspective and the result is the completion method. The historical data is tabulated between claims paid prior to the accounting date under study and claims paid after the date. The completion ratio is the proportion of total claims which have been paid before the accounting date, or in other words, the proportion of the total claims which are completed on the accounting date. The example calculates the reserves for 12-31-86 based on the historical study of 12-31-80. In practice, the experience of several prior study dates would be reviewed.

Historical Data

Months Disabled on 12-31-80	Claims Paid Prior to 12-31-80	Claims Paid after 12-31-80	Completion Ratio on 12-31-80
0 - 1	6,000	24,000	.20
1 - 2	8,000	24,000	.25
2 - 3	12,000	28,000	.30

12-31-86 Claim Reserve

The claim payments on known claims on the valuation date are summarized by the number of months specified. These totals are divided by the completion factor to produce total projected claims. Claim reserves for 12-31-86 are the total projected claims less the paid claims.

Months Disabled on 12-31-86	Claims Paid Prior to 12-31-86	Completion Factor	Total Projected Claims	Claim Reserves
0 - 1	9,000	.20	45,000	36,000
1 - 2	13,000	.25	52,000	39,000
2 - 3	18,000	.30	60,000	42,000

TOTAL FACTOR METHOD

One method in use recognizes that the total claim reserve is the key number. A total claim reserve is developed from the factor method. Subsidiary calculations are made to separate the total claim reserve into its subdivisions. Where sufficient data is available, the study should be done by class of lender.

A prior accounting date is selected, then a tabulation is made of all claim payments made after the accounting date where the date of disability is prior to the accounting date. This total is divided by a base number. One common base is the number of dollars of monthly benefits on all open claims on the accounting date. Consider the following claims:

Claim Number	Date of Disability	Date Reported	Monthly Benefit	Amount Paid Prior to 12-31-80	Amount Paid After 12-31-80	Type
1	1-1-80	3-1-80	200	2,200	1,400	Continuing
2	6-1-80	8-1-80	100	600	500	Continuing
3	9-1-80	11-15-80	200	600	1,450	Continuing
4	11-1-80	12-15-80	150	-0-	600	CCS
5	12-1-80	1-15-81	175	-0-	1,900	IBNR
Total					5,850	

This study is done as of 12-31-85, and no other claims were reported with a date of disability before 12-31-80. In hindsight, the reserve should have been $5,850 on 12-31-80. The problem is to calculate claim reserves for 12-31-85. A factor is needed which can be applied to a known quantity at 12-31-85 to predict future claim payments.

One known quantity is the dollars of monthly benefit on the claims received as of 12-31-85 (continuing and CCS). On 12-31-80, the monthly benefit was $650 on known claims at that time (claim numbers 1 through 4). A factor is calculated:

$$= \frac{\text{(All claim payments after 12-31-80)}}{\text{(Dollars of monthly benefit on reported claims at 12-31-80)}}$$

$$= \frac{5{,}850}{650}$$

$$= 9.0$$

The monthly benefit on all open claims at 12-31-85 is tabulated and multiplied by 9.0 to produce the total claim reserves at 12-31-85.

A secondary factor study is done for IBNR claims. Claim number 5 is an IBNR claim. A factor is needed representing the portion of the IBNR claims between the date of disability and 12-31-80. Since one month would have been earned, the amount is $175 and the factor is:

$$\frac{175}{650} = .27$$

The IBNR reserve at 12-31-85 is .27 times the dollars of monthly benefit on open claims.

CCS is done by direct tabulation based on open claims at 12-31-85. Using claim number 4 as an example, the CCS liability is the benefit between November 1 and December 31, or two months of benefit at $150 per month.

The Continuing Reserve is simply the total claim reserve less the IBNR and CCS.

The following total reserve factors are representative of a typical book of credit business for a regional or national company:

Auto Dealer Business	10.0 - 12.5
Bank Business	8.5 - 10.5
Credit Union Business	10.5 - 12.5
Finance Company Business	9.0 - 11.0

To make a general review of credit disability reserves of an insurer, approximate the dollars of open monthly benefits by dividing the annual incurred disability benefits by 12. This ratio can be multiplied by the appropriate factors to estimate the total claim reserves.

These factors have two components. One piece represents the average remaining claim duration on known claims. This segment constitutes about one-half of the factor. The second component inflates known claims to provide for IBNR claims. This component is affected by the reporting time of claims. A one-state insurer may have factors lower than the range shown due to the proximity of claimants to the insurer. An insurer paying claims nationwide from one claim office may have higher factors because of mail delivery time.

It is interesting to analyze the factors. Automobile dealers and credit unions have the highest factors. This is unexpected at first, since automobile dealer business has the lowest loss ratios and credit unions have the highest loss ratios. Credit unions experience a higher number of claims per dollar of premium, but this is independent of the parameters of the claim reserves. Since automobile dealers usually write loans of 48 months, their average claim duration tends to be longer than that of the other classes. The automobile dealer's independence from the corporation actually providing the financing may create a delay in filing claims. Credit unions tend to have slow claims reporting and a longer average claim duration than banks and finance companies. The lower factors for banks and finance companies reflect quick claim reporting and a shorter average claim duration due to shorter term policies.

A primary advantage of this factor method is that it can be applied at any level of reporting; i.e., by branch location, lender, state, or class of business. Once companywide factors are developed, they can be applied at the individual lender level. In preparing an accounting for a lender's experience, the dollars of monthly benefit on open claims for that lender's business are tabulated. The lender's claim reserve is the product of its open claims times the companywide factor for the lender's class of business.

This is an advantage because lenders can see their claim reserves go up or down as their level of reported claims varies.

For small lenders, a problem arises if there are only one or two open claims. A reserve may be created equal to twelve months of claim payments while the claimant's policy has only four months to expiration. This method will produce a reasonable estimate with about twenty-five open claims. However, on a rapidly growing block, the method may understate the claim reserve. On the other hand, there is a definite overstatement on a closed block of business. No method is perfect.

One technical aspect in implementing the method is the coding of claims; i.e., when does a claim come off the open claim file? Some claims are known to be complete because of the nature of the claim, as in the death of the insured, or the expiration of the policy. These claims are coded "final" and are removed from the file quickly. In many cases, no notification is received that the claim is finished. The claimant just quits sending in monthly claim forms. An insurer will have a procedure to remove these claims after several months of inactivity, usually 2-6 months. The amount of time is not a concern, as long as there is consistency in the procedure between the base experience years and the current accounting date.

At the company level, this factor method works extremely well, particularly in the estimation of the IBNR component. While the lag method and case reserves may be superior for known claims, the methods of calculating the IBNR component are weaker.

OTHER FACTOR METHODS

Another use of the factor method is to calculate the IBNR component for use in conjunction with the lag method or the case reserve method. One alternative is to use the preceding procedure for the IBNR component. Generally, if an insurer is going to develop the data processing system for this approach, the insurer might as well use it for all components.

Another alternative is to develop a factor as a function of unearned premiums on the accounting date, or paid claims for the year. Again, a prior accounting date is selected. The IBNR claims are tracked for a number of years after the accounting date. The final total is divided by the unearned premiums on the prior accounting date to produce a factor. The IBNR for the current valuation date is the product of the factor times the current unearned premium. Along the same lines, the total IBNR claims may be divided by the paid claims in the year preceding the prior accounting date, producing a claims factor. For the current valuation, the claims factor is multiplied by the paid claims for the current year to produce the IBNR estimate at the end of the current year.

These methods work reasonably well on a stable block of business, but often produce inappropriate reserves on blocks of business which are growing or declining.

In all claim reserving calculations there is a significant margin of error. Even on relatively large blocks of business, claims fluctuate rather widely. Large blocks may have a potential error margin of 10% using the best of methods. Since this margin can easily represent one year of earnings on a book of credit business, the importance of claim reserves is clear. A subjective review is necessary once the basic calculations are finished. The actuary must consider trends and known problems with claim reporting. Divergent factors may be produced by various prior accounting dates. For better or worse, the quality of the actuary's work is evident in the financial results of the next one or two years.

CHAPTER SIX
MEASUREMENT OF PROFITABILITY

Successful operation in the credit insurance business requires that the financial results be measured and monitored periodically. Each individual account should be reviewed annually, significant blocks of business should be reviewed quarterly, and the overall book of business reviewed monthly. Financial statements must be prepared which provide additional information on the profitability of the book of business from different perspectives. Many states require an annual submission of an insurer's experience on business written in the state which provides yet another view of the financial results.

Profitability of an individual account is determined by net income for a period. Quarterly accountings are usually prepared on a year-to-date basis and an inception-to-date basis, which display the historical results of an account and current trends. Quarterly reviews allow an insurer to take corrective action by adjusting commissions, canceling business, or filing for rate deviations. Individual accountings may be grouped for review by logical business segments.

In this chapter, the term *case* may apply to a single account, or refer to a combined group of accounts to be studied as a business segment or for rate deviation purposes. In other words, a case is the unit of experience being evaluated, and may consist of one or more accounts. The term *written premiums* refers to gross premiums collected less refunded premiums.

To grasp the measurement of profits, an understanding of three concepts is needed–loss ratios, reserves, and credibility. A loss ratio is the proportion of the premium necessary to pay claims, normally expressed as a percentage. To accurately determine the loss ratio, reserves must be calculated. Credibility is the degree of confidence that can be placed on the calculated loss ratio as a predictor of the true experience of a case, which is usually determined by the amount of earned premium, number of lives insured, or number of claims. The loss ratio experience of a small case fluctuates significantly from quarter to quarter. Larger accounts have less fluctuation, so their experience is more credible.

PRO RATA AND RULE OF 78 UNEARNED PREMIUMS

The basic concept involved in the measurement of profitability is to match the premiums of the period with the claims of the period. This is best done by calculating *earned premiums* and *incurred claims*. Unearned premium reserves and claim reserves provide the accounting mechanisms to accurately determine earned premiums and incurred claims.

The need for reserves is easily understood for single premium credit insurance. At the inception of a policy, a single premium is collected which provides for insurance coverage spanning several years. From an accounting standpoint, a mechanism is needed to hold back a portion of the premium to pay for future claims. If a portion is not withheld, the single premium will flow directly into net income.

For ease of calculation, consider a four-month single premium policy. Since the coverage spans four months, a method must be devised to determine when the premium is included in net income. A liberal approach would include the premium in income on the day collected. A conservative approach would wait until the policy expires. However, to accurately measure experience over short time periods, the premium must be earned throughout the term of the policy. The key is to earn the premiums in proportion to the claims which are occurring. If one-fourth of the claims occur in the first month, one-fourth of the premium should be earned in the first month. At the end of the first month, three-fourths of the premium is said to be unearned.

The general formula for earned premiums is:

Written premiums for the period,

plus Unearned premiums at the beginning of the period,

less Unearned premiums at the end of the period.

Assuming that one-fourth of the claims occur each month, unearned premium factors are calculated based on expected experience. The factor is the ratio of remaining claims to total claims. For example:

Month	Percentage Of Total Claims Occurring in Month	Remaining Claims at End of Month	Ratio of Remaining Claims to Total Claims
1	25%	75%	.75
2	25%	50%	.50
3	25%	25%	.25
4	25%	-0-	-0-
Total	100%		

The ratio is multiplied by the original gross premium to obtain the unearned premium at the end of each month.

If the four-month policy has a premium of $10, the earned premium by month is:

Month	Written Premiums	Unearned Premium Beginning of Month	Unearned Premium End of Month	Earned Premium for the Month
1	10.00	-0-	7.50	2.50
2	-0-	7.50	5.00	2.50
3	-0-	5.00	2.50	2.50
4	-0-	2.50	-0-	2.50

At the beginning of the first month, unearned premiums are zero, because there is no business in force. When the policy is issued on the first day of the month the unearned premium is the full gross premium, since none of the coverage has elapsed. By the same token, the unearned premium after four months is zero, since all coverage has elapsed.

These tables demonstrate *pro rata* unearned premiums. Pro rata in this situation means that the premium is earned in equal increments over the term of the policy. In each month, one-fourth of the premium is earned.

Selection of the proper unearned premium method depends on the expected pattern of claims. For a level credit life policy, the amount in force is the same throughout the term of the policy. Over this short term period, it can reasonably be assumed that the probability of death is constant. Since the likelihood of claim is the same and the death benefit is constant, one would expect that an equal amount of claims would occur each month. Pro rata unearned premiums result in the earning of premium in equal increments. Therefore, there is a matching of the premium earned to the expected claim pattern.

Gross coverage decreasing credit life insurance requires a different set of unearned premium factors. While one may continue to assume that the probability of death is the same for each month, the death benefit is different. If the four-month example has a $100 monthly payment, the death benefit in the first policy month is $400 for gross coverage. The amount in force in any month is equal to the sum of the remaining monthly payments.

Month	Remaining Monthly Payments	In Force During Month	Probability of Death	Expected Claims
1	$400	$400	.01	$4
2	300	300	.01	3
3	200	200	.01	2
4	100	100	.01	1

For proper matching, the unearned premium factors should be the ratio of future claims to total claims. By using the assumption that the probability of death is constant, the factors are equal to the ratio of the remaining coverage to the total coverage provided by the policy. Over this term, $10 in claims could be anticipated. At the end of the first month the unearned premium factor is:

Remaining Claims / Total Claims

$$= (3+2+1) / (4+3+2+1)$$

$$= .6$$

The numerator is the sum of the digits from 1 to 3, where three is the remaining number of monthly payments. The denominator is the sum of the digits from 1 to 4, where four is the original number of monthly payments. A general formula for the sum of the digits from 1 to "n", where n is any number, is:

$$n \times (n+1) / 2$$

This is known as the **Rule of 78**. Its name comes from the fact that the sum of the digits from 1 to 12 is 78; i.e., (12 x 13) / 2 = 78.

Coverage which decreases in equal monthly installments, like gross coverage decreasing credit life insurance, results in the following simplified formula for unearned premium factors:

{t x (t+1)/2} / {n x (n+1)/2} =

{t x (t+1)} / {n x (n+1)}

Where t = remaining number of monthly payments
n = original number of monthly payments

Since both the numerator and denominator represent the Rule of 78, unearned premiums for gross coverage decreasing term credit life policies are said to be held on the Rule of 78. The factors for the four-month policy are:

Month	Remaining Payments at End of Month	Sum of Remaining Payments at EOM	Unearned Premium Factor
1	3	6	.6
2	2	3	.3
3	1	1	.1
4	0	0	-0-

Again, with a $10 gross premium:

Month	Written Premium	Unearned Premium Beginning of Month	Unearned Premium End of Month	Earned Premium
1	$10.00	-0-	$6.00	$4.00
2	-0-	$6.00	3.00	3.00
3	-0-	3.00	1.00	2.00
4	-0-	1.00	-0-	1.00

Here the portion of premium earned in the first month is larger than the premium earned in other months. One expects this result, since the death benefit is larger than in any other month.

For credit disability insurance, there is no consensus as to the pattern by which claims are incurred. Use of Rule of 78 unearned premiums results in earning the premium too rapidly. This understates the true loss ratio, particularly during the early years, on a block of business. Use of pro rata unearned premiums earns the premium too slowly, overstating the loss ratio. Unearned premiums based on the arithmetic mean of the Rule of 78 and pro rata are the most widely accepted basis for earning the premium. An alternative is the Single Premium Method, also called the Rule of Anticipation. A discussion of these methods, along with a comparison of the resulting factors, is contained in Chapter Five.

The Rule of 78, pro rata, and the Single Premium Method are based on assumptions which are not satisfied in the real world. For Rule of 78 unearned premiums to be accurate, all disability claims must continue until the end of the policy term. This is not true since many claims terminate prior to maturity because the disability ceases or the claimant dies. For pro rata to be proper, an equal number of claims must occur each month, with each month's claims having the same average duration. This condition is not met since claims occurring at early policy durations have a longer period of potential benefits. A claim occurring in the last policy month can have only one month of benefits regardless of the severity of the claim.

The use of the mean between the Rule of 78 and pro rata is based on its ease of calculation, and its reasonableness from the application of general logic. There have not been any published studies which confirm the accuracy of the method.

The Single Premium Method makes theoretical sense. The unearned premium factor equals:

$$\frac{\text{Single Premium for the Remaining Term and Benefit}}{\text{Original Gross Premium}}$$

Suppose a state specifies the following rates per $100 of initial indebtedness for a 14-day retroactive benefit for each of the original terms shown:

Term	Rate per $100
1	$0.66
2	0.82
3	0.93
4	1.03

For a four-month single premium policy with monthly payments of $100 per month, the initial gross indebtedness is $400. The gross premium equals:

$$\frac{400}{100} \times 1.03 = \$4.12$$

At the end of the first month, the remaining term is 3 months and the remaining gross coverage is $300. The factor for the Single Premium Method at the end of the first month is:

$$\frac{(300/100) \times .93}{4.12} = \frac{2.79}{4.12} = .68$$

The resulting factors for the end of the second, third, and fourth months are .40, .16, and zero respectively.

This method is correct if the gross premiums charged by month are an accurate reflection of the relationship of the claim costs between the various terms. This is probably not the case. Almost all state rates are based either on the relationship by term in the 1968 NAIC Disability Study, or on an ad hoc scale derived by negotiation. In addition, most states use the NAIC recommendation in calculating prima facie gross premiums. This includes the use of a constant in the expense component which results in an increasing expected loss ratio as the original term increases. For these reasons, any accuracy between the Single Premium Method factors and the true pattern of claims is coincidental. In most states, the Single Premium Method unearned premium factors are reasonably close to the mean unearned premium factors.

For monthly outstanding balance business, the formula for earned premiums is the same. If all premiums are due on the first of the month, the unearned premiums at the end of any month are zero, so written premiums equal earned premiums. Where premiums are due throughout the month (i.e., policies are not all dated on the first of the month), an unearned premium equal to one-half of the prior month's written premium is usually established, and the formula for the earned premiums is the same as for single premium policies.

INCURRED CLAIMS

Unearned premiums represent the portion of the original premium withheld to pay future claims. More precisely, this refers to claims for which the date of death or original disability is after the accounting date. Earned premiums represent the portion of the original premiums associated with claims for which the date of death or the original disability date is prior to the accounting date. These are incurred claims. The general formula for incurred claims is:

Paid claims

less Claim reserves at the beginning of the period,

plus Claim reserves at the end of the period.

When preparing an accounting for a period, the amount of paid claims is known, however this may not represent the total payments for claims where death or disability is prior to the end of the accounting period. The basic rule is that a claim reserve must be established to estimate all claim payments to be made after the accounting date, for which the date of death or disability is prior to the accounting date. The intent is to charge the accounting period with the entire cost of any claim which happens during the accounting period.

Consider the accounting period from October 1 to December 31, with the following death claim payments:

Claim Number	Amount of Claim	Date of Death	Date Claim Paid
1	$ 500	September 15	October 15
2	750	October 15	November 15
3	1,000	November 15	December 15
4	1,250	December 15	January 15

At September 30, the beginning claim reserve is $500, and at December 31, the ending claim reserve is $1,250, if the estimate of the claim reserves proves to be exactly correct. The incurred claims for the quarter are:

Paid Claims - Beginning claim reserves + Ending claim reserves

= (500 + 750 + 1,000) - 500 + 1,250

= 3,000

Subtracting the $500 beginning claim reserve results in allocating the $500 claim to the prior accounting quarter. This is proper since the death occurred prior to October 1. Adding the ending claim reserve to this quarter's claims is proper since the $1,250 claim occurred prior to December 31. There were $3,000 of claims for which the deaths occurred during the quarter. The formula accurately calculates this result. If the estimate of the claim reserve at the end of the period is different from the subsequent actual experience, the difference will fall into a subsequent accounting period. After all policies expire and all claim payments are made, claim reserves are zero and paid claims equal incurred claims.

LOSS RATIOS

Once incurred claims and earned premiums are calculated, the *incurred-earned loss ratio* (also called the *incurred loss ratio*) can be calculated by dividing incurred claims by earned premiums. This measure of losses is the most accurate method for estimating the true loss ratio for a group of policies. The true loss ratio is not known until all policies expire and all claims are complete. Since it's not feasible to wait five to ten years to determine if an account has acceptable loss experience, the incurred-earned loss ratio is the best indicator of the true loss experience prior to completion. Small blocks measured over short time spans can be expected to have erratic experience, but the incurred-earned loss ratio is a good predictor with a minimum amount of experience.

Other loss ratios misrepresent the true experience of business. The most common variation is a *paid loss ratio* (paid claims divided by written premiums). A paid loss ratio will severely understate the loss experience of a block of business early in its history. Another variation is the *paid-earned loss ratio* (paid claims divided by earned premiums). For credit life insurance, this method is fairly accurate, since claim reserves are small. For credit disability, this method will understate the loss ratio rather substantially. When the block has expired, the inception-to-date loss ratio on all three bases will be the same. The question is which loss ratio best predicts the ultimate loss ratio. Figure 6.2 shows the actual history of a block of disability business from inception to completion. Figure 6.1 illustrates the distortion created by using any loss ratio other than the incurred-earned loss ratio.

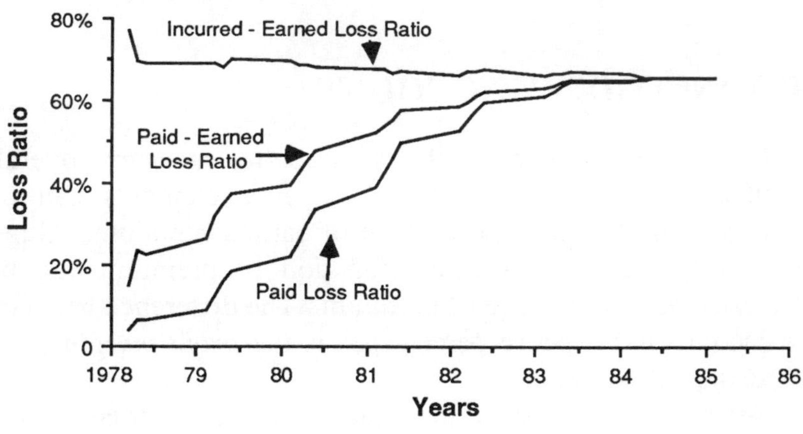

Fig. 6.1 Comparison of loss ratios for various methods of calculation.

STUDY OF VARIOUS LOSS RATIOS FOR A BLOCK OF CREDIT DISABILITY BUSINESS

ALL AMOUNTS SHOWN ARE ON AN INCEPTION-TO-DATE BASIS
INCEPTION DATE IS APRIL 1, 1978

END OF QUARTER	WRITTEN PREMIUMS	ENDING UNEARNED	EARNED PREMIUMS	PAID CLAIMS	ENDING CLAIM RESERVE	INCURRED CLAIMS	LOSS RATIOS PAID	LOSS RATIOS PAID-EARNED	LOSS RATIOS INCURRED-EARNED
6-30-78	334,071	250,814	83,257	12,451	51,615	64,066	3.7	15.0	76.9
9-30-78	521,352	379,286	142,066	32,918	65,633	98,551	6.3	23.2	69.4
12-31-78	944,335	664,332	280,003	62,837	130,141	192,978	6.7	22.4	68.9
3-31-79	1,111,302	725,629	385,673	101,282	165,295	266,577	9.1	26.3	69.1
6-30-79	1,250,342	752,935	497,407	158,407	184,008	342,415	12.7	31.8	68.8
9-30-79	1,310,612	709,045	601,567	209,778	198,746	408,524	16.0	34.9	67.9
12-31-79	1,443,933	718,070	725,863	268,840	240,002	508,842	18.6	37.0	70.1
3-31-80	1,487,262	656,570	830,692	325,672	250,994	576,666	21.9	39.2	69.4
6-30-80	1,533,739	601,572	932,167	391,846	246,782	638,628	25.5	42.0	68.5
9-30-80	1,573,080	543.626	1,029,454	467,004	237,657	704,661	29.7	45.4	68.5
12-31-80	1,610.587	485,925	1,124,662	538,659	225,211	763,870	33.4	47.9	67.9
3-31-81	1,619,874	412,605	1,207,269	629,314	185,834	815,148	38.8	52.1	67.5
6-30-81	1,622,213	340,918	1,281,295	685,892	177,829	863,721	42.3	53.5	67.4
9-30-81	1,625.124	280,608	1,344,516	743,483	150,620	894,103	45.7	55.3	66.5
12-31-81	1,625,235	228,512	1,396,723	803,855	130,832	934,687	49.5	57.6	66.9
3-31-82	1,617,871	167,981	1,449,890	849,565	109,392	958,957	52.5	58.6	66.1
6-30-82	1,613,691	125,385	1,488,306	889,404	109,249	998,653	55.1	59.8	67.1
9-30-82	1,610,965	91,798	1,519,167	928,184	92,848	1,021,032	57.6	61.1	67.2
12-31-82	1,609,771	66,691	1,543,080	957,741	85,844	1,043,585	59.5	62.1	67.6
3-31-83	1,608,744	46,614	1,562,130	983,874	51,974	1,035,848	61.2	63.0	66.3
6-30-83	1,607,758	31,510	1,576,248	1,002,482	50,452	1,052,934	62.4	63.6	66.8
9-30-83	1,607,407	21,363	1,586,044	1,022,052	35,839	1,057,891	63.6	64.4	66.7
12-31-83	1,606,787	13,735	1,593,052	1,034,207	31,944	1,066,151	64.4	64.9	66.9
3-31-84	1,606,646	9,010	1,597,636	1,040,834	23,706	1,064,540	64.8	65.1	66.6
6-30-84	1,606,490	5,537	1,600,953	1,045,057	12,321	1,057,378	65.1	65.3	66.0
9-30-84	1,606,486	3,777	1,602,709	1,047,563	6,047	1,053,610	65.2	65.4	65.7
12-31-84	1,606,456	2,632	1,603,824	1,051,185	3,070	1,054,255	65.4	65.5	65.7
3-31-85	1,606,438	0	1,606,438	1,051,758	0	1,051,758	65.5	65.5	65.5

Fig 6.2 Experience data and loss ratios by quarter for Figure 6.1.

NET INCOME BY ACCOUNT

The loss ratio approach is used to measure overall profitability. Most income and expense elements can be expressed directly as a percentage of earned premium. Other items which are not a direct function of premium can be converted to a percentage of premium. The difference between the income and expense percentages is the *profit margin* (as a percentage of premium).

Underwriting profit is the premiums less all claims and expenses. Total income before federal income tax is calculated by adding investment income to the underwriting profit. A simple example assumes the following amounts for an accounting period:

Paid Items:	Premiums written		$105,000
	Claims paid		50,000
	Commissions paid		31,500
	Premium taxes paid		2,100
	General expenses paid		10,000
	Investment income		7,000
Reserves:	Unearned premium	- beginning	110,000
		- ending	115,000
	Claim reserves	- beginning	25,000
		- ending	30,000

Earned premiums and incurred claims are calculated to produce the incurred-earned loss ratio. One concept involves viewing the loss ratio as the wholesale cost of the product being sold. Commissions, state premium taxes, and general expenses comprise the loading, or expense, elements. Commissions and premium taxes are a percentage of premium and are paid at issue. Just as the premium is earned during the term of the policy, the charge to earnings for these items must be spread over the policy term by developing unearned expense amounts. These are assets, because cash has been paid out for an expense which has a future value. The formula for earned commissions and premium taxes is:

Commissions and taxes paid,

plus Unearned commissions and premium taxes at the beginning of the period,

less Unearned commissions and premium taxes at the end of the period.

Commissions and premium taxes are a percentage of the initial gross single premium. The unearned portion is the same percentage times the remaining unearned premium.

For the example:

Commission rate = (commissions paid) / (premium written)
= 31,500 / 105,000
= .30 or 30%

Premium tax rate = (premium taxes paid) / (premium written)
= 2,100 / 105,000
= .02 or 2%

Total commission and premium tax rate = .30 + .02
= .32

Unearned commissions and premium taxes - beginning
= rate x (beginning unearned premiums)
= .32 x 110,000
= 35,200

Unearned commissions and premium taxes - ending
= rate x (ending unearned premiums)
= .32 x 115,000
= 36,800

Refunds take care of themselves in the computation, since they are processed as negative premiums. Premiums written are called *G-R premiums*–gross premiums collected minus refund premiums–or *net written premiums.* Written premiums are the net of the gross premium collected on new issues less the refunds paid on terminated policies. The lender has a chargeback of commission on refunds. Commissions paid are determined by multiplying the commission rate by the net written premiums. Premium taxes paid are also calculated as the state premium tax rate times net written premiums. In this manner, refunds are negative premiums which produce negative expenses.

When new business for an account ceases, the net written premium will be negative as the policies in force mature and only refunds are reported. The unearned premium begins to decline during runoff, so the earned premium remains positive.

The overall accounting becomes:

	Dollars	Percent
Paid premiums	$105,000	
Unearned premiums - beginning	110,000	
Unearned premiums - ending	115,000	
Earned premiums	100,000	100%
Paid claims	50,000	
Claim reserves - beginning	25,000	
Claim reserves - ending	30,000	
Incurred claims	55,000	55%
Paid commissions and taxes	33,600	
Unearned - beginning	35,200	
Unearned - ending	36,800	
Incurred commissions and taxes	32,000	32%
General expenses	10,000	10%
Total expenses	97,000	97%
Underwriting profit	3,000	3%
Investment income	7,000	7%
Profit before federal income tax	10,000	10%

HOME OFFICE EXPENSES

General expenses often represent the most difficult item of a profitability analysis. Total general expenses of the insurer are known, but the allocation to an account can only be estimated at best. The starting point is a functional cost study. The study takes the total corporate expenses, allocates the expenses by line of business, then subdivides the line expenses by function. Common function groups are:

Operating Departments

Claims Administration

Commission Accounting

Policy Issue

Premium Booking

Sales

Sales Administration

Underwriting

Service Departments

Corporate Overhead

Sales includes the internal sales force and the internal sales management group who are salaried personnel. Sales administration is responsible for setting up new accounts, handling service requests from lenders, and providing rate charts and policy forms.

Service departments provide support for the other operating departments. Examples of service departments are data processing, personnel, legal, actuarial, procurement, and word processing. Corporate overhead includes the departments and expenses necessary for the corporate operation not directly related to the day-to-day operation of the business. Examples include executive management, financial reporting, and investments.

Operating departments must separate expenses by function and line of business. Personnel are interviewed to determine the time spent by each person for each line of business and function. Service departments must allocate their expenses to the different operating departments. The service expense allocated to an operating department is then allocated by function and line of business, usually based on the percentages developed from the allocation of the particular operating department expenses. Corporate overhead is then spread over the operating departments. In this manner, all corporate expenses are allocated to the cost of operations by line and function. For credit insurance, the dollars of expense for each function are usually expressed as a percentage of earned premium for the year.

Allocation by line and function is a time-consuming process and only results in an approximate allocation. The allocation of some departments is fairly clear. The claims department expense is usually identifiable from a functional standpoint, but the line of business allocation may not be precise. Even for a department with clear functional and line of business allocations, the allocation of service and corporate overhead costs is subjective.

Once expenses are determined as a percentage of earned premium, the costs can be allocated by account. In a broad study of profitability, only the overall expense rate by line is needed. A company may determine that general expenses are 8% of earned premium for life insurance and 10% of earned premium for disability. These percentages are multiplied by the appropriate earned premium for the account to allocate general expenses at the account level.

This result is the average expense rate and may not be appropriate for a specific account. The most obvious differences between accounts are by class of business and size of account. Monthly outstanding balance business is much easier to process than single premium business. Automobile business may involve processing thousands of individual certificates, while a large bank may report on computer tape. Size of account is important, since costs are not directly related to premium. The allocation of expenses by size of account applies to some operating departments, but service and overhead expenses are also affected. The size of an account may not affect the cost of preparing financial statements, but using overall corporate expense rates causes more expenses to be allocated to larger accounts, since the base is earned premium.

Loss experience is important. An account with a low loss ratio should be less expensive to administer than an account with a high loss ratio, given the same dollars of earned premium, since there are fewer claims to pay. In reality, each element of expense varies somewhat by account. The maxim is that 20% of the business produces 80% of the problems. Sales may spend an inordinate amount of time on certain accounts. Accounts in Pennsylvania and New York may require more rate charts because of required periodic rate deviations. Accounts writing disability insurance covering preexisting conditions are easier to administer by the claims department. The list is endless.

To analyze the profitability of an account, one should use as much detail as possible. This detail will be limited by the available functional cost data. Expense variation by account is considered when a reasonable allocation and measurement of the expense is possible. The expense allocation will always contain some approximation and will involve the omission of some individual account expense variations.

The task is not finished. Allocated costs must be charged to the proper accounting period. Should expenses be charged when paid or should a portion be deferred over the term of the policies? Consider premium accounting and policy booking costs. These functions relate to the costs of booking the premium at issue and adding the policy to the in force. Except for refunds, these costs are incurred at issue, but the expense should be charged over the term of the policy. Claim expenses are spread over the term of the policy as claims are paid. It is appropriate to charge these expenses to earnings as they are paid, since they are paid in rough proportion to the premiums earned. The allocation of sales and sales administration is even more difficult. Initial sales costs are incurred before the lender first selects the insurer as its carrier, but should be spread over the lifetime of the lender's business. This is difficult, since no one knows how long the lender will remain with the insurer.

General expenses are often charged to earnings as they are paid. While deferral is appropriate for some expenses, the decision to add a deferral element depends on the magnitude of the expenses and the refinement desired in the profitability analysis program. Rules are specified for deferral if an insurer prepares GAAP financial statements, but an insurer may determine the need for a different deferral in preparing internal studies.

Investment income can be allocated by account if desired. Some insurers just analyze business on the basis of underwriting profit. However, an allocation of investment income is often enlightening with regard to the profitability of certain accounts.

Investment income depends primarily on the level of commissions paid and the nature of any deposit arrangement. Automobile dealer business generally involves regular cash flow without any deposit arrangement. Investment income reflects the commission paid and the premium rate level. Premiums, less commissions and premium taxes, comprise the investable funds. A cash flow analysis is performed, reflecting each element of paid expense against the premium income flow. An assumed earnings rate is applied to the flow of funds, generally using representative short-term interest rates. Investment income expressed as a percentage of premium for a representative book of business runs between 6% and 8% if the funds are invested in six-month certificates of deposit yielding 9%.

Insurers writing credit insurance for financial institutions may offer to maintain deposits in the institution for competitive reasons. A common requirement for obtaining the lender's credit insurance is for the insurer to maintain deposits roughly equal to one year of premiums produced by the lender.

If a state permits compensating balances, the deposit may be in a non-interest-bearing checking account. This definitely affects investment income to the insurer. In the early years, the investment income can even be negative, since the insurer must pay claims out of its own funds. Where compensating balances are not permitted, the deposits may be in an interest-bearing checking account or a savings account. Profitability is affected somewhat, since the interest rates on these accounts are about 5%. Where possible, insurers maintain deposits in certificates of deposit with the lender.

Some credit life business and all credit disability business produces a loss of net income in the statutory financial statement on the day issued. This is called *surplus drain.* For life business, the loss depends on the relationship among the gross premiums charged, the mortality reserves on the business, and the commission and premium taxes paid. For disability business, the amount of drain is usually equal to the commission and premium taxes paid. In traditional studies of profitability of insurance products, called *asset shares* in ordinary insurance, an expense item is introduced for the use of the insurer's surplus needed to produce the business. As business matures, this initial paper loss is recovered along with any actual profit on the business.

The cost of surplus is usually introduced into the profit model as a percentage of the outstanding surplus drain at the beginning of the period. One method for setting the percentage is to estimate the cost that would be paid if surplus relief reinsurance were purchased. This is approximately 1% per quarter times the outstanding surplus drain at the beginning of the quarter. Another approach is for management to determine a reasonable return expected on invested surplus. An annual percentage of from 5% to 10% is common.

Many credit insurers buy surplus relief reinsurance, particularly on disability business. For these insurers, the cost of surplus drain is a real expense and should definitely be a part of any profitability analysis.

For example, consider a new block of credit life business with the following first quarter experience.

Premiums for the quarter:	$100,000
Claims for the quarter:	10,000
Commissions and premium taxes:	32,000
Mortality reserves end of quarter:	70,000
Claim reserves end of quarter:	5,000

Beginning of quarter reserves are zero, so the increase in reserves is $70,000 and the incurred claims are $15,000 (10,000 - 0 + 5,000).

The statutory income statement for the quarter on this business, ignoring investment income and general expenses, is:

Premium income	$100,000
Incurred claims	(15,000)
Increase in reserves	(70,000)
Commissions and premium taxes	(32,000)
Net income	(17,000)

This is surplus drain. The profitability analysis would have a cost of surplus in the second quarter. Given a 1% charge per quarter, the cost is:

$$.01 \times 17{,}000 = 170$$

To facilitate the evaluation of profitability, an insurer will develop pro forma profit models.

REINSURANCE TO CAPTIVES

Business reinsured to a captive must be analyzed separately. In the captive situation, the underwriting risk and profit are the property of the captive reinsurer to the extent of the percentage of risk assumed. One role of the direct writer is that of a service organization. On the business reinsured on a written basis, direct writer profits are the excess of the administration charge (retention) over the actual cost of processing the business. The direct writer may earn a little investment income on the cash flow. The direct writer may get to hold the premiums for thirty days, but it must also pay claims and await reimbursement. Business ceded on an earned basis generally produces the same investment income to the direct writer as if the business were not reinsured.

A direct writer with a significant volume of captive business has a more difficult job with expense allocation. Captive reinsurers are operated by producers with large volumes of business. The functional cost study must address the issue of allocated costs by size of account. Some of the individual lender variations must be considered for the expense allocation to be valid. Costs of the reinsurance accounting department must be considered. One approach is to consider captive reinsurance business as a separate line of business.

The cost of excess of loss reinsurance or other reinsurance arrangements must also be considered in a profitability analysis.

CREDIBILITY OF EXPERIENCE

Once net income is produced, decisions must be made based on the results. Is the experience a reliable measure of the true value of the block of business? The true experience will not be known until the business in force expires. Is the current experience an accurate portrait of what the final result will be? The answers to these questions are needed to determine the need and justification for rate deviations and to make decisions about the profitability of accounts.

A whole section of statistical theory is devoted to *credibility*. Credibility is the measure of confidence that current demonstrated experience is a true reflection of underlying claims distribution. Credibility theory is based on the theory of large numbers. The larger the sampling of experience, the more likely that the actual experience reflects the underlying claim distribution. If a coin is flipped six times, it's unlikely that the actual result will reflect the underlying distribution, but if the coin is flipped 6,000 times, the degree of confidence is very high. The objective is to get an optimal estimate of the underlying distribution, based on actual experience.

For credit insurance the question arises, how long do you wait before the measured results provide a basis for a good business decision? If an account is unprofitable after three months, should it be canceled? When is it time to take action? Credibility theory is helpful, but it has limited applicability to the real world without expertise and the time and ability to apply this complex statistical process. Few credit insurers have personnel with this expertise. Even most actuaries have limited knowledge about this field of statistics. In most cases, credit insurance business decisions are made by people without the availability of this expertise and are based on intuition or reliance on the few methods adopted in state regulations–methods which evolved based on available data and practical compromise rather than reliance solely on a theoretical framework.

Until recent years, credibility in credit insurance was measured by earned premium levels. The common benchmark was that experience was credible after $50,000 of premium was earned, but earned premium is usually a poor basis for determining credibility. While premium does relate to the amount of insurance in force (the exposure), the $50,000 standard produces uneven results. If one block is written at a 40¢/100/year rate and a second block at 60¢/100/year, the exposure associated with $50,000 of earned premium will be materially different. Also, applying the same standard to life and disability may not produce comparable levels of exposure. On the other hand, earned premium can be an excellent basis to measure credibility if premiums are converted to a standardized set of premium rates and the proper theory is applied.

The newer methods in practice measure credibility by the amount of exposure or the frequency of occurrence. For example, exposure for life insurance is often based on dollars-life-years exposed. A unit is one dollar of insurance in force, for a year, on one insured. With conversions and approximations, a value can be determined based on the average insurance in force during the year.

A widely used measure is based on *frequency of occurrence*; i.e., the number of claims incurred. For life insurance, each death claim is counted. For disability insurance, the number of initial disability payments is counted. The greater the number of actual claims, the more credible the experience.

The following credibility table was adopted by the NAIC for rate deviations in the 1979-80 Model Regulation. The derivation of the table began with a theoretical approach, but the final table was the result of practical and political compromises. There is no simple answer to be found. Credit insurers must select from the available approaches, however limited, and apply the results in the day-to-day business decisions.

CREDIBILITY TABLE					
Credit Life	Average Number of Life Years Credit and Accident and Health Plans Retroactive and Nonretroactive Waiting Periods			Incurred Claim Count	Credibility Factor
	7 DAY	14 DAY	30 DAY		
1	1	1	1	1	.00
1,800	95	141	209	9	.25
2,400	126	188	279	12	.30
3,000	158	234	349	15	.35
3,600	189	281	419	18	.40
4,600	242	359	535	23	.45
5,600	295	438	651	28	.50
6,600	347	516	767	33	.55
7,600	400	594	884	38	.60
9,600	505	750	1,116	48	.65
11,600	611	906	1,349	58	.70
14,600	768	1,141	1,698	73	.75
17,600	926	1,375	2,047	88	.80
20,600	1,084	1,609	2,395	103	.85
25,600	1,347	2,000	2,977	128	.90
30,600	1,611	2,391	3,558	153	.95
40,000	2,106	3,125	4,651	200	1.00

The above integral numbers represent the lower end of the bracket for each Z factor. The upper end is 1 less than the lower end for the next higher Z factor.

Fig. 6.3 Credibility table.

The following example demonstrates application of the credibility table. Although the actual loss ratio is 60%, the number of claims is not sufficient to consider the experience fully credible. When experience is less than fully credible, credibility theory dictates that a weighted average of actual and expected experience is the best estimate of the underlying experience.

A = actual observed loss ratio

= .60

E = expected loss ratio

= .50

Number of actual claims = 48

Z = credibility factor from the table

= .65

T = credible loss ratio

= Z x A + (1-Z) x E

= .65 x .60 + (1-.65) x .5

= .565

CHAPTER SEVEN

STATUTORY AND GAAP ACCOUNTING

Annually, every insurer is required to prepare a statutory financial statement, as of December 31, based on *Statutory Accounting Principles* (SAP). This statement is so named because the accounting principles which must be observed are embodied in the state statutes. These principles differ substantially from *Generally Accepted Accounting Principles* (GAAP) which are the basis of accounting of U.S. corporations other than life insurance companies. Stock life insurance companies usually prepare both statutory and GAAP financial statements. Mutual insurers usually prepare only statutory statements. This chapter provides a comprehensive discussion of these accounting principles as they affect the credit insurance industry. The general reader may not have a need for all the specific details provided here. If that is the case, sections of this chapter may be skipped.

The purposes of the two accounting systems are different. Statutory accounting is prepared for state regulators as a conservative test of the solvency of the insurer. Consequently, it focuses on the balance sheet–the pages showing the company's assets, liabilities, and net worth. GAAP is designed for the owners of the company. Since its purpose is to accurately measure net income for the accounting period, the focus is on the statement of net income. This goal reflects the desire to present financials which accurately portray the financial success or failure for the accounting period.

From the early days of insurance, insurers were required to publish their financial condition annually. In the non-regulated environment of the late 1800s, disclosure of the financial condition was considered sufficient regulation. In the 1890s, some insurance companies began to abuse this lack of close scrutiny by regulators. Non-financial abuses led to the Armstrong Investigation of 1905. Recommendations from that investigation included certain rules affecting the presentation of an insurer's financial condition. Many of the constraints imposed by statutory accounting today can be traced to the recommendations stemming from the Armstrong Investigation.

In both GAAP and SAP systems, the fundamental accounting equation applies:

$$\text{Assets} = \text{Liabilities} + \text{Net Worth}$$

The fundamentals of cash accounting apply to both GAAP and SAP. However, the difference between the two systems lies in the methods and assumptions used to value assets and liabilities. This difference has a direct impact on the income of an accounting period. GAAP values assets and liabilities using realistic assumptions, resulting in a realistic measure of income. SAP values assets and liabilities on a conservative basis, resulting in a conservative measure of income. Profits tend to be recognized in later accounting periods under SAP.

Neither system has an impact on ultimate profitability. When all is said and done, profit is the difference between income received and expenses paid. Owners of insurance companies do not want to wait until all policies expire to find out if the company is profitable. Corporations calculate earnings monthly, quarterly or annually, so accounting systems are designed to measure financial results for these accounting periods. Differences between GAAP and statutory accounting principles are timing differences. In the long run, GAAP profits equal SAP profits. An example may help clarify the concept of timing differences.

Suppose a life insurance company buys a small computer for $2,000, with a useful life of five years. One SAP principle is that expenses must be charged to earnings in the year the expense is incurred. In year one, the SAP income statement will reflect the $2,000 expense. GAAP recognizes that this computer has a useful life of five years. Therefore, it is appropriate to spread the expense against the income of the entire five years. A GAAP statement would charge earnings $400 a year in each of the five years, assuming the straight line method of depreciation; i.e., the cost is spread equally over the useful life of the asset. At the end of year one, an asset for equipment is established for $1,600. In year one, the assets (and the earnings) would be $1,600 higher under GAAP than SAP. At the end of four years, the cumulative GAAP earnings would be $400 higher than SAP. When the computer is fully depreciated, both statements contain a cumulative expense of $2,000. The expense was recognized earlier under SAP, so the earnings were lower in the first four years. In other words, use of SAP resulted in the deferral of the recognition of income.

GAAP attempts to realistically match the income of an accounting period with its associated expenses. This matching results in a realistic measure of income. GAAP fulfills the logical expectation of the purpose of an accounting system. Why does SAP exist? SAP is a measure of solvency. State regulators are not primarily concerned with whether the insurance company makes a profit. Indeed, prior to 1951, the statutory financials did not even contain a true statement of income. Instead, regulators are properly concerned that the company has the financial wherewithal to meet its long-term obligations to its policyholders. SAP places conservative valuations on assets and liabilities. By undervaluing an asset, net worth is decreased. By overvaluing liabilities, net worth is decreased. If an insurer has the minimum required level of net worth after these conservative valuations, the regulators and policyholders can feel secure that the insurer has the resources necessary to fulfill its contractual obligations. SAP attempts to calculate the net worth as if the company had to be liquidated on December 31.

What is the value of the computer if the company must be liquidated? Its value is certainly subjective. Statutory principles demand that assets may not be overvalued. One way to be sure that the asset is not overvalued is to assign no value to it. This results in charging income and net worth with the full expense in the year the expense is incurred.

GAAP values assets and liabilities on a *going concern* basis. GAAP recognizes that the company is not likely to need to sell the computer to raise cash. At the end of year one, the company has used only one-fifth of the value of the computer. An asset is established for the unamortized cost of the computer. The asset (cash) is decreased by $2,000, but an asset for equipment is established. At the end of year one, there would be an asset of $1,600, so net worth is decreased only $400 in year one.

DETAILS OF THE STATUTORY STATEMENT AFFECTING CREDIT INSURERS

All life insurance companies must prepare a statutory statement portraying their financial condition as of December 31 each year. State laws specify that the financial statement be prepared based on the form and principles decreed by the National Association of Insurance Commissioners (NAIC). This form has various names such as the *convention blank*, the *blue book* (from its traditional light blue cover), or simply the *statutory statement*. Annually, the Blanks Committee of the NAIC reviews the form for revision. While the general content has remained the same for thirty years, revisions have been made over the years.

Pages 1-15, as well as certain supplementary pages applicable to credit insurance of the 1985 NAIC blank follow this discussion. The scope of this discussion is limited to the aspects of statutory accounting uniquely applicable to credit insurance. The discussion assumes a basic knowledge of accounting and statutory principles.

The general format of the blank is that the financial condition is summarized on Pages 2-4 (Assets, Liabilities, and Summary of Operations). Exhibits numbered 1-14 support portions of the summary pages. Numerous Schedules (not reproduced) support the Exhibits or portray certain details not shown elsewhere. Scattered throughout the blank are informational pages (Page 1, Pages 14A and 14B, Page 15). Page numbers are standardized. Several pages are commonly referenced by their page number (Page 5, Page 6, Page 15).

Pages 2, 3, 4 and 4A apply to the total corporate financial position, and entries are prepared in the same manner for all lines of business. Exhibits 2, 3, and 4 detail investment income of the entire company. Exhibits 5 (General Expenses) and 6 (Taxes) also apply to total corporate results separated only by life, health, and investment sections. Exhibits 7 and 10 are rarely used in credit insurance. Exhibits 12, 13, and 14, which develop the admitted assets, apply to all corporate assets. The remaining Exhibits, Pages 5, 6, and 15, and Schedule H contain separate columns for credit life and disability insurance.

All columns relative to credit insurance reference a footnote "business not exceeding 120 months duration." They also contain the subtitle "group and individual." All credit business with original terms under 121 months is included in the credit insurance column regardless of whether the policy form is group or individual. If a policy has an original term in excess of 120 months, its financial details are to be excluded from the credit insurance columns. Such a policy must be classified in the appropriate column based on its policy form. Individual policy data goes in the ordinary column, and group policy data goes in the group column. This requirement causes considerable trouble for credit insurers, since the administrative systems have no other need for distinguishing by term. Some companies ignore the footnote and include all credit insurance in the credit columns.

Page 5 (Analysis of Operations by Lines of Business) separates the total company income and expenses by line of business. Formulas and procedures are adopted and applied to allocate each income and expense item by line of business. The same methods are used for credit insurance as for other lines. Page 6 (Analysis of Increase in Reserves) is calculated using formulas in the Instructions to the blank. The credit insurance formulas are straightforward. This page has little significance, since several items may require gross approximations.

EXHIBIT 1

Exhibit 1 (Premiums and Commissions) contains the first section where the unique aspects of credit insurance are noticeable. Most credit insurance is single premium, so entries are shown on line 10. One requirement of line 10 is that it (plus lines 6 and 16) must balance with the cash premiums in Exhibit 12. This assumes that there are no deferred and uncollected premiums on single premium business. This is logical, since a direct written single premium cannot be uncollected–the policy is not in force until the premium is paid. With only one premium, a credit insurance policy does not have deferred premiums. Therefore, a problem does not exist for direct business, but unfortunately, there may be an uncollected assumed or ceded premium.

A direct writer collects the premium from the insured in December and includes this amount in collected direct premiums. At the end of December, ceded premiums for the month are tabulated. A check is sent to the reinsurer in early January. For the direct writer, the amount is an uncollected ceded premium. Since line 10 does not permit accrual items for deferred and uncollected premiums, some companies show the uncollected amounts in the First Year or Renewal section. This produces unusual numbers in these sections, but line 20 (total incurred premium) is correct. For this reason, some companies code all credit premiums in the First Year or Renewal section. The assuming reinsurer has the same problem in recording the transaction.

There is an interrelationship of various lines within the statement, referred to as *cross-checks*. There are several hundred of these cross-checks. As stated above, cash premiums, lines 6 + 10 + 16, must equal the cash premiums shown in Exhibit 12. If reinsurance is involved, an alternative approach might be to develop a supplementary worksheet for line 10 providing for the uncollected ceded premiums; then line 10 would reflect incurred premiums instead of cash premiums. This is not advisable. State insurance departments often perform the cross-checks and write the company inquiring why a cross-check is violated. In this case, the insurer has a perfectly good explanation which would be acceptable. This might be worth the effort if one explanation would suffice, but a widely licensed company may receive the same inquiry from several states. In addition, the inquiry may become an annual ritual–state departments may ask the same question the following year. In general, it is better to find some way to record a transaction within the framework of the cross-check rather than to violate a cross-check.

A second problem is the classification of monthly outstanding balance premiums. They are not considered single premiums, so the single premium section is rarely used. Since insurers do not maintain the First Year/Renewal premium distinction for MOB business, one of these sections is generally selected and used for all MOB business.

EXHIBIT 8

Exhibit 8 (Life Reserves) contains the active life reserves which provide for the estimated future death claims on all policies in force on December 31. The entries are mortality reserves calculated by applying a mortality table and an assumed rate of interest to the in force policy parameters. Less than one-half of the state regulations specify a mortality table for credit insurance. The accepted standard is the 1958 Commissioners Extended Term table (1958 CET), or its equivalent–130% of the 1958 Commissioners Standard Ordinary table (1958 CSO). Other tables used by a few states are 100% of 1958 CSO or the

1960 Commissioners Standard Group table (1960 CSG). Reserves on the 1960 CSG table are about 88% of the 1958 CET reserves. The maximum interest rate permitted in calculating the reserves is generally 4.5%.

Some companies calculate reserves for all policies using the reserve basis required by their state of domicile. Others use the reserve basis specified by state regulations of the insured's state of residence. Regulations often do not address this point, so either approach is generally acceptable. The final test of acceptability is whether the reserves are accepted on the triennial examination.

The question occasionally arises whether life insurance reserves should be based on unearned premium reserves. Unearned premiums are used for measurement of profitability and for the reserves in GAAP statements. Tradition and taxes are the primary reasons that mortality reserves are used. All other lines of life insurance have reserves based on mortality reserves. Also, for an insurer to qualify as a life insurance company, more than 50% of its reserves must be life insurance reserves. To qualify as life insurance reserves for tax purposes, reserves must be calculated on a recognized mortality table and an assumed rate of interest.

Credit insurers typically have entries only in section A (Life Insurance). Occasionally, disability insurance is written as a rider to a life policy. Active life reserves for these riders would be entered in section E (Disability-Active Lives) rather than Exhibit 9, Part A. The claim reserves would be entered in section F (Disability-Disabled Lives) rather than Exhibit 9, Part B.

Statutory principles require a special reserve in section G (Miscellaneous Reserves) for "surrender values in excess of reserves otherwise required and carried in this schedule." Refunds on credit life policies are not considered surrender values; they are a return of premium. Some insurers do consider it necessary to carry a reserve if the unearned premiums for their business exceed the mortality reserves in section A. The relationship between mortality reserves and unearned premium reserves varies depending on the gross premiums charged by a particular insurer. In the event of a refund, the full unearned premium is paid to the insured. Insurers holding this extra reserve are taking the position that the full unearned premium amount would be payable if all policies terminated. This is a conservative approach. Few insurers hold the reserve, but those who do not are sometimes asked to defend their reasons for the omission.

First of all, it is unlikely that more than 30% of the business in force will be refunded prior to expiration. Holding the full unearned premium as a reserve assumes 100% of the policies will refund. This is redundant. Second, the mortality reserves contain a substantial margin of conservatism. Overall, 1958 CET reserves are about 50% above the current claim costs. Statutory accounting does require a large margin for conservatism. The 1958 CET margins are sufficient to meet statutory principles and provide for some excess to cover any deficiency on refunded policies. Third, commissions are charged in the year incurred. On refunds, the insurer usually receives a return commission on refunded policies. The net cash outlay on a refund is less than the full unearned premium. Finally, the reserve is not a deductible expense for tax purposes.

EXHIBITS 9 AND 11

Exhibit 9, Part A contains the active life reserves for disability policies. All credit disability reserves are gross unearned premium reserves and shown on line 1. There has been considerable debate over the basis of calculating these unearned premiums. State regulations in this area may be one of the few situations where statutory reserves are liberal.

Most states have laws which require gross pro rata unearned premium reserves on all accident and health policies. Pro rata in this context does not necessarily mean "in equal proportions"–the usual interpretation of pro rata. Rather, the law is requiring that the reserve be "proportionate" to the pattern of claim incurral. Most states interpret the pro rata requirement to be met for credit disability business if Rule of 78 unearned premiums are held. Only a few states still require pro rata (equal proportions) unearned premium reserves. A few other states have intermediate requirements, such as the mean of the Rule of 78 and pro rata, or the Single Premium Method.

To resolve the issue, the purpose of the reserve must be determined. If the purpose is simply to provide a reserve sufficient to meet future claim payments, the Rule of 78 is adequate in most cases. Remember that 20% to 40% of the premium goes for insurer expenses and producer compensation. These expenses have already been charged off at issue under statutory accounting. Future claims should be significantly less than the gross unearned premiums under either reserve basis. On the average, Rule of 78 unearned premiums are about 30% less than pro rata, but the relationship varies by the mix of business. The consensus "true" basis is about midway between the two bases, so Rule of 78 reserves are about 15% light. The expense element usually exceeds 15%, so the reserves generally are sufficient to mature claims. A further investigation of the adequacy of the Rule of 78 reserves should be undertaken on a block of business with a loss ratio of over 80% or on a closed block of business. Rule of 78 reserves tend to become inadequate as business runs off the books.

If the goal is to reflect the proper earning of premium, the Rule of 78 reserves will result in earning the premium too rapidly. In this case, one of the intermediate reserve bases should be held. While the proposition seems reasonable, it must be recognized that all expenses have been charged off, so statutory net income is already distorted. In summary, the Rule of 78 is acceptable for most business, but the margin for conservatism is slim by statutory standards. One of the intermediate reserve bases would fit better with the traditional statutory approach.

Disability claim reserves and claim liabilities are contained in Exhibit 9, Part B and Exhibit 11, Part 1. Although the total of these two sections is the overriding concern, the statutory statement makes a fine distinction between a reserve and a liability. Normally, the terms "reserve" and "liability" are used interchangeably. Here the statement distinguishes between an accrued or unaccrued amount. Consider an IBNR claim incurred on December 1. At December 31, the insured has accrued, or earned, one month of disability benefits. At December 31, this amount is considered a liability of the company, since the insured needs only to complete the claim form to qualify for the money. The claimant may remain disabled after December 31, so a provision must be made for these payments. These are reserves because the amount is an estimate of the unaccrued benefits; i.e., the insured has yet to earn the benefits.

Credit disability claim reserves are entered on line 1 of Exhibit 9, Part B (Present Value of Future Unaccrued Benefits). The term "present value" implies that the future payments would be discounted with interest back to December 31. Some credit insurers use an interest discount in calculating this reserve. Approximately 60% of the reserved benefits will be paid in the following year, and 30% in the succeeding year. About 10% will be paid more than two years after the accounting date. Introducing an interest discount in the calculation reduces the reserves about 5%-8%. Many insurers omit the interest discount and consider the omission as a margin for conservatism.

Exhibit 11, Part 1 displays the claim liabilities for both life and disability. The determination of these items is described in the Reserve chapter. Otherwise, Part 1 and Part 2 (incurred claims) follow the usual rules for all lines of business including credit insurance.

PAGE 15

Page 15 (Exhibit of Life Insurance) displays the number of policies or certificates in force, and the transactions for the year by line of business. Credit insurance follows the usual rules. The beginning and ending amounts in force are obtained from reserve valuation runs. An exact count is made for the transactions–issued during the year, deaths, expirations, and refunds. Refunds may be shown on line 14 (Surrender) or line 15 (Lapse) or as a write-in item on lines 19 or 20. For the amount of insurance in force, line 17 (Decreased(net)) is a balancing item. This represents the portion of the insurance which decreased on all of the decreasing credit life policies. No one attempts to calculate this amount directly by analyzing the thousands of policies in force during the year.

On monthly outstanding balance business, the insurer may not receive reports of the detail transactions except for deaths. The change in the in force for the year, excluding deaths, is entered on line 5 or line 17, whichever is appropriate. A few companies enter the in force at the end of the year on line 2 (Issued) for those new groups underwritten during the year.

SCHEDULE H

Following the Exhibits in the statutory statement are numerous Schedules. Only Schedule H has a separation of credit insurance data.

Schedule H (Accident and Health Exhibit) contains important information about credit disability experience. Part 1 (Analysis of Underwriting Operations) essentially provides more detail about the accident and health columns of Page 5. Only underwriting profit is shown. With the addition of investment income and federal income taxes, the totals must balance to Page 5. The items in Part 1 are net of reinsurance.

Presentation of premiums and claims differs from Page 5 and follows a GAAP presentation. Premiums earned are based on net written premium, less the increase in unearned premiums. Claims incurred are paid claims, plus the increase in the claim reserves and liabilities. The increase in Exhibit 9, Part A, line 1 reduces premium in Schedule H rather than showing up as an expense item for increase in reserves. Also, the increase in the claim reserves in Exhibit 9, Part B is added to claims rather than an increase in reserves. Other active life reserves (Exhibit 9, Part A, lines 2 through 4) are separated. These reserves are zero for credit disability insurance.

Each line is displayed in dollar amounts and as a percentage of line 2 (earned premium). This display is an easy reference to the loss and expense ratios of an insurer. The only problem is that the unearned premiums are based on the statutory unearned premiums, often the Rule of 78. Use of the Rule of 78 tends to understate the true loss ratio.

Part 2 (Reserves and Liabilities) and Part 4 (Reinsurance) simply display some of the detail behind the amounts shown in Part 1.

Part 3 (Test of Previous Year's Claim Reserves and Liabilities) is a significant test from a regulatory and operational standpoint. The section is a one-year test of the adequacy of the claim reserves and liabilities held on December 31 of the prior year. Importance is added to the test since the results are carried into Page 14B (Five-Year Historical Data).

The claim reserves and liabilities at the prior year-end were established to fund all future claim payments on any claim incurred prior to that date. One year later, the actual claim payments, plus the new estimate of remaining payments on prior year claims, is compared to the prior reserve established. The test is satisfied if the actual payments plus the new reserve are about equal to the prior claim reserve established. A negative result on line 3c is desirable, but a small positive result is acceptable.

To perform the test, a separation is made of the actual claim payments for the current year. Payments are tabulated by claims incurred prior to the current year and claims incurred during the current year. Next, the total claim reserves and liabilities at the end of the current year are separated. If the reserve applies to a claim incurred prior to the current year, it is included in line 2a. The remainder goes on line 2b. Line 3a represents the actual payments plus the estimate of the remaining payments on claims incurred prior to the current year. The goal is for this amount to be about equal to the reserve established for these claims at the prior year-end.

EXAMPLE OF SCHEDULE H CLAIM RESERVE TEST

Statement date: 12-31-86
Claim reserves and liabilities 12-31-85: $6,200

Claims paid in 1986

Claim Number	Date of Disability	Claim Payments in 1986	Estimate of Remaining Payments after 12-31-86
1	9-15-84	$ 600	-0-
2	6-20-85	1,200	$ 600
3	12-10-85	1,800	750
4	5-10-86	900	1,000
5	10-1-86	400	800
IBNR	before 1986	-0-	1,000
IBNR	1986	-0-	2,500
Total		$4,900	$6,650

"IBNR-before 1986" represents the estimate of the claim payments after 12-31-86 on claims which had a date of disability prior to 12-31-85, but still had not been reported on 12-31-86. "IBNR-1986" represents the estimate of the claim payments after 12-31-86 on claims which had a date of disability in 1986, but had not been reported on 12-31-86.

Claims paid in current year: 4,900

On claims incurred prior to current year = 600 + 1,200 + 1,800
= 3,600

On claims incurred during current year = 900 + 400
= 1,300

Claim reserve and liabilities 12-31-86: 6,650

On claims incurred prior to current year = 600 + 750 + 1,000
= 2,350

On claims incurred during current year = 1,000 + 800 + 2,500
= 4,300

Schedule H, Part 3

1. Claims paid during the year:

a. On claims incurred prior to current year	=	3,600
b. On claims incurred during current year	=	1,300

2. Claim reserves and liabilities, 12-31-86:

a. On claims incurred prior to current year	=	2,350
b. On claims incurred during current year	=	4,300

3. Test:

a. Line 1a and 2a	=	5,950
b. Claim reserves and liabilities, 12-31-85	=	6,200
c. Line a minus line b	=	(250)

This test is one measure of the quality of the method used to set claim reserves. Adequate claim reserves are critical to continued profitable operations in credit insurance. Inadequate reserves understate the loss experience of the business and can mislead the company in setting commissions and evaluating overall profitability.

Setting of claim reserves is not an exact science. Although an insurer may use valid procedures and reserving methods, the Part 3 test may produce positive results for some years. Over a number of years, an insurer should display more negative results than positive results. Several years of substantial positive results indicates a deficiency in the reserving methods used, and may indicate a large unrecognized liability which will come due in the future.

Insurers with reinsurance ceded have difficulty completing the test as it is designed. General practice is to perform the test as designed for direct business. The results are then applied on a percentage basis to the net retained business after reinsurance ceded. The problem arises because reinsurance is often quota share coinsurance. Captives and other reinsurers may change the coinsurance percentage during a year. This distorts the separation of paid claims and claim reserves relative to the reserves being tested. Distortions also arise because ceded claims are booked on the ledger in different months than the direct claims.

If an insurer realizes that prior reserves were inadequate, and strengthens reserves in the current year, the Schedule H test will still show a positive result, since the test is of the prior year's reserves. Paid claims are unaffected by the change, but the new estimate of the remaining claims will reflect the strengthening. Since action has been taken, a regulatory problem should not exist, but an explanation may be required.

From an operational standpoint, this test is the first measure of reserve adequacy. Although the statutory statement makes no requirement, claims should be tracked until completion.

LIFE AND ACCIDENT AND HEALTH COMPANIES–ASSOCIATION EDITION

Form 1

ANNUAL STATEMENT

For the Year Ended December 31, 1985

OF THE CONDITION AND AFFAIRS OF THE

____

NAIC Group Code __________ NAIC Company Code __________ Employer's ID Number __________

Organized under the Laws of the State of ______________________, made to the

INSURANCE DEPARTMENT OF THE STATE OF

PURSUANT TO THE LAWS THEREOF

Incorporated ______________________ Commenced Business ______________________

Home Office ______________________ (Street and Number), ______________________ (City or Town, State and Zip Code)

Mail Address ______________________ (Street and Number), ______________________ (City or Town, State and Zip Code)

Main Administrative Office ______________________ (Area Code) ______________________ (Telephone Number)

Contact Person and Phone Number ______________________

OFFICERS

President ______________________

Secretary ______________________

Treasurer ______________________

Actuary ______________________

Vice-Presidents ______________________

DIRECTORS OR TRUSTEES

State of ....
County of .... } SS

.... President, ... Secretary, ... Treasurer

of the ...., being duly sworn, each for himself deposes and says that they are the above described officers of the said insurer, and that on the thirty-first day of December last, all of the herein described assets were the absolute property of the said insurer, free and clear from any liens or claims thereon, except as herein stated, and that this annual statement, together with related exhibits, schedules and explanations therein contained, annexed or referred to are a full and true statement of all the assets and liabilities and of the condition and affairs of the said insurer as of the thirty-first day of December last, and of its income and deductions therefrom for the year ended on that date, according to the best of their information, knowledge and belief, respectively.

....
President

....
Secretary

....
Treasurer

....
Actuary

Subscribed and sworn to before me this

.... day of ...., 1986

....

2 ANNUAL STATEMENT FOR THE YEAR 1985 OF THE .... (Name) Form 1

ASSETS	1 Current Year	2 Previous Year
1. Bonds		
2. Stocks:		
2.1 Preferred stocks		
2.2 Common stocks		
3. Mortgage loans on real estate		
4. Real estate:		
4.1 Properties occupied by the company (less $ .... encumbrances)		
4.2 Properties acquired in satisfaction of debt (less $ .... encumbrances)		
4.3 Investment real estate (less $ .... encumbrances)		
5. Policy loans		
6. Premium notes, including $ .... for first year premiums		
7. Collateral loans		
8.1 Cash on hand and on deposit		
8.2 Short-term investments		
9.		
10. Other invested assets		
10A. Subtotals, cash and invested assets (Items 1 to 10)		
11. Reinsurance ceded:		
11.1 Amounts recoverable from reinsurers		
11.2 Commissions and expense allowances due		
11.3 Experience rating and other refunds due		
11.4		
12.		
13. Electronic data processing equipment		
14. Federal income tax recoverable		
15.		
16.		
17. Life insurance premiums and annuity considerations deferred and uncollected		
18. Accident and health premiums due and unpaid		
19. Investment income due and accrued		
20. Net adjustment in assets and liabilities due to foreign exchange rates		
21. Receivable from parent, subsidiaries and affiliates		
22.		
23.		
24.		
25.		
26. Subtotals (Items 10A to 25)		
27A. From Separate Accounts Statement		
27B. From Variable Life Insurance Separate Accounts Statement		
28. Totals (Items 26 to 27B)		

NOTE: The items on this page to agree with Exhibit 13, Col. 4

The Notes to Financial Statements are an integral part of this statement.

	LIABILITIES, SURPLUS AND OTHER FUNDS	1 Current Year	2 Previous Year
1.	Aggregate reserve for life policies and contracts $ .... (Exh. 8, Line H) less $ .... included in Item 7.3		
2.	Aggregate reserve for accident and health policies (Exhibit 9, Line C, Col. 1)		
3.	Supplementary contracts without life contingencies (Exhibit 10, Line 7, Col. 5)		
4.	Policy and contract claims:		
	4.1 Life (Exhibit 11, Part 1, Line 4d, Column 1 less sum of Columns 9, 10 and 11)		
	4.2 Accident and health (Exhibit 11, Part 1, Line 4d, sum of Columns 9, 10 and 11)		
5.	Policyholders' dividend and coupon° accumulations (Exhibit 10, Line 7, Col. 6 plus Col. 7)		
6.	Policyholders' dividends $ .... and coupons $ .... due and unpaid (Exhibit 7 Line 10)		
7.	Provision for policyholders' dividends and coupons payable in following calendar year — estimated amounts:		
	7.1 Dividends apportioned for payment to ...., 19		
	7.2 Dividends not yet apportioned		
	7.3 Coupons and similar benefits		
8.	Amount provisionally held for deferred dividend policies not included in Item 7		
9.	Premiums and annuity considerations received in advance less $ .... discount; including $ .... accident and health premiums (Exhibit 1, Part 1, Col. 1, sum of Lines 4 and 14)		
10.	Liability for premium and other deposit funds		
11.	Policy and contract liabilities not included elsewhere:		
	11.1 Surrender values on cancelled policies		
	11.2 Provision for experience rating refunds		
	11.3 Other amounts payable on reinsurance assumed		
	11.4		
12.			
13.	Commissions to agents due or accrued — life and annuity $ .... accident and health $		
13A.	Commissions and expense allowances payable on reinsurance assumed		
14.	General expenses due or accrued (Exhibit 5, Line 12, Col. 4)		
14A.	Transfers to Separate Accounts due or accrued, excluding Variable Life Insurance (net)		
14B.	Transfers to Variable Life Insurance Separate Accounts due or accrued (net)		
15.	Taxes, licenses and fees due or accrued, excluding federal income taxes (Exhibit 6, Line 9, Col. 4)		
15A.	Federal income taxes due or accrued, including $ .... on capital gains (excluding deferred taxes)		
16.	"Cost of collection" on premiums and annuity considerations deferred and uncollected in excess of total loading thereon		
17.	Unearned investment income (Exhibit 3, Line 10, Col. 2)		
18.	Amounts withheld or retained by company as agent or trustee		
19.	Amounts held for agents' account, including $ .... agents' credit balances		
20.	Remittances and items not allocated		
21.	Net adjustment in assets and liabilities due to foreign exchange rates		
22.	Liability for benefits for employees and agents if not included above		
23.	Borrowed money $ .... and interest thereon $		
24.	Dividends to stockholders declared and unpaid		
25.	Miscellaneous liabilities (give items and amounts):		
	25.1 Mandatory securities valuation reserve (Page 29A, final Item)		
	25.2 Reinsurance in unauthorized companies		
	25.3 Funds held under reinsurance treaties with unauthorized reinsurers		
	25.4 Payable to parent, subsidiaries and affiliates		
	25.5 Drafts outstanding		
	25.6		
	25.7		
	25.8		
	25.9		
25A	From Separate Accounts Statement		
25B.	From Variable Life Insurance Separate Accounts Statement		
26.	Total Liabilities (Items 1 to 25B)		
27A.	Common capital stock		
27B.	Preferred capital stock		
27C.	...		
28.	Gross paid in and contributed surplus (Page 3, Item 28, Col. 2 plus Page 4, Item 46a, Col. 1)		
29A.	Special surplus funds:		
	(a)		
	(b)		
	(c)		
29B.	Unassigned funds (surplus)		
29C.	Less treasury stock, at cost:		
	(1) .... shares common (value included in Item 27A $ ....)		
	(2) .... shares preferred (value included in Item 27B $ ....)		
29D.	Surplus (total Items 27 + 28 + 29A + 29B − 29C)		
30.	Totals of Items 27A, 27B and 29D (Page 4, Item 50)		
31.	Totals of Items 26 and 30 (Page 2, Item 28)		

° Includes coupons, guaranteed annual pure endowments and similar benefits.

SUMMARY OF OPERATIONS (Excluding Capital Gains and Losses)	1 Current Year	2 Previous Year
1. Premiums and annuity considerations (Exhibit 1, Part 1, Line 20d, Col. 1)		
1A. Annuity and other fund deposits		
2. Considerations for supplementary contracts with life contingencies (Exhibit 12, Line 3)		
3. Considerations for supplementary contracts without life contingencies and dividend accumulations (Exhibit 12, Lines 4 and 5)		
3A. Coupons left to accumulate at interest (Exhibit 12, Line 5A)		
4. Net investment income (includes $ .... equity in undistributed income or loss of subsidiaries) (Exhibit 2, Line 7)		
5. Commissions and expense allowances on reinsurance ceded (Exhibit 1, Part 2, Line 26a, Col. 1)		
5A. Reserve adjustments on reinsurance ceded (Exhibit 12, Line 10A)		
6.		
7. Totals (Items 1 to 6)		
8. Death benefits		
9. Matured endowments (excluding guaranteed annual pure endowments)		
10. Annuity benefits (Exhibit 11, Part 2, Line 6d, Cols. 4+8)		
11. Disability benefits and benefits under accident and health policies		
11A. Coupons, guaranteed annual pure endowments and similar benefits (Exhibit 7, Line 15, Cols. 3 + 4)		
12. Surrender benefits		
13. Group conversions		
14. Interest on policy or contract funds		
15. Payments on supplementary contracts with life contingencies (Exhibit 12, Line 22.1)		
16. Payments on supplementary contracts without life contingencies and of dividend accumulations (Exhibit 12, Lines 22.2 + 23)		
16A. Accumulated coupon payments (Exhibit 12, Line 23A)		
17. Increase in aggregate reserves for life and accident and health policies and contracts		
18. Increase in reserve for supplementary contracts without life contingencies and for dividend and coupon accumulations		
19.		
20. Totals (Items 8 to 19)		
21. Commissions on premiums and annuity considerations (direct business only) (Exhibit 1, Part 2, Line 30, Col. 1)		
21A. Commissions and expense allowances on reinsurance assumed (Exhibit 1, Part 2, Line 26b, Col. 1)		
22. General insurance expenses (Exhibit 5, Line 10, Cols. 1 + 2)		
23. Insurance taxes, licenses and fees, excluding federal income taxes (Exhibit 6, Line 7, Cols. 1 and 2)		
24. Increase in loading on and cost of collection in excess of loading on deferred and uncollected premiums		
24A. Net transfers to (+) or from (−) Separate Accounts (excluding Variable Life Insurance)		
24B. Net transfers to (+) or from (−) Variable Life Insurance Separate Accounts		
25.		
26. Totals (Items 20 to 25)		
27. Net gain from operations before dividends to policyholders and federal income taxes (Item 7 minus Item 26)		
28. Dividends to policyholders (Exhibit 7, Line 15, Cols. 1 and 2)		
29. Net gain from operations after dividends to policyholders and before federal income taxes (Item 27 minus Item 28)		
30. Federal income taxes incurred (excluding tax on capital gains)		
31. Net gain from operations after dividends to policyholders and federal income taxes (excluding tax on capital gains) (Item 29 minus Item 30)		
CAPITAL AND SURPLUS ACCOUNT		
32. Capital and surplus, December 31, previous year (Page 3, Item 30, Col. 2)		
33. Net gain (Item 31)		
34. Net capital gains (Exhibit 4, Line 10.2)		
35. Change in non-admitted assets and related items (Exhibit 14, Item 13, Col. 3)		
36. Change in liability for reinsurance in unauthorized companies, increase (−) or decrease (+) (Page 3, Item 25.2, Col. 1 minus 2)		
37. Change in reserve on account of change in valuation basis, increase (−) or decrease (+) (Exh. 8A, Line 7, Col. 4)		
38. Change in mandatory securities valuation reserve, increase (−) or decrease (+) (Page 3, Item 25.1, Col. 1 minus 2)		
39.		
40.		
41. Change in treasury stock, increase (−) or decrease (+) (Page 3, Items 29C (1) & (2) Col. 1 minus 2)		
42.		
43. Change in surplus in Separate Accounts Statement		
44. Change in surplus in Variable Life Insurance Separate Accounts Statement		
45. Capital changes:		
(a) Paid in		
(b) Transferred from surplus (Stock Dividend)		
(c) Transferred to surplus (Exhibit 12, Line 29)		
46. Surplus adjustments:		
(a) Paid in		
(b) Transferred to capital (Stock Dividend) (Exhibit 12, Line 30, inside amount for stock $)		
(c) Transferred from capital (Exhibit 12, Line 29)		
47. Dividends to stockholders		
48.		
49. Net change in capital and surplus for the year (Items 33 through 48)		
50. Capital and surplus, December 31, current year (Items 32 + 49) (Page 3 Item 30)		

NOTE: Items 1 to 31 to agree with Page 5, Col. 1, Items 1 to 31.

Form 1 **ANNUAL STATEMENT FOR THE YEAR 1985 OF THE** 4A
(Name)

CASH FLOW	1 Current Year	2 Previous Year*
1. Premiums and annuity considerations		
2. Annuity and other fund deposits		
3. Other premiums, considerations and deposits		
4. Allowances and reserve adjustments received on reinsurance ceded		
5. Investment income received (excluding realized gains/losses and net of investment expenses)		
6. Other income received		
7. Total (Items 1 to 6)		
8. Life and accident and health claims paid		
9. Surrender benefits paid		
10. Other benefits to policyholders paid		
11. Total (Items 8 to 10)		
12. Commissions, other expenses and taxes paid (excluding FIT)		
13. Net transfers to (+) or from (−) Separate Accounts (operational items only)		
14. Total (Items 12 to 13)		
15. Dividends to policyholders paid		
16. Federal income taxes paid (excluding tax on capital gains)		
17. Net increase (+) or decrease (−) in policy loans and premium notes		
18. Other operating expenses paid		
19. Total (Items 15 to 18)		
20. Net cash from operations (Item 7 minus Item 11 minus Item 14 minus Item 19)		
21. Proceeds from investments sold, matured or repaid:		
21.1 Bonds		
21.2 Stocks		
21.3 Mortgage loans		
21.4 Real estate		
21.5 Collateral loans		
21.6 Other invested assets		
21.7 Net gains (+) or losses (−) on cash and short-term investments		
21.8 Miscellaneous proceeds		
21.9 Total investment proceeds (Items 21.1 to 21.8)		
22. Tax on capital gains		
23. Total (Item 21.9 minus Item 22)		
24. Other cash provided:		
24.1 Capital and surplus paid in		
24.2 Borrowed money $ .... less amounts repaid $		
24.3 Other sources		
24.4 Total other cash provided (Items 24.1 to 24.3)		
25. Total (Item 20 plus Item 23 plus Item 24.4)		
26. Cost of investments acquired (long-term only):		
26.1 Bonds		
26.2 Stocks		
26.3 Mortgage loans		
26.4 Real estate		
26.5 Collateral loans		
26.6 Other invested assets		
26.7 Miscellaneous applications		
26.8 Total investments acquired (Items 26.1 to 26.7)		
27. Other cash applied:		
27.1 Dividends to stockholders paid		
27.2 Other applications (net)		
27.3 Total other cash applied (Items 27.1 and 27.2)		
28. Total (Items 26.8 and 27.3)		
29. Net change in cash and short-term investments (Item 25 minus Item 28)		
RECONCILIATION		
30. Cash and short-term investments:		
30.1 Beginning of year		
30.2 End of year (Item 29 plus Item 30.1)		

*Optional for 1985

Form 1

ANNUAL STATEMENT FOR THE YEAR 1985 OF THE

(Name)

ANALYSIS OF OPERATIONS BY LINES OF BUSINESS (Gain and Loss Exhibit) (Excluding Capital Gains and Losses)

	1	2	Ordinary			6	Group		Accident and Health			
	Total	Industrial Life	3 Life Insurance	4 Individual Annuities	5 Supplementary Contracts	Credit Life [a] (Group and Individual)	7 Life Insurance†	8 Annuities	9 Group	10 Credit [a] (Group and Individual)	11 Other	
1. Premiums and annuity considerations					X X X							1.
1A. Annuity and other fund deposits					X X X							1A.
2. Considerations for supplementary contracts with life contingencies			X X X	X X X					X X X	X X X	X X X	2.
3. Considerations for supplementary contracts without life contingencies and dividend accumulations												3.
3A. Coupons left to accumulate at interest												3A.
4. Net investment income												4.
5. Commissions and expense allowances on reinsurance ceded												5.
5A. Reserve adjustments on reinsurance ceded												5A.
6.												6.
7. Totals (Items 1 to 6)												7.
8. Death benefits				X X X				X X X	X X X	X X X	X X X	8.
9. Matured endowments (excluding guaranteed annual pure endowments)				X X X				X X X	X X X	X X X	X X X	9.
10. Annuity benefits			X X X			X X X	X X X		X X X	X X X	X X X	10.
11. Disability benefits and benefits under accident and health policies												11.
11A. Coupons, guaranteed annual pure endowments and similar benefits												11A.
12. Surrender benefits				X X X				X X X	X X X	X X X	X X X	12.
13. Group conversions				X X X				X X X				13.
13A. Transfers on account of group package policies and contracts	X X X	X X X	X X X	X X X	X X X						X X X	13A.
14. Interest on policy or contract funds												14.
15. Payments on supplementary contracts with life contingencies			X X X	X X X					X X X	X X X	X X X	15.
16. Payments on supplementary contracts without life contingencies and of dividend accumulations												16.
16A. Accumulated coupon payments												16A.
17. Increase in aggregate reserves for life and accident and health policies and contracts												17.
18. Increase in reserve for supplementary contracts without life contingencies and for dividend and coupon accumulations												18.
19.												19.
20. Totals (Items 8 to 19)												20.
21. Commissions on premiums and annuity considerations (direct business only)												21.
21A. Commissions and expense allowances on reinsurance assumed												21A.
22. General insurance expenses												22.
23. Insurance taxes, licenses and fees, excluding federal income taxes												23.
24. Increase in loading on and cost of collection in excess of loading on deferred and uncollected premiums												24.
24A. Net transfers to (+) or from (−) Separate Accounts (excluding Variable Life Insurance)												24A.
24B. Net transfers to (+) or from (−) Variable Life Insurance Separate Accounts												24B.
25.												25.
26. Totals (Items 20 to 25)												26.
27. Net gain from operations before dividends to policyholders and federal income taxes (Item 7 minus Item 26)												27.
28. Dividends to policyholders												28.
29. Net gain from operations after dividends to policyholders and before federal income taxes (Item 27 minus Item 28)												29.
30. Federal income taxes incurred (excluding tax on capital gains)												30.
31. Net gain from operations after dividends to policyholders and federal income taxes (excluding tax on capital gains) (Item 29 minus Item 30).												31.

Form 1

ANNUAL STATEMENT FOR THE YEAR 1985 OF THE .... (Name)

ANALYSIS OF INCREASE IN RESERVES DURING THE YEAR

(Gain and Loss Exhibit)

	1 Total	2 Industrial Life	Ordinary			6 Credit Life[a] (Group and Individual)	Group		
			3 Life Insurance	4 Individual Annuities	5 Supplementary Contracts		7 Life Insurance	8 Annuities	
1. Reserve Dec. 31 of previous year									1
2. Tabular net premiums or considerations									2
3. Considerations for supplementary contracts without life contingencies and dividend accumulations									3
4. Present value of disability claims incurred					X X X				4
5. Tabular interest									5
6. Tabular less actual reserve released		X X X							6
7. Increase in reserve on account of change in valuation basis									7
8. Other increases (net)									8
9. Totals (Items 1 to 8)									9
10. Tabular cost					X X X				10
11. Reserves released by death				X X X	X X X			X X X	11
12. Reserves released by other terminations (net)									12
13. Annuity, supplementary contract, disability and accumulated dividend payments									13
13A. Net transfers to (+) or from (−) Separate Accounts (excluding Variable Life Insurance)									13A
13B. Net transfers to (+) or from (−) Variable Life Insurance Separate Accounts									13B
14. Total deductions (Items 10 to 13B)									14
15. Reserve Dec. 31 of current year									15

[a] Business not exceeding 120 months duration.

EXHIBIT 1—PART 1—PREMIUMS AND ANNUITY CONSIDERATIONS

	1 Total	2 Industrial Life	Ordinary 3 Life Insurance	Ordinary 4 Individual Annuities	5 Credit Life [a] (Group and Individual)	Group 6 Life Insurance	Group 7 Annuities	Accident and Health 8 Group	Accident and Health 9 Credit [a] (Group and Individual)	Accident and Health 10 Other	
FIRST YEAR (other than single)											
Current Year: 1. Uncollected											1
2. Deferred											2
3. Deferred & uncollected:											3
a. Direct											a.
b. Reinsurance assumed											b.
c. Reinsurance ceded											c.
d. Net (Line 1 + Line 2)											d.
4. Advance											4
5. Line 3d – Line 4											5
6. Collected during year:											6.
a. Direct											a.
b. Reinsurance assumed											b.
c. Reinsurance ceded											c.
d. Net											d
7. Line 5 + Line 6d											7
8. Previous year (uncollected + deferred – advance)											8
9. First year premiums and considerations:											9
a. Direct											a
b. Reinsurance assumed											b
c. Reinsurance ceded											c
d. Net (Line 7 – Line 8)											d
SINGLE											
10. Single premiums and considerations:											10
a. Direct											a
b. Reinsurance assumed											b
c. Reinsurance ceded											c
d. Net											d
RENEWAL											
Current Year: 11. Uncollected											11
12. Deferred											12
13. Deferred & uncollected:											13
a. Direct											a
b. Reinsurance assumed											b
c. Reinsurance ceded											c
d. Net (Line 11 + Line 12)											d
14. Advance											14
15. Line 13d – Line 14											15.
16. Collected during year:											16.
a. Direct											a.
b. Reinsurance assumed											b.
c. Reinsurance ceded											c.
d. Net											d.
17. Line 15 + Line 16d											17.
18. Previous year (uncollected + deferred – advance)											18
19. Renewal premiums and considerations:											19
a. Direct											a
b. Reinsurance assumed											b
c. Reinsurance ceded											c
d. Net (Line 17 – Line 18)											d
TOTAL											
20. Total premiums and annuity considerations:											20
a. Direct											a
b. Reinsurance assumed											b
c. Reinsurance ceded											c
d. Net (Lines 9d + 10d + 19d)											d

[a] Business not exceeding 120 months duration.

EXHIBIT 1—PART 2—DIVIDENDS AND COUPONS* APPLIED, REINSURANCE COMMISSIONS AND EXPENSE ALLOWANCES AND COMMISSIONS INCURRED (direct business only)

	1 Total	2 Industrial Life	Ordinary		5 Credit Life[a] (Group and Individual)	Group		Accident and Health			
			3 Life Insurance	4 Individual Annuities		6 Life Insurance	7 Annuities	8 Group	9 Credit[a] (Group and Individual)	10 Other	
DIVIDENDS AND COUPONS* APPLIED (included in Part 1)											
21. To pay renewal premiums (Exhibit 7, Line 1)											21.
22. All other (Exhibit 7, Lines 2, 3 & 4)											22.
REINSURANCE COMMISSIONS AND EXPENSE ALLOWANCES INCURRED											
23. First year (other than single):											23.
a. Reinsurance ceded											a.
b. Reinsurance assumed											b.
c. Net ceded less assumed											c.
24. Single:											24.
a. Reinsurance ceded											a.
b. Reinsurance assumed											b.
c. Net ceded less assumed											c.
25. Renewal											25.
a. Reinsurance ceded											a.
b. Reinsurance assumed											b.
c. Net ceded less assumed											c.
26. Totals:											26.
a. Reinsurance ceded (Page 5, Item 5)											a.
b. Reinsurance assumed (Page 5, Item 21A)											b.
c. Net ceded less assumed											c.
COMMISSIONS INCURRED (direct business only)											
27. First year (other than single)											27.
28. Single											28.
29. Renewal											29.
30. Totals (to agree with Page 5, Item 21)											30.

[a] Business not exceeding 120 months duration.
*Includes coupons, guaranteed annual pure endowments and similar benefits.

8 ANNUAL STATEMENT FOR THE YEAR 1985 OF THE .... (Name) Form

EXHIBIT 2—NET INVESTMENT INCOME

1. Gross investment income (Exhibit 3, Line 10, Col. 7)	
2. Investment expenses (Exhibit 5, Line 10, Col. 3)	
3. Investment taxes, licenses and fees, excluding federal income taxes (Exhibit 6, Line 7, Col. 3)	
4. Depreciation on real estate and other invested assets	
5.	
6. Total (Lines 2 through 5)	
7. Net Investment Income—Line 1 less Line 6 (to Page 4, Item 4)	
8. Ratio of net investment income to mean assets (see instructions)	

†Includes $ .... investment expenses and $ .... investment taxes, licenses and fees, excluding federal income taxes, attributable to Separate Acc

EXHIBIT 3—GROSS INVESTMENT INCOME

	1 Collected During Year	Current Year 2 Unearned	 3 Due	 4 Accrued	 5 Non-Admitted	6 Previous Year 3 + 4 − 2 − 5	7 Earned Du 1 − 2 + 3 +
1. U.S. government bonds	*						
1.1 Bonds exempt from U.S. tax	*						
1.2 Other bonds (unaffiliated)	*						
1.3 Bonds of affiliates	*						
2.1 Preferred stocks (unaffiliated)	‡						
2.11 Preferred stocks of affiliates	‡						
2.2 Common stocks (unaffiliated)							
2.21 Common stocks of affiliates							
3. Mortgage loans	**						
4. Real estate	§						
5. Premium notes, policy loans and liens							
6. Collateral loans							
7.1 Cash on hand and on deposit							
7.2 Short-term investments	†						
8. Other invested assets							
9.							
9.1 Financial options and futures							
10. Totals							

*Includes $ .... accrual of discount less $ .... amortization of premium and less $ .... paid for accrued interest on purchases.

†Includes $ .... accrual of discount less $ .... amortization of premium and less $ .... paid for accrued interest or

‡Excludes $ .... paid for accrued dividends on purchases.

**Includes $ .... accrual of discount less $ .... amortization of premium and less $ .... paid for accrued interest on purchases.

§Includes $ .... for company's occupancy of its own buildings; and excludes $ .... interest on encumbrances.

*EXHIBIT 4—CAPITAL GAINS AND LOSSES ON INVESTMENTS

	1 Increase in Book Value	2 Profit on Sale or Maturity	3 Decrease in Book Value	4 Loss on Sale or Maturity	5 Net Gain (+) or Loss (−) From Change in Difference Between Book and Admitted Values	6 Net Gains (+) or 1 + 2 − 3 −
1. U.S. government bonds						
1.1 Bonds exempt from U.S. tax						
1.2 Other bonds (unaffiliated)						
1.3 Bonds of affiliates						
2.1 Preferred stocks (unaffiliated)						
2.11 Preferred stocks of affiliates						
2.2 Common stocks (unaffiliated)						
2.21 Common stocks of affiliates						
3. Mortgage loans						
4. Real estate			**			
5. Premium notes, policy loans and liens						
6. Collateral loans						
7.1 Cash on hand and on deposit						
7.2 Short-term investments						
8. Other invested assets			**			
9. Foreign exchange	X X X	X X X	X X X	X X X		
9.1 Financial options and futures						
9.2						
10. Totals						
10.1 Less federal income taxes incurred on capital gains						
10.2 Balance to Surplus Account, Page 4, Item 34						

Distribution of Line 10.2, Col. 6. (Attach statement or memorandum explaining basis of division.)

11. Net realized capital gains (+) or losses (−) on assets disposed of during the year $ .... less $ .... reflected in previous years' statements and less $ .... federal income tax incurred on capital gains

12. Net unrealized capital gains (+) or losses (−) of the year

*Adjustments due to amortization to be reported in Exhibit 3.

**Excluding $ .... depreciation on real estate and $ .... depreciation on other invested assets included in Exhibit 2, Line 4.

EXHIBIT 5—GENERAL EXPENSES

	Insurance		3 Investment	4 Total
	1 Life	2 Accident and Health		
1. Rent				
2. Salaries and wages				
3.11 *Contributions for benefit plans for employees				
3.12 *Contributions for benefit plans for agents				
3.21 Payments to employees under non-funded benefit programs				
3.22 Payments to agents under non-funded benefit programs				
3.31 Other employee welfare				
3.32 Other agent welfare				
3.4				
4.1 Legal fees and expenses				
4.2 Medical examination fees				
4.3 Inspection report fees				
4.4 Fees of public accountants and consulting actuaries				
4.5 Expense of investigation and settlement of policy claims				
4.6				
5.1 Traveling expenses				
5.2 Advertising				
5.3 Postage, express, telegraph and telephone				
5.4 Printing and stationery				
5.5 Cost or depreciation of furniture and equipment				
5.6 Rental of equipment				
5.7				
6.1 Books and periodicals				
6.2 Bureau and association dues				
6.3 Insurance, except on real estate				
6.4 Miscellaneous losses				
6.5 Collection and bank service charges				
6.6 Sundry general expenses				
6.7 Group service and administration fees				
6.8				
7.1 Agency expense allowance				
7.2 Agents' balances charged off (less $ .... recovered)				
7.3 Agency conferences other than local meetings				
8.1				
8.2				
9.1 Real estate expenses				
9.2 Investment expenses not included elsewhere				
9.3				
10. General Expenses Incurred Reconciliation with Exhibit 12	(To Page 4, Item 22)		(To Exhibit 2, Line 2)	
11. General expenses unpaid December 31, previous year				
12. General expenses unpaid December 31, current year				
13. General expenses paid during year (10 + 11 − 12)	XXX	XXX	XXX	(To Exhibit 12, Line 27)

ORDINARY LIFE INSURANCE AND INDIVIDUAL ANNUITY BUSINESS ONLY

A. Compensation to agents on a plan other than commissions, included in Col. 1: First year $ .... Renewal $ ....
B. Agency supervision, except home office, included in Col. 1: Line 2 $ .... Line 5.1 $ .... Line ..... $ ....
C. Branch office expenses other than those in A and B included in Col. 1: Line 1 $ .... Line 2 $ .... All other lines $ ....

*These items include $ .... on account of prior service.

EXHIBIT 6—TAXES, LICENSES AND FEES (EXCLUDING FEDERAL INCOME TAXES)

	Insurance		3 Investment	4 Total
	1 Life	2 Accident and Health		
1. Real estate taxes				
2. State insurance department licenses and fees				
3. State taxes on premiums				
4. Other state taxes, incl. $ .... for employee benefits				
5. U.S. Social Security taxes				
6. All other taxes				
7. Taxes, Licenses and Fees Incurred Reconciliation with Exhibit 12	(To Page 4, Item 23)		(To Exhibit 2, Line 3)	
8. Taxes, licenses and fees unpaid December 31, previous year				
9. Taxes, licenses and fees unpaid December 31, current year				
10. Taxes, licenses and fees paid during year (7 + 8 − 9)	XXX	XXX	XXX	(To Exhibit 12, Line 28.1)

NOTE: Canadian and other foreign taxes are included appropriately in Lines 1, 2, 3, 4 and 6.

EXHIBIT 7—DIVIDENDS AND COUPONS* TO POLICYHOLDERS

	Dividends		Coupons*	
	1 Life	2 Accident and Health	3 Life	4 Accident and Health
1. Applied to pay renewal premiums				
2. Applied to shorten the endowment or premium-paying period				
3. Applied to provide paid-up additions				
4. Applied to provide paid-up annuities				
5. Total Lines 1-4				
6. Paid in cash				
7. Left on deposit with the company				
8.				
9. Total Lines 5-8				
10. Amount due and unpaid (Item 6, Page 3)				
11. Provision for annual dividend and coupon* policies (Item 7, Page 3, in part)				
11A. Terminal dividends (Item 7, Page 3, in part)				
12. Provision for deferred dividend policies (Item 7, Page 3, in part)				
12A. Amount provisionally held for deferred dividend policies not included in line 12 (Item 8, Page 3)				
13. Total Lines 10-12A				
14. Line 13 of previous year				
15. Total Dividends and Coupons* to Policyholders (Lines 9 + 13 − 14)	(To Page 4, Item 28)		(To Page 4, Item 11A)	

*Includes coupons, guaranteed annual pure endowments and similar benefits.

10 **ANNUAL STATEMENT FOR THE YEAR 1985 OF THE** .... (Name) **Form 1**

EXHIBIT 8—AGGREGATE RESERVE FOR LIFE POLICIES AND CONTRACTS

1 Valuation Standard	2 Total	3 Industrial	4 Ordinary	5 Credit [a] (Group and Individual)	6 Group
A. LIFE INSURANCE:					
1.					
2.					
3.					
4.					
5.					
6.					
7.					
8.					
9.					
10.					
11.					
12.					
13.					
14.					
15.					
16.					
17.					
18.					
19.					
20.					
21.					
22.					
23.					
24.					
25.					
26.					
27.					
28.					
29. Totals (Gross)					
30. Reinsurance ceded					
31. Totals (Net)					
B. ANNUITIES (excluding supplementary contracts with life contingencies):					
1.		X X X		X X X	
2.		X X X		X X X	
3.		X X X		X X X	
4.		X X X		X X X	
5.		X X X		X X X	
6.		X X X		X X X	
7.		X X X		X X X	
8.		X X X		X X X	
9.		X X X		X X X	
10.		X X X		X X X	
11.		X X X		X X X	
12.		X X X		X X X	
13.		X X X		X X X	
14.		X X X		X X X	
15.		X X X		X X X	
16.		X X X		X X X	
17. Totals (Gross)		X X X		X X X	
18. Reinsurance ceded		X X X		X X X	
19. Totals (Net)		X X X		X X X	
C. SUPPLEMENTARY CONTRACTS WITH LIFE CONTINGENCIES:					
1.					
2.					
3.					
4.					
5. Totals (Gross)					
6. Reinsurance ceded					
7. Totals (Net)					
D. ACCIDENTAL DEATH BENEFITS:					
1.					
2.					
3.					
4.					
5. Totals (Gross)					
6. Reinsurance ceded					
7. Totals (Net)					
E. DISABILITY—ACTIVE LIVES:					
1.					
2.					
3.					
4.					
5.					
6.					
7. Totals (Gross)					
8. Reinsurance ceded					
9. Totals (Net)					
F. DISABILITY—DISABLED LIVES:					
1.					
2.					
3.					
4.					
5.					
6.					
7. Totals (Gross)					
8. Reinsurance ceded					
9. Totals (Net)					

[a] Business not exceeding 120 months duration.

EXHIBIT 8—AGGREGATE RESERVE FOR LIFE POLICIES AND CONTRACTS (Continued)

1 Valuation Standard	2 Total	3 Industrial	4 Ordinary	5 Credit[a] (Group and Individual)	6 Group
scellaneous Reserves:					
. For excess of valuation net premiums over corresponding gross premiums on respective policies, computed according to the standard of valuation required by this state					
. For non-deduction of deferred fractional premiums or return of premiums at the death of the insured					
. For surrender values in excess of reserves otherwise required and carried in this schedule					
Totals (Gross)					
Reinsurance ceded					
Totals (Net)					
Grand Totals (Net)—(Item 1, Page 3)					

EXHIBIT 8A—CHANGES IN BASES OF VALUATION DURING THE YEAR

(Including supplementary contracts set up on a basis other than that used to determine benefits)

1 Description of Valuation Class	Valuation Bases 2 Changed From	 3 Changed To	4 Increase in Actuarial Reserve Due to Change
Total (Item 7, Page 6)			

. Has the company ever issued both participating and non-participating policies? Answer:

. Does the company at present issue both participating and non-participating policies? Answer:
If not, state which kind is issued.
Answer:

Has the company any assessment or stipulated premium policies in force? Answer: If so, state:
Amount of insurance $
Amount of reserve $

Basis of reserve:
Basis of regular assessments:

Basis of special assessments:

Assessments collected during year $

4. If the policy loan interest rate guaranteed in any one or more of its currently issued policies is less than 5%, not in advance, state the policy loan rate guarantees on any such policies. Answer:

5. Does the company hold reserves for any annuity contracts which are less than the reserves that would be held on a standard basis?

Answer:. . . . . .If so, state the amount of reserve on such policies (a) on the basis actually held: $ . . . .; (b) which would have been held (on an exact or approximate basis) using the actual ages of the annuitants; the interest rate(s) used in (a); and the same mortality basis used by the company for the valuation of comparable annuity benefits issued to standard lives. If the company has no comparable annuity benefits for standard lives to be valued, the mortality basis shall be the table most recently approved by the state of domicile for valuing individual annuity benefits: $. . . . .; and (c) attach statement of methods employed in their valuation.

EXHIBIT 9—AGGREGATE RESERVE FOR ACCIDENT AND HEALTH POLICIES

	1 Total	2 Group Accident and Health	3 Credit[a] (Group and Individual)	4 Collectively Renewable	Other Individual Policies 5 Non-Cancellable	 6 Guaranteed Renewable	 7 Non-Renewable for Stated Reasons Only	 8 Other Accident Only	 9 All Other
A. ACTIVE LIFE RESERVE									
Unearned premium reserve									
Additional reserves[◦]									
Reserve for future contingent benefits (deferred maternity and other similar benefits)									
Reserve for rate credits									
Totals (Gross)									
Reinsurance ceded									
Totals (Net)									
B. CLAIM RESERVE									
Present value of amounts not yet due on claims[◦◦]									
Reserve for future contingent benefits (deferred maternity and other similar benefits)									
Totals (Gross)									
Reinsurance ceded									
Totals (Net)									
GRAND TOTALS (Net) (Item 2, Page 3)									
Tabular Interest on policy funds									

[a]Attach statement as to valuation standard used in calculating this reserve, specifying reserve bases, interest rates and methods.
[◦]Includes reserves for unaccrued benefits on incurred but unreported claims. Accrued benefits should be reported in Exhibit 11, Part 1, Lines 2.2 and 3.
[◦◦]Business not exceeding 120 months duration.

EXHIBIT 10—SUPPLEMENTARY CONTRACTS WITHOUT LIFE CONTINGENCIES, DIVIDEND ACCUMULATIONS, AND COUPON* ACCUMULATIONS

	1 Valuation Rate	2 Contract Rate or Rates‡	Supplementary Contracts Without Life Contingencies 3 Present Value of Amounts Not Yet Due	 4 Amounts Left on Deposit	 5 Totals	6 Dividend Accumulations	7 Coupon[◦] Accumulations
1.							
2.							
3.							
4.							
5.	**Totals (Gross)**						
6.	**Reinsurance Ceded**						
7.	**Totals (Net) (Items 3 and 5, Page 3)**						

‡Show contract rate or rates corresponding to each valuation rate. [◦]Includes coupons, guaranteed annual pure endowments and similar benefits.

ANNUAL STATEMENT FOR THE YEAR 1985 OF THE ....
(Name)

EXHIBIT 11—POLICY AND CONTRACT CLAIMS
PART 1—Liability End of Current Year

	1 Total	2 Industrial Life	Ordinary			6 Credit Life [a] (Group and Individual)	Group		Accident and Health		
			3 Life Insurance	4 Individual Annuities	5 Supplementary Contracts		7 Life Insurance	8 Annuities	9 Group	10 Credit [a] (Group and Individual)	11 Other
1. Due and Unpaid:											
a. Direct											
b. Reinsurance assumed											
c. Reinsurance ceded											
d. Net											
2. In course of settlement:											
2.1 Resisted a. Direct									X X X	X X X	X X X
b. Reinsurance assumed									X X X	X X X	X X X
c. Reinsurance ceded									X X X	X X X	X X X
d. Net			†	†		†	†		X X X	X X X	X X X
2.2 Other a. Direct											
b. Reinsurance assumed											
c. Reinsurance ceded											
d. Net			†	†		†	†		†	†	†
3. Incurred but unreported — net as to reinsurance			†	†		†	†		†	†	†
4. TOTALS a. Direct											
b. Reinsurance assumed											
c. Reinsurance ceded											
d. Net		°	°				°				

°Including matured endowments (but not guaranteed annual pure endowments) unpaid amounting to $ .... in Column 2, $ .... in Column 3 and $ .... in Column 7.

†Include only portion of disability and accident and health claim liabilities applicable to assumed "accrued" benefits. Reserves (including reinsurance assumed and net of reinsurance ceded) for unaccrued benefits for Ordinary Life Insurance $ ...., Individual Annuities $ ...., Credit Life (Group and Individual) $ ...., and Group Life $ ...., are included in Page 3, Item 1, (See Exhibit 8, Section F) and for Group Accident and Health $ ...., Credit (Group and Individual) Accident and Health $ .... and Other Accident and Health $ .... are included in Page 3, Item 2, (See Exhibit 9, Section B).

[a] Business not exceeding 120 months duration.

EXHIBIT 11—POLICY AND CONTRACT CLAIMS
PART 2—Incurred During the Year

	1 Total	2 Industrial Life°	Ordinary			6 Credit Life[a] (Group and Individual)	Group		Accident and Health		
			3 Life Insurance°°	4 Individual Annuities	5 Supplementary Contracts		7 Life Insurance°°°	8 Annuities	9 Group	10 Credit[a] (Group and Individual)	11 Other
1. Settlements during the year:											
a. Direct											
b. Reinsurance assumed											
c. Reinsurance ceded											
d. Net	†										
2. Liability December 31, current year from Part 1:											
a. Direct											
b. Reinsurance assumed											
c. Reinsurance ceded											
d. Net											
3. Amounts recoverable from reinsurers December 31, current year (Schedule S, Part 1, Col. 3)											
4. Liability December 31, previous year:											
a. Direct											
b. Reinsurance assumed											
c. Reinsurance ceded											
d. Net											
5. Amounts recoverable from reinsurers December 31 previous year											
6. Incurred Benefits:											
a. Direct											
b. Reinsurance assumed											
c. Reinsurance ceded											
d. Net											

°Including matured endowments (but not guaranteed annual pure endowments) amounting to $ .... in Line 1a, $ .... in Line 1d.
$ .... in Line 6a and $ .... in Line 6d

°°Including matured endowments (but not guaranteed annual pure endowments) amounting to $ .... in Line 1a, $ .... in Line 1d.
$ .... in Line 6a and $ .... in Line 6d

°°°Including matured endowments (but not guaranteed annual pure endowments) amounting to $ .... in Line 1a, $ .... in Line 1d.
$ .... in Line 6a and $ .... in Line 6d

†Equals sum of Exhibit 12, Lines 16.1, 16.2, 17, 22.1 and 22.2 Includes $ .... premiums waived under total and permanent disability benefits.

[a]Business not exceeding 120 months duration

EXHIBIT 12—RECONCILIATION OF LEDGER ASSETS

INCREASES IN LEDGER ASSETS

1. Premiums on life policies and annuity considerations
1A. Annuity and other fund deposits
2. Accident and health cash premiums, including $ .... policy, membership and other fees (Schedule T, Line 98, Col. 5)
3. Considerations for supplementary contracts with life contingencies
4. Considerations for supplementary contracts without life contingencies, including $ .... disability
5. Dividends left with the company to accumulate at interest
5A. Coupons* left with the company to accumulate at interest
6. Gross investment income (Exhibit 3, Line 10, Col. 1)
7. Increase of paid up capital during the year
8. From other sources (give items and amounts):
   8.1
   8.2
   8.3
9. Borrowed money gross $ .... less amount repaid $
10. Commissions and expense allowances on reinsurance ceded
10A. Reserve adjustments on reinsurance ceded
11.
12.
13. From sale or maturity of ledger assets (Exhibit 4, Line 10, Column 2)
14. By adjustment in book value of ledger assets (Exhibit 4, Line 10, Column 1)
15. Total Increases in Ledger Assets (Lines 1 through 14)

DECREASES IN LEDGER ASSETS

16. Policy and contract claims (Exhibit 11, Part 2):
   16.1 Life
   16.2 Accident and health
17. For annuities with life contingencies excluding payments on supplementary contracts (including cash refund payments)
18. Premium notes and liens voided by lapse, less $ .... restorations
19. Surrender values
19A. Group conversions
19B. Interest on policy or contract funds
20. Dividends to policyholders:
   20.1 Life insurance and annuities (Exhibit 7, Line 9, Col. 1)
   20.2 Accident and health (Exhibit 7, Line 9, Col. 2)
20A. Coupons, guaranteed annual pure endowments and similar benefits (Exhibit 7, Line 9, Cols. 3 + 4)
21. Total Paid Policyholders
22. Paid for claims on supplementary contracts:
   22.1 With life contingencies
   22.2 Without life contingencies
23. Dividends and interest thereon held on deposit disbursed during the year
23A. Coupons* and interest thereon held on deposit disbursed during the year
24.
25.
26. Commissions to agents (direct business only):
   26.1 Life insurance and annuities, including $ .... commuted commissions
   26.2 Accident and health, including $ .... commuted commissions
   26.3 Policy, membership and other fees retained by agents
26A. Commissions and expense allowances on reinsurance assumed
27. General expenses (Exhibit 5, Line 13, Col. 4)
28.1 Taxes, licenses and fees, excluding federal income taxes (Exhibit 6, Line 10, Col 4)
28.2 Federal income taxes, including $ .... on capital gains
29. Decrease of paid up capital during the year
30. Paid stockholders for dividends (cash $ .... stock $ ....)
31. Borrowed money repaid gross $ .... less amount borrowed $
32. Interest on borrowed money
32A. Net transfers to (+) or from (−) Separate Accounts (excluding Variable Life Insurance)
32B. Net transfers to (+) or from (−) Variable Life Insurance Separate Accounts
33.
34.
35.
36. From sale or maturity of ledger assets (Exhibit 4, Line 10, Column 4)
37. By adjustment in book value of ledger assets (Exhibit 4, Line 10, Column 3 and Exhibit 2, Line 4)
38. Total Decreases in Ledger Assets (Lines 16 through 37)

RECONCILIATION BETWEEN YEARS

39. Amount of ledger assets December 31st of previous year
40. Increase (+) or decrease (−) in ledger assets during the year (Line 15 minus Line 38)
41. Total = Ledger Assets December 31st of Current Year (Exhibit 13, Line 26, Col. 1)

*Includes coupons, guaranteed annual pure endowments and similar benefits.

1 **ANNUAL STATEMENT FOR THE YEAR 1985 OF THE** 14

(Name)

EXHIBIT 13—ASSETS

	1 Ledger Assets	2 Non-Ledger Assets	3 Assets Not Admitted	4 Net Admitted Assets (Cols. 1 + 2 − 3)
Bonds (Schedule D, Part 1)				
Stocks:				
2.1 Preferred stocks (Schedule D, Part 2, Section 1)				
2.2 Common stocks (Schedule D, Part 2, Section 2)				
Mortgage loans on real estate (Schedule B, Part 1, Sec. 1):				
3.1 First liens				
3.2 Other than first liens				
Real estate (Schedule A, Part 1):				
4.1 Properties occupied by the company (less $ .... encumbrances)				
4.2 Properties acquired in satisfaction of debt (less $ .... encumbrances)				
4.3 Investment real estate (less $ .... encumbrances)				
Policy loans				
Premium notes, including $ .... for first year premiums				
Collateral loans (Schedule C, Part 1)				
Cash on hand and on deposit:				
a. Cash in company's office				
b. Cash on deposit (Schedule E)				
Short-term investments (Schedule DA, Part 1)				
Other invested assets (Schedule BA, Part 1)				
Reinsurance ceded:				
11.1 Amounts recoverable from reinsurers (Schedule S, Part 1)				
11.2 Commissions and expense allowances due				
11.3 Experience rating and other refunds due				
11.4				
Other assets (give items and amounts):				
12.1 Agents' balances (gross debit $ .... less $ .... for doubtful accounts less				-0-
$ .... credit balances)				-0-
12.2 Bills receivable				-0-
12.3 Furniture and equipment				-0-
12.4 Cash advanced to or in hands of officers or agents				-0-
12.5 Loans on personal security, endorsed or not				
12.6				
Electronic data processing equipment				
Federal income tax recoverable				
Life insurance premiums and annuity considerations deferred and uncollected on in force Dec. 31st of current year (less premiums on reinsurance ceded and less $ .... loading)				
Accident and health premiums due and unpaid				
Investment income due and accrued				
Net adjustment in assets and liabilities due to foreign exchange rates				
Receivable from parent, subsidiaries and affiliates				
Totals (Lines 1 to 25)				
A. From Separate Accounts Statement				
B. From Variable Life Insurance Separate Accounts Statement				
Total (Lines 26 to 27B)				

EXHIBIT 14—ANALYSIS OF NON-ADMITTED ASSETS AND RELATED ITEMS

(Excluding Investment Adjustments Not Listed)

	1 End of Previous Year	2 End of Current Year	3 Changes for Year Increase (−) or Decrease (+)
1. Loans on company's stock			
2. Supplies, stationery, printed matter			
3. Furniture and equipment			
4. Commuted commissions			X X X
5. Agents' balances (net)			
6. Cash advanced to or in the hands of officers or agents			
7. Loans on personal security, endorsed or not			
8. Bills receivable			
9. Premium notes, etc., in excess of net value and other policy liabilities on individual policies			X X X
10. Accident and health premiums due and unpaid			
11. Other assets not admitted (itemize):			
11.1			
11.2			
11.3			
12. Agents' credit balances (Page 3, Item 19 inside)			
13. Total Change	X X X	X X X	*

*(Carry to Item 35, Page 4) [a]Business not exceeding 120 months duration.

14A ANNUAL STATEMENT FOR THE YEAR 1985 OF THE .... (Name)

FIVE-YEAR HISTORICAL DATA

All Figures Taken From or Developed From Annual Statements of Corresponding Years

Show amounts in whole dollars only, no cents
Items from prior years should be included only if they are available from prior year's statements

	1 1985	2 1984	3 1983	4 1982	5 1981
Life Insurance in Force (Page 15)					
1. Ordinary – Whole Life and Endowment (Line 31D)					
2. Ordinary – Term (Line 22, Col. 4, less Line 31D, Col. 4)					
3. Credit Life (Line 22, Col. 6)					
4. Group, excluding FEGLI/SGLI (Line 22, Col. 9 less Lines 38 & 39, Col. 4)					
5. Industrial (Line 22, Col. 2)					
6. FEGLI/SGLI (Lines 38 & 39, Col. 4)					
7. Total (Line 22, Col. 10)					
New Business Issued (Page 15)					
8. Ordinary – Whole Life and Endowment (Line 31D)					
9. Ordinary – Term (Line 2, Col. 4, less Line 31D)					
10. Credit Life (Line 2, Col. 6)					
11. Group (Line 2, Col. 9)					
12. Industrial (Line 2, Col. 2)					
13. Total (Line 2, Col. 10)					
Premium Income (Exhibit 1–Part 1)					
14. Ordinary and Industrial Life – First Year (Line 9d, Cols. 2 & 3)					
15. Ordinary and Industrial Life – Single and Renewal (Line 10d, Line 19d, Cols. 2 & 3)					
16. Other Life (Line 20d, Cols. 5 & 6)					
17. Annuity (Line 20d, Cols. 4 & 7)					
18. A & H (Line 20d, Cols. 8, 9 and 10)					
19. Total (Line 20d, Col. 1)					
Balance Sheet Items (Pages 2 & 3)					
20. Total Admitted Assets Excluding Separate Account Business (Page 2, Item 26)					
21. Total Liabilities Excluding Separate Account Business (Page 3, Item 26 less Items 25A & 25B)					
22. Aggregate Life Reserves (Page 3, Item 1)					
23. Aggregate A & H Reserves (Page 3, Item 2)					
24. Mandatory Securities Valuation Reserve (Page 3, Item 25.1)					
25. Capital (Page 3, Items 27A and 27B)					
26. Surplus (Page 3, Item 29D)					
Percentage Distribution of Assets (Page 2) (Item No. ÷ Page 2, Item 10A) × 100.0					
27. Bonds (Item 1)					
28. Stocks (Items 2.1 and 2.2)					
29. Mortgage Loans on Real Estate (Item 3)					
30. Real Estate (Items 4.1, 4.2 and 4.3)					
31. Policy Loans (Item 5)					
32. Premium Notes (Item 6)					
33. Collateral Loans (Item 7)					
34. Cash and short-term investments (Items 8.1 and 8.2) (1981 Item 8)					
35. Other Invested Assets (Item 10)					
36. Cash and Invested Assets (Item 10A)	100.0	100.0	100.0	100.0	100.0

Form 1 **ANNUAL STATEMENT FOR THE YEAR 1985 OF THE** .... (Name) **14B**

FIVE-YEAR HISTORICAL DATA

(Continued)

	1 1985	2 1984	3 1983	4 1982	5 1981
Investments in Parent, Subsidiaries and Affiliates					
37. Affiliated Bonds (Page 29, Line 29, Col. 6)					
38. Affiliated Preferred Stocks (Page 29, Line 47, Col. 3)					
39. Affiliated Common Stocks (Page 29, Line 65, Col. 3)					
40. Affiliated short-term Investments (subtotal included in Schedule DA, Part 1, Col. 10)					
41. Total of above Lines 37 to 40					
Total Nonadmitted and Admitted Assets					
42. Total Nonadmitted Assets (Page 14, Line 26, Col. 3)					
43. Total Admitted Assets (Page 14, Line 28, Col. 4)					
Investment Data (Page 8)					
44. Ratio of Net Investment Income to Mean Assets (Exhibit 2, Line 8) (To 2 decimal places)					
45. Net Investment Income (Exhibit 2, Line 7)					
46. Realized Capital Gains (Losses) (Exhibit 4, Line 11, Col. 6)					
47. Unrealized Capital Gains (Losses) (Exhibit 4, Line 12, Col. 6)					
48. Total of above Lines 45, 46 & 47					
Benefits and Reserve Increases (Page 5)					
49. Total Policy Benefits—Life (Items 8, 9, 10, 11, 11A & 12, Col. 1, less Items 11 & 11A, Cols. 9, 10, & 11)					
50. Total Policy Benefits—A & H (Items 11 & 11A, Cols. 9, 10 & 11)					
51. Increase in Life Reserves—Other than Group and Annuities (Item 17, Cols. 2 and 3)					
52. Increase in A & H Reserves (Item 17, Cols. 9, 10 & 11)					
53. Dividends to Policyholders (Item 28, Col. 1)					
Operating Ratios					
54. Insurance Expense Ratio (Page 5, Col. 1, Items 21, 21A & 22 less Item 5) ÷ (Page 5, Col. 1, Item 1 plus group annuity contribution funds) × 100					
55. Lapse Ratio (Ordinary Only) [(Page 15, Col. 4, Lines 14 & 15) × 100 ÷ ½(Lines 1 & 22)]					
56. A & H Loss Ratio (Schedule H, Part 1, Lines 3 and 4, Col. 1, %)					
57. A & H Expense Ratio (Schedule H, Part 1, Line 8, Col. 1, %)					
A & H Claim Reserve Adequacy					
58. Incurred Losses on Prior Years' Claims—Group Health (Schedule H, Part 3, Line 3a, Col. 2)					
59. Prior Years' Claim Liability and Reserve—Group Health (Schedule H, Part 3, Line 3b, Col. 2)					
60. Incurred Losses on Prior Years' Claims—Health other than Group (Schedule H, Part 3, Line 3a, Col. 1 less Col. 2)					
61. Prior Years' Claim Liability and Reserve—Health other than Group (Schedule H, Part 3, Line 3b, Col. 1 less Col. 2)					
Net Gains From Operations After Federal Income Taxes by Lines of Business (Page 5, Item 31)					
62. Industrial Life (Col. 2)					
63. Ordinary-Life (Col. 3)					
64. Ordinary-Individual Annuities (Col. 4)					
65. Ordinary-Supp. Contracts (Col. 5)					
66. Credit Life (Col. 6)					
67. Group Life (Col. 7)					
68. Group Annuities (Col. 8)					
69. A & H—Group (Col. 9)					
70. A & H—Credit (Col. 10)					
71. A & H—Other (Col. 11)					
72. Total (Col. 1) (Page 5, Item 31, Col. 1)					

ANNUAL STATEMENT FOR THE YEAR 1985 OF THE .... (Name)

SCHEDULE H—ACCIDENT AND HEALTH EXHIBIT

	1 Total		2 Group Accident and Health		3 Credit[a] (Group and Individual)		4 Collectively Renewable		Other Individual Policies: 5 Non-Cancellable		6 Guaranteed Renewable		7 Non-Renewable for Stated Reasons Only		8 Other Accident Only		9 All Other	
	Amount	%†	Amount	%†	Amount	%†	Amount	%†	Amount	%†	Amount	%†	Amount	%†	Amount	%†	Amount	%†
PART 1.—ANALYSIS OF UNDERWRITING OPERATIONS																		
1. Premiums written																		
2. Premiums earned (see note b)																		
3. Incurred claims																		
4. Increase in policy reserves																		
5. Commissions*																		
6. General insurance expenses																		
7. Taxes, licenses and fees																		
8. Total expenses incurred																		
9. Gain from underwriting before dividends to policyholders																		
10. Dividends to policyholders																		
11. Gain from underwriting after dividends to policyholders																		
PART 2.—RESERVES AND LIABILITIES																		
A. Premium Reserves:																		
1. Unearned premiums																		
2. Advance premiums																		
3. Reserve for rate credits																		
4. Total premium reserves, current year																		
5. Total premium reserves, previous year																		
6. Increase in total premium reserves																		
B. Policy Reserves:																		
1. Additional reserves																		
2. Reserve for future contingent benefits (deferred maternity and other similar benefits)**																		
3. Total policy reserves, current year																		
4. Total policy reserves, previous year																		
5. Increase in policy reserves																		
C. Claim Reserves and Liabilities:																		
1. Total current year																		
2. Total previous year																		
3. Increase																		
PART 3.—TEST OF PREVIOUS YEAR'S CLAIM RESERVES AND LIABILITIES																		
1. Claims paid during the year:																		
a. On claims incurred prior to current year																		
b. On claims incurred during current year																		
2. Claim reserves and liabilities, December 31, current year:																		
a. On claims incurred prior to current year																		
b. On claims incurred during current year																		
3. Test:																		
a. Line 1a and 2a																		
b. Claim reserves and liabilities, December 31, previous year																		
c. Line a minus Line b																		
PART 4.—REINSURANCE																		
A. Reinsurance Assumed:																		
1. Premiums written																		
2. Premiums earned (see note b)																		
3. Incurred claims																		
4. Commissions																		
B. Reinsurance Ceded:																		
1. Premiums written																		
2. Premiums earned (see note b)																		
3. Incurred claims																		
4. Commissions																		

a Business not exceeding 120 months duration.

†In each column of Part 1, show the percentages of Line 2 for Lines 3 through 11 inclusive.

*Includes $ .... reported as "Policy, membership and other fees retained by agents."

**If not included in claim reserves.

... for the increase in policy reserves which has been treated as a separate deduction

SUPPLEMENTARY EXHIBITS

Special reporting of certain credit life and disability experience is required by the following supplementary reports in the statutory statement:

- Page 46 (State Page) - credit insurance section
- Credit Life Statistical Report
- Credit Life and Accident and Health Exhibit

These pages have limited usefulness. They are scheduled to be deleted from the statement after 1986, and a new experience reporting supplement will replace them. This supplement is optional for 1985 experience and required for 1986 experience.

PAGE 46 (STATE PAGE)

Page 46 (State Page) is prepared for each state where the insurer is licensed. The data displayed applies only to direct business written in the particular state. At the bottom of the page is a section displaying credit insurance data separately.

The credit insurance data is required separately for individual and group insurance. Group insurance is further divided based on whether the original term was 1-60 months or 61-120 months. Insurers are required to maintain the ability to make these distinctions, although the distinction is not needed in the body of the statement or for general operations. The distinction is a carryover from data that was necessary years ago when many state regulations limited credit insurance to terms of 60 months or less.

Several technical problems limit the usefulness of the data. Insurers are inconsistent in the presentation of earned premiums for life insurance. Some insurers calculate earned premiums as written premiums less the increase in the mortality reserves for the year. Most show the earned premiums as the written premiums less the increase in the unearned premiums for the year. A footnote on Page 46 states that "The figures shown in these columns should be consistent with the corresponding figures in the Credit Life and Accident and Health Exhibit."

This exhibit calls for mortality reserves, but there is little use for earned premiums based on the change in the mortality reserves. In addition, many states require annual statistical reporting on a special form (see later discussion). Many of these forms use unearned premiums and are supposed to balance to Page 46. For disability, the unearned premiums are on the statement basis, usually the Rule of 78.

The primary deficiency is that written and earned premiums are based on actual premiums charged. One can easily calculate an incurred claim-earned premium loss ratio from the data shown, but this may not provide much insight to the regulator wanting to test the reasonableness of the state's prima facie rates. If an insurer charges premiums different from prima facie rates, or if the prima facie rates have changed in recent years, the loss ratio displayed is on a different basis than the current prima facie rates. The new 1985 Experience Reporting Form solves this deficiency by adjusting earned premiums to the amount which would have been earned if the state's current prima facie rates had been charged.

CREDIT LIFE STATISTICAL REPORT

This report displays earned premiums and incurred losses for all group credit life policies. Experience on individual policies is separated between level and decreasing plans of insurance. Earned premiums are clearly based on the written premium less the increase in unearned premiums, but the Page 46 problem of actual versus prima facie premiums remains. The various group and individual distinctions have no useful purpose.

CREDIT LIFE AND ACCIDENT AND HEALTH EXHIBIT

This exhibit follows the format of Schedule H using the distinctions of the Credit Life Statistical Report. In the life insurance section, line 5 would correspond to earned premiums, but the calculation uses the change in the mortality reserve. Since most disability insurance is group coverage, this section is just a rehash of Schedule H.

Form 1 ANNUAL STATEMENT FOR THE YEAR 1985 OF THE ....
Name

DIRECT BUSINESS IN THE STATE OF .... **DURING THE YEAR**

NAIC GROUP CODE: **LIFE INSURANCE** NAIC COMPANY CODE:

(1)	(2)	(3)	(4)	(5)	(6)
DIRECT PREMIUMS AND ANNUITY CONSIDERATIONS (Excluding Reinsurance Accepted and without deduction of Reinsurance Ceded)	ORDINARY	CREDIT LIFE[a] (Group and Individual)	GROUP	INDUSTRIAL	TOTAL
1. Life Insurance					
2. Annuity considerations					
3.					
4. Totals					
4.1 Annuity and other fund deposits - based on residence of identifiable individuals		X X X		X X X	
DIRECT DIVIDENDS TO POLICYHOLDERS (Excluding Reinsurance Accepted and without deduction of Reinsurance Ceded)					
Life insurance:					
5.1 Paid in cash or left on deposit					
5.2 Applied to pay renewal premiums					
5.3 Applied to provide paid-up additions or shorten the endowment or premium paying period					
5.4 Other					
5.5 Totals (Sum of 5.1 to 5.4)					
Annuities:					
6.1 Paid in cash or left on deposit					
6.2 Applied to provide paid-up annuities					
6.3 Other					
6.4 Totals (Sum of 6.1 to 6.3)					
7. Grand Totals (Lines 5.5 plus 6.4)					
DIRECT CLAIMS AND BENEFITS PAID (Excluding Reinsurance Accepted and without deduction of Reinsurance Ceded)					
8. Death benefits					
9. Matured endowments					
10. Annuity benefits					
11. Surrender values					
12.					
13. All other benefits, except Accident and Health					
14. Totals					

DIRECT DEATH BENEFITS AND MATURED ENDOWMENTS INCURRED (Excluding Reinsurance Accepted and without deduction of Reinsurance Ceded)	ORDINARY		CREDIT LIFE[a] (Group and Individual)		GROUP		INDUSTRIAL		TOTAL	
	No.	Amount	No. of Ind. Pols. & Gr. Certifs.	Amount	No. of Certifs.	Amount	No.	Amount	No.	Amount
15. Unpaid December 31, previous year										
16. Incurred during current year										
Settled during current year:										
17.1 By payment in full										
17.2 By payment on compromised claims										
17.3 Totals paid										
17.4 Reduction by compromise										
17.5 Amount rejected										
17.6 Total settlements										
18. Unpaid Dec. 31, current year (15+16—17.6)										
POLICY EXHIBIT (Excluding Reinsurance Accepted and without deduction of Reinsurance Ceded)					No. of Policies					
19. In force December 31, previous year				†						
20. Issued during year										
21. Ceased to be in force during year (Net)										
22. In force December 31 of current year				†						

†Includes Individual Credit Life Insurance: previous year $................; current year $................
Includes Group Credit Life Insurance: Loans less than or equal 60 months at issue, previous year $................; current year $................
Loans greater than 60 months at issue BUT NOT GREATER THAN 120 MONTHS previous year $................; current year $................

NOTE: This company's participations in the FEGLI and SGLI policies are shown in this Policy Exhibit as direct business.

ACCIDENT AND HEALTH INSURANCE

(1)	(2) DIRECT PREMIUMS (Excluding Reinsurance Accepted and without deduction of Reinsurance Ceded)	(3) DIRECT PREMIUMS EARNED	(4) DIVIDENDS PAID OR CREDITED ON DIRECT BUSINESS	(5) DIRECT LOSSES PAID	(6) DIRECT LOSSES INCURRED
23. Group Policies					
23.1 Credit (Group and Individual)[a]					
23.2 Collectively Renewable Policies					
Other Individual Policies:					
24.1 Non-cancellable					
24.2 Guaranteed renewable					
24.3 Non-renewable for stated reasons only					
24.4 Other accident only					
24.5 All other					
24.6 Totals (Sum of 24.1 to 24.5)					
25. Totals (Lines 23+23.1+23.2+24.6)					

CREDIT LIFE AND ACCIDENT AND HEALTH INSURANCE
(Included in the above schedules)

(1)	(2) DIRECT PREMIUMS (Excluding Reinsurance Accepted and without deduction of Reinsurance Ceded)	(3) DIRECT PREMIUMS EARNED* (prior to Dividends and Retrospective Rate Credits Paid or Credited)	(4) DIVIDENDS AND RETROSPECTIVE RATE CREDITS PAID OR CREDITED ON DIRECT BUSINESS*	(5) DIRECT LOSSES PAID	(6) DIRECT LOSSES INCURRED*
26. Individual life policies					
27.1 Group life policies—loans OF 60 OR LESS months' duration					
27.2 Group life policies—loans OF GREATER THAN 60 MONTHS' DURATION BUT NOT GREATER THAN 120 MONTHS					
28. Totals (Lines 26+27.1+27.2)					
29.1 Group A & H policies—loans of 60 OR LESS months' duration					
29.2 Group A & H policies—loans of GREATER THAN 60 MONTHS' DURATION BUT NOT GREATER THAN 120 MONTHS					
30. Other A & H policies					
31. Totals (Lines 29.1+29.2+30)					
32. Totals (Lines 28+31)					

*The figures shown in these columns should be consistent with the corresponding figures in the Credit Life and Accident and Health Exhibit.
[a]Business not exceeding 120 months duration.

CREDIT LIFE INSURANCE STATISTICAL REPORT OF THE

(Company) OF (Location)

To be filed on or before April 1 to report the experience on credit life insurance for the

Calendar Year 19.......

CLASSIFICATION (Accrual Basis)	DIRECT BUSINESS		
	Group Policies	Individual Policies: Level Amount	Individual Policies: Decreasing Amount
1. Gross premiums			
2. Less return premiums on cancelled policies			
3. Line 1 minus Line 2			
4. Gross premiums unearned beginning of year			
5. Gross premiums unearned end of year			
6. Earned premiums (Line 3 plus Line 4 minus Line 5)			
7. Losses paid during year			
8. Unpaid losses end of year			
9. Unpaid losses beginning of year			
10. Losses incurred (Line 7 plus Line 8 minus Line 9)			

SPECIAL INSTRUCTIONS

Amounts reported on Lines 1, 2, and 3 should be the same as on the corresponding lines of Part 1 of the Credit Life and Accident and Health Exhibit.

Gross premiums unearned on Lines 4 and 5 should be computed using the sum of the digits method for decreasing amounts and the pro-rata method for level amounts.

Losses reported on Line 10 should agree with the sum of Lines 6(a) and 6(b) of Part 1 of the Credit Life and Accident and Health Exhibit.

If this Report is filed bound with the Annual Statement, signatures required on this report may be omitted.

Officer Completing Report ....

Subscribed and sworn to before me this ....day of ...., 19.......

....

CREDIT LIFE AND ACCIDENT AND HEALTH EXHIBIT

Supplement to the December 31, 19...... Annual Statement of the .... Insurance Company

To Be Filed on or Before May 1

PART 1—CREDIT LIFE INSURANCE

CLASSIFICATION (Accrual Basis)	GROUP POLICIES			INDIVIDUAL POLICIES			
	Direct	Reinsurance		Level Amount Direct	Decreasing Amount Direct	Reinsurance	
		Assumed	Ceded			Assumed	Ceded
1. Gross premiums							
2. Less return premiums on cancelled policies							
3. Line 1 minus line 2							
4.* Increase in reserve liability							
5. Line 3 minus line 4							
6. Losses (a) Death benefits							
(b) Other benefits							
7. Loss expense							
8. Commissions							
9. General insurance expense							
10. Taxes, licenses and fees							
11.							
12. Total (lines 6-11 inclusive)							
13. Net gain from operations before dividends and retrospective rate credits (line 5 minus line 12)							
14. Dividends and retrospective rate credits							
15. Net gain from operations after dividends and retrospective rate credits (line 13 minus line 14)							
16. Amount of insurance in force, December 31, previous year							
17. Amount of insurance in force, December 31, current year							

*State reserve basis, including valuation standards, used..

PART 2—CREDIT ACCIDENT AND HEALTH INSURANCE

CLASSIFICATION (Accrual Basis)	GROUP POLICIES			INDIVIDUAL POLICIES		
	Direct	Reinsurance		Direct	Reinsurance	
		Assumed	Ceded		Assumed	Ceded
1. Gross premiums						
2. Less return premiums on cancelled policies						
3. Line 1 minus line 2						
4. Increase in unearned premium reserve						
5. Earned premiums (line 3 minus line 4)						
6. Losses						
7. Loss expense						
8. Commissions						
9. General insurance expense						
10. Taxes, licenses and fees						
11. Other reserve increase						
12. Total (lines 6-11 inclusive)						
13. Net gain from operations before dividends and retrospective rate credits (line 5 minus line 12)						
14. Dividends and retrospective rate credits						
15. Net gain from operations after dividends and retrospective rate credits (line 13 minus line 14)						

SPECIAL INSTRUCTIONS

Credit life insurance is defined as that form of insurance under which the life of a borrower of money or purchaser of goods is insured in connection with a specific loan or credit transaction. Credit Accident and Health insurance is that form of insurance under which a borrower of money or a purchaser of goods is indemnified in connection with a specific loan or credit transaction against loss of time resulting from accident or sickness. If a single insurance contract combines both Life and Accident and Health coverage, proper allocation should be made to the appropriate Parts of this Exhibit. These definitions shall not include Life insurance or Accident and Health insurance in connection with loans of more than 120 months' duration.

This Exhibit should be completed on the accrual, i.e., earned and incurred basis. Certain items may be either positive or negative, and should be entered accordingly.

"Direct" means that reinsurance ceded has not been deducted and reinsurance assumed is excluded.

LINE 1—GROSS PREMIUMS—Amounts should be reported before (a) dividends and retrospective rate credits, (b) returned premiums on cancelled policies, and (c) adjustment for unearned premium reserves, but should include membership and policy fees and any other charge made in connection with insurance policies or certificates.

LINE 6—LOSSES—Losses should include only actual benefits incurred during the year to beneficiaries or assignees in accordance with the policy provisions.

LINE 8—COMMISSIONS—Commissions should include policy, membership and other fees retained by agents.

LINES 16 AND 17—AMOUNTS OF INSURANCE IN FORCE, DECEMBER 31 PREVIOUS AND CURRENT YEARS—The amounts of insurance in force should be based on actual amounts of insured outstanding indebtedness, rather than on original amounts of loans.

C-4

STATE EXPERIENCE REPORTS

For many years, states regulators have faced the problem of setting and adjusting prima facie rates. Solving the problem requires an accurate measure of the loss experience. Nationwide experience, as reported in the annual statement and the supplementary exhibits is not considered relevant to rate-making for a particular state. Page 46 shows the state's data, but contains the aforementioned flaws. Consequently, some states now require another set of experience reporting forms. Some states require the reports to be submitted annually, while others just issue a special call for data every few years, usually when a rate change is being considered.

States have been inconsistent in developing a standard form. Prior to 1975, most states used the form now called the *old NAIC form.* An improved form was adopted in 1973 and amended in 1980. States generally use some variation of the 1980 NAIC form now. Both forms will be discussed since they have current relevance.

OLD NAIC FORM

This form uses different methods to evaluate life and disability experience. Life insurance experience is calculated as a claim cost per $100 per year, comparable to the prima facie rate basis. Data is reported separately by:

- Single premium, level or decreasing
- Monthly Outstanding Balance

One year of experience (listed separately for various classes of business) is shown. Only direct business is included.

Incurred losses per $100 of mean insurance in force are calculated. In essence, this is a monthly outstanding balance claim cost. The result is converted to a single premium basis, and divided by the average premium rate charged to get a loss ratio.

From a theoretical view, the approach is valid, but practical considerations limit the usefulness of the final result. In the following example, the application of the procedure is shown. Line 1 calls for the mean insurance in force. Insurers generally use the average of the beginning-of-year and end-of-year amounts. This causes a distorted result when the pattern of in force is changing during the year. To minimize the distortion, some states require insurers to use the average of the monthly in force amounts. Improvement in data processing systems in recent years has allowed for more precise calculation of this item, but complete confidence cannot be placed in this measure.

Incurred claims are properly calculated as the paid claims plus the change in the claim reserves. Multiplying the incurred claims by 100 and dividing the result by the mean insurance in force gives an annual claim cost per $100 of in force. Dividing the annual claim cost by 12 gives an MOB claim cost which is converted to a single premium claim cost using the standard conversion formula:

Single premium claim cost per $100 at 12 months

= MOB cost per $1000 x (n+1) / 20
= MOB cost per $100 x (n+1) / 2
= annual claim cost per $100 x (n+1) / 24
= annual claim cost per $100 x (13/24)

The assumption is that the policies have an average term of 12 months. As described in Chapter Five, one must select the appropriate average term to have an accurate result. While the 12-month assumption may have been valid when the form was designed, the assumption does not fit current business.

Next, the minimum and maximum gross premiums charged are shown along with the weighted average premium. In all likelihood, the values displayed are only a reasonable approximation. Dividing the claim cost by the average premium results in a loss ratio.

Over the years, this report should produce a reasonable estimate of the true results. States use the reports as a guideline, so the form serves its purpose. The results should be considered an approximation which may have a considerable margin of error.

For disability insurance, incurred claims and earned premiums are determined and a loss ratio shown. This display is a further breakdown of Page 46. The same distortions arise–earned premiums are not converted to a standard base and unearned premiums are usually on the Rule of 78.

States attempting to change prima facie rates based on the data from these forms faced an onslaught of criticism attacking the practical and technical deficiencies of the data. Prima facie rates were usually set by negotiation rather than by the displayed experience.

Figures 7.1 and 7.2 display the form by line of business with sample values.

CREDIT LIFE INSURANCE EXPERIENCE EXHIBIT

All Credit Life Insurance Written Under the NAIC Model Credit Insurance Bill in the State of Delaware

Experience of Calendar Year 1986

I. Single Premium Paid in Advance, Reducing Term

A. Other than Commercial and Savings Banks

a. Cash Loans (Small Loans, Industrial Bank Loans,etc)

1. Mean Insurance in force*		$2,776,288.00
2. Losses paid	$14,638.50	
3. Increase (+) or decrease (-) in loss reserves, including incurred but unreported.	270.00	
4. Losses incurred (Item 2 + Item 3).		$ 14,908.50
5. Losses per $100 mean insurance in force (100 x Item 4 / Item 1)		$ 0.54
6. Losses per $100 initial amount on basis of 12 months policy (13/24 x Item 5)		$ 0.29
7. Premium rate per $100 initial amount on basis of 12 months policy: (a) minimum .62 (b) maximum .65 (c) average, weighted by amounts of mean insurance in force.		$ 0.63
8. Eligibility requirements (Explain). None		
9. Underwriting limitations (Explain). None		
10. Other limits on coverage (Explain). None		
11. Loss ratio (Item 6 / Item 7 (c)).		46.03%

*Mean of insurance in force beginning and end of year after appropriate deduction for reducing term provisions and termination.

Fig 7.1 Old NAIC Form for life insurance.

CREDIT ACCIDENT AND HEALTH EXPERIENCE EXHIBIT ALL CREDIT ACCIDENT AND HEALTH INSURANCE WRITTEN UNDER "THE MODEL ACT FOR THE REGULATION OF CREDIT LIFE INSURANCE AND CREDIT ACCIDENT AND HEALTH INSURANCE"

( ) ALL MODEL ACT STATES — 1986 CALENDAR YEAR

(X) STATE OF DELAWARE — POLICY YEAR

1.	GROSS PREMIUMS WRITTEN (A)	10,000.00
2.	REFUNDS ON TERMINATION	3,156.88
3.	NET PREMIUM WRITTEN (1-2)	6,843.12
4.	PREMIUM RESERVE AT START OF PERIOD	14,251.53
5.	PREMIUM RESERVE AT END OF PERIOD	3,867.13
6.	EARNED PREMIUMS (3+4-5)	17,227.52
7.	CLAIMS PAID	29,516.69
8.	RESERVE FOR CLAIMS AT END OF PERIOD	16,523.00
9.	RESERVE FOR CLAIMS AT BEGINNING OF PERIOD	34,171.00
10.	INCURRED LOSSES (7+8-9)	11,868.69
11.	LOSS RATIO - RATIO OF LINE 10 TO LINE 6	68.89

FORM NO. (B) P1054		
INDICATE:	GROUP (X)	OR INDIVIDUAL ( )
		(X) RETROACTIVE
TYPE OF COVERAGE	(C) 14 DAY	( ) ELIMINATION
PREMIUM RATES (A)	2.20 100/12 MONTHS, $3.00/24 MONTHS, $3.80/36 MONTHS	
ELIGIBILITY REQUIREMENTS (D)	NONE	
UNDERWRITING LIMITATIONS (L)	NONE	
OTHER LIMITATIONS ON COVERAGE	NONE	
CLASS OF BUSINESS (F)	( ) CREDIT UNION ( ) BANK (X) SMALL LOANS ( ) SALES FINANCE	
MODE OF PREMIUM PAYMENT	( ) MONTHLY PREMIUM (X) SINGLE PREMIUM	

Fig. 7.2 Old NAIC Form for disability insurance

1980 NAIC FORM

Included in the 1979-80 NAIC Model Regulation was a revised, and improved, experience report. Although the Model Regulation has been virtually ignored by the states, the reporting form has found wide acceptance. Most states insisted on some modifications, so standardization remains elusive. Still, the form corrected the critical flaws of prior forms. States now have a good basis for evaluating current experience in the state.

Data is required in rather fine detail, but one can combine the data to reach various levels of summarization. Business is displayed separately by class and by premium mode. Life insurance experience is separated into single and joint coverage, level and decreasing plans, and gross and net payoff in some states. Disability experience is shown by plan. Three years' experience is displayed, giving a good view of trends.

For life insurance, earned premiums are properly based on written premium less the change in unearned premiums. The unearned premium bases are specified by most states, so the industry should be reporting consistent values. The major improvement is that actual earned premiums are also converted to the comparable premiums which would have been earned if prima facie rates had been charged.

Form B converts the actual premiums to prima facie premiums. The conversion must be done for each set of rates different from prima facie. For disability insurance, prima facie and actual rates for terms of 12, 24 and 36 months are shown and the ratios taken. The average of the three ratios is multiplied by the actual earned premiums to get the prima facie earned premiums. Since deviated premiums are usually a percentage adjustment of the prima facie rates, the ratio for all three terms is often the same.

For disability insurance, insurers may still be inconsistent in the unearned premium basis. Some states now specify the mean of pro rata and the Rule of 78 for these forms.

Incurred claims are paid claims plus the change in the claim reserves. The form requires a separation of unreported claims and claim reserves, but only the combined total is important.

The three-year display overcomes some of the insurer's reporting inconsistencies. With three years of data, the unearned premium basis has a smaller effect on the combined loss ratio. In the same manner, the year-to-year variations in claim reserves are smoothed.

The final result is a loss ratio based on prima facie earned premiums, which is a consistent basis on which to compare the experience of different insurers. Statewide experience can be compiled at whatever level of detail is desired. One can multiply the prima facie loss ratio times the prima facie rate to obtain a reasonably accurate claim cost. The form does not solve all of the problems, but the results are far superior to any other available data. Assuming that the combined experience is of credible size, the experience should represent the true experience with a narrow margin of error.

Several remaining deficiencies should be noted. For instance, insurers may have reporting problems in the definition of class of business, since neither states nor insurers have uniform definitions. Some companies either cannot separate net payoff experience or may use the Rule of 78 for net payoff unearned premiums.

The major deficiency is that this form does not provide any insight into the validity of the slope of the disability premiums. Only one loss ratio representing a composite average term is shown. The composite may be the result of a low loss ratio on twelve-month original term business and a high loss ratio on forty-eight month business. This question will remain unanswered until insurers can reach a new level of data processing sophistication.

CREDIT LIFE & DISABILITY INSURANCE EXPERIENCE REPORT
STATE OF ______________
CALENDAR YEAR OF 1986

FORM A

CLASSES OF BUSINESS: Check one:

__ (a) credit unions;
x (b) commercial & savings banks;
__ (c) finance companies;
__ (d) motor vehicle dealers;
__ (e) other sales finance
__ (f) production credit associations; bank agricultural loans;
__ (g) all others

Mode of Premium Payment: x Single Premium __ Outstanding Balance (Monthly Premium)

Plan of Benefits

x Credit Life: x Decreasing x Single Life x Gross
__ Level __ Joint Life __ Net

__ Credit Disability _____ Days, __ Retro __ Non-Retro

	1984	1985	1986	Total
1. Actual Earned Premiums				
a. Gross premium written (before deduction for Dividends and Experience Rating Credits)	___	___	57,796	57,796
b. Refunds on terminations	___	___	6,636	6,636
c. Net (a - b)	___	___	51,160	51,160
d. Premium reserve, beginning of period	___	___	30,055	30,055
e. Premium reserve, end of period	___	___	49,621	49,621
f. Actual earned premiums (c + d - e)	___	___	31,594	31,594

Fig 7.3 Form A of 1980 NAIC Experience Reporting Form.

g. Earned premiums at prima facie rate (Form B)	___	___	28,722	28,722
2. Incurred Claims				
a. Claims paid	___	___	21,810	21,810
b. Unreported claims, beginning of period	___	___	1,151	1,151
c. Unreported claims, end of period	___	___	2,798	2,798
d. Claim reserve, beginning of period	___	___	0	0
e. Claim reserve, end of period	___	___	0	0
f. Incurred Claims (a - b + c - d + e)	___	___	23,457	23,457
3. Loss Ratios				
a. Actual loss ratio (2f / 1f)	___	___	74.24	74.24
b. Loss ratio at prima facie rate (2f / 1g)	___	___	81.27	81.67

____
(Company)

____
(Signature)

____
(Title)

Fig. 7.3 Form A of 1980 NAIC experience reporting form (continued).

CREDIT LIFE INSURANCE EXPERIENCE REPORT
STATE OF ______________
PRIMA FACIE EARNED PREMIUM

FORM B 1

Class of business Bank Calendar Year 1986

Premium Mode Single Premium Plan of Benefits Single Life Gross

	Actual Earned Premiums Col.1	Prima Facie Rate Col.2	Actual Premium Rate Col.3	Prima Facie Earned Premiums Col.4
A. Earned premiums at prima facie rate	0	XXX	XXX	0
B. Earned premiums at other than prima facie rates:				
1.	31,594	.50	.55	28,722
2.				
3.				
4.				
5.				
6.				
Totals	31,594 To Form A Line 1f	XXX	XXX	28,722 To Form A, Line 1g

Fig. 7.4 Form B of 1980 NAIC experience reporting form.

1985 NAIC ANNUAL STATEMENT EXPERIENCE REPORT

Regulators recognize the limitations of Page 46 and the limitations of the supplementary exhibits. They recognize a need for standardized reporting forms to replace the variety of state experience forms. With a standard form, the compilation of data by the NAIC central office is possible. Insurers agree with these concerns. The diversity of forms precludes automation, causes errors, and results in inconsistent reporting. In June 1985, the Blanks Committee adopted a new form which is considered part of the annual statement. The new form will replace the credit insurance section of Page 46 and the two supplementary exhibits. The goal is for the new form to replace annual or special state experience reports.

Most state regulations specify that the annual statement follow the NAIC format. The adoption by the NAIC will make the form mandatory for all insurers. Similarly, the deletions adopted by the NAIC must be accepted by the states unless they adopt specific regulations reinstating the deleted pages. The current state experience reports are not a part of the annual statement requirements, but are required because most state regulations specify that insurers must maintain statistical data available on request from the Commissioner. Many states require annual filing of the experience on specified forms. Since these regulations are distinct from the annual statement reporting, there is no guarantee that the states will accept the new form in lieu of their current reporting requirements. In all probability, some states will insist on their current form, but most states seem willing to accept the new form.

The new form must be filed by June 30 each year showing the experience of the prior calendar year. The forms and the instructions follow. In general, the form follows the 1980 NAIC Experience Reporting Form, except that the data is not separated in such fine detail.

On certain classes of credit business, the NAIC felt regulation was unnecessary, so these classes are exempt from reporting.

Otherwise, all credit insurance is included regardless of term or form of policy. Experience is reported by state for direct business only. Gross premiums before dividends to policyholders and experience rating refunds are shown. For these reasons, the total of all state reports will not balance with annual statement items for most companies.

Credit life experience is reported separately for single and joint life coverages, but a separation is not made for level versus decreasing, gross or net payoff, or class of business. Earned premiums are calculated using the change in unearned premiums. Actual earned premiums are also converted to prima facie earned premiums. Incurred claims represent the usual calculation using paid claims plus the change in claim reserves. Loss ratios are calculated based on actual earned premiums and on prima facie earned premiums.

A separate calculation is provided using the old NAIC form concept. Line 4 calls for the mean insurance in force. On line 5, the losses incurred are multiplied by 1,000 and divided by the mean insurance in force. The result is an annual claim cost per $1,000 of mean insurance in force. Dividing by 12 converts the answer to a monthly rate per $1,000. Then the usual conversion formula can be used to calculate the single premium claim cost per $100 per year. To do this calculation, a representative average term must be selected.

The claim costs can also be derived by multiplying the prima facie loss ratio on line 3b, times the state's MOB prima facie rate or the single premium prima facie rate. Again, care must be taken in the selection of terms and premium mode at which the comparison is made. This answer should match the claim cost based on the mean in force. It will not. In most cases, the two results will be similar and will provide the range of reasonable answers. If the two answers are materially different, the insurer should recheck the underlying data. A wide difference may be valid where there is a substantial swing in amounts in force during the year.

Consider the sample form completed for Ohio business. The prima facie rate is specified as an MOB rate of 80¢/1000/month.

Single premiums are calculated using the usual formula:

Single premium per \$100 at n months =
(MOB rate per \$1,000) x (n+1) / 20

Given the sample data for single life coverage, the annual claim cost per \$1,000 is \$5.28. Dividing by 12 gives an MOB claim cost of 44¢/1000/month. Using the prima facie rates, the claim cost is:

(Prima facie loss ratio) x (Prima facie MOB rate) =

.542 x (80¢/1000/month) = 43.4¢/1000/month

Suppose the same data applied to a state which specified its prima facie rate as 49¢/100/year. Here the mean in force claim cost must be converted to a single premium per \$100 per year. The conversion is made using the average remaining term on business in force. Since this value is difficult to calculate and is constantly changing, only an estimate is possible. A greater difference in the two methods in this situation might be expected. Assume an average term of 36 months. Using the mean in force, the claim cost is:

Single premium claim cost per \$100 at 36 months =

.44 x (37 / 20) = .814

This is compared to the prima facie loss ratio times the single premium at 36 months:

Single premium claim cost per \$100 at 36 months =

.49 x (36/12) x .542 = .797

Identical calculations are done for joint life business. If the loss ratios for single and joint life are reasonably close, this is an indication that the state's joint life multiple approximates the difference in mortality costs between the two coverages.

Data for disability experience is presented using the loss ratio approach by plan. The determination of earned premiums and incurred claims follow the procedures for life insurance. However, no insight is given to the loss ratio by term of coverage.

The new format is the best available considering the constraints of industry administration procedures. States will have valid data from all insurers on a consistent basis. While the form does not contain the detail of the 1980 NAIC form, sufficient data is presented for prima facie rate-setting in most states. Once several years of experience are accumulated, the industry and its regulators will have a valuable tool for accurate determination of the claim costs.

SUPPLEMENT TO THE 1986 ANNUAL STATEMENT
OF THE SOUND AND SECURE LIFE INSURANCE COMPANY
TO BE FILED ON OR BEFORE JUNE 30

NAIC GROUP CODE ___ NAIC GROUP CODE ___

DIRECT BUSINESS IN THE STATE OF OHIO

PART 1 - CREDIT LIFE INSURANCE

	SINGLE	JOINT	TOTAL
1. EARNED PREMIUMS			
A. GROSS WRITTEN PREMIUM	95,000	85,300	180,300
B. REFUNDS ON TERMINATIONS	20,000	10,000	30,000
C. NET WRITTEN PREMIUMS (A - B)	75,000	75,300	150,300
D. PREMIUMS RESERVES, START OF PERIOD	95,000	103,000	198,000
E. PREMIUM RESERVES, END OF PERIOD	90,000	109,000	199,000
F. ACTUAL EARNED PREMIUMS (C + D - E)	80,000	69,300	149,300
G. EARNED PREMIUMS AT PRIMA FACIE RATES	80,200	69,300	149,500
2. INCURRED CLAIMS			
A. CLAIMS PAID	43,000	41,580	84,580
B. UNREPORTED CLAIM RESERVE, START OF PERIOD	2,000	2,200	4,200
C. UNREPORTED CLAIM RESERVE, END OF PERIOD	2,500	2,200	4,700
D. CLAIMS RESERVES, START OF PERIOD	0	0	0
E. CLAIMS RESERVES, END OF PERIOD	0	0	0
F. INCURRED CLAIMS (A - B + C - D + E)	43,500	41,580	85,080
3. LOSS RATIO			
A. ACTUAL LOSS RATIO (2F / 1F)	54.4%	60.0%	57.0%
B. LOSS RATIO AT PRIMA FACIE RATES (2F / 1G)	54.2%	60.0%	56.9%
4. MEAN INSURANCE IN FORCE	8,240,000	4,500,000	12,740,000
5. LOSSES PER $1,000 MEAN INSURANCE IN FORCE ((1,000 x 2f) / 4)	5.28	9.24	6.68

Fig. 7.5 1985 NAIC experience reporting form.

PART 2 - CREDIT ACCIDENT & HEALTH INSURANCE

	7 DAY RETRO	14 DAY RETRO	14 DAY NON-RETRO	30 DAY RETRO	30 DAY NON-RETRO	OTHER	TOTAL
EARNED PREMIUMS							
A. Gross Written Preiums	____	85,000	____	____	____	____	85,000
B. Refunds On Terminations	____	8,000	____	____	____	____	8,000
C. Net Written Premiums (A-B)	____	77,000	____	____	____	____	77,000
D. Preiums Rererves, Start Of Period	____	82,000	____	____	____	____	82,000
E. Premium Reserves, End Of Period	____	84,000	____	____	____	____	84,000
F. Actual Earned Premium (C + D - E)	____	75,000	____	____	____	____	75,000
G. Earned Premiums At Prima Facie Rates	____	74,545	____	____	____	____	74,545
INCURRED CLAIMS							
A. Claims Paid	____	48,000	____	____	____	____	48,000
B. Unreported Claim Reserve, Start Of Period	____	500	____	____	____	____	500
C. Unreported Claim Reserve, End Of Period	____	75	____	____	____	____	750
D. Claim Reserves, Start Of Period	____	4,500	____	____	____	____	4,500
E. Claims Reserves, End Of Period	____	5,000	____	____	____	____	5,000
F. Incurred Claims (A - B + C - D + E)	____	48,750	____	____	____	____	48,750
LOSS RATIO							
A. Actual Loss Ratio (2F / 1F)	____	65.0%	____	____	____	____	65.0%
B. Loss Ratio At Prima Facie Rates (2F / 1G)	____	65.4%	____	____	____	____	65.4%

Fig. 7.5 1985 NAIC experience reporting form (continued).

EARNED PREMIUM CONVERSION WORKSHEET
CREDIT LIFE INSURANCE
STATE OF OHIO
CALENDAR YEAR 1986

Single Life _X_ Joint Life __

		Actual Earned Premiums Col.(1)	Prima Facie Rate Col.(2)	Actual Premium Rate Col.(3)	Prima Facie Earned Premium Col.(4) [(1)x(2)/(3)]
A. Earned premiums at prima facie rate		75,000	XXX	XXX	75,000
B. Earned premiums at other than prima facie rates:					
	1.	5,000	.80	.7692	5,200
	2.				
	3.				
	4.				
	5.				
	6.				
Totals		80,000	XXX	XXX	80,200
		To Line 1.F., Part 1			To Line 1.G., Part 1

C. State method used to calculate unearned premiums: Rule of 78 for decreasing life and pro rata for level life.

Note: Companies making a direct calculation of prima facie earned premium will complete only Col. 1 and Col. 4 totals, and Line C.

Fig. 7.6 Form B for life insurance.

EARNED PREMIUM CONVERSION WORKSHEET
CREDIT ACCIDENT & HEALTH INSURANCE
STATE OF OHIO
CALENDAR YEAR 1986

Plan of Benefits 14-Day Retroactive

	Actual Earned Premium	Premium Rates:			Prima Facie Earned Premium
		12 mo.	24 mo.	36 mo.	
	Col.1	Col.2	Col.3	Col.4	Col.5*
A. Earned Premium at prima facie rate	70,000	2.47	3.12	3.56	70,000
B. Earned Premium at other than prima facie rate:					
1. a. Actual Rate	XXX	2.72	3.43	3.92	XXX
b. Ratio	XXX	.908	.910	.908	XXX
c. Average Ratio of Columns 2 - 3 - 4	XXX	XXX	.909	XXX	XXX
d. Earned Premium	5,000	XXX	XXX	XXX	4,545
2. a. Actual Rate	XXX	____	____	____	XXX
b. Ratio	XXX	____	____	____	XXX
c. Average Ratio of Columns 2 - 3 - 4	XXX	XXX	____	XXX	XXX
d. Earned Premium	____	XXX	XXX	XXX	____

Fig.. 7.7 Form B for disability insurance.

3. a. Actual Rate	XXX	_____	_____	_____	XXX
b. Ratio	XXX	_____	_____	_____	XXX
c. Average Ratio of Columns 2 - 3 - 4	XXX	XXX	_____	XXX	XXX
d. Earned Premiums	_____	XXX	XXX	XXX	_____
Totals	75,000	XXX	XXX	XXX	75,545
	To Line 1.f., Part 2				To Line 1.g., Part 2

C. State method used to calculate unearned premiums: ( ) Rule of 78; ( ) Straight Line; (x) Average Rule of 78 and Straight Line; ( ) Tabular Basis; ( ) Other, specify basis ____

____

____

* Prima Facie Earned Premium in Column (5) are found by multiplying the Actual Earned Premium (Col.1) by the Average Ratio shown in line (c).

Note: Companies making a direct calculation of prima facie earned premium will complete only Column 1 and Column 5 totals.

Fig. 7.7 Form B for disability insurance (continued).

CREDIT LIFE AND ACCIDENT & HEALTH EXPERIENCE EXHIBIT

INSTRUCTIONS:

1. Data is to be reported for all life insurance and all accident and health insurance written in the state for which the exhibit is being prepared in connection with loans or other credit transactions entered into for personal, family or household purposes, under which the creditor is the primary beneficiary, without regard to the scope of any applicable credit insurance statute, the term of the insurance or the duration of the credit transaction, but excluding the following: insurance written on a non-contributory basis; insurance written in connection with agricultural loans or other agricultural credit transactions through banks or production credit associations; insurance written in connection with loans or other credit transactions secured by purchase money liens on residential real property; insurance written in connection with isolated transactions not related to a plan or agreement of the insurer for insuring the debtors of the creditor. In view of the differences between these specifications and those applicable to other Annual Statement exhibits, the data may not balance with the credit insurance data exhibited elsewhere in the Annual Statement.

2. The data reported is to be the direct business of the reporting insurer only; reinsurance ceded is not to be deducted and reinsurance assumed is not to be included.

3. Copies of all work papers, calculations and other data used in preparing this Exhibit, including forms used in the conversion of actual earned premiums to earned premiums at prima facie rates, must be maintained at the home office of the insurer and be available for examination by or submission to the respective insurance departments upon request. In addition, each company

Fig. 7.8 Instructions for completing 1985 Experience Reporting Form.

shall prepare a nationwide summary of the state exhibits, which shall also be available for submission to the respective insurance departments upon request.

4. Gross Written Premiums (Line 1.A - Parts 1 and 2). Report gross premiums before deductions for dividends or experience rating refunds or credits.

5. Earned Premiums at Prima Facie Rates (Line 1.G - Parts 1 and 2). Actual earned premiums are to be adjusted to the amount which would have been earned if all the insurance in force during the year had been written at rates actuarially equivalent to the current prima facie or statutory rates (the rates in effect at the end of the reporting year). Utilizing credit life or credit accident and health earned premium conversion worksheets, the conversion must be performed for each premium rate (or schedule of rates) which is not actuarially equivalent to the current prima facie rate and which had premiums earned during the year. (For the conversion of actual earned premiums on business for which prima facie rates have not been promulgated, see paragraph C. Special Instructions). Both earned premium conversion worksheets call for actual earned premiums at prima facie rates on Line A; this is for balancing purposes only. If all actual earned premiums are written at rates actuarially equivalent to current prima facie rates, Lines 1.F and 1.G will be equal and earned premium conversion worksheets need not be completed. Earned premium conversion worksheets are not to be submitted with the Exhibit, but are to be retained in accordance with Instruction 3.

A. Credit Life Earned Premium Conversion Worksheet. Actual earned premiums are converted to prima facie earned premiums by using a conversion factor which is the ratio of the current prima facie rate to the premium rate actually charged.

B. Credit Accident & Health Earned Premiums Conversion Worksheet. Actual earned premiums are converted to prima facie earned premiums by using a conversion factor which is the

Fig. 7.8 Instructions for completing 1985 Experience Reporting Form (continued).

average of the ratios of the current prima facie rates to the premium rates actually charged for 12, 24 and 36 month terms.

C. Special Instructions. In the absence of specific instructions adopted by an insurance department for the conversion of actual earned premiums on unregulated business in that state, the following shall apply:

(1) For business written in states which have not promulgated any prima facie rates, actual earned premiums need not be converted; the amounts shown on Lines 1.F and 1.G will be equal.

(2) For business written in states which have promulgated prima facie rates that apply only to insurance written in connection with transactions of specific durations, e.g., 10 years or less, the conversion factor for actual earned premiums on unregulated business, i.e., over 10 years, shall be based on the prima facie rate for regulated business, observing any class of business rate differentials, where applicable.

6. Mean Insurance In Force (Line 4 - Part 1 only). The average of the monthly amounts of insurance in force should be calculated and entered, without adjustment for reinsurance assumed or ceded

Fig. 7.8 Instructions for completing 1985 Experience Reporting Form (continued).

GENERALLY ACCEPTED ACCOUNTING PRINCIPLES (GAAP)

GAAP statements are prepared for the owners of the insurance company. A requirement to prepare and publish GAAP statements applies only to stock life insurance companies registered with the Securities and Exchange Commission (SEC). Closely held life companies normally do not register with the SEC. Although no regulatory body requires GAAP, most of these insurers voluntarily calculate and publish GAAP financials. Stock insurers prepare an annual report to stockholders which is based on GAAP financials if GAAP financials are prepared.

GAAP requirements are specified by pronouncements of the American Institute of Certified Public Accountants (AICPA). The pronouncements are contained in audit guides and principles adopted by the AICPA. A special audit guide applies to life insurers–the *Audit Guide for Stock Life Insurance Companies*. A knowledge of general accounting and GAAP is assumed in the following discussion.

Since cash and other items are the same for SAP and GAAP, most insurers prepare the statutory statement, and then make adjusting entries to convert the SAP financial to GAAP. Some insurers maintain a ledger for both SAP and GAAP, then GAAP statements are prepared directly from the GAAP ledger. The conversion of a SAP financial to a GAAP financial is relatively simple for a credit insurer writing only direct business.

The following total corporate items must be addressed to convert a statutory financial statement to a GAAP financial statement:

- Admitted assets
- Non-admitted assets
- MSVR liability
- Deferred tax liability

- Valuation of subsidiaries
- Presentation

Admitted assets of bonds and stocks generally are carried at the same value for SAP and GAAP. Bonds in default have SAP values prescribed by the NAIC, but GAAP carries the bonds at market. Certain preferred stocks are valued at market for GAAP, versus at cost for SAP.

Under SAP, certain assets must be valued at zero; i.e., the asset is a *non-admitted asset* for statutory purposes. This is a foreign concept under GAAP–an asset either has value or it is not an asset. Each statutory non-admitted asset is reviewed to determine the realistic value of the asset. One significant item is furniture and equipment, which includes all items except data processing hardware equipment (which may be carried at depreciated value under SAP). Office furnishings, company cars, company airplanes, and data processing application software packages are all valued at zero under SAP. These items are carried at their depreciated value in the GAAP statement. Other SAP non-admitted items include:

- Premiums due from agents
- Cash loaned to officers or agents
- Unsecured personal loans
- Premiums in course of collection over 90 days old
- Due and accrued investment income on defaulted securities

Each of these items would be individually evaluated for collectability. Any portion deemed collectable would be included in the GAAP assets.

SAP requires establishing a liability called the Mandatory Securities Valuation Reserve (MSVR). This is not a true liability, just a fluctuation reserve to protect an insurer from swings in surplus caused by changes in the value of securities. GAAP restores this liability to surplus.

SAP financials are the basis of federal income taxation. Generally, GAAP recognizes the profits in earlier accounting periods than SAP, but taxes do not have to be paid until the earnings emerge on SAP. The GAAP profits must be reduced by the taxes which will be paid when the earnings emerge on SAP. A liability for the deferred taxes is established for the ultimate tax to be paid on the profits which have emerged under GAAP, but have not emerged under SAP.

Subsidiaries of life insurance companies are conservatively valued under SAP. If the subsidiary is a life insurance company, the value carried is the statutory book value. Non-life insurance subsidiaries are valued at book value, but statutory rules apply. The book value of a subsidiary must be reduced if a portion of the book value is attributable to an asset not admitted under SAP. GAAP values the subsidiaries at GAAP book value.

Several differences in presentation affect the values in the statements but do not affect net worth:

1. On the income statement, the change in the active life reserves for credit insurance is a reduction to premium income rather than an item of expense. Premium income becomes earned premium under GAAP.

2. Realized capital gains, net of taxes, are included in net income under GAAP, rather than an adjustment to surplus under SAP.

3. Intercompany transactions with consolidated subsidiaries are eliminated under GAAP.

Only two adjustments are needed beyond the overall corporate adjustments:

- Calculation of deferred acquisition costs
- Calculation of reserves

DEFERRED ACQUISITION COSTS

The fundamental difference between SAP and GAAP is the deferral of expenses associated with the acquisition of new business. Insurers pay a significant portion of the initial premium dollars as compensation for the solicitation of new business. The nature of insurance also requires the outlay of money to process an application for insurance, underwrite a risk, and issue a policy. SAP requires that all of these expenses be charged to the accounting period when the expense is incurred, while GAAP recognizes that these expenses should be spread over the policy lifetime. An asset is established for the unamortized acquisition expenses.

Deferred acquisition costs (DAC) are the portion of expenses paid to acquire the business which may be deferred and charged to earnings over the policy lifetime. For credit insurance, the Audit Guide requires that expenses be charged to earnings in proportion to premium earned in the accounting period. Deferred expenses are amortized over the term of the policies. Only those expenses which "both vary with and are directly related to the production of new business" qualify for deferral.

MOB premiums are usually earned as they are collected, so the associated expenses are charged as they are incurred. Expenses are deferred on single premium business. Credit insurers defer the front compensation and premium taxes, since these expenses vary directly with the amount of new business written. Since both expenses are a percentage of premium, the determination of the unamortized portion of the DAC is easy. The unearned premium represents the portion of the premium remaining for the unexpired term. To obtain the unamortized DAC, multiply the compensation and tax percentage times the applicable unearned premium.

Calculations are made on a policy-by-policy basis or a year-of-issue basis. A seriatim valuation is done when an individual in force is available containing the state of issue and the compensation paid on the policy. The premium tax rate for the state plus the front compensation rate are multiplied times the policy's unearned premium.

The year-of-issue approach uses the average compensation rate and premium tax rate for the policies issued each year. On the accounting date, the unearned premium for the company is tabulated by year of issue. The compensation and tax rate is multiplied times the unearned premium for each year. A simple example is:

	--------New Business in Year--------		
	1984	1985	1986
Premium written	100,000	150,000	200,000
Compensation paid	30,000	48,000	62,000
Premium taxes paid	2,000	3,300	4,200
Compensation percentage	30.0%	32.0%	31.0%
Premium tax percentage	2.0%	2.2%	2.1%

UNAMORTIZED DAC AT DECEMBER 31, 1986

	Unearned Premium at 12-31-86	Commission and tax rate for year	Unamortized DAC
Business issued in 1984	40,000	32.0%	12,800
Business issued in 1985	80,000	34.2%	27,360
Business issued in 1986	180,000	33.1%	59,580
All Business	300,000		99,740

Some companies also defer a portion of the policy issue expenses. This would include the cost of policy forms and costs associated with issuing the policy and adding the policy to the in force. A functional cost analysis is performed. The expenses are usually expressed as a percentage of premium, so that the year-of-issue approach may be utilized. These costs are small and have only a small impact on the DAC. One generally finds it difficult to justify more than 1%-3% of premiums for these costs.

Annually, the insurer must make *recoverability tests* to establish the validity of the DAC. An asset cannot be established for unamortized expenses unless the expenses can be recovered from the future earnings of the block of business. The guiding principle is that profits must be recognized over the term of the policies, but losses must be recognized as soon as they are apparent. Recoverability tests are straightforward for credit insurance based on a loss ratio test. The tests are performed by line of business rather than by segments finer than line of business. Some companies make the test separately by credit life and disability; others consider all credit insurance as one line of business. This decision is between the insurer and its independent auditors. For the preceding data, the average unamortized DAC is (99,740/300,000) = 33%. A margin is added for all maintenance expenses, primarily the cost of claims administration, that must be incurred to mature the business, usually about 4%. If the incurred loss ratio for the year is less than 63% (100% - 33% - 4%), the line of business meets the recoverability test and the DAC may be established. If the loss ratio exceeds 63%, part or all of the expenses are not recoverable. The DAC must then be reduced to a level where the recoverability test is satisfied. If the loss ratio exceeds 96%, an additional liability must be established.

RESERVES

SAP reserves are based on conservative methods and assumptions. GAAP reserves are based on a realistic valuation of the liability. For credit insurance, reserves must be established which result in premium being earned in direct proportion to the coverage provided. Credit life business is reserved on an unearned premium basis rather than mortality reserves.

GAAP reserves follow the same logic as valuing the profitability of a block of business. Active life reserves are based on unearned premiums. The accepted standards are:

Single premium life decreasing gross coverage	Rule of 78
Single premium life level coverage	Pro rata
Single premium life net payoff	Single Premium Method
Single premium disability coverage	Mean of Rule of 78 and Pro rata

If the volume of net payoff life business is not material, it may be valued on the Rule of 78, possibly with an adjustment factor to estimate the Single Premium Method. Some variation is found for disability reserves. A few insurers hold Rule of 78 reserves; others hold a split different from the mean; i.e., 60% pro rata plus 40% Rule of 78. The Single Premium Method is also acceptable. An insurer selects the method which it feels most accurately reflects the pattern of incurred claims on its business.

Reserves for MOB business may be zero if all policies are dated on the first of the month, although the usual practice is to hold an active life reserve equal to one-half of the prior month's collected gross premiums. In the latter case, a DAC element is included for the compensation and premium taxes paid on MOB business.

Claim reserves are usually carried at the statutory statement values. If the statutory statement reserves contain an explicit margin for conservatism, some or all of the margin may be removed for GAAP purposes.

Certain other liabilities may need adjustment for the GAAP statement. One example is contingent commissions and experience rating refunds. When these items are calculated at the time of payment, some conservatism may be introduced. A common method is to calculate these items with pro rata unearned premiums on disability business, which defers the recognition of profit and the payment of contingent commissions or experience refunds. Thus, an insurer protects itself from a deterioration in experience. At year-end, a liability is established for the contingent payments which have been earned but not paid. For GAAP financials, the liability should be revalued on a realistic basis without the conservatism.

If a portion of the business is reinsured, this business may be treated separately. Traditional excess reinsurance and captive reinsurance on a written basis are handled in the same manner as direct business. Ceded cash items are deducted, and there is a reserve credit for the ceded reserves. The DAC percentages are applied to the unearned premiums net of reinsurance ceded. If the amount is material, a test should be made to insure that the percentages are appropriate to the net retained business.

In a typical captive reinsurance deal, the entire risk is reinsured by the captive. The direct writer simply retains a fee for administering the business. On business reinsured on a written basis, the direct writer receives a percentage of the written premium for its administrative fee. Since some services, such as claims administration, are performed over the term of the policies, it is proper to defer the recognition of a portion of the fee. An unearned income liability is established. Since the income is a percentage of premium, it can be amortized based on the unearned premium. An administrative fee might be allocated:

Rate charts, policy forms, policy issue costs and premium processing	4.0%
Premium taxes	2.5%
Refund processing	.5%
Claims administration	3.0%
Profit and risk charge	2.0%
Total	12.0%

The portions for rate charts, forms, issue costs, premium processing and premium taxes represent front expenses to the direct writer. The portion of the administration fee applicable to these items should be included in income on a written basis. Expenses for processing refunds and administering claims occur over the term of the policies; therefore, this portion of the fee should be earned over the term of the reinsured policies. The profit and risk charge should be earned over the term of the policies or in proportion to the earning of the fees for the other services. Materiality of the amounts involved will affect the decision about whether to establish the liability.

Adjustments are needed for business reinsured on an earned basis. In the statutory statement, the business appears to belong to the direct writer. Statutory reserves and cash items are not ceded in the ledger or in accrual calculations. As profits or losses emerge, the net profit is transferred to the reinsurer. For GAAP statements, adjusting entries are made to convert the presentation as if the business were ceded on a written basis, since the risk is ultimately transferred to the reinsurer. The adjustments are complicated and only need to be made by those direct writers having a material volume of these transactions.

STATUTORY SURPLUS DRAIN

The requirement that expenses be charged to earnings in the accounting period incurred causes a unique accounting result, called *surplus drain* or *surplus strain*. At the time of issue, even profitable business may result in a loss to net income on the statutory income statement. This paper loss is created because the premium must be earned over the term of the policy, while expenses are charged when incurred. For single premium credit insurance, the premium is earned over the policy term, about three years as an average. In contrast, the front commissions, premium taxes and issue costs are incurred when the business is issued, so these expenses must be charged to the accounting period when the policy is sold.

As a policy progresses through the term of coverage, the paper loss is recovered along with any real profits on the business. For a new company, or an insurer with a growing book of business, statutory losses are likely. These losses will reduce surplus, hence the term surplus drain. An insurer will require a substantial amount of surplus to absorb the drain and remain in operation until the profits emerge.

Surplus drain is not a bad situation for an insurer with adequate surplus. Insurers are taxed based on statutory accounting. The phenomenon defers the recognition of profits, but also defers the taxation of those profits. If an insurer cannot fund the surplus drain, it must reinsure a portion of its business to a reinsurer with the requisite surplus using *surplus relief reinsurance*. Reinsurers charge a fee for the reinsurance which adds to the direct writer's cost of doing business. From the direct writer's standpoint, the transaction is like borrowing money, not receiving any cash, and paying interest on the borrowed funds. Annual surplus relief reinsurance fees are about 4% of the amount of relief outstanding.

The following example shows how the drain arises and illustrates some of the differences between statutory and GAAP. Consider a credit disability policy issued on December 31, 1986 with a 12-month term. The gross premium is $100. Commissions and premium taxes are 40% of premium or $40. Assume general expenses and investment income are zero. During 1987, the insured has a claim for $60.

Since the policy has just been issued, the unearned premium at December 31, 1986 is the full gross premium. On December 31, 1987, the policy has expired so the reserve is zero. In 1986, the change in the reserve for the year is $100. In 1987, the reserve begins at $100 and decreases to zero. The change in reserves is ($100). The statutory statements for the two years are shown in Figure 7.9.

DECEMBER 31, 1986					
Assets	Cash	60			
	Total		60		
Liabilities	Reserves	100			
	Surplus	(40)			
	Total		60		
Income Statement	Premium Income			100	
	Total Income				100
	Claims			-0-	
	Increase in Reseves			100	
	Commissions and Taxes			40	
	Total Expenses				140
	Net Income				(40)

DECEMBER 31, 1987					
Assets	Cash	0			
	Total		0		
Liabilities	Reserves	0			
	Surplus	0			
	Total		0		
Income Statement	Premium Income			0	
	Total Income				0
	Claims			60	
	Increase in Reserves			(100)	
	Commissions and Taxes			0	
	Total Expenses				(40)
	Net Income				40

Fig. 7.9 Statutory results.

Here is the experience of a policy on which the insurer made no profit. Yet, the statutory statement shows a loss in the year of issue and a profit as the policy matures. This is not an isolated example. It occurs on all disability business and some life business. Statutory accounting creates artificial losses when the business is issued and paper profits as the business matures.

On single premium disability business, the insurer must hold a gross unearned premium reserve. Under any method for calculating unearned premiums, the initial reserve is the gross premium collected. This means an insurer will have a loss from income (and surplus drain) equal to the front compensation, premium taxes, and issue costs.

For life insurance, the statutory statement requires mortality reserves. Mortality reserves are calculated based on the characteristics of the particular policy. The reserve is the same for identical policies issued in all states, and is independent of the gross premium charged. The amount of surplus drain will depend on the relationship between the mortality reserves, the gross premiums, and the front expenses. At issue the surplus drain is:

Gross premium collected,

less Mortality reserve at issue,

less Front compensation, premium taxes, and issue costs.

Not all life insurance business results in surplus drain. Some life business actually produces a statutory profit on the day issued. Until recently, life insurance did not produce significant drain except in certain states with very low prima facie rates. As states have reduced gross premium levels, more life business has created surplus drain. The situation can only be alleviated by reducing front compensation or lowering mortality reserve requirements. The marketplace will not permit the former solution, and the regulators dislike reducing reserve requirements. Insurers with adequate surplus have no reason to encourage a change, since surplus drain defers taxes and makes life tougher on the competition with less surplus. The 1958 CET contains a substantial margin for conservatism even for statutory principles. The 1980 CET can be expected to gradually replace the 1958 CET as the basis of mortality reserves for credit insurance in order to reduce the surplus drain.

Surplus drain does not exist under GAAP. This follows from the basic premise that net income is to be measured accurately. At issue, the insurer has not earned any profits or incurred any losses. Profits and losses are reflected as they occur over the term of the business. GAAP uses the deferred acquisition cost asset to correct the statutory results.

An asset is established for the front compensation and premium taxes. These expenses are charged to earnings over the term of the policy in proportion to the premium earned. The DAC is established at issue and decreases as the policy matures. Standard presentation considers the change in the DAC an expense item, so an increase in the DAC is a negative expense. The GAAP statements for the example are shown in Figure 7.10.

This is the expected result. The insurer did not make any profit on this policy. Net income for both years is zero.

DECEMBER 31, 1986					
Assets	Cash	60			
	Deferred Acquisition Costs	40			
	Total		100		
Liabilities	Reserves	100			
	Surplus	0			
	Total		100		
Income Statement					
	Premium Income			100	
	Change in Unearned Premium Reserves			100	
	Earned Premium				0
	Claims Incurred			0	
	Commissions, Taxes Paid			40	
	Change in DAC			(40)	
	Expenses Incurred				0
	Net Income				0

DECEMBER 31, 1987					
Assets	Cash	0			
	Deferred Acquisition Costs	0			
	Total		0		
Liabilities	Reserves	0			
	Surplus	0			
	Total		0		
Income Statement					
	Premium Income			0	
	Change in Unearned Premium Reserves			(100)	
	Earned Premium				100
	Claims Incurred			60	
	Commissions, Taxes Paid			0	
	Change in DAC			40	
	Expenses Incurred				100
	Net Income				0

Fig. 7.10 GAAP results.

CHAPTER EIGHT

FEDERAL INCOME TAXATION OF LIFE INSURANCE COMPANIES

Life insurance companies are taxed at the federal level by special sections of the Internal Revenue Code. The applicable laws were totally revised by the Deficit Reduction Act of 1984. This chapter is intended to describe the taxation in a general way as it affects credit insurance operations.

Methods of taxation of life insurance companies have always attempted to apply the usual corporate rules and tax rates, while recognizing the unique aspects created by the long-term nature of the insurance product and the industry's accounting practices. Prior to the early 1970s, life insurance companies prepared financial statements only on the basis of statutory accounting principles, so these principles have always been the basis of taxation.

From 1921 to 1959, life insurance companies were taxed only on taxable investment income. Small companies could invest solely in tax-exempt investments and avoid federal income tax altogether. Several specialty credit insurance companies did this. One purpose of the 1959 Tax Act was to impose a tax on these credit insurance companies.

1959 TAX ACT

In 1959 a new act was adopted which served as the basis of life insurance company taxation for twenty-five years. The law adopted a three-phase approach to taxation. For a *phase-one company*, taxable income was *taxable investment income, (TII)*. As a continuation of the pre-1959 concepts, this remained the basis of taxation for most mutual insurance companies. A second phase of taxable income was imposed if the *taxable gain from operations (GFO)* exceeded taxable investment income. This situation applied to most stock life insurance companies, which included most credit insurance companies. One-half of the excess of GFO over TII was added to TII to get taxable income for the year. The other half of (GFO - TII) was not taxed currently. This deferred portion, maintained in a memorandum account, was called the *Policyholder Surplus Account, (PSA)*. Taxation on the PSA was deferred as long as certain conditions were met.

For example, if:

TII	= \$100,000
GFO	= \$300,000
Taxable Income	= TII + .5 x (GFO - TII)
	= 100,000+ .5 x (300,000 - 100,000)
	= 200,000

The taxable income of \$200,000 was taxed at the usual corporate rates. The remainder equal to {.5 x (300,000 - 100,000)} was not subject to taxation in the current tax year. This amount was added to the PSA.

The taxable income, after reduction for taxes paid, was added to a second memorandum account, the *Shareholder Surplus Account*. Other non-taxed income, such as tax-exempt interest and the small business deduction, was also added to this account. Dividends to stockholders were subtracted from this account.

A stock company where GFO exceeded TII was a *phase-two positive company.* If GFO was less than TII, the company was taxed on GFO. It was a *phase-two negative company.* If a company paid policyholder dividends, the formulas were more complex.

The amount in the PSA could not exceed the greatest of:

1. 50% of premium income for the year,

2. 15% of the life insurance reserves, or

3. 25% of the increase in life insurance reserves since 1959.

As a practical matter, the first test applied to credit insurance companies. Life insurance reserves for credit insurance were relatively small. The second or third test applied only to a declining book of credit insurance business, or an insurer with ordinary insurance business. If the PSA exceeded the limit, the excess was removed from the PSA and included in taxable income. This was a *phase-three tax.* Dividends to stockholders in excess of the amount in the Shareholder Surplus Account also triggered a phase-three tax. This tax applied in addition to the tax imposed on current year operations.

Gain from operations was defined on the basis of statutory accounting. Conservatism in statutory accounting rules resulted in the deferral of the recognition of income. As the basis of taxation, this had the pleasant effect of deferring taxes.

The law provided various special deductions from statutory investment income and gain from operations to produce taxable investment income and taxable gain from operations. The combination of deductions gave insurance companies a tax-favored status. Many stock insurance companies had overall tax rates under 25%, a rate significantly lower than the general corporate tax rate. Measured as a percent of GAAP earnings, the tax rate was even lower.

Reinsurance companies are taxed on the same basis as a direct writer. Consequently, the basis of taxation prompted the formation of captive credit insurance companies. A producer receives compensation for the sale of the product. This produces commission income in the corporate entity taxed at corporate rates (currently 46%). If the producer is willing to accept the underwriting risk, the producer could accept lower compensation and allow the remainder to be earned as underwriting profits in the captive at a much lower tax rate. By 1980, most producers of credit insurance writing $500,000 or more of annual credit insurance premiums owned a captive.

The price for this tax-favored status included compliance with one of the most complex set of tax laws ever devised by man. As the environment of non-credit products changed in the late 1970s, the 1959 Tax Act became inadequate. Universal life and deferred annuities were not clearly handled from a tax standpoint. Mutual companies found reinsurance mechanisms to reduce taxable investment income. The 1959 Tax Act was significantly modified by the temporary provisions of the Tax Equity and Fiscal Responsibility Act of 1982, (TEFRA). TEFRA was adopted for two years in order for a complete revision in the tax code to take place. TEFRA had little impact on credit insurance operations. The revision was adopted into law in 1984.

1984 TAX ACT

The 1984 Tax Act provides a definition of insurance to cope with the ever-changing marketplace. Provisions in the law resulted from compromises by all concerned parties. Countless hours were involved, and the result was a far simpler basis of taxation. Gone is the three-phase system under the 1959 Act. Many of the 1959 Act's contested issues between the IRS and insurers were resolved. The 1984 Tax Act is applicable to 1984 and subsequent tax years.

QUALIFICATION AS A LIFE INSURANCE COMPANY

The Act defines an insurance company for the first time, while retaining the prior tests to determine whether an insurance company is a life insurance company. To qualify for taxation as a life insurance company, three tests must be met:

1. An insurance company test,
2. A business activity test, and
3. A reserve test.

An insurance company is a corporation where more than one-half of the business during the year is the issuance of insurance policies or annuity contracts, or the reinsurance of such policies or contracts. Forthcoming regulations may specify more definitive tests. In general, one would expect net income to be a reasonable test. Other tests might include corporate resources or facilities allocated to insurance operations.

The business activity test just specifies that the company issues or reinsures the types of insurance policies or contracts deemed to be life insurance by the IRS. These are :

1. Ordinary or term life insurance,
2. Annuities, and
3. Non-cancellable accident and health policies.

Credit life insurance qualifies as a life insurance policy, but the IRS does not consider credit disability insurance as meeting the requirements for inclusion as a non-cancellable accident and health policy.

Finally, the reserve test specifies that more than 50% of the total company reserves must be life insurance reserves. The *qualification ratio* is a fraction calculated using statutory reserves. The numerator includes life insurance reserves; the denominator includes total insurance reserves.

Life insurance reserves must:

1. Be calculated on a recognized mortality or morbidity table,

2. Include an assumed rate of interest in the calculation,

3. Be necessary to mature future unaccrued claims on life insurance business involving contingencies of life, health or accident, and

4. Be required by law.

Total insurance reserves include:

1. Life insurance reserves, and

2. Unearned premiums and unpaid losses on accident and health policies.

In terms of the statutory accounting, the qualification ratio for credit insurance products is:

$$\frac{\text{Exhibit 8 Reserves}}{\text{Exhibit 8 Reserves} + \text{Exhibit 9 Reserves} + \text{Exhibit 11, Part 1 (col.10) Liabilities}}$$

Any reserves in Exhibit 8 which do not meet the tests of life insurance reserves must be excluded from the numerator. Calculations for a tax year are based on the average of these reserves at the beginning and the end of the tax year.

A life insurance company may be taxed as a non-life company. This occurs when the company meets the definition of an insurance company but fails the life reserve test. The non-life status is the basis on which property and casualty insurance companies are taxed. Essentially, a non-life insurance company for tax purposes is taxed in the same manner as other corporations, but the basis of taxation is still the statutory financial statement concept. A deduction from income is permitted for the increase in active life and claim reserves.

In some situations, a direct writer or captive credit insurer may prefer to be taxed as a non-life company. Some of the provisions of the 1984 Tax Act do not apply to non-life companies including the new definitions of reserve bases for tax purposes if unearned premium reserves are held. Also, tax-exempt interest is effectively taxed in a life insurance company because of the workings of the various formulas used to determine taxable investment income. However, the interest is not taxed by the formulas used for non-life companies. Offsetting these advantages is the applicable tax rate. Non-life companies are taxed at the usual corporate tax rates.

LIFE INSURANCE COMPANY TAXABLE INCOME

Having met the qualifications as a life company, the tax must be calculated. Standard corporate tax rates are applied to the *life insurance company taxable income (LICTI).* LICTI is the difference between gross income and deductions. Gross income consists of the usual statutory items of premium income, net investment income, and other income. For tax purposes, a decrease in reserves is an income item rather than a negative expense.

Net investment income is gross investment income less deductions. The deduction for investment expenses is defined as 10% of gross investment income. This should resolve many disagreements originating from the 1959 Act over which expenses qualified as investment expenses. A second deduction is allowed for the policyholder share of investment income. Generally, the objective is to exclude from taxable income the portion of investment income required to support the reserves.

Deductions from income include the usual corporate deductions and two special life insurance company deductions. Usual deductions include:

1. Policy benefits incurred,

2. Increase in reserves,

3. Policyholder dividends, and

4. All other deductions permitted in computing a corporation's taxable income; e.g., general expenses, commissions, state and local taxes.

Two special deductions retain much of the tax-favored status of the prior law–a small company deduction and a general life company deduction. If a company qualifies as a small life insurance company, taxation is much lower. To qualify, it must meet an assets test and an earnings test. The assets test is met if the insurer has total assets of less than $500,000,000. If the company is a member of a controlled group under the usual tax rule of 80% ownership, all assets of the controlled group are included. Credit insurance captives are one of the primary targets of this test. With the controlled group definition, captives of most banks and other financial institutions will not qualify for the small company deduction.

The earnings test applies to *tentative LICTI*. Tentative LICTI is gross income less deductions, before the two special deductions are calculated. It also includes the controlled group delineation. Only income from the life insurance business of the controlled group is included in the calculation of the deduction. Life insurance business includes investment activities normally conducted by insurance companies. Real estate sale and development is specifically included as insurance income.

A company meeting the assets test is permitted to deduct 60% of the first $3,000,000 of tentative LICTI. The deduction is reduced by 15% of the excess of tentative LICTI over $3,000,000. At a tentative LICTI of $15,000,000, the reduction eliminates the small company deduction entirely. The table displays the deduction.

Tentative LICTI	Small Company Deduction
$ 1,000,000	.6 x 1,000,000 = 600,000
$ 2,000,000	.6 x 2,000,000 = 1,200,000
$ 3,000,000	.6 x 3,000,000 = 1,800,000
$ 4,000,000	.6 x 3,000,000 - .15 (4,000,000 - 3,000,000) = 1,650,000
$ 5,000,000	.6 x 3,000,000 - .15 (5,000,000 - 3,000,000) = 1,500,000
$ 10,000,000	.6 x 3,000,000 - .15 (10,000,000 - 3,000,000) = 750,000
$ 15,000,000	.6 x 3,000,000 - .15 (15,000,000 - 3,000,000) = -0-

A second special deduction is permitted for all life insurance companies. The deduction is made after the small company deduction is calculated. The deduction permitted is 20% of: (tentative LICTI less the small company deduction). As in the small company deduction, the controlled group is used. Only income relative to insurance activity, or related investment activity, qualifies for the deduction. A sample calculation for a company would be:

Tentative LICTI	$ 2,000,000
Small Company Deduction	1,200,000
Net	800,000
Life Company Deduction (.20 x 800,000)	160,000
LICTI	640,000

TAX RATES

The usual corporate taxes are:

Taxable Income	Tax Rate
First $25,000	15%
Next $25,000	18%
Next $25,000	30%
Next $25,000	40%
Amounts over $100,000	46%

In effect, if taxable earnings exceed $100,000, the first $100,000 of taxable earnings is taxed at a corporate rate of 25.75%:

.15 x 25,000 =	3,750
.18 x 25,000 =	4,500
.30 x 25,000 =	7,500
.40 x 25,000 =	10,000
Total	25,750

Tax rate = 25,750 / 100,000 = 25.75%

This reduced tax rate on the first $100,000 of taxable income is called the surtax exemption. The maximum amount of the surtax exemption is $20,250; i.e., [(.46 x $100,000)-$25,750]. If taxable income exceeds $1,000,000, the surtax exemption is gradually eliminated by imposing an additional tax equal to 5% of the taxable income in excess of $1,000,000. The additional tax is imposed until the tax on all income reaches the 46% rate.

For a small life insurance company, the tax rate on the first $312,500 of earnings (tentative LICTI) is only 8.24%:

Tentative LICTI	$312,500
Small Company Deduction	187,500
Life Company Deduction	25,000
LICTI	100,000
Corporate Tax Rate	.2575
Taxes Due	25,750
Tax as a percentage of Tentative LICTI	.0824

The tax rate for tentative LICTI of $3,000,000 or less can be computed by the formula:

(1 - Small Company Deduction Rate) x
(1 - Life Company Deduction Rate) x (General Corporate Rate)

= (1 - .60) x (1 - .20) x (General Corporate Rate)

= .32 x (General Corporate Rate)

Tentative LICTI between $312,500 and $3,000,000 is taxed at a corporate rate of 46%, so the tax rate is:

.32 x .46 = .1472

The overall tax rate for tentative LICTI up to $3,000,000 is the weighted average of the amount taxed at 8.24% and the amount taxed at 14.72%. At a tentative LICTI of $3,000,000 the overall tax rate is 14.05%.

For a tentative LICTI between $3,000,000 and $15,000,000, the small company deduction and the surtax exemption are gradually eliminated. The overall tax rate rises to the tax rate for companies not qualifying for the small company deduction.

If a company does not qualify for the small company deduction, the formula for the overall tax rate is:

(1 - Life Company Deduction Rate) x (General Corporate Rate)

= .8 x (General Corporate Rate)

For amounts in excess of a tentative LICTI of $125,000, the tax rate is:

.8 x .46 = .368 or 36.8%

The overall tax rate will be slightly lower because of the lower tax rates applicable to the first $100,000 of taxable income until taxable income reaches the level where the surtax exemption is eliminated

Applying the usual corporate tax rates, the tax rates for a small life insurance company would be:

Tentative LICTI	LICTI	Taxes	Overall Tax Rate	Marginal Tax Rate
$ 1,000,000	320,000	126,950	12.70%	14.72%
$ 3,000,000	960,000	421,350	14.05%	42.32%
$ 3,043,478	1,000,000	439,750	14.45%	46.91%
$ 3,483,696	1,405,000	646,300	18.55%	42.32%
$ 10,000,000	7,400,000	3,404,000	34.04%	42.32%
$ 15,000,000	12,000,000	5,520,000	36.80%	36.80%

The *marginal tax rate* is the rate applied to the next higher dollar of taxable income. Note that the marginal tax rate on earnings between $3,000,001 and $15,000,000 exceeds the 36.80% maximum rate because of the gradual elimination of the small company deduction. In addition, the marginal tax rate is even higher on earnings between $3,043,478 and $3,483,696 as the surtax exemption is also eliminated.

The new law will have a mixed impact on captives. A captive for an automobile dealer or one owned by a general agent has tremendous appeal. These captives would generally qualify as small companies and be subject to the 14.72% tax rate. On the other hand, a tax rate of 36.8% may not be attractive to a financial institution. Many financial institutions have leasing or other operations which generate substantial tax credits.

TAXATION OF AMOUNTS IN THE POLICYHOLDER SURPLUS ACCOUNT

Many stock life companies still have earnings in the policyholder surplus account which have not been taxed. The PSA is frozen at the December 31, 1983 level. Taxation of these amounts will be required if the conditions set by the prior law are not met. Any amounts withdrawn from the PSA are taxed at regular corporate rates. For example, if a company has $1,000,000 in the PSA and has only $1,500,000 in premium income in 1986, the law limits the PSA to 50% of $1,500,000 or $750,000 (assuming the applicable test is the premium income test). Therefore, $250,000 is removed from the PSA and included in LICTI after the special deductions are calculated.

TAX RESERVE BASES

The 1984 Tax Act modified the prior law in defining life insurance reserves included in the calculation of taxable investment income and gain from operations. Insurers were required to recalculate reserves on the new tax bases as of January 1, 1984. These new bases were to be used for future tax returns. The difference between the statutory reserves on December 31, 1983 and the new tax reserves on January 1, 1984 was forgiven. Companies were given a *fresh start* on the new tax reserves.

Statutory reserves are conservative, far too conservative for the IRS's taste. Tax requirements were a compromise between the IRS position of unnecessary conservatism and the company's position that statutory reserves were the proper basis of tax reserves. Under The 1984 Tax Act, life insurance reserves are the greater of the net surrender value of the policy or the tax reserves, with the caveat that the tax reserve cannot be greater than the statutory reserve. Since credit insurance does not have surrender values, the reserve basis is the tax reserves.

Tax reserves are determined by applying the tax reserve method and an assumed mortality table and interest rate.

Commissioners Reserve Valuation Method (CRVM) is the tax reserve method. For single premium business, this method is equal to the Net Level Reserve Method. Therefore, no change is dictated for credit life insurance.

The assumed mortality table is the most recent table prescribed by the NAIC and permitted by the laws of 26 states. The assumed interest rate is the highest rate applicable in 26 states. If these conditions are not sufficient to define the items, the IRS is to issue guidelines. Fewer than 26 states specify a mortality table and an interest rate for credit life reserves. In 1985, the American Council of Life Insurance (ACLI) recommended a basis for credit life reserves. To date, the IRS has not issued any guidelines. Most insurers prepared their 1984 tax return based on the ACLI recommendations. A few insurers just used statutory reserves.

The ACLI recommendation specified the 1958 CET as the assumed mortality table. This table is the prevailing industry standard and is accepted by most states. The ACLI proposed that the assumed interest rate be the prevailing standard for ordinary insurance. Rates vary by the issue year of the policy. These rates are:

Year of Issue	Initial Policy Term	Interest Rate
1948 -74	All	3.50%
1975 - 79	All	4.00%
1980 - 82	All	4.50%
1983 - 86	0 - 10 years	7.25%
	11 - 20 years	6.75%
	over 20 years	6.00%

Since most insurers hold statutory reserves on the 1958 CET, the tax reserves are not significantly different from statutory reserves. Each 1% increase in the assumed interest rate reduces reserves about 1.5%. Overall, most tax reserves are 5%-8% below statutory reserves.

Insurers with less than $100,000,000 in assets at December 31, 1983 (controlled group rules apply) and with tentative LICTI of less than $3,000,000 for 1984 are permitted a special election. They may continue to use statutory reserves as the tax reserves for business issued prior to January 1, 1989. The election is irrevocable.

ISSUES IN TAXATION FOR CREDIT INSURERS

CURRENT TAX RESERVE BASES

Insurers have several concerns. While the ACLI recommendation is reasonable, there is no guarantee that it will be acceptable to the IRS.

Second, ordinary insurance tax reserves are sex distinct. For single life coverage, credit insurers generally use a male table. This adds to the conservatism since male reserves are higher than female reserves. However, sex of the insured is usually not included in credit insurance data processing records. One method is to sample the distribution of insureds' sex. Industry personnel estimate that about 20% of the single life insureds are female. An insurer could calculate separate reserve factors for males and females or use the assumption that the female reserves are equal to the male reserves with a six-year age setback. A set of blended reserve factors can be developed using 80% of the male reserve and 20% of the female reserve. These blended factors could be applied to all business. One insurer using this approach found that the blended factors reduced reserves about 6%. This is just one method to achieve sex distinct reserves; other methods are possible.

PRIOR TAX RESERVE BASES

Credit life reserves calculated based on a recognized mortality table qualify as life reserves. Until 1984, the 1958 CET table was commonly used for tax reserves, but other recognized tables in use included the 1941 CSO table, 1958 CSO table, and the 1960 CSG table. For ages applicable to credit insurance, the 1958 CET table is equal to 130% of the 1958 CSO table. Some states require 130% of the 1958 CSO. The IRS initially maintained that the 1958 CET was a recognized mortality table, but 130% of the 1958 CSO was not a recognized table. The service finally acquiesced, but only if each individual reserve factor were multiplied by 130% and then applied to the policy parameters. Calculating the reserve based on 1958 CSO factors and then multiplying the total by 130% is not acceptable, although the two results are nearly identical.

EARNED REINSURANCE TREATIES

Credit insurers have been subject to considerable controversy and litigation over tax issues. Of basic concern is the IRS general position that credit insurance more nearly fits the classification of casualty insurance. After various Circuit Court decisions, the issue was resolved in the insurers' favor by the U.S. Supreme Court in the 1967 Alinco Life Insurance Company case. (Alinco Life Insurance Company vs. U.S. 373F 2d 336, 19 AFTR 2d. 745, Ct.Cl. 1967, Par No. 1.09; 1.22).

Non-cancellable accident and health insurance has a specific definition in the eyes of the IRS. Credit disability does not meet the test, and the courts have agreed with the IRS on this issue. In the typical mix of credit insurance business, disability reserves will exceed life insurance reserves. Therefore, a direct writer issuing only credit insurance must cede a portion of its disability business in order to meet the 50% test.

Captive reinsurers maintain life status by assuming only a portion of their disability business on a written basis. The remainder is not reinsured, or else it is reinsured on an earned basis. Reinsurance on a written basis is more favorable to a captive. Coinsurance percentages are set to maximize the portion which is assumed on a written basis while retaining life status for tax purposes.

The IRS felt earned reinsurance was a circumvention of the law and wanted to impute the reserves held by the direct writer to the captive. Imputing the unearned premiums and claim reserves would disqualify the captive as a life insurance company. In the Consumers Life Insurance Company case, the Supreme Court rejected the IRS position. (Consumer Life Insurance Company vs. U.S. 725, 39 AFTR 2d 77-1261, 1977, Par No. 1.22; 8.17; 14.07; 14.10; 20.09; 25.24). Tax basis is defined by statutory accounting, which ascribes the reserves to the direct writer on earned reinsurance treaties. This position was later broadened in the Western Diversified Life Insurance Company case. (Western Diversified Life Insurance Company vs. U.S. 49 AFTR 2d 82-353, Ct.Cl. 1981, Par No. 1.22; 2.23; 8.13).

In 1978, the Arizona Insurance Department shocked the credit insurance industry by adopting a statutory reserve requirement that the reserves must be imputed to the reinsurer on an earned reinsurance treaty. Disability business reinsured on a written basis results in surplus drain if front compensation is paid. The surplus drain reduces an insurer's capital and surplus. Under earned reinsurance, the surplus drain remains with the direct writer. Since the reinsurer had the underwriting risk associated with the business, the Department felt that the reinsurer's financial statement did not properly reflect its statutory financial condition. While the logic was not based on the IRS position, the result would have the same impact by disqualifying a captive from life status.

After January 1, 1979, the reinsurer was forced to carry reserves as if the reinsurance were on a written basis. While the Department allowed an offsetting asset for funds due from the direct writer, the damage was done. Arizona, home of over half of the credit insurance captives, had now set statutory accounting practices matching the IRS position. After some intense discussions, the Department modified its position to say that reserves need only be established for the period the captive is obligated to reinsure the business. Earned reinsurance treaties were modified to give the captive the right to terminate the treaty on 30 days written notice. This left the direct writer in a position where a captive can terminate an unprofitable block of disability business and continue to reinsure a profitable life insurance block. In a few cases, this has happened. The direct writer was left with losses on disability, even though the intent of the arrangement was to reinsure all of the risk to the captive.

GENERAL TREATMENT OF REINSURANCE TRANSACTIONS

TEFRA changes provided the IRS with a new power to reallocate items on the tax return for related party reinsurance transactions. The 1984 Tax Act expanded this power to include reinsurance between unrelated parties. Section 845 of the Code reads:

> *(a) ALLOCATION IN CASE OF REINSURANCE AGREEMENT INVOLVING TAX*
>
> *AVOIDANCE OR EVASION - In the case of 2 or more related persons (within the meaning of section 482) who are parties to a reinsurance agreement (or where one of the parties to a reinsurance agreement is, with respect to any contract covered by the agreement, in effect an agent of another party to such agreement or a conduit between related persons), the Secretary may*
>
> > *1. Allocate between or among such persons income (whether investment income, premium, or otherwise), deductions,*

assets, reserves, credits, and other items related to such agreement,

2. *Recharacterize any such items, or*

3. *Make any other adjustment,*

if he determines that such allocation, characterization or adjustment is necessary to reflect the proper source and character of the taxable income (or any item described in paragraph (1) relating to such taxable income) of each such person.

(b) REINSURANCE CONTRACT HAVING SIGNIFICANT TAX AVOIDANCE EFFECT -

If the Secretary determines that any reinsurance contract has a significant tax avoidance effect on any party to such contract, the Secretary may make proper adjustments with respect to such party to eliminate such tax avoidance effect (including treating such contract with respect to such party as terminated on December 31 of each year and reinstated on January 1 of the next year).

Section 845 (b) is broad. The power to reclassify is granted if there is significant tax avoidance effect. The industry is uncertain as to its meaning or the transactions which will be subject to reclassification. Given such a broad statement, one would expect IRS guidelines to define its meaning; however, several tax experts do not expect guidelines to be issued. The IRS may use the power where deemed applicable and let the courts make interpretations. The primary difficulty is that it will be many years before the section is clearly defined. Insurers must operate with the knowledge that reinsurance transactions may be subject to revision years from now. One possible application of the powers would be to mount a new attack on earned reinsurance treaties.

Another disturbing feature of Section 845 (b) is the power of the IRS to make adjustments in the tax return of one party without a corresponding adjustment to the other party's tax return. In theory, a reinsurance transaction which provides a taxable loss for one company and a taxable gain for the other company could be taxed in a manner which eliminates the loss but preserves the gain.

SUMMARY

The 1984 Tax Act provides a simpler form of taxation for life insurers. The Act is not definitive in some areas, and credit insurers are left with many unanswered questions. These questions pose difficult operational problems, since business must go on without assurance of the amount of ultimate taxation on the profits.

1986 TAX REFORM ACT

As this book was going to press, Congress was considering a complete revision of the tax code. In general, the insurance industry was successful in their position that a substantial effort was involved in the adoption of the 1984 Act, so a complete revision of insurance taxation was unwarranted. The primary change being proposed was the elimination of the 20% general life insurance company deduction. This reflected the drop in the general corporate tax rate to a level below the 36.8% rate which resulted from the application of the 20% deduction to the 46% corporate rate. The small company deduction was retained.

Form **1120L** — Department of the Treasury, Internal Revenue Service

U.S. Life Insurance Company Income Tax Return

For calendar 1985, or tax year beginning ...., 1985, and ending ...., 19....

► For Paperwork Reduction Act Notice, see page 1 of the instructions.

OMB No. 1545-0128

1985

Please type or print

Name	A Employer identification number
Number and street	B Date incorporated
City or town, state, and ZIP code	C Check box if this is a consolidated return . . ► ☐
	D Check box if non-life insurance companies are included . . . . ► ☐

E Check box if address changed from previous year . . . ► ☐

Taxable Income

1 Life insurance company taxable income (LICTI)—(Schedule A, line 22)	1	
2 Limitation on noninsurance losses (Schedule P, line 9)	2	
3 Amount subtracted from policyholder surplus account (enter the smaller of Schedule N, line 1 or line 3)	3	
4 Total taxable income—Add lines 1, 2 and 3; however, the total may not be less than line 3	4	

Tax

5 Check if you are a member of a controlled group (see sections 1561 and 1563). . . . . . ☐ If checked, see instructions and enter your share of the $25,000 amount in each taxable income bracket: a $......... b $......... c $......... d $.........				
6 Income tax (see instructions to figure the tax). If you use the alternative tax, check this box ☐ and enter the tax from your attached schedule			6	
7 a Foreign tax credit (attach Form 1118)	7a			
b Other credits (see instructions)	7b			
c General business credit. Check if from: ☐ Form 3800 ☐ Form 3468 ☐ Form 5884 ☐ Form 6478 ☐ Form 8007	7c			
8 Add lines 7a through 7c.			8	
9 Balance of tax (subtract line 8 from line 6)			9	
10 Foreign corporations—tax on income not connected with U.S. business (see Tax Computation Instructions)			10	
11 Increase in tax from refiguring an earlier year investment credit (attach Form 4255)			11	
12 Minimum tax on tax preference items (see instructions—attach Form 4626)			12	
13 Total tax (add lines 9 through 12)			13	
14 a Overpayment from 1984 allowed as a credit	14a			
b 1985 estimated tax payments	14b			
c Less refund of 1985 estimated tax applied for on Form 4466	14c	( )		
d Tax deposited with Form 7004	14d			
e Credit from regulated investment companies (attach Form 2439)	14e			
f Federal tax on gasoline and special fuels (attach Form 4136)	14f			
g U.S. income tax paid or withheld at source	14g			
h Other payments (see instructions)	14h			
i Total refundable credits (combine lines 14a through 14h)			14i	
15 Enter any **PENALTY** for underpayment of estimated tax—Check ► ☐ if Form 2220 is attached			15	
16 **TAX DUE**—If the total of lines 13 and 15 is larger than line 14i, enter AMOUNT OWED			16	
17 **OVERPAYMENT**—If line 14i is larger than the total of lines 13 and 15, enter AMOUNT OVERPAID			17	
18 Enter amount of line 17 you want: **Credited to 1986 estimated tax** ► $ **Refunded** ►			18	

Please Sign Here

Under penalties of perjury, I declare that I have examined this return, including accompanying schedules and statements, and to the best of my knowledge and belief, it is true, correct, and complete. Declaration of preparer (other than taxpayer) is based on all information of which the preparer has any knowledge.

► Signature of officer — Date — ► Title

Paid Preparer's Use Only

Preparer's signature ►	Date	Check if self-employed ► ☐	Preparer's social security no.
Firm's name (or yours, if self-employed) and address ►		E.I. No. ►	
		ZIP Code ►	

Form **1120L** (1985)

Form 1120L (1985) Page **2**

SCHEDULE A **Life Insurance Company Taxable Income (LICTI) (Section 801(b))**

1	**a** Gross premiums, etc. .... **b** Less return premiums, etc. .... Balance ▶		
2	Decrease in reserves (see instructions)		
3	10% of any decrease in reserves under section 807(f)(1)(B)(ii)		
4	Investment income (Schedule C, line 8)		
5	Net capital gain (line 10, Schedule D (Form 1120))		
6	Other amounts (attach schedule)		
7	Life insurance company gross income (add lines 1 through 6)		
8	Death benefits, etc		
9	Increase in reserves (Schedule B, line 12)		
10	10% of any increase in reserves under section 807(f)(1)(B)(i)		
11	Policyholder dividends (Schedule E, line 7)		
12	Assumption by another person of liabilities under insurance, etc., contracts		
13	Reimbursable dividends		
14	Other deductions (attach schedule—see instructions)		
15	Dividends-received deduction (Schedule G, column (c), line 12—see instructions for limitation and attach schedule if applicable), enter here and on Schedule M, line 2c		
16	Operations loss deduction (attach schedule)		
17	Total deductions (add lines 8 through 16)		
18	Gain or (loss) from operations (subtract line 17 from line 7), enter here and, if a gain, on Schedule H, line 1		
19	Small life insurance company deduction (Schedule H, line 12)		
20	Special life insurance company deduction (Schedule J, line 5)		
21	Add lines 19 and 20, enter here and on line 2b, Schedule M		
22	LICTI (line 18 less line 21), enter here and on page 1, line 1		

SCHEDULE B **Increase Or (Decrease) In Reserves (Section 807)**

		(a) Beginning of tax year	(b) End of tax year
1	Life insurance reserves (section 807(c)(1))		
2	Unearned premiums and unpaid losses (section 807(c)(2))		
3	Supplementary contracts (section 807(c)(3))		
4	Dividend accumulations and other amounts (section 807(c)(4))		
5	Advance premiums (section 807(c)(5))		
6	Special contingency reserves (section 807(c)(6))		
7	Total (add lines 1 through 6 in both columns)		
8	Increase (decrease) in reserves (column (b) less column (a)) (see instructions)		
9	Policyholders' share of tax-exempt interest (Schedule C, line 9 times Schedule K, line 26)		
10	Line 8 less line 9		
11	Excess ownership differential adjustment (Schedule E, line 8)		
12	Net increase (decrease) in reserves (If an increase, enter here and on Schedule A, line 9. If a (decrease), enter here and on Schedule A, line 2.)		

SCHEDULE C **Gross Investment Income (Section 812(d))**

1	Interest (excluding tax-exempt interest)	
2	Dividend income (Schedule G , column (a), line 12)	
3	Gross rents	
4	Gross royalties	
5	Leases, terminations, etc.	
6	Excess of net-short term capital gain over net long-term capital loss (line 9, Schedule D (Form 1120))	
7	Gross income from trade or business other than insurance (attach schedule)	
8	Investment income (add lines 1 through 7), enter here and on Schedule A, line 4	
9	Tax-exempt interest, enter here and on Schedule K, line 5 and on Schedule M, line 2d	
10	Add lines 8 and 9	
11	Subsidiaries 100% dividends (sections 805(a)(4)(C) and (D))	
12	Gross investment income (line 10 less line 11), enter here and on Schedule K, line 1	

Form 1120L (1985) Page 3

SCHEDULE E Policyholder Dividends (Section 808)

1	Amounts paid or accrued	
2	Excess interest	
3	Premium adjustments	
4	Experience-rated refunds	
5	Total (add lines 1 through 4)	
6	Differential earning amount for mutual company only (Schedule F, line 15)	
7	Deductible policyholder dividends (line 5 minus line 6, but not less than zero), enter here and on Schedule A, line 11 and Schedule K, line 10	
8	Excess ownership differential adjustment (excess, if any, of line 6 over line 5), enter here and on Schedule B, line 11	
9	Deductible percentage (line 7 divided by line 5)	%

SCHEDULE F Differential Earnings Amount—Mutual Companies Only (Section 809)

		(a) End of preceding tax year	(b) End of this tax year
1	Annual statement surplus and capital		
2	Nonadmitted financial assets (attach schedule)		
3	Excess of statutory reserves over tax reserves on section 807(c) items		
4	Deficiency reserves		
5	Mandatory securities valuation reserve		
6	Other voluntary reserves		
7	50% of the amount of any provision for policyholder dividends payable in the next tax year		
8 a	Subtotal (add lines 1 through 7)		
b	Adjustment for equity allocable to noncontiguous Western Hemisphere countries and other adjustments		
c	Total of lines 8a and 8b, both columns		
9	Total of line 8c, columns (a) and (b)		
10	Tentative average equity base—Enter 50% of line 9		
11	Other adjustments		
12	Total of lines 10 and 11		
13	High surplus adjustment (section 809 (i))—attach schedule		
14	Average equity base (line 12 less line 13)		
15	Differential earnings amount (line 14 times the differential earnings rate), enter here and on line 6, Schedule E	see instructions	

SCHEDULE G Dividend Income and Dividends-Received Deduction (See instructions)

	Dividends subject to proration	(a) Gross taxable dividends	(b) Deduction rate	(c) Deduction (column (a) times column (b))
1	Certain domestic corporations		.85	
2	Certain debt-financed stock		see instructions	
3	Certain public utility corporations		.5913	
4	Certain foreign corporations		.85	
5	Certain foreign corporations		1.00	
6	Certain affiliated company dividends		1.00	
7	Gross dividends-received deduction (add lines 1 through 6 of column (c))			
8	Company share percentage (Schedule K, line 25)			
9	Prorated amount (line 7 times line 8)			
	Dividends not subject to proration			
10	Affiliated company dividends		see instructions	
11	Other corporate dividends			
12	Total (add lines 1 through 11 in column (a) and lines 9 and 10 in column (c))—Enter the amount from line 12, column (a) on Schedule C, line 2, and enter the amount from line 12, column (c) on Schedule A, line 15			

Form 1120L (1985) Page 4

SCHEDULE H Small Life Insurance Company Deduction (Section 806(b))—If assets (Schedule O, Part I) are $500,000,000 or more, complete lines 1 through 5, line 11, and enter zero on line 12. (See instructions)

1	Gain from operations (Schedule A, line 18)		
2	a Noninsurance income .... b less noninsurance deductions .... c Balance ▶		
3	a Line 1 less line 2c		
	b Adjustments (attach schedule)		
	c Tentative LICTI (Total of lines 3a and 3b)		
4	Controlled group tentative LICTI (Schedule I, line 8)		
5	Combined tentative LICTI (line 3c plus line 4). Enter here and on Schedule J, line 1. If $15,000,000 or more, omit lines 6 through 10. Enter zero on line 12, and line 19, Schedule A		
6	Small life insurance company deduction before adjustment (line 5 times .6, but not more than $1,800,000)	× .6	
7	Maximum statutory amount	3,000,000	
8	Subtract line 7 from line 5, but not less than zero		
9	Reduction rate (15%)—Line 8 times .15, but not over $1,800,000	× .15	
10	Tentative small life insurance company deduction (line 6 less line 9), enter here and on line 2, Schedule J		
11	Taxpayer's share (line 3c divided by the sum of line 3c and Schedule I, column (a), line 6)		
12	Allowable small life insurance company deduction (line 11 times line 10), enter here and on Schedule A, line 19		

SCHEDULE I Controlled Group Information— (See instructions)

	Company	Tentative LICTI	
		(a) Income	**(b)** (Loss)
1			
2			
3			
4			
5			
6	Total—Add lines 1 through 5 in both columns		
7	Enter amount from (Loss) column		
8	Net controlled group tentative LICTI (line 6 less line 7). Enter here and on line 4, Schedule H		

SCHEDULE J Special Life Insurance Company Deduction (Section 806(a))

1	Combined tentative LICTI (Schedule H, line 5)		
2	Tentative small life insurance company deduction (Schedule H, line 10)		
3	Line 1 less line 2		
4	Tentative special life insurance company deduction (line 3 times .20 (taxable income adjustment rate))	× .20	
5	Taxpayer's share of special deduction (line 4 times Schedule H, line 11), enter here and on Schedule A, line 20		

SCHEDULE K Company/Policyholder Share Percentage (Section 812)—Part I (See instructions)

1	Gross investment income (Schedule C, line 12)		
2	Policy interest (Schedule L, line 5)		
3	Line 1 less line 2		
4	Life insurance company gross income		
5	Tax-exempt interest (Schedule C, line 9)		
6	Add lines 4 and 5		
7	Increase (decrease) in reserves (Schedule B, line 8)		
8	Line 6 less line 7		
9	Investment income ratio (line 3 divided by line 8)		
10	Deductible policyholder dividends (Schedule E, line 7)		
11	Deductible excess interest (Schedule L, line 2)		
12	Deductible dividends on employee pension funds		
13	Deductible dividends on deferred annuities		
14	Deductible premium and mortality charges for contracts paying excess interest		
15	Add lines 11 through 14		
16	Line 10 less line 15		
17	Investment portion of dividends (line 9 times line 16)		
18	Policy interest (Schedule L, line 5)		
19	Policyholder share amount (add lines 17 and 18)		

Form 1120L (1985) Page **5**

SCHEDULE K **Part II**

20	Gross investment income (line 1)		
21	Net investment income (line 20 times .9)	× .9	
22	Policyholder share amount (line 19)		
23	Company share of net investment income (line 21 less line 22)		
24	Total share percentage		100%
25	Company share percentage (line 23 divided by line 21), enter here and on Schedule G, line 8		
26	Policyholders' share percentage (line 24 less line 25)		

SCHEDULE L **Policy Interest (Section 812(b)(2))**

1	Required interest on reserves under sections 807(c)(1),(3),(4),(5) and (6) —attach schedule	
2	Deductible excess interest (Schedule E, line 2 times Schedule E, line 9) enter here and on Schedule K, line 11	
3	Deductible amounts credited to employee pension funds	
4	Deductible amounts credited to deferred annuities	
5	Total policy interest (add lines 1 through 4), enter here and on lines 2 and 18 of Schedule K	

SCHEDULE M **Shareholders' Surplus Account (Section 815(c))**

1	a	Balance at the beginning of the tax year	
	b	Transfers under pre-1984 section 815(d)(1) and (4) for preceding year	
	c	Balance at the beginning of the tax year (add lines 1a and 1b)	
2	a	LICTI (Page 1, sum of lines 1 and 2, but not less than zero)	
	b	Special deductions allowed by sections 806(a) and 806(b) (Schedule A, line 21)	
	c	Dividends-received deduction (Schedule A, line 15)	
	d	Tax-exempt interest (Schedule C, line 9)	
3		Total (add lines 1c through 2d)	
4		Tax liability for year without regard to section 815 (figure the tax on line 2a as if line 2a were taxable income)	
5		Line 3 less line 4 (do not enter less than zero)	
6		Direct or indirect distributions in the tax year (not more than line 5)	
7		Balance at the end of the tax year (line 5 less line 6)	

SCHEDULE N **Policyholders' Surplus Account (Section 815(d))**

1		Balance at the beginning of the tax year		
2	a	Direct or indirect distributions that are more than Schedule M, line 5		
	b	Tax increase on line 2a		
	c	Subtractions under pre-1984 sections 815(d)(1) and (4) (see instructions)		
	d	Tax increase on line 2c		
	e	Subtraction required under pre-1984 section 815(d)(2) due to termination		
3		Total—Add lines 2a through 2e, but not more than line 1		
4		Balance at the end of the tax year (line 1 less line 3)		

SCHEDULE O **Total Assets and Total Insurance Liabilities**

Part I—Total Assets (Section 806(b)(3)(C))

		As of Close of Tax Year
1	Real property	
2	Stocks	
3	Proportionate share of partnership assets	
4	Other assets (attach schedule)	
5	Total assets of controlled groups	
6	Total (add lines 1 through 5)	

Form 1120L (1985) Page **6**

SCHEDULE O **Total Assets and Total Insurance Liabilities—continued**

PART II—Total Insurance Liabilities (Section 813(a)(4)(B))

Item	(a) Section	(b) Description of item	(c) Liabilities at close of tax year
1	816(c)(1)	Reserve for life policies and contracts	
2	816(c)(2)	Reserve for accident and health policies	
3	807(c)(3)	Supplementary contracts without life contingencies	
4	816(c)(2)	Policy and contract claims, life	
5	816(c)(3)	Policy and contract claims, accident and health	
6	807(c)(4)	Policyholders' dividend and coupon accumulations	
7	807(c)(5)	Premiums and annuity considerations received in advance	
		Less: Discount	
8	807(c)(5)	Liability for premium and other deposit funds	
9		Miscellaneous insurance liabilities, not included above:	
	807(c)(6)	**a** Special contingency reserves for group life, health and accident insurance	
	807(c)(3)	**b** Amounts held at interest under insurance, annuity or deposit administration contracts or pension trust side funds	
	807(c)(3)	**c** Funds held to provide for future conversion of policies or contracts	
	807(c)(3)	**d** Amounts held pending issue of contracts supplementary to insurance or annuity contracts	
	816(c)(3)	**e** Other insurance liability or adjustments:	
		(i) Reserves for mortality fluctuations	
		(ii) Liability for insurance or annuity benefits for employees and agents	
	816(c)(3)	**f** Other items (please describe):	
10		**Total**	

SCHEDULE P **Limitation on Noninsurance Losses (Section 806(c)(3)(C))**

1	Noninsurance income (attach schedule)	
2	Noninsurance deductions (attach schedule)	
3	Noninsurance operations loss deductions	
4	Add lines 2 and 3	
5	Noninsurance loss (line 4 less line 1). If line 1 is greater than line 4, omit lines 5 through 8, and enter zero on line 9	
6	Enter 35% of line 5	
7	Enter 35% of Schedule A, line 22 less any noninsurance loss included in Schedule A	
8	Enter the lesser of line 6 or line 7	
9	Line 5 less line 8—Enter here and on page 1, line 2	

Form 1120L (1985) Page 7

SCHEDULE Q Additional Information Required (See instructions)

	Yes	No
F Check if you are a:		
(1) ☐ Legal reserve company—if checked: Kind of company: ☐ Stock ☐ Mutual. Principal business: ☐ Life insurance ☐ Health and accident insurance		
(2) ☐ Fraternal or assessment association		
(3) ☐ Burial or other insurance company		
G Enter the percentage that the total of your life insurance reserves (section 816(b)) plus unearned premiums and unpaid losses (whether or not ascertained) on noncancellable life, health or accident policies not included in life insurance reserves, is to your total reserves (section 816(c)) ______ %. Attach a schedule of your computation.		
H Do you have any variable annuity contracts outstanding?		
I (1) Did you, at the end of the tax year, own, directly or indirectly, 50% or more of the voting stock of a domestic corporation (for rules of attribution, see section 267(c))?		
If "Yes," attach a schedule showing: *(a)* Name, address, and identifying number; *(b)* Percentage owned; and *(c)* Taxable income or (loss) before NOL or special deductions from line 28, page 1, Form 1120 (or line 24, page 1, Form 1120-A) of that corporation for the tax year ending with or within your tax year.		
(2) Did any individual, partnership, corporation, estate, or trust, at the end of the tax year, own, directly or indirectly, 50% or more of your voting stock (for rules of attribution, see section 267(c))?		
If "Yes," attach a schedule showing— *(a)* Name, address, and identifying number. *(b)* Percentage owned.		
(c) If the owner of that voting stock was a person other than a U.S. person (see instructions), check "Yes" and show owner's country ▶ ______		
Note: *If question I(2)(c) is checked "Yes," the corporation may have to file Form 5472.*		

	Yes	No
J Did you claim a deduction for:		
(1) Entertainment facility (boat, resort, ranch, etc.)?		
(2) Living accommodations (except for employees on business)?		
(3) Employees attending conventions or meetings outside the North American area? (See section 274(h).)		
(4) Employees' families at conventions or meetings?		
If "Yes," were any of these conventions or meetings outside the North American area? (See section 274(h).)		
(5) Employee or family vacations not reported on Form W-2?		
K Were you a U.S. shareholder of any controlled foreign corporation? (See sections 951 and 957, and the instructions.) If "Yes," attach Form 5471 for each corporation.		
L At any time during the tax year, did you have an interest in or a signature or other authority over a financial account in a foreign country (such as a bank account, securities account, or other financial account)? (See the instructions for exceptions and filing requirements for Form TD F 90-22.1.) If "Yes," write the name of the foreign country ▶ ______		
M Were you ever the grantor of or transferor to a foreign trust which existed during the current tax year, whether or not you have any beneficial interest in it? (See instructions.) If "Yes," you may be required to file Forms 926, 3520, or 3520A.		
N During the tax year did you maintain any of your accounting/tax records on a computerized system?		
O Check method of accounting: **(1)** ☐ Accrual **(2)** ☐ Other (Specify) ______		

SCHEDULE R Reconciliation (See instructions)

SCHEDULE S Compensation of Officers (See instructions)

☆ U.S. GOVERNMENT PRINTING OFFICE: 1985—463-186

CHAPTER NINE

HISTORY OF THE INDUSTRY AND ITS REGULATION

THE MORRIS PLAN INSURANCE SOCIETY

The idea of credit insurance was conceived and implemented by one man, Arthur J. Morris. A man of many accomplishments, he was also responsible for bank consumer lending as we know it today. Some of his contemporaries credit him with being the founder of consumer lending and laying the foundation for consumer borrowing practices which have revolutionized consumption of consumer goods in this century.

Even today, many borrowers feel that banks lend money only to those who can prove that they do not need it. At the turn of the century, this was literally true. Bankers would not make loans unless the borrower had deposits at the bank or could provide unimpeachable collateral.

Morris practiced law in Norfolk, Virginia in 1906, and was often approached by individuals asking for his assistance in securing loans because of his contacts in the banking industry. With the growing number of requests, Morris realized that a significant number of credit-worthy people were only able to obtain loans from small loan operations and loan sharks.

He dispatched a group of people to travel around the country to study the credit environment. From the survey, he concluded that 80% of working people and small business owners had no ready access to credit. Banks would not lend money simply on the earning power of the borrower.

Morris developed an idea for the "democratization of credit." He felt a bank should be willing to lend money if the borrower could show good character and the earning power to repay the debt. The concept was not unique. Mutual banks already existed in Europe, organized similar to today's credit unions and mutual savings banks. In 1910, Morris organized a bank in Norfolk on these principles.

Arthur Morris had a dream far bigger than owning a bank in Norfolk. He was one of the first individuals to consider the concept of franchising. Along with other local individuals, he formed a bank in Atlanta. The Georgia newspapers soon began an expose on loan sharks. The Atlanta bank was prominently portrayed as a viable alternative for working people.

As publicity about the Atlanta bank spread, a number of inquiries about his banking plan poured in. He formed the Fidelity Corporation of America, the first bank holding company to aid in establishing the other local banks. The holding company owned 20%-25% of each local bank. After fourteen banks were formed, Morris took the program nationwide. He traveled to New York and met with prominent financiers, who agreed to provide additional financial backing. The strategy called for Morris to travel throughout the country, meeting with the prominent businessmen, gaining support for a local Morris Plan Bank. Banks would be formed with 75%-80% local ownership, with the holding company owning the remainder. Standardized procedures, forms, and advertising were provided to the local operation.

At the initial New York meeting, one of the businessmen suggested the name Morris Plan Banks. Those who knew Morris doubted if it took much effort to convince him to accept the honor. At the peak, 170 Morris Plan Banks were formed. Over the years, these banks evolved into regular banks or became finance companies. The Morris Plan concept was somewhere between the two. A few Morris Plan Banks still exist today.

The Morris Plan concept required one or two co-makers on the loan. Morris soon realized that the death or disability of the borrower cut off the earning power which was the basis of the loan. Collecting from a borrower's co-maker was fairly successful in those days, but the task was unpleasant. Morris decided that insurance was needed to complete the concept.

He visited several of the major insurers of the day. With little data on which to base rates, the insurers were unwilling to venture into this new field. Undaunted, he formed his own insurance company in 1917–the Morris Plan Insurance Society, with the motto, "No man's debt should live after him."

The original policy was a level term individual life policy sold with weekly premiums based on the age of the insured. Weekly premiums soon gave way to monthly premiums, with an option to pay annually in advance. In those days both loans and insurance coverage were for 12-month terms. The first decreasing term policy was introduced in 1922. Although the company is no longer a force in the credit insurance industry, it is still in business today as Bankers Security Life Insurance Society.

OTHER EARLY CREDIT INSURERS

One stop on Morris' itinerary was the industrial town of Springfield, Ohio, where a local Morris Plan Bank was formed in 1917. The relationship between the New York holding company and the local bank was never particularly good. The local management chose not to enter the insurance program of the Morris Plan Insurance Society. Instead, a portion of each loan was set aside, with the stipulation that the loan was paid in full in the event of the primary borrower's death. On a routine bank examination in 1925, the bank examiner declared that this was insurance and ruled this stipulation illegal, saying only life insurance companies could provide life insurance protection.

The ruling caused consternation at the Springfield bank. Officers knew the practice was popular with its borrowers. They submitted a proposal to the Ohio Insurance Department to form an insurance company for the purpose of providing this insurance. The proposal was initially met with skepticism. After legal counsel was employed, the bankers were successful in obtaining the approval of the Department, and The Credit Life Insurance Company was formed in 1925.

In early 1926, the Company issued the first group credit policy in the United States to the Springfield Morris Plan Company. The policy provided life insurance for the amount of the loan as well as total and permanent disability coverage. Both coverages paid the remaining unpaid weekly payments owed by the borrower. All borrowers up to age sixty were accepted for amounts up to $1,000 at a premium rate equal to 1% of the gross note. This rate evolved into the common standard of $1.00 per $100 per year.

The Springfield Morris Plan Company eventually converted to a regular bank and is still in business today as a locally-owned bank. The insurance company grew steadily through the years. The Credit Life Insurance Company is now one of the top credit life insurance writers today–licensed in all fifty states and Canada. The group insurance concept its founders developed is the basis of most credit insurance written today.

Both The Credit Life Insurance Company and the Morris Plan Insurance Society charged borrowers for the insurance. The current top two writers of credit insurance entered the field shortly afterwards with a different concept. In 1928, Prudential Insurance Company of America wrote a group policy for the National City Bank of New York. Under their policy, the lender paid the premium as a part of its loan expenses. The lender was charged a monthly premium per $1,000 of outstanding loans. In 1941, Prudential began writing the credit insurance for General Motors Acceptance Corporation, which financed General Motors' automobile loans. For many years, this was the largest group policy in the world.

A fourth company entered the field in 1931 using the contributory approach. Old Republic Life Insurance Company, as it is now known, was a significant force in the marketplace during the formative years. Old Republic Life was initially active in the finance company market but also recognized an unmet insurance need in the agricultural community. The company originated the writing of credit insurance to cover farm loan commitments and still remains a major writer in the Production Credit Association and agriculture loan market segment. Old Republic continues as an active force in the credit insurance industry.

Credit unions, which began in the United States in 1909, were recognizing the need for credit insurance protection. When the Credit Union National Association held its first national board meeting in January, 1935, the first order of business was to address the insurance needs of the credit union movement. The Board voted to establish the CUNA Mutual Insurance Society which was incorporated in May, 1935 as a Wisconsin life insurance company.

With a $25,000 loan from Edward A. Filene of Boston, a staff of two people opened the doors of the company for business in August, 1935 in an old rented mansion in Madison, Wisconsin. The first claim, in the amount of $40, was paid in October when a Milwaukee railroad switchman died. The company was guided during its formative years by Roy F. Bergengren, managing director.

CUNA Mutual first offered life insurance on an individual basis only. However, Bergengren felt that in keeping with the credit union ideals of cooperation and risk-sharing, group insurance should be on all borrowers and paid for by the credit union. In 1936, Loan Protection Insurance was introduced to provide non-contributory group life coverage.

By 1937, merely two years after it had been established, CUNA Mutual had more credit life insurance in force than any other insurer–a position it still holds in 1986. That same year, a total and permanent disability rider was offered with the Loan Protection Insurance.

In 1938, CUNA Mutual began to expand beyond credit insurance by offering group insurance on credit union member savings up to $1,000. Since then, CUNA Mutual Insurance Society has become the CUNA Mutual Insurance Group, which encompasses nine companies, offering a full line of life, health, accident, and casualty insurance protection to credit union members throughout the world.

By 1946, fifty-one companies were writing credit insurance, but by 1955 the number of insurers mushroomed to 237. The phenomenal growth was a response to the growth in consumer debt and continuing demand for the coverage. Now there are 443 U.S. and Canadian insurers writing credit insurance. Figure 9.2 shows the 100 leading companies today.

GROWTH OF CREDIT LIFE INSURANCE

Growth of credit life insurance was steady between 1917 and 1941. In 1941, World War II necessitated Regulation "W" sharply curtailing purchases of consumer goods, and credit life insurance in force declined. A spectacular period of growth occurred in the decade following the war. Consumer spending grew, but the percentage of insured loans grew even faster. Insured loans grew from 9% of all loans in 1946 to 47% by 1956. The growth of insurance was also spurred by the product's acceptance by lenders. Broadening of state laws to include the product also opened new markets. Figure 9.1 illustrates the growth of credit life insurance in force.

Credit Life Insurance In Force

In the United States (000 omitted)

Year	No. of Policies and Certificates	Amount	Year	No. of Policies and Certificates	Amount
1917	1	•	1972	78,439	$ 93,410,000
1920	22	$ 4,000	1973	77,574	101,154,000
1925	81	18,000	1974	83,860	109,623,000
1930	363	73,000	1975	79,708	112,032,000
1935	559	101,000	1976	78,230	123,569,000
1940	2,563	380,000	1977	79,259	139,402,000
1945	2,110	365,000	1978	83,725	163,081,000
1950	10,819	3,844,000	1979	84,435	179,250,000
1955	27,900	14,493,000	1980	78,446	165,215,000
1960	43,087	29,101,000	1981	73,055	162,356,000
1965	62,599	53,020,000	1982	66,758	161,144,000
1970	77,516	77,392,000	1983	64,386	170,659,000
1971	76,041	81,931,000			

Fig. 9.1 Growth of credit life insurance in force. (**1984 Life Insurance Fact Book**, a publication of the American Council of Life Insurance).

Company	1984 Rank	1984 Credit in Force
CUNA Mutual	1	31,827,909,000
Prudential	2	9,394,632,000
Credit Life	3	7,758,319,000
Canada Life, Can.	4	7,264,980,000
Sun Life, Can.	5	6,218,970,000
Confed. Life, Can.	6	6,009,861,000
Globe Life, Ill.	7	6,006,886,000
Minnesota Mutual	8	4,898,173,000
Ford Life	9	4,553,066,000
American Bankers Life	10	4,527,634,000
Old Republic Life, Ill.	11	4,311,913,000
John Hancock	12	4,256,170,000
CUMIS Life, Can.	13	4,181,678,000
Central National, Neb.	14	3,981,078,000
Sterling Life, Ohio	15	3,954,587,000
Alex. Hamilton Life	16	3,145,787,000
Union Security Life	17	3,126,862,000
Metropolitan Life	18	3,083,421,000
Aetna Life	19	2,990,091,000
National Life, Can.	20	2,890,345,000
USLIFE Credit Life, Ill.	21	2,757,173,000
Great-West, Can.	22	2,544,692,000
MIC Life	23	2,429,574,000
Cooperators Life, Can.	24	2,364,064,000
Heritage Life, Ariz.	25	2,361,719,000
Sierra General Life	26	2,356,878,000
Monumental General	27	2,331,550,000
Omaha Financial Life	28	2,310,922,000
Security of America, Pa.	29	2,298,177,000
Cumberland Life	30	2,169,599,000
Imperial Life, Can.	31	2,094,127,000
Provident Alliance	32	2,075,110,000
NRG America Life Re.	33	2,043,888,000
PHF Life, Mich.	34	2,038,501,000
North Central Life	35	1,822,418,000
Family Guardian Life	36	1,810,060,000
Transamer. Occid., Calif.	37	1,727,712,000
Mutual of Omaha	38	1,696,011,000
Northwestern Security	39	1,627,301,000
Centurion Life	40	1,606,841,000
Tempco Life	41	1,586,359,000
Transport Life	42	1,563,008,000
Lyndon Ins., Mo.	43	1,507,093,000
Durham Life	44	1,402,244,000
American Way Life	45	1,351,872,000
Alabama Reassur.	46	1,339,084,000
Employers Life, Wis.	47	1,337,993,000
Merit Life, Ind.	48	1,306,262,000
World Service Life, Colo.	49	1,274,004,000
ITT Lyndon Life	50	1,248,538,000
First Protection Life	51	1,221,923,000
Life Assur. of Pa.	52	1,170,218,000
American Health & Life	53	1,153,697,000
Acceleration Life, Ohio	54	1,129,633,000
League Life	55	1,120,040,000
American Heritage Life	56	1,114,526,000
Voyager Life	57	1,107,311,000
Washington National	58	1,076,242,000
Foremost Life	59	1,038,025,000
Western Diversified	60	1,022,304,000
Security Assurance	61	1,021,989,000
Mutual Life of Canada	62	1,012,142,000
Mass. Indemnity & Life	63	997,338,000
Life Investors, Iowa	64	996,788,000
American Annuity Life	65	962,585,000
Combined Ins., Ill.	66	948,166,000
Centennial Life, Kan.	67	942,379,000
United Fidelity, Tex.	68	935,106,000
Montgomery Ward	69	933,177,000
BA Insurance	70	926,064,000
Enterprise Life, Tex.	71	919,120,000
Chrysler Life, Mich.	72	911,663,000
JMIC Life	73	906,859,000
Crown Life, Can.	74	898,509,000
Service Life & Casualty	75	884,471,000
Volunteer State Life	76	874,385,000
Chartered Protective Life	77	873,914,000
Maritime Life, Can.	78	866,122,000
Puritan Life	79	865,476,000
Central States H&L, Neb.	80	853,787,000
Monogram Reins.	81	843,974,000
Consumers Life, Del.	82	843,304,000
Pilot Life	83	842,536,000
Universal Underwriters	84	806,021,000
Individual Assur.	85	784,425,000
Integon Life	86	755,041,000
Mid-South Life	87	752,425,000
Peninsular Life	88	752,194,000
Industrial Life, Tex.	89	737,395,000
Arcadia National Life	90	728,615,000
Lincoln National Life	91	633,175,000
Gulf Atlantic	92	631,631,000
Mountain Life	93	629,520,000
Vista Life	94	603,054,000
Continental Assurance	95	595,871,000
First Life Assur., Okla.	96	591,156,000
Superior Life, S.C.	97	583,933,000
John Alden Life, Minn.	98	574,680,000
First Continental L&A	99	573,718,000
Standard Life, Miss.	100	569,962,000

Fig. 9.2 Top 100 writers of credit life insurance, as reported by Best's Review, September, 1985.

Some of the growth of credit insurance was due to the increases in the cost of consumer goods, as well as increases in the number of consumer purchases. Postwar economic expansion and availability of installment lending made a vast array of consumer goods available to many Americans. Automobiles became a necessity, along with television and other modern appliances. Inflation created a steady increase in the cost of most consumer goods over time. As a result, the average amount in force per policy has risen sharply over the years.

Year	Average Amount In Force Per Policy or Certificate
1920	$ 182
1930	201
1940	148
1950	355
1960	675
1970	998
1980	2,106
1983	2,882

The size of new loans has paralleled rising costs. Automobile loans can easily exceed $10,000. In several market segments there is now a demand for credit insurance on large loans in amounts similar to ordinary insurance–second mortgage loans, home equity loans, and lines of credit can go up to $100,000; mobile home and recreational vehicle loans can exceed $100,000. Commercial loans are also substantial.

As the cost of consumer goods rose, lenders began to extend the term of loans. In 1955, 65% of all loans were for one year or less. The average term for all loans now is about 36 months.

The advent of the 48-month new car loan in the late 1970s dramatically extended the average term of credit insurance policies. Second mortgage and home improvement loans usually exceed five years.

GROUP VERSUS INDIVIDUAL POLICIES

Before 1960, the industry was generally divided between insurers writing under the group policy form and those writing the individual policy form. Both provided virtually identical coverage. However, there were significant differences in premiums, but those differences were not due to the form of the insurance policy, but were a result of fundamental differences in philosophy on credit insurance.

Both Prudential and CUNA Mutual initially wrote individual policies for a brief period, because group statutes did not envision creditor groups. As permissive statutes were adopted, the mutual companies wrote a traditional group policy. Noncontributory credit life coverage was their primary product. Administration was simpler under this form–monthly outstanding balance premiums were charged based on the total loan portfolio; an individual in force record was not maintained. By 1950, Prudential was writing a significant amount of contributory coverage and single premium business, but the group administration practices were retained.

Specialty credit insurers wrote individual policies and maintained individual in force files. The existing group statutes were a factor in selecting the individual policy approach. The fundamental difference was the belief that lenders should make the coverage available voluntarily, and that the lender should receive compensation for the sale of the product. Cost of operation for specialty insurers was higher due to the administrative procedures and the cost of compensation.

In time, the specialty companies converted to the group policy form, but retained the administrative procedures and compensation structure of their former approach. Once enacted, permissive group statutes provided the insurers more flexibility than individual statutes and regulations. The 1959 Tax Act provided a special deduction for group business. No deduction was available for individual credit business because of the short policy terms. By 1970, 84% of all credit life business was written on the group plan of insurance.

CREDIT DISABILITY INSURANCE

Several of the early insurers provided a total and permanent disability benefit. This lump sum benefit paid off the loan if the insured met the conditions for being totally and permanently disabled. A few casualty insurers wrote the product in the 1930s.

Around 1935, Old Republic introduced the first disability plan similar to those used today. Growth was slow. Policies were written on an individual policy form because of group statutes. The mutual companies only offered total and permanent disability coverage. By 1956, the total credit disability premiums were just $32 million.

Rapid growth has occurred in the last twenty years. Practically all business is now on a group policy form, primarily using fourteen-day retroactive and thirty-day non-retroactive benefits. All market segments have contributed to the growth. The product is now offered almost everywhere credit life is sold.

Disability coverage has been generally limited to terms of sixty months or less. For longer terms, the cost of single premium coverage is prohibitive and anti-selection by the insureds is evident in loss experience. In the late 1970s, the critical period product was introduced. Other partial coverage plans followed, such as truncated disability coverage. These plans provided a disability product for long-term loans.

MARKET SEGMENTS

Adoption of credit insurance programs by different types of financial institutions involved not only change in consumer preference and business practices, but also vigorous debate and revision of banking and lending laws. Morris Plan Banks adopted the credit insurance concept quickly. By 1940, the idea had spread to the small loan companies and industrial banks, but large scale adoption by these institutions was delayed by World War II and completion of vigorous debate in the 1950s over the development and adoption of a revised regulatory framework.

In the early part of the century, loan sharks were the scourge of the lending environment. In order to eradicate the blight, the Russell Sage Foundation developed a model Uniform Small Loan Act which was published in 1916. The Act was designed to protect borrowers of small amounts from exorbitant interest rates and other abuses, including the use of tie-in sales as a cloak for usurious loan charges.

The bill provided protection to the borrower through five basic principles:

1. A clearly defined loan area, originally loans up to $300.00,

2. A maximum interest rate,

3. An all-inclusive simple interest rate covering all charges,

4. A fair contract in writing, and a prohibition on false, misleading or deceptive advertising, and,

5. State licensing and supervision of lenders.

A common clause in small loan laws implementing the all-inclusive rate principle reads:

In addition to the interest herein provided for, no further charge or amount whatsoever for any examination, service,

> *brokerage, commission, expense, fee or bonus or other thing or otherwise shall be directly or indirectly charged, contracted for, or received.*

States adopted laws and regulations based on the provisions of the Act, but variations by state were sometimes significant. These laws and regulations set the stage for a battle over credit insurance in the 1950s between the two largest finance companies, Household Finance Corporation and Beneficial Corporation.

Household defended the all-inclusive rate principle and argued that the language was clear, if not explicit. If a lender charged the maximum interest rate, no further charge could be made. Any charge for insurance had to be included in the calculation of the interest rate.

Beneficial argued that credit insurance was a factor in the collateral of the loan, not a part of the loan itself. They felt the product was particularly needed by small loan borrowers. Effective regulations would provide the borrower with any necessary protection.

The issue was debated at every available forum during the early and mid-1950s. Debate took place at the NAIC level and on a state-by-state basis. The issue was finally resolved by the development of the NAIC Model Regulations and by the amendment of state banking and loan laws to specifically authorize financial institutions to offer credit insurance with a separate contributory charge. Both companies now sell the product nationwide through their own direct-writing insurance company subsidiaries.

Finance companies were in the forefront of forming captive insurers. Beginning in 1953, several companies formed direct-writing insurers or reinsurers. Several of these captives are large writers of credit insurance today. A few have branched out to write credit insurance for other lenders and to write ordinary insurance products.

Recently, the large finance companies have modified or expanded operations to include larger loans. They have been a prime proponent of the home-equity loan, which allows the borrower to obtain a loan by placing a second mortgage on his home. These companies have led the way in developing new coverages to insure these long-term loans, including truncated life, net plus life, and critical period disability coverage.

Commercial banks did not enter the installment lending arena on a direct basis until after 1946. Before 1946, they purchased loans *(indirect paper)* from sales finance companies and made unsecured personal loans. Soon after, banks quickly became a dominant force in installment lending. Initially, some banks were reluctant to sell credit insurance, choosing to ignore the product or to purchase group coverage without an identifiable charge to the borrower.

However, many banks offered the product with a separate charge. By 1960, banks were writing a significant amount of credit insurance. The Federal Reserve Board's decision in 1972 to permit a bank holding company to own an insurance subsidiary spurred further interest in the product. Practically all banks now offer credit insurance on a contributory basis. Most bank holding companies have captive insurers as a part of their corporate group.

Sales finance operations have existed since the turn of the century. Retail stores selling high-cost consumer goods, such as furniture and appliances, have arranged to provide financing at the store through an arrangement with a bank to purchase the loan paper or through an in-house revolving charge program. Some large retail outlets have their own financing subsidiaries. Credit insurance is offered at the retail outlet when the purchase is financed.

Automobile financing quickly became the most significant segment of consumer lending. Automobile manufacturers formed corporations to provide a financing package for the purchaser available from the dealers with credit insurance an optional feature of the financing package. Many manufacturers eventually formed direct-writing insurers to write the credit insurance.

Automobile dealers do not always participate in the factory financing and insurance programs. Arrangements are possible with local banks to purchase the loans. At first, banks provided the credit insurance through their own group coverage, but in the 1960s, banks began to allow the automobile dealer to offer the insurance and receive the compensation. Credit insurance business produced directly by automobile dealers has become a major portion of the overall credit insurance market.

Credit unions began to provide credit life insurance as a part of their loan package in the 1930s. This trend has continued with this segment having stiff rate competition. Since the individual credit unions pay for the coverage, they want the lowest cost for their members. Before 1971, they could not receive any commission from the sale of insurance. Premiums did not provide any commission, so the premiums have always been below prevailing rates.

Standard plans of credit disability insurance were usually not offered, although total and permanent disability coverage was often included. Beginning in 1971, the credit unions could receive fee income. Credit insurers began to offer contributory credit disability insurance to the credit unions. Loss experience in the mid-1970s was poor. This market segment produced claim costs far in excess of the other market segments. Credit unions of heavy industry had claim costs two and three times the usual levels. Credit unions resisted upward rate deviations. For a period of years, new insurers were entering the market who were willing to write a case at prima facie when the old insurer wanted to raise rates. By the late 1970s, the insurers learned their lesson. Insurers were successful in obtaining deviations and finding an acceptable rating mechanism for this class of business.

TRADE ASSOCIATIONS

Insurers have formed several trade associations to promote the industry and to assist in development of regulations. The primary trade association for credit insurers is the Consumer Credit Insurance Association (CCIA). Founded in 1951, CCIA now has 212 member companies, including practically all of the major credit insurers. The association has four purposes stated in its Articles of Incorporation:

1. To act as a trade association of insurance companies engaged in the business of underwriting creditor's life insurance and allied lines of insurance;

2. To promote high ethical standards for the consumer credit insurance business and related lines of insurance;

3. To disseminate information and provide for the exchange of ideas among and between its members; and

4. To aid and advance the business of its members by any and all proper means.

CCIA holds two conventions each year--the annual membership meeting in the spring and the Fall Executive Planning Conference. Speakers at both meetings provide discussion on technical aspects of the product and updates on legislative and other matters of topical interest. Seminars are sponsored on topics requiring special attention.

At various times, CCIA has presented its highest award to persons who have made major contributions to the development of credit insurance. The award is named after the developer of credit insurance, Arthur J. Morris. The award has been presented to 13 people:

1969	James H. Jarrell
1970	Dwight W. Hollenbeck
1972	W. L. Harlan
1973	Ralph R. Lounsbury
1975	Paul F. Boyer
1976	G. Cecil Woods
1979	John D. Mace
1980	Maurice G. Olson
1980	Charles T. Hargrove

1981	Robert N. Tyler
1982	Edward A. Dunbar
1983	Ronald Roberts
1984	R. Donald Quackenbush

Since its inception, CCIA has played an important role in the development of credit insurance regulations. The organization has been a strong proponent of effective state regulation of the product. CCIA has been active in all of the work at the NAIC level. Association personnel travel around the country giving testimony and providing technical assistance as regulations are written or revised.

The American Council of Life Insurance (ACLI) is an organization representing the entire scope of the life insurance industry. As such, credit insurance is only a minor aspect of the scope of their activities. While the membership of ACLI is broad, the association is primarily comprised of the mutual insurers and the larger stock insurers. ACLI was formed by the merger of the American Life Convention (ALC) and the Life Insurance Association of America (LIAA). These forerunners were active in the development of credit insurance regulations in the 1950s.

A second association, the National Association of Life Companies (NALC), also serves the broad spectrum of life insurers. NALC's membership is primarily comprised of small and medium-sized stock insurers. Credit insurance is not a major part of their activities, but is included as a part of their concerns about the entire scope of insurance products.

The Health Insurance Association of America (HIAA) performs activities similar to those of the ACLI and NALC, with emphasis on health insurance products. This organization often works in concert with CCIA, ACLI and NALC on issues like credit insurance where both life and health coverages are involved.

REGULATION

NAIC involvement in the regulation of credit insurance was first initiated in a speech by NAIC President J. E. Larson in 1948. The dramatic growth of the product following World War II resulted in abusive practices in certain segments of the industry. A subcommittee was appointed that year to investigate reported abuses. In June, 1949, the subcommittee reported that the following abuses had been uncovered:

- Failure to disclose coverage
- Failure to deliver evidence of insurance
- Overcharge of premium
- Failure to notify insureds of cancellation (pyramiding)
- Failure to refund unearned premiums
- Coercion to buy insurance
- Coercion to buy insurance from a particular company

The report was not a blanket indictment of the industry, since most insurers were operating honorably. Lenders were responsible for the majority of abusive practices, but the regulators felt the insurers had an obligation to monitor their product and protect the industry's reputation.

Credit insurers did consider the issues to be serious. They recommended a set of rules which were adopted by the NAIC in 1949. These rules specified that:

- An insured must be informed of the coverage and its cost.
- An insured had the option to refuse the insurance.
- Policies must be filed.

- Coverage must be provided for the full term of the loan.
- The premium charged the insured must not exceed the premium the insurer charged the lender.
- Notice of cancellation must be given to the insured.
- Unearned premium refunds must be paid on cancellation.
- The insurer was responsible for payment of claims.

Another NAIC subcommittee was appointed in 1952. Model Rules and Regulations, recommended by the subcommittee and supported by the CCIA, were adopted by the NAIC in 1954. The rules addressed the abuses found in 1949 and generally followed the industry recommendations. Since current regulations are still built around these rules, a review of the rules (shown in italics) and their rationale is useful.

- ***Excessive Insurance***. The original credit life policies were level term insurance. Although industry practice soon evolved to decreasing term coverage, some insurers continued to sell level term policies. In some cases, the policy term exceeded the loan term–an attempt by some insurers to become providers of ordinary insurance. *Credit insurance was limited to the unpaid indebtedness, with a $5.00 margin, and the policy term could not exceed the loan term by more than 15 days unless the term was extended without an extra charge to the insured.*

- ***Pyramiding***. Pyramiding is the sale of a new insurance policy on a refinanced loan without cancellation of the old policy. In its worst form, the loan was repaid on the death of the insured without paying the excess insurance to the estate. *Cancellation of an existing policy was required on renewal or refinancing. An unearned premium refund, based on formulas filed with the insurance department, was* *required. The policy and certificate had to specify the termination provisions. The cancellation and refund payment were considered a responsibility of the agent and the insurer.*

- ***Overcharging.*** Some lenders purchased the coverage from an insurer on a group basis, but some lenders added a mark-up. Insureds were charged more than the lender paid for the insurance. *Premium rates had to be filed with the insurance department. Any identifiable charge to the insured had to be consistent with the group policy premiums.*

- ***Evidence of Insurance.*** Some lenders forgot to inform the borrowers that a charge was made for insurance or that the borrower had purchased insurance. Naturally, no policy or certificate was provided. *A policy or certificate must be delivered to the insured stating amount of insurance, premium, term, description of coverage, exceptions, limitations, and restrictions. All forms were to be filed with or approved by the insurance department.*

- ***Denial of Claims.*** Some lenders were permitted to retain premiums and pay claims. Claims were denied unjustly since they reduced the lender's profit. *Only insurers could retain funds for claims. All claims were to be reported to the insurer and files maintained. Claims must be paid by the insurer's drafts or checks. Only the company or its designated claim agent could adjust claims. Agents, brokers, and lenders could not be claim agents, except group policyholders were permitted to issue drafts on the insurer's account subject to audit and review by the insurer.*

- ***Coercion.*** Some lenders applied undue pressure or required the borrower to purchase credit insurance from the lender. *If insurance was required, the insured must be notified of the right to use existing insurance or to furnish equivalent coverage obtained from an insurer chosen by the borrower.*

- ***Unlicensed Agents.*** Some business was being sold through unlicensed agents. *All policies were to be issued by authorized insurers through licensed agents.*

An onerous example of the practices which led to these rules was the infamous 90/10 Plan. The insurer would issue a group policy to the lender. Ten percent of the premium was remitted to the insurer. A lender retained ninety percent and was responsible for processing claims and claim payments. Needless to say, providing the insured with a certificate was considered an unnecessary burden and expense, and the lack of evidence of insurance had a tendency to reduce claims. Fortunately, for the industry and its consumers, the plan was not widely sold.

A separate recommendation was made concerning the reserve basis for credit life insurance. Single premium decreasing term business required the use of a gross unearned premium reserve based on the Rule of 78 or mortality reserves based on tables permitted in the state. An experience exhibit, to be included in the statutory annual statement, was adopted. Experience was displayed for life and disability insurance, separately for individual and group coverage.

Significantly, the rules did not specify anything about premium rates or lender compensation. Much debate took place over both issues. In the end, these issues were left for another day. Only a handful of states adopted the rules.

The subcommittee stated that questions concerning the legality of the sale of the product, or the implications of antitrust laws, were beyond the scope of the report. Although the subcommittee was discharged in June, it was reactivated in December of 1954.

Following the NAIC's adoption of the 1954 Rules and Regulations, attention focused on premium rates and lender compensation. Interested parties were divided on both issues. The stock insurers, generally supported by CCIA, ALC, and HIAA, believed that neither premium nor compensation needed regulation. Mutual companies writing group coverage felt rate regulation was needed, but did not want to confront the specter of rate regulation for all life insurance. Some parties believed rate regulation was the only answer. Others strongly urged that lenders should only receive compensation for actual cost of providing the service. The National Association of Life Underwriters (NALU) proposed that lenders should not receive any compensation. The majority of credit insurers felt that producers should be compensated like other insurance agents. The battle lines were drawn.

In November 1955, a joint proposal was made by the ALC and the LIAA to limit lender compensation. They agreed that some control was needed over either premium rates or compensation and decided control of compensation was better. For loans under $500, credit life compensation was limited to 40¢/100/year and disability compensation was limited to 60¢/100/12 months (with appropriate adjustment for longer terms). Loans over $500 and captive reinsurance were not addressed. A revised model bill was presented to the NAIC in 1956. At the same time, CCIA recommended a set of twelve principles which included acceptance of the ALC-LIAA compensation limit.

During 1957, the results of an industry mortality study were released. Life claim costs were 27¢/100/year in 1955 and 28.5¢/100/year in 1956. Combined experience was 28¢/100/year. A sidelight of the study showed that the percentage of loans covered by credit life insurance had risen from 9% in 1946 to 47% in 1956. These statistics added emphasis to the need for regulation.

In December of 1957, a new Model Bill was adopted. The NAIC specifically declined to limit compensation or to set a maximum premium rate, but a significant addition was Section 7B–policies could be disapproved if the "benefits provided were not reasonable to the premium charged." Revisions were made in 1958 and 1960. During these years, the majority of states adopted versions of these three bills, and they remain the basis of most state regulations today.

Changes made to the NAIC Model Bill during this period include:

1. The scope of credit regulation was limited to loan terms of five years or less,
2. The $5.00 leeway on the amount of insurance exceeding the indebtedness was removed,
3. An optional provision was added permitting agricultural and educational loans to be insured for the full commitment,
4. Insurance was required to be terminated on renewal or refinancing before any new insurance could be issued on the renewed or refinanced loan,
5. Policy form requirements were expanded,
6. All policies were required to be approved, with the Commissioner given 30 days after filing to disapprove (deemer clause), and
7. The Commissioner was given the authority to disapprove policies if the policy language was misleading, unjust, etc., in addition to the benefits/premiums test.

In 1959, the NAIC adopted a position that a rate which produced a loss ratio of less than 50% was considered excessive in relation to the benefits provided. Given the mortality studies showing a claim cost of about 30¢/100/year, several groups wanted the NAIC to adopt a recommended prima facie credit life rate of 60¢/100/year. Conceptually, the prima facie rate would be a maximum, but insurers would be permitted upward deviations if they could demonstrate loss ratios in excess of the benchmark loss ratio.

Several groups opposed the 60¢/100/year rate, although the concept of prima facie rates was generally accepted. On one side was the position adopted by New York. New York proposed a decremental scale requiring higher loss ratios for lenders writing larger amounts of credit insurance. The argument was that these lenders have economies of scale which reduce unit expenses. Several states adopted the decremental scale, but only a few states continue to use the concept today.

On the other hand, many insurers and some regulators felt the prima facie rate should be at least 75¢/100/year. The mortality studies indicated a wide range of claim costs by individual insurer. A low prima facie rate would result in a large number of deviation filings and could endanger insurer solvency. Many states were not prepared to handle deviations and were as concerned as the insurers. Debate also began over the proper method of calculating deviations and measuring the credibility of the experience. Twenty-five years later, the debate is still not settled.

The discussion over these issues continued at a lively pace during the 1960s at the NAIC level, while regulatory action took place on a state-by-state basis. Gradually, states began to adopt prima facie rates which set a maximum on the rate an insurer could charge without documentation of the need for higher rates.

States also began to set caps on the maximum compensation rate, beginning with California in 1964. Currently, twenty-one states have a percentage limitation on compensation (see Appendix D). Caps ranged from 20% to 50%. Caps were good in concept but poor in practice; the lack of regulatory manpower often resulted in a voluntary compliance system. Most insurers and lenders complied, while a few insurers found ways to circumvent the caps, or simply violated them. States began to remove or ignore caps after 1965. CCIA withdrew its endorsement of compensation caps in 1966. Pennsylvania is one of the few states where the caps have been successfully enforced, but its regulation is comprehensive and includes experience filings and mandatory rate deviations.

A second mortality study was instituted in 1962, with the results published in 1964. Results of the study were disputed, but the report was adopted. Overall mortality costs were 29.3¢/100/year. Claim costs by class changed slightly from the earlier study. Only small differences were found between group and individual coverages. A major disappointment was the study's inability to produce reliable experience on disability claim costs.

A regulatory milestone was the adoption of the 1966 *Richmond Resolution.* (NAIC positions have a tendency to be named after the convention site where the position was adopted.) Presented by the CCIA and endorsed by the ALC, LIAA, and HIAA, the Resolution called for:

1. Enactment of the model bill in all states (31 states had some form of the model bill),

2. Adoption and enforcement of the 50% minimum loss ratio benchmark,

3. Promulgation of prima facie rates,

4. Adoption of a simple, reasonable deviation procedure,

5. Use of all available data, including the 1964 mortality study, and

6. Continuation of the Mortality and Morbidity Subcommittee to work on disability claim costs.

Many believed that this resolution defined the NAIC position and that debate would move on to the state level, but the NAIC debate was only the beginning. The central question became, "Did the 50% benchmark loss ratio specified in the resolution represent the maximum loss ratio a state should adopt or did it represent the minimum a state should adopt?" CCIA, ALC, and HIAA felt 50% was the maximum benchmark. LIAA said any prima facie rate over 60¢/100/year was excessive. Prudential recommended the decremental scale and a 50% minimum benchmark. The *Las Vegas Resolution* in 1968 settled the issue at the NAIC level. This resolution reaffirmed the Richmond Resolution, but specified that a state may adopt a benchmark in excess of 50%.

During 1966-68, the NAIC Experience Reporting Form was developed and adopted. Initially, disability unearned premiums were specified on the true pro rata basis. The specification was removed in 1969 after the parties were unable to agree on the proper basis. The form required the insurer to specify the method used. A study was also initiated to determine the need and method to extend the scope of the Model Bill beyond five years. After considerable discussion, the scope was extended in 1968 to credit transactions of ten years or less.

In 1968, the National Conference of Commissioners on Uniform State Laws adopted a model Uniform Consumer Credit Code, which related to lender transactions. Article 4 covers credit insurance as it applies to the lender.

The study of disability claim costs for 1965-66 experience was released in 1967 and adopted by the NAIC in 1968. Few people were satisfied with the results, due to the limitations of the underlying data. Lacking other experience, the NAIC had little alternative but to accept the results. Separate tables of claim costs for 14-day and 30-day plans were specified. Claim costs were expressed per $100 of initial indebtedness, separately by term of coverage. Claim costs were shown for terms of 60 months and less. After the scope of the model bill was extended, the NAIC asked the study group to extend the claim costs to 120 months, even though the study did not have credible experience over 60 months. The study group extended the claim costs to 120 months with the caveat that the extended rates "may not reflect the true cost of insurance."

In 1969, work continued on the deviation procedures. A proposal was adopted which modified the Richmond Resolution. Deviations were not permitted unless the demonstrated loss ratio exceeded 60%. If the loss ratio was less than 50%, the insurer was required to reduce rates or show cause why rates should not be reduced. *Portability* was also introduced. Once a case had its rate deviated, the rate stayed in effect until experience demonstrated the need for a change. The concern was that an insurer deviating downward would have the case stolen by an insurer able to write the case at prima facie rate.

In a separate action, CCIA introduced its recommendations on deviations. Minimum credibility was specified based on $50,000 of earned premiums. CCIA recognized that this was not the best basis, but it was the only basis which could be produced by all insurers. Deviations were not required if the new rate was within 5¢ of the existing rate. Separate groups were successful in promoting the concept that upward deviations should not increase lender compensation. The deviation should only provide additional money to meet increased claim costs and possibly increased insurer expenses associated with higher levels of claim costs.

The availability of disability claim costs sparked debate on the method of using the data. Prudential successfully promoted the concept that loss ratios should vary by plan. Since 14-day plans had higher claims costs, a uniform loss ratio would result in larger expense margins on costlier plans. The *O'Hare Resolution* in 1970 modified the Richmond Resolution by removing all references to disability. The O'Hare Resolution called for higher loss ratios on disability which varied by plan. Upward deviations were permitted only where the loss ratio exceeded the benchmark by 10%.

The discussion continued into 1971. CCIA, ALC, and HIAA recommended that disability loss ratios vary by amount, term, and plan. From the Ohio University study, a three-factor approach was proposed. Finally, the NAIC adopted a recommendation that prima facie rates should be 125% of the claim costs plus a 60¢ constant. These rates were adopted by and remain the prima facie rates in many states.

During 1968-70, debate raged over the use of the Rule of 78 as the basis of unearned premium refunds, particularly on disability. No one disputed that the Rule of 78 resulted in a surrender charge on disability. Advocates of the Rule of 78 stressed the understandability and widespread use of the method; and the acceptability of a modest surrender charge on early termination. The NAIC retained the Rule of 78 as the basis of refund calculations.

Several minor items occurred in 1970. First, the 1969 mortality claim costs were released. Consistent with prior studies, the overall result was about 30¢/100/year. In addition, a credit life statistical report, with earned premiums based on gross unearned premium (not mortality reserves), was adopted for the statutory annual statement. Also, debate continued over the use of unlicensed agents under group plans. The Richmond Resolution was again revised to include a deviation procedure and credibility standards.

By 1973, forty-five states had adopted some version or variation of the 1960 Model Bill. Work on deviation procedures and other changes culminated in a new Model Regulation being adopted by the NAIC in 1973. The significant change was the addition of the deviation procedure. Previous work on rates and deviations generally assumed the use of companywide or intercompany data for prima facie rates and deviations. Embodied in the new regulation was the growing trend that statewide experience be used for prima facie rates and case experience for deviations. Non-contributory business, which had always been written below prevailing rates, was exempt from prima facie standards and deviations. A new experience reporting form was included in the Model which changed the method of determining life claim costs.

In the period 1974-85, the NAIC activity concentrated on several projects which often spanned many years. A project analysis is more helpful than a chronological tracing of the activities.

From 1973 to 1979, significant effort went into developing a separate model bill for long-term credit insurance. Although the short-term model extended to ten years, the long-term bill applied to business in excess of five years. Ordinary insurance pricing techniques were included with age-banded premiums. Development of the long-term bill did produce useful studies and debates. After the long-term bill was adopted by the NAIC, the scope of the NAIC short-term bill was reduced back to five years; however, states have not followed the NAIC in this regard. No state has adopted the long-term model bill, so further discussion is unwarranted.

Claim costs for disability insurance received attention, but a definitive study remains elusive today. The 1974 Disability Study was based on experience of 1971-72. Claim costs were significantly higher than in the 1968 Study, about 50% overall. The study had its technical flaws, again stemming from the quality of the underlying data base. The industry felt claim costs were rising. Recent changes in policy forms and exclusions were expected to exacerbate the trend. (The principal change was a trend by states to reduce the preexisting condition exclusion from two years to six months.) Regardless of the technical flaws, the costs shown were more realistic than the 1968 results. After long deliberation, the NAIC chose only to "receive" the study, not to adopt it. In 1977, the NAIC removed the 1968 table from the recommended list. States are now left without any official guidance to set prima facie rates for disability insurance.

Tables of California experience for 1973-4 and 1975-6 were prepared by the California Insurance Department. Since experience was limited to California, the NAIC only "received" the tables. A pilot study of credit life and disability experience was undertaken by the Society of Actuaries, but the study has not produced meaningful results. Changes in prima facie disability rates have been based on guesswork for more than a decade now.

Interest in regulation of credit property insurance revived in 1976. By 1980, the discussion reached the point where a model regulation was drafted; then interest disappeared. The NAIC Proceedings during this period contain discussion papers from groups with different viewpoints. These papers are a good starting point for someone interested in credit property insurance.

Several items of importance occurred in 1979. The *Chicago Resolution* was adopted which finally rescinded the oft-amended

Richmond Resolution. In its place, a minimum loss ratio of 60% for credit life and disability was accepted as the NAIC position. In December, a revised Model Regulation for credit transactions was adopted without a section on deviations. A deviation procedure section was added in 1980.

In 1983, a new NAIC Credit Life and Disability Task Force was formed. The primary objective of the Task Force is to consider refinement of NAIC recommendations in the following areas:

- Uniform reporting of experience, central collection of data, and analysis on an annual basis,
- Long-term credit insurance issues,
- Gross versus net payoff life coverage,
- Financing of single premiums and refunds on long-term loans,
- Compensation limits,
- Loss ratio benchmarks, and
- Premium levels and calculation parameters.

An industry advisory group was named by the NAIC. In 1985, the advisory group proposed a new reporting form, which was adopted by the NAIC as a part of the statutory annual statement requirements. The filing of the form was optional in 1986 for 1985 experience, but becomes mandatory beginning in 1987 for 1986 experience. Reports must be filed by June 30 each year. By the NAIC action, the following items will be eliminated:

- Page 46 (section on credit insurance)
- Credit Insurance Statistical Report
- Credit Life and Accident and Health Exhibit
- Accident and Health Policy Experience Exhibit (credit insurance section)

State regulations specify that the annual statement follow NAIC requirements. These changes will automatically be made unless a state takes action. The intent is that states will also accept the new form in lieu of annual state experience filings. The NAIC Central Office is directed to prepare and publish an annual summary of the experience reported.

1954 MODEL RULES AND REGULATIONS

MODEL RULES AND REGULATIONS FOR CREDIT INSURANCE ADOPTED BY THE NAIC IN 1954

SECTION I. - DEFINITION AND SCOPE

A. On and after ______________________________, the following rules and regulations shall govern the sale of Credit Life and Credit Accident and Health Insurance. Provided, however, that these regulations shall not apply to life or accident and health insurance sold on an individual contract basis in connection with real estate loans of more than 36 months duration.

B. Credit insurance is defined as follows:

1. Credit Life Insurance is that form of insurance under which the life of a borrower of money or purchaser of goods is insured in connection with a specific loan or credit transaction.

2. Credit Accident and Health Insurance is that form of insurance under which a borrower of money or a purchaser of goods is indemnified in connection with a specific loan or credit transaction against loss of time resulting from accident or sickness.

SECTION II. - AMOUNT OF INSURANCE

A. Credit Life Insurance
The amount of credit life insurance written under one or more policies shall not exceed by more than $5.00 the original face amount of the specific contracts of indebtedness in connection with which it is written, pro-

vided, however, that where the indebtedness if repayable in installments the amount of insurance shall never exceed the approximate unpaid balance of the loan.

B. Credit Accident and Health Insurance
The total indemnities provided under the term of credit accident and health coverage shall not exceed by more than $5.00 the amount of the initial indebtedness.

SECTION III. - TERM OF INSURANCE

The term of such coverages shall not extend more than fifteen (15) days beyond the term of the indebtedness except where extended without additional cost to the insured borrower or purchaser.

SECTION IV. - PREMIUM FOR INSURANCE

A. The premium rates for Credit Life and Credit Accident and Health Insurance shall be filed with the Commissioner of Insurance.

B. If through prepayment, renewal or refinancing, the indebtedness is discharged prior to the scheduled maturity date, cancellation of the credit insurance then in force shall be mandatory. In the event of cancellation, the return premium shall be promptly paid to the person entitled thereto. The formula to be used in computing the amount of the return premium shall be filed with and approved by the Commissioner of Insurance. The policy form shall contain a termination clause in accordance with the foregoing provision. The responsibility for the enforcement of these conditions shall be upon the agent and company alike and failure on the part of the agent to enforce the provisions of this section shall be cause for the cancellation of such agent's license.

C. No company shall execute any contract or agreement with any person, firm or corporation which permits such person, firm or corporation to retain any portion of the premium for payments of losses incurred or to be incurred under policies or certificates of insurance issued by said company.

D. Where an identifiable charge for group credit insurance is made to insured borrowers or purchasers such charge shall be consistent with the premium provided for in the group policy issued to the creditor.

SECTION V. - POLICIES AND POLICY PROVISIONS

A. All Credit Insurance sold shall be evidenced by a policy, certificate or statement of insurance which shall be delivered to the insured borrower or purchaser.

B. Said policy, certificate or statement shall describe the amount and term of the coverage, the amount of the premium and a description of the coverage including any exceptions, limitations or restrictions.

C. Said policy, certificate or statement shall be delivered to the insured borrower or purchaser at the time the indebtedness is incurred except as hereinafter provided.

D. If the policy, certificate or statement is not delivered to the insured borrower or purchaser at the time the indebtedness is incurred, a copy of the application for such policy or certificate shall set forth the amount of the premium, the amount and the term of the coverage provided, and a brief description thereof, which shall be delivered to the purchaser at the time of such application. Upon approval of such application and within thirty (30) days of the date upon which the indebtedness is incurred, the insurance company shall cause to be delivered to the insured borrower or purchaser the policy or certificate. Said application shall serve as a binder and the coverage provided shall become effective as of the date the indebtedness is incurred.

E. If the policy certificate or statement is not delivered to the insured borrower or purchaser at the time the indebtedness is incurred, and if no application is taken, then the insured borrower or purchaser shall be furnished at the time the indebtedness is incurred a statement setting forth a brief description of the coverage provided. Said statement may be made a part of the contract of indebtedness. Said statement shall serve as a binder and the coverage provided shall become effective as of the date the indebtedness is incurred.

F. All policies, certificates, binders or statements of insurance, applications, endorsements, riders and other forms constituting a part of the contract or contracts of insurance with the insured borrower or purchaser shall be filed with or approved by the Commissioner of Insurance of that state in which the policy is issued.

G. Where insurance is required as additional security, the debtor shall have the right to furnish as security an existing policy or to procure the necessary coverage through any insurer authorized to transact business within the state.

SECTION VI. - LICENSED AGENT OR BROKER

A. All claims shall be promptly reported to the insurance company or its designated claim agent or representative by the agent and the company shall maintain adequate claim files.

B. All claims shall be settled strictly in accordance the policy terms.

C. All claims shall be paid either by draft drawn upon the company or by check of the company to the order of the claimant to whom payment of the claim is due pursuant to the policy provisions, or upon direction of such claimant to one specified. In the case of Credit Life Insurance, separate payment shall be made to the creditor beneficiary and to the named second beneficiary, if any, as their interests may appear. If the policy contains no provision for the designation of a second beneficiary, then it shall contain a facility of payment clause authorizing the company to pay any insurance in excess of the unpaid balance of the indebtedness of the estate, wife, husband, children, or other blood relative, or other person equitably entitled thereto as determined by the company.

D. No plan or arrangement shall be used whereby any person, firm or corporation other than the company or its designated claim agent or representative shall be authorized to settle or adjust claims. Agents, brokers, or persons affiliated with a creditor may not be designated as claim agents or representatives for the insurance company in adjusting claims. Provided, that a group creditor policy may, by arrangement with the Group insurer, draw drafts or checks in payment of claims due to the creditor-policy holder subject to audit and review by the insurance company.

Fig. 9.3 1954 Model Rules and Regulations (Reprinted by permission of the National Association of Insurance Commissioners.)

1960 Model Bill With Amendments

MODEL BILL TO PROVIDE FOR THE REGULATION OF CREDIT LIFE INSURANCE AND CREDIT ACCIDENT AND HEALTH INSURANCE

Table of Contents

BE IT ENACTED BY THE STATE OF (insert state).
(adapt caption and formal portions to local requirements and statutes)

Section 1. Purpose.

The purpose of this Act is to promote the public welfare by regulating credit life insurance and credit accident and health insurance. Nothing in this Act is intended to prohibit or discourage reasonable competition. The provisions of thisAct shall be liberally construed.

Section 2. Scope and Definitions.

A. Citation and Scope

(1) This Act may be cited as "The Model Act for the Regulation of Credit Life Insurance and Credit Accident and Health Insurance."

(2) All life insurance and all accident and health insurance in connection with loans or other credit transactions shall be subject to the provisions of this Act, except such insurance in connection with a loan or other credit transaction of more than ten years duration; nor shall insurance be subject to the provisions of this Act where the issuance of such insurance is an isolated transaction on the part of the insurer not related to an agreement or a plan for insuring debtors of the creditor.*

*[**Editor's Note**: Originally adopted as loans or other credit transactions in duration of five years or more. See 1958 NAIC Proceedings I 106-112.]

B. Definitions

For the purpose of this Act:

(1) "Credit life insurance means insurance on the life of a debtor pursuant to or in connection with a specific loan or other credit transaction;

(2) "Credit accident and health insurance" means insurance on a debtor to provide indemnity for payments becoming due on a specific loan or other credit transaction while the debtor is disabled as defined in the policy;

(3) "Creditor" means the lender of money or vendor or lessor of goods, services, or property, rights or privileges, for which payment is arranged through a credit transaction, or any successor to the right, title or interest of any such lender, vendor, or lessor, and an affiliate, associate or subsidiary of any of them or any director, officer or employee of any of them or any other person in any way associated with any of them;

(4) "Debtor" means a borrower of money or a purchaser or lessee of goods, services, property, rights or privileges for which payment is arranged through a credit transaction;

(5) "Indebtedness" means the total amount payable by a debtor to a creditor in connection with a loan or other credit transaction;

(6) "Commissioner" means (Insurance Supervisory Authority of the State).

Section 3. Forms of Credit Life Insurance and Credit Accident and Health Insurance.

Credit life insurance and credit accident and health insurance shall be issued only in the following forms:

A. Individual policies of life insurance issued to debtors on the term plan;

B. Individual policies of accident and health insurance issued to debtors on a term plan or disability benefit provisions in individual policies of credit life insurance;

C. Group policies of life insurance issued to creditors providing insurance upon the lives of debtors on the term plan;

D. Group policies of accident and health insurance issued to creditors on a term plan insuring debtors or disability benefit provisions in group credit life insurance policies to provide such coverage.

Section 4. Amount of Credit Life Insurance and Credit Accident and Health Insurance.

A. Credit Life Insurance

(1) The initial amount of credit life insurance shall not exceed the total amount repayable under the contract of indebtedness and, where an indebtedness is repayable in substantially equal installments, the amount of insurance shall at no time exceed the scheduled or actual amount of unpaid indebtedness, whichever is greater.

Note: If desired the following provisions may be added as subsection (2) and (3).

(2) Notwithstanding the provisions of the above paragraph, insurance on agricultural credit transaction commitments, not exceeding one year in duration may be written up to the amount of the loan commitment, on a non-decreasing or level term plan.

(3) Notwithstanding the provisions of paragraph A (1) of this or any other subsection, insurance on educational credit transaction commitments may be written for the amount of the portion of such commitment that has not been advanced by the creditor.

B. Credit Accident and Health Insurance

The total amount of periodic indemnity payable by credit accident and health insurance in the event of disability, as defined in the policy, shall not exceed the aggregate of the periodic scheduled unpaid installments of the indebtedness; and the amount of each periodic indemnity payment shall not exceed the original indebtedness divided by the number of periodic installments.

Section 5. Term of Credit Life Insurance and Credit Accident and Health Insurance.

The term of any credit life insurance or credit accident and health insurance shall, subject to acceptance by the insurer, commence on the date when the debtor becomes obligated to the creditor, except that, where a group policy provides coverage with respect to existing obligations, the insurance on a debtor with respect to such indebtedness shall commence on the effective date of the policy. Where evidence of insurability is required and such evidence is furnished more than thirty (30) days after the date when the debtor becomes obligated to the creditor, the term of the insurance may commence on the date on which the insurance company determines the evidence to be satisfactory, and in such event there shall be an appropriate refund or adjustment of any charge to the debtor for insurance. The term of such insurance shall not extend more than fifteen days beyond the scheduled maturity date of the indebtedness except when extended without additional cost to the debtor. If the indebtedness is discharged due to renewal or refinancing prior to the scheduled maturity date, the insurance in force shall be terminated before any new insurance may be issued in connection with the renewed or refinanced indebtedness. In all cases of termination prior to scheduled maturity, a refund shall be paid or credited as provided in Section 8.

Section 6. Provisions of Policies and Certificates of Insurance: Disclosure to Debtors.

A. All credit life insurance and credit accident and health insurance shall be evidenced by an individual policy, or in the case of group insurance by a certificate of insurance, which individual policy or group certificate of insurance shall be delivered to the debtor.

B. Each individual policy or group certificate of credit life insurance, and/or credit accident and health insurance shall, in addition to other requirements of law, set forth the name and home office address of the insurer, the name or names of the debtor or in the case of a certificate under a group policy, the identity by name or otherwise of the debtor, the premium or amount of payment, if any, by the debtor separately for credit life insurance and credit accident and health insurance, a description of the coverage including the amount and term thereof, and any exceptions, limitations and restrictions, and shall state that the benefits shall be paid to the creditor to reduce or extinguish the unpaid indebtedness and, wherever the amount of insurance may exceed the unpaid indebtedness, that any such excess shall be payable to a beneficiary, other than the creditor, named by the debtor or to his estate.

C. Said individual policy or group certificate of insurance shall be delivered to the insured debtor at the time the indebtedness is incurred except as hereinafter provided.

D. If said individual policy or group certificate of insurance is not delivered to the debtor at the time the indebtedness is incurred, a copy of the application for such policy or a notice of proposed insurance, signed by the debtor and setting forth the name and home office address of the insurer, the name or names of the debtor, the premium or amount of payment by the debtor, if any, separately for credit life insurance and credit accident and health insurance, the amount, term and a brief description of the coverage provided, shall be delivered to the debtor at the time such indebtedness is incurred. The copy of the application for, or notice of proposed insurance, shall also refer exclusively to insurance coverage, and shall be separate and apart from the loan, sale or other credit statement of account, instrument or agreement, unless the information required by this subsection is prominently set forth therein. Upon acceptance of the insurance by the insurer and within thirty (30) days of the date upon which the indebtedness is incurred, the insurer shall cause the individual policy or group certificates of insurance to be delivered to the debtor. Said application or notice of proposed insurance shall state that upon acceptance by the insurer, the insurance shall become effective as provided in Section 5.

E. If the named insurer does not accept the risk, then and in such event the debtor shall receive a policy or certificate of insurance setting forth the name and home office address of the substituted insurer and the amount of the premium to be charged, and if the amount of premium is less than that set forth in the notice of proposed insurance an appropriate refund shall be made.

Section 7. Filing, Approval and Withdrawal of Forms.

A. All policies, certificates of insurance, notices of proposed insurance, applications for insurance, endorsements and riders delivered or issued for delivery in this State and the schedules of premium rates pertaining thereto shall be filed with the Commissioner.

B. The Commissioner shall within thirty (30) days after the filing of any such policies, certificates of insurance, notices of proposed insurance, applications for insurance, endorsements and riders, disapprove any such form if the benefits provided therein are not reasonable in relation to the premium charge, or if it contains provisions which are unjust, unfair, inequitable, misleading, deceptive or encourage misrepresentation of the coverage, or are contrary to any provision of the Insurance Code or of any rule or regulation promulgated thereunder.

C. If the Commissioner notifies the insurer that the form is disapproved, it is unlawful thereafter for such insurer to issue or use such form. In such notice, the Commissioner shall specify the reason for his disapproval and state that a hearing will be granted within twenty (20) days after request in writing by the insurer. No such policy, certificate of insurance, notice of proposed insurance, nor any application, endorsement or rider, shall be issued or used until the expiration of thirty (30) days after it has been so filed, unless the Commissioner shall give his prior written approval thereto.

D. The Commissioner may, at any time after a hearing held not less than twenty (20) days after written notice to the insurer, withdraw his approval of any such form on any ground set forth in subsection B above. The written notice of such hearing shall state the reason for the proposed withdrawal.

E. It is not lawful for the insurer to issue such forms or use them after the effective date of such withdrawal.

F. If a group policy of credit life insurance or credit accident and health insurance

(i) has been delivered in this State before the effective date of this Act, or

(ii) has been or is delivered in another State before or after the effective date of this Act,

the insurer shall be required to file only the group certificate and notice of proposed insurance delivered or issued for delivery in this State as specified in subsections B and D of Section 6 of this Act and such forms shall be approved by the Commissioner if they conform with the requirements specified in said subsections and if the schedules of premium rates applicable to the insurance evidenced by such certificate or notice are not in excess of the insurer's schedules of premium rates filed with the Commissioner; provided, however, the premium rate in effect on existing group policies may be continued until the first policy anniversary date following the date this Act becomes operative as provided in Section 12.

G. Any order or final determination of the Commissioner under the provisions of this section shall be subject to judicial review.

Section 8. Premiums and Refunds.

A. Any insurer may revise its schedules of premium rates from time to time, and shall file such revised schedules with the Commissioner. No insurer shall issue any credit life insurance policy or credit accident and health insurance policy for which the premium rate exceeds that determined by the schedules of such insurer as then on file with the Commissioner.

B. Each individual policy, or group certificate shall provide that in the event of termination of the insurance prior to the scheduled maturity date of the indebtedness, any refund of an amount paid by the debtor for insurance shall be paid or credited promptly to the person entitled thereto; provided, however, that the Commissioner shall prescribe a minimum refund and no refund which would be less than such minimum need be made. The formula to be used in computing such refund shall be filed with and approved by the Commissioner.

C. If a creditor requires a debtor to make any payment for credit life insurance or credit accident and health insurance and an individual policy or group certificate of insurance is not issued, the creditor shall immediately give written notice to such debtor and shall promptly make an appropriate credit to the account.

D. The amount charged to a debtor for any credit life or credit health and accident insurance shall not exceed the premiums charged by the insurer, as computed at the time the charge to the debtor is determined.

Note: Where a state prohibits payments for insurance by the debtor in connection with credit transactions, the following paragraph may be included.

E. Nothing in this Act shall be construed to authorize any payments for insurance now prohibited under any statute, or rule thereunder, governing credit transactions.

Section 9. Issuance of Policies.

All policies of credit life insurance and credit accident and health insurance shall be delivered or issued for delivery in this state only by an insurer authorized to do an insurance business therein, and shall be issued only through holders of licenses or authorizations issued by the Commissioner.

Section 10. Claims.

A. All claims shall be promptly reported to the insurer or its designated claim representative, and the insurer shall maintain adequate claim files. All claims shall be settled as soon as possible and in accordance with the terms of the insurance contract.

B. All claims shall be paid either by draft drawn upon the insurer or by check of the insurer to the order of the claimant to whom payment of the claim is due pursuant to the policy provisions, or upon direction of such claimant to one specified.

C. No plan or arrangement shall be used whereby any person, firm or corporation other than the insurer or its designated claim representative shall be authorized to settle or adjust claims. The creditor shall not be designated as claim representative for the insurer in adjusting claims; provided, that a group policyholder may, by arrangement with the group insurer, draw drafts or checks in payment of claims due to the group policyholder subject to audit and review by the insurer.

Section 11. Existing Insurance — Choice of Insurer.

When credit life insurance or credit accident and health insurance is required as additional security for any indebtedness, the debtor shall, upon request to the creditor, have the option of furnishing the required amount of insurance through existing policies of insurance owned or controlled by him or of procuring and furnishing the required coverage through any insurer authorized to transact an insurance business within this state.

Section 12. Enforcement.

The Commissioner may, after notice and hearing, issue such rules and regulations as he deems appropriate for the supervision of this Act. Whenever the Commissioner finds that there has been a violation of this Act or any rules or regulations issued pursuant thereto, and after written notice thereof and hearing given to the insurer or other person authorized or licensed by the Commissioner, he shall set forth the details of his findings together with an order for compliance by a specified date. Such order shall be binding on the insurer and other person authorized or licensed by the Commissioner on the date specified unless sooner withdrawn by the Commissioner or a stay thereof has been ordered by a court of competent jurisdiction. The provisions of Sections 5, 6, 7 and 8 of this Act shall not be operative until ninety (90) days after the effective date of this Act, and the Commissioner in his discretion may extend by not more than an additional ninety (90) days the initial period within which the provisions of said sections shall not be operative.

Section 13. Judicial Review.

Any party to the proceeding affected by an order of the Commissioner shall be entitled to judicial review by following the procedure set forth in (insert applicable section).

Section 14. Penalties.

In addition to any other penalty provided by law, any person, firm or corporation which violates an order of the Commissioner after it has become final, and while such order is in effect, shall, upon proof thereof to the satisfaction of the court, forfeit and pay to the State of (insert state) a sum not to exceed $250.00 which may be recovered in a civil action, except that if such violation is found to be willful, the amount of such penalty shall be a sum not to exceed $1,000.00. The Commissioner, in his discretion, may revoke or suspend the license or certificate of authority of the person, firm or corporation guilty of such violation. Such order for suspension or revocation shall be upon notice and hearing, and shall be subject to judicial review as provided in Section 13 of this Act.

Section 15. Separability Provision.

If any provision of this Act, or the application of such provision to any person or circumstances, shall be held invalid, the remainder of the Act, and the application of such provision to any person or circumstances other than those as to which it is held invalid, shall not be affected thereby.

Legislative History (all references are to the Proceedings of the NAIC).

1958 Proc. I 106-112
1959 Proc. I 126-130
1961 Proc. I 300-305
1968 Proc. II 499

Fig 9.4 1960 Model Bill (Reprinted by permission of the National Association of Insurance Commissioners).

1979 Model Regulation

MODEL REGULATION FOR

SHORT TERM CREDIT LIFE AND ACCIDENT AND HEALTH INSURANCE

(MINIMUM REQUIREMENTS)

Table of Contents

Section 1. Purpose and Authority.

The purpose of this regulation is to protect the interests of debtors and the public in this state by providing a system of rate, policy form, and operating standards for the transaction of short term credit life and credit accident and health insurance. This rule interprets and implements the (insert state) Statutes, including but not limited to the following sections:

Section 2. Definitions.

As used in this regulation:

(1) "Compensation" means money or anything else of value.

(2) "Credit accident and health insurance" means insurance as defined in Section (insert applicable section) of the (insert state) Statutes.

(3) "Credit insurance" means both credit life insurance and credit accident and health insurance.

(4) "Credit life insurance" means insurance as defined in Section (insert applicable section) of the (insert state) Statutes.

(5) "Short term" means a credit transaction of less than 61 months.

(6) "Net written premium" means gross written premium minus refunds on termination.

(7) "Indebtedness" means total amount repayable including principal, interest and finance charges.

Section 3. Rights and Treatment of Debtors.

(1) Multiple Plans of Insurance. If a creditor makes available to the debtors more than one plan of credit life insurance or more than one plan of credit accident and health insurance, all debtors must be informed of such plans.

(2) Substitution. When a creditor requires credit life insurance, credit accident and health insurance, or both, as additional security for an indebtedness, the debtor shall be given the option of furnishing the required amount of insurance through existing policies of insurance owned or controlled by the debtor procuring and furnishing the required coverage through any insurer authorized to transact insurance business in this state. If this subsection is applicable, the debtor shall be informed by the creditor of the right to provide alternative coverage before the transaction is completed.

(3) Evidence of Coverage.

(a) All credit insurance shall be evidenced by an individual policy, or, in the case of group insurance, by a certificate of insurance. The individual policy or certificate of insurance shall be delivered to the debtor in accord with Section (insert applicable section) of the Credit Insurance Law.

(b) Each individual policy or certificate of insurance shall set forth such information as is required by Sections (insert applicable sections) of the Credit Insurance Law and any other appropriate sections of the (state) Statutes.

(4) Claims Processing. All credit insurance claims shall be processed in accord with Section (insert appropriate section) of the Credit Insurance Law and with regulation No. (insert applicable citing) as amended.

(5) Termination of group credit insurance policy.

(a) If a debtor is covered by a group credit insurance policy providing for the payment of single premiums to the insurer, then provision shall be made by the insurer that in the event of termination of the policy for any reason, insurance coverage with respect to any debtor insured under such policy shall be continued for the entire period for which the single premium has been paid.

(b) If a debtor is covered by a group credit insurance policy providing for the payment of premiums to the insurer on a monthly outstanding balance basis, then the policy shall provide that, in the event of termination of such policy for whatever reason, termination notice thereof shall be given to the insured debtor at least 30 days prior to the effective date of termination except where replacement of the coverage by the same or another insurer in the same or greater amount takes place without lapse of coverage. The notice required in this paragraph shall be given by the insurer or, at the option of the insurer by the creditor.

(6) Interest on Premiums. If the creditor adds identifiable insurance charges or premiums for credit insurance to the indebtedness, and any direct or indirect finance, carrying, credit, or service charge is made to the debtor on such insurance charges or premiums, the creditor must remit and the insurer shall collect such premium within sixty (60) days after it is added to the indebtedness.

(7) Renewal or Refinancing of Indebtedness. If the indebtedness is discharged due to renewal or refinancing prior to the scheduled maturity date, the insurance in force shall be terminated before any new insurance may be issued in connection with the renewed or refinanced indebtedness. In all cases of such termination prior to scheduled maturity, a refund shall be paid or credited to the debtor as provided in Section 9. In any renewal or refinancing of the indebtedness, the effective date of the coverage as respects any policy provision shall be deemed to be the first date on which the debtor became insured under the policy covering the indebtedness which was renewed or refinanced, at least to the extent of the amount and term of the indebtedness outstanding at the time of renewal and refinancing of the debt.

(8) Maximum Aggregate Provisions. A provision in a policy or certificate that sets a maximum limit on total payments must apply only to that policy or certificate.

(9) Voluntary Prepayment of Indebtedness. If a debtor prepays the indebtedness other than as a result of death or through a lump sum disability payment:

(a) Any credit life insurance covering such indebtedness shall be terminated and an appropriate refund of the credit life insurance premium shall be paid to the debtor in accordance with Section 9; and

(b) Any credit accident and health insurance covering such indebtedness shall be terminated and an appropriate refund of the credit accident and health insurance premium shall be paid to the debtor in accordance with Section 9. If a claim under such coverage is in progress at the time of prepayment, the amount of refund may be determined as if the prepayment did not occur until the payment of benefits terminates. No refund need be paid during any period of disability for which credit accident and health benefits are payable. A refund shall be computed as if prepayment occurred at the end of the disability period.

(10) Involuntary Prepayment of Indebtedness. If an indebtedness is prepaid by the proceeds of a credit life insurance policy covering the debtor or by a lump sum payment of a disablility claim under a credit insurance policy covering the debtor, then it shall be the responsibility of the insurer to see that the following are paid to the insured debtor if living or the beneficiary, other than the creditor, named by the debtor or to the debtor's estate:

(a) In the case of prepayment by the proceeds of a credit life insurance policy, or by the proceeds of a lump sum total and permanent disability benefit under credit life coverage, an appropriate refund of the credit accident and health insurance premium in accordance with Section 9;

(b) In the case of prepayment by a lump sum disability claim, an appropriate refund of the credit life insurance premium in accordance with Section 9;

(c) In either case, the amount of the benefits in excess of the amount required to repay the indebtedness after crediting any unearned interest or finance charges.

(11) Amounts to be Insured:

(a) Credit life insurance may provide benefits not exceeding the amount of indebtedness outstanding or, at the option of the insurer, provide benefits not exceeding the amount of indebtedness outstanding less the unearned interest or finance charges. Premium charges shall be computed on the same basis as the benefits provided.

(b) Credit accident and health insurance may provide benefits not exceeding the amount of outstanding indebtedness inclusive of unearned interest or finance changes.

Section 4. Policy Forms and Related Material.

(1) Permissible Forms. Credit life and credit accident and health insurance shall be issued only in the forms described in Section (insert applicable section) of the Credit Insurance Law.

(2) Filing Requirements. All policy forms, certificates of insurance, notices of proposed insurance, applications for insurance, endorsements and riders to be delivered or issued for delivery in this state and the schedules of maximum premium rates pertaining thereto shall be filed with the Commissioner as required by Section (insert applicable section) of the Credit Insurance Law.

Section 5. Determination of Reasonableness of Benefits in Relation to Premium Charge.

(1) General Standard. Under the Credit Insurance Law, benefits provided by credit insurance policies must be reasonable in relation to the premium charged. This requirement is satisfied if the premium rate charged develops or may be reasonably expected to develop a loss ratio of not less than 60%.

(2) Nonstandard Coverage. If any insurer files for approval of any form providing coverage more restrictive than that described in Sections 7 and 8, the insurer shall demonstrate to the satisfaction of the Commissioner that the premium rates to be charged for such restricted coverage will develop or may be reasonably expected to develop a loss ratio not less than that contemplated for standard coverage at the premium rates described in these sections.

(3) Coverage Without Separate Charge. If no specific charge is made to the debtor for credit insurance the standards of Section 5 are not required to be used but any premium rates resulting from such standards as are used which exceed the premium rate standards set out in Section 7 and 8 must be filed with the Commissioner. For purposes of this subsection, it will be considered that the debtor is charged a specific amount for insurance if an identifiable charge for insurance is disclosed in the credit or other instrument furnished the debtor which sets out the financial elements of the credit transactions, or if there is a differential in finance, interest, service or other similar charge made to debtors who are in like circumstances, except for their insured or noninsured status.

Section 6. Limitation on Compensation. (optional provision)

(1) An insurer shall not pay compensation in excess of 30% of the prima facie premium of which no more than 25% may be paid to a creditor and no more than 5% to a producing agent.

Drafting note: This is an optional provision subject to the statutory provision of the state or jurisdiction.

Section 7. Credit Life Insurance Rates.

(1) Premium Rate. Credit life insurance premium rates for the insured portion of an indebtedness repayable in equal monthly installments, where the insured portion of the indebtedness decreases uniformly by the amount of the monthly installment paid, shall be as set forth in Paragraphs (a) and (b). Paragraphs (c), (d) and (e), refer to premium rates for other types of benefits either alone or in combination with the type of benefits applicable to (a) and (b).

(a) ________per month per $1,000 of outstanding insured indebtedness if premiums are payable on a monthly outstanding balance basis.

(b) If premiums are payable on a single premium basis, the following formula shall be used to develop single premium rates from the outstanding balance rate:

$Sp = \frac{n + 1\ Op}{20}$ where Sp is the single term premium per $100 of initial insured indebtedness, n is the credit term in months, and Op is monthly outstanding balance rate per $1,000 of outstanding insured indebtedness.

(c) If premiums are payable on a single premium basis when the benefit provided is level term, the following formula shall be used to develop single premium rates from the outstanding balance rate:

$Sp = \frac{n}{10}\ Op$ where Sp is the single term premium per $100 of initial insured indebtedness, n is the credit term in months, and Op is the monthly outstanding balance rate per $1,000 of outstanding insured indebtedness.

(d) Joint coverage on either of the basis in (a), (b), or (c), of Subsection 1, shall be one hundred and forty percent of the specific rate for that type of coverage.

(e) A combination of the appropriate rate for level term and the appropriate rate for decreasing term (with equal decrements), if coverage provided is a combination of level term and decreasing term (with equal decrements).

(f) If the benefits provided are other than those described in Subsection (1) above, rates for such benefits shall be actuarially consistent with the rates provided in Paragraphs (a), (b), (c) and (d).

Drafting note: Credit life insurance premium rates have not been included in the model regulation. Each state should adopt rates which reflect the experience developed within that state or regionally if a state lacks sufficient credible data. A state may also establish rates by creditor class of business wherever warranted. These rates shall be calculated so as to provide a minimum loss ratio of 60%. It is recognized that the rates set up in this section are computed on an annual basis, and no discount for mortality or interest has been provided. A state with the capability of developing and enforcing such discount is urged to do so.

(2) The premium rates in subsection (1) shall apply to policies providing credit life insurance to be issued with or without evidence of insurability, to be offered to all debtors, and containing:

(a) No exclusions other than suicide within six months of the incured indebtedness; and

(b) Either no age restrictions or age restrictions making ineligible for coverage debtors 65 or over at the time the indebtedness is incurred or debtors having attained age 66 or over on the maturity date of the indebtedness.

(c) A revolving credit insurance policy may exclude from the classes eligible for insurance, classes of debtors determined by age, and provide for the cessation of insurance or reduction in the amount of insurance upon attainment of not less than age 65.

Section 8. Credit Accident and Health Insurance.

(1) Premium Rate. Credit accident and health insurance premium rates for the insured portion of an indebtedness repayable in equal monthly installments, where the insured portion of the indebtedness decreases uniformly by the amount of the monthly installment paid, shall be as set forth in Paragraphs (a) and (b). Paragraphs (c), (d), and (e), refer to premium rates for other types of benefits either alone or in combination with the type of benefits applicable to (a) and (b).

(a) As set forth in Appendix I if premiums are payable on a single-premium basis for the duration of the coverage; or

(b) If premiums are paid on the basis of a premium rate per month per thousand of outstanding insured indebtedness, these premiums shall be computed according to the following formula or according to a formula approved by the Commissioner which produces rates actuarially equivalent to the single premium rates in Appendix I:

$$OP_n = \frac{20}{n+1} SP_n$$

Where SP_n= Single Premium Rate per $100 of initial insured indebetedness repayable in n equal monthly installments (Appendix I).

OP_n = Monthly Outstanding Balance Premium Rate per $1,000.

n = Original repayment period, in months.

(c) The actuarial equivalent of Paragraphs (a) and (b) shall be used if the coverage provided is a constant maximum indemnity for a given period of time.

(d) An appropriate combination of the premium rate for a constant maximum indemnity for a given period of time and the premium rate for a maximum indemnity which decreases in even amounts per month, if the coverage provided is a combination of a constant maximum indemnity for a given period of time after which the maximum indemnity begins to decrease in even amounts per month.

(e) If the benefits provided are other than those described in Subsection (1) above, rates for such benefits shall be actuarially consistent with rates provided in Paragraphs (a), (b), (c) and (d).

(f) The outstanding balance rate for credit accident and health insurance, may be either a term specified rate or may be a single composite term outstanding balance rate applicable to all loans made under an open-end credit plan.

(2) The premium rates in Subsection (1) shall apply to policies providing credit accident and health insurance to be issued with or without evidence of insurability, to be offered to all eligible debtors, and containing:

(a) No provision excluding or denying a claim for disability resulting from pre-existing conditions except for those conditions for which the insured debtor received medical advice, diagnosis, or treatment within six months preceding the effective date of the debtor's coverage and which caused loss within the six months following the effective date of coverage.

(b) No other provision which excludes or restricts liability in the event of disability caused in a specific manner except that it may contain provisions excluding or restricting coverage in the event of normal pregnancy and intentionally self-inflicted injuries.

(c) No Actively at Work Test may require that the debtor be employed more than thirty (30) hours per week.

(d) No age restrictions or only age restrictions making ineligible for coverage debtors 65 or over at the time the indebtedness is incurred or debtors who will have attained age 66 or over on the maturity date of the indebtedness;

(e) A daily benefit equal in amount to one-thirtieth of the monthly benefit payable under the policy for the indebtedness;

(f) A definition of "disability" which provides that during the first 12 months of disability the insured shall be unable to perform the duties of his occupation at the time the disability occurred, and thereafter the duties of any occupation for which the insured is reasonably fitted by education, training, or experience. This paragraph shall not apply to lump sum disability coverage.

(g) A revolving credit insurance policy may exclude from the classes eligible for insurance classes of debtors determined by age, and provide for the cessation of insurance or reduction in the amount of insurance upon attainment of not less than age 65.

Section 9. Refund Formulas.

(1) Refund formulas which any insurer desires to use must be filed with and approved by the Commissioner prior to use. The following methods are deemed appropriate for the plans described:

(a) Pro Rata Method. The pro rata unearned gross premium method shall be used for level term credit life insurance, credit accident and health insurance wherein the insured is covered for a constant maximum indemnity begins to decrease in even amounts per month, and for credit insurance coverage under which premiums are collected from the debtor on a basis other than the single premium basis.

(b) "Sum of the Digits Method." The "Rule of 78" or "sum of the digits" unearned premium method for coverages other than those included in paragraph (a) shall be used.

(c) Combination Methods. An appropriate combination of the pro rata method and the Rule of 78 shall be used or, at the option of the insurer, the pro rata method for credit life insurance provided as a combination of level and decreasing term coverage and for credit accident and health insurance wherein the insured is covered for a constant maximum indemnity for a given period of time, after which the maximum indemnity begins to decrease in even amounts per month.

(2) In the event of termination, no charge for credit insurance may be made for the first 15 days of a loan month and a full month may be charged for 16 days or more of a loan month.

(3) The requirements of the Credit Insurance Law that refund formulas be filed with the Commissioner shall be considered fulfilled if the refund formulas are set forth in the individual policy or group certificate filed with the Commissioner. If the appropriate refund formula is the "sum of the digits" formula, commonly known as the "Rule of 78", it shall be sufficient to refer to it by either phrase.

(4) No refund of $1 or less need be made.

Section 10. Experience Reports.

(1) Each insurer doing credit insurance business in this state shall submit experience reports as provided in this section for the experience period of each class of business.

(2) "Class of business" means any of the following:

(a) Credit unions;

(b) Commercial and savings banks;

(c) finance companies;

(d) motor vehicle dealers;

(e) other sales finance;

(f) production credit associations; bank agricultural loans;

(g) all others.

Drafting note: It is recommended that experience be gathered by classes of business to enable the regulator to determine whether rates ought to be established by creditor class. These classes are the minimum number of classes which may be validly used, and states may elect to designate other classes although it is urged that such classes not be inconsistent with the above specified classes.

(3) The reports required by this section shall be submitted in the manner prescribed by Forms A, B, and C attached to these regulations. Insurers are expected to reproduce the form for use according to their needs. Such experience reports shall be submitted not later than June 1st of each calendar year following the effective date of this regulation.

(4) The experience reports required by this section shall replace all other annual reports of credit insurance experience except for reports required by the National Association of Insurance Commissioners annual statements. The experience reports required by this section are separate and distinct from the NAIC annual statement and are not used in any manner to determine the financial condition of the company.

Section 11. Use of Rates—Direct Business Only.
(Long Form With Standard Case Rating)

(See Glossary of "terms and definitions" herein.)

(1) *Minimum Loss Ratio Test.*

(a) *Loss Ratio Test.* Benefits will be considered reasonable in relation to the premium charged if the ratio of claims incurred to premium earned during the most recent experience period at the rates in use produces a loss ratio that equals or exceeds the Minimum Loss Ratio Standard specified in Section 5.

(b) *Broad Test.* This test will be made separately for:

(i) the total credit life insurance experience of the insurer in this state for all classes of business and plans of insurance combined, and for

(ii) the total credit accident and health insurance experience of the insurer in this state for all classes of business and plans of insurance combined, provided, however,

(iii) a separate test is not required for each class of business or plan of insurance therein.

(c) *Scope of Test When Deviated Rates are in Use.* If an insurer has deviated rates approved under (3)(a) or (3)(b), the test will exclude the experience of the accounts for which deviated rates are in use. The reasonableness of rates for those accounts will be determined by subsection (3).

(d) *Frequency of Test.* The test will be made each year when submitting the experience reports required by Section 10.

(2) *Use of Prima Facie Rates.*

An insurer that has rates which are equal to or lower than prima facie rates may retain on file and use those rates without further proof of their reasonableness while the experience of the insurer in this state for the accounts to which they are applied continues to satisfy the Minimum Loss Ratio Test specified in subsection (1). An insurer may at any time use a rate for an account that is lower than its filed rate without notice to the Commissioner.

(3) *Use of Deviated Rates.*

(a) *Use of Rates Higher Than Prima Facie Rates.*

If the Minimum Loss Ratio Test produces a loss ratio that exceeds the Minimum Loss Ratio Standard, the insurer may file for approval and use rates that are higher than prima facie rates if it can be expected that the use of such higher rates will continue to produce a loss ratio for the accounts to which they are applied that will satisfy the Minimum Loss Ratio Test.

(b) *Use of Rates Lower Than Prima Facie Rates.*

If the Minimum Loss Ratio Test produces a loss ratio that is lower than the Minimum Loss Ratio Standard, the insurer shall either file adjusted rates that can be expected to produce a loss ratio that will satisfy the Minimum Loss Ratio Test or submit reasons acceptable to the Commissioner why it should not be required to do so.

(c) *Determination of Deviated Rates.*

If deviated rates are to be filed under (a) or (b) above, the insurer may file rates for approval that will be:

(i) Applied uniformly to all accounts of the insurer.

(ii) applied on an equitable basis approved by the Commissioner to only one or more accounts of the insurer for which the experience has been more favorable or less favorable than expected, or

(iii) applied according to a case rating procedure on file with the Commissioner (an insurer electing to file a case rating procedure may either file its own plan for the approval of the Commissioner or may use the Standard Case Rating Procedure specified herein by notice to him.)

The rate for each account which has been deviated must be redetermined on the same basis thereafter or until the rate for the account is no longer deviated.

(4) *Use of Rates Determined by Standard Case Rating Procedure.*

An insurer, by written notice to the Commissioner of its election to do so, may file and use premium rates determined by this Standard Case Rating Procedure. If elected, the procedure will be used by the insurer to rate all of its credit insurance in this State. Once elected, the procedure will remain in effect for the insurer until a different procedure has been filed with the Commissioner and approved by him.

(a) *Determination of Case Rate.*

An insurer may use a rate for an account not greater than the case rate for that account as follows:

(i) Single Account Cases and Multiple Account Cases.

If the account is within the definition of a single account case or of a multiple account case as filed by the insurer, the case rate for the account or for each account comprising the multiple account case will be determined by the formula set forth in (b) below.

(ii) Pooled Account Cases.

If the account is in a pooled account case, the case rate for each account comprising the case will be the case rate for that pooled account case as determined by the formula set forth in (b) below.

(iii) New Accounts Without Experience.

If a new account of an insurer has no experience in this State, the case rate for the account will be the prima facie rate under Sections 7 and 8.

(b) *Calculation of Case Rate.*

(i) Symbols and Definitions.

NCR = New Case Rate (redefined in (ii) below)
= PFR (CLR) + AE
PFR = Prima Facie Rate
ALR = Actual Loss Ratio for case at Prima Facie Rate Basis
ELR = Minimum Loss Ratio Required by Section 5
SLR = the loss ratio at prima facie rates based on the most recent published State experience for the applicable plan of insurance and class of business. If appropriate published experience is not available, then
SLR = ELR.
Z = Credibility Factor for Case
CLR = Credibility Adjusted Case Loss Ratio at Prima Facie Basis
= Z(ALR) + (1 − Z)(SLR)
E = Expense Loading in prima facie rate
= (1 − ELR)PFR
AE = Adjusted Expense Loading (defined in (ii) below)

(ii) New Case Rate.

((a)) If CLR is less than ELR for credit life insurance or for credit accident and health insurance.
AE = E
NCR = PFR [1 − (ELR − CLR)]

((b)) If CLR is greater than ELR for credit life insurance
AE = E + .1(CLR − ELR)
NCR = PFR [1 + 1.1(CLR − ELR)]

((c)) If CLR is greater than ELR for credit accident and health insurance
AE = E + .2(CLR − ELR)
NCR + PFR [1 + 1.2(CLR − ELR)]

(c) *Minimum Changes.*

If the new case rate does not differ by more than 5% from the current case rate, the new case rate will be the current case rate.

(d) *Case Rate Period.*

A case rate will be in effect for a period of time not longer than the experience period used to establish the case rate (i.e. 1 year, 2 years, 3 years). An insurer may file for a new case rate before the end of a case rate period, but not more often than once during any 12 month period.

(e) *Change of Insurers.*

If a creditor changes insurers, the case rate in effect for his account on the date of the change will continue to be in effect for the account with the succeeding insurer for the remainder of the case rate period or until a new case rate for his account is established if sooner.

(5) *Filing of Rates.*

When submitting the Experience Reports required by Section 10, an insurer who has elected to file higher rates under (3)(a) above or who is required to file reduced rates under (3)(b) above, or who has elected the Standard Case Rating Procedure shall also file a new schedule of rates as determined by those subsections. If the Commissioner does not disapprove the new schedule of rates within 30 days after receipt of filing, or July 1, whichever is later, rates not higher than the new rates shall be placed in effect on September 1 next following unless a different effective date has been approved by the Commissioner. In no event, however, may a rate increase be placed in effect earlier than the date rate decreases are required to be placed in effect.

(6) *Glossary of Terms and Definitions as Used in this Section 11.*

(a) "*Account*" means the aggregate credit life insurance or credit accident and health insurance coverage for a single plan of insurance and for a single class of business written through a single creditor by the insurer whether coverage is written on a group or individual policy basis. With the approval of the Commissioner, the account may also mean the credit life insurance or the credit accident and health insurance of two or more plans of insurance or two or more classes of business of a single creditor.

(b) "*Case*" means either a "Single Account Case" or a "Multiple Account Case" or a "Pooled Account Case" as follows:

(i) "Single Account Case," means an account that is at least as credible as the minimum level of credibility elected by the insurer for defining a single account case excluding all of these accounts which have been included in multiple account cases.

An insurer may make this election by notice to the Commissioner, in writing, of the minimum credibility factor it will use to define a "Single Account Case." Once notified, the minimum credibility factor will remain in effect for the insurer until a different factor has been filed by the insurer and approved by the Commissioner. If an insurer makes no written election, its minimum credibility factor will be 100%.

(ii) "Multiple Account Case" means, with the approval of the Commissioner, two or more accounts of the same insurer having similar underwriting characteristics are combined by the insurer for premium rating purposes, excluding all cases defined in (i) above and which, when combined, are at least as credible as the minimum level of credibility elected in (i) above.

(iii) "Pooled Account Case" means a combination of all the insurer's accounts of the same plan of insurance and class of business which combination has experience in this State, excluding all cases defined in (i) and (ii) above.

(c) "*Plan of Insurance*" unless otherwise filed and approved means

(i) credit life insurance on a flat rated basis other than revolving accounts (i.e. including joint and single life coverage, decreasing and level insurance, outstanding balance and single premium),

(ii) credit life insurance on a revolving account basis,

(iii) credit life insurance on an age-graded basis,

(iv) credit accident and health insurance other than on revolving accounts combining outstanding balance and single premium but separately for each combination of waiting period and retroactive or non-retroactive.

(v) credit accident and health insurance on a revolving account basis separately for each combination of waiting period and retroactive or non-retroactive.

(**NOTE**: For states which have a sufficient volume of business, the definition of the term "plan of insurance" may be more complex.)

(d) "*Class of business*" means a grouping of the classes of business in Section 10 having the same prima facie rate.

(e) "*Experience*" means "earned premiums," incurred claims, "incurred claim count," number of life years insured, and "average amount of insurance" during the experience period.

(f) "*State experience*" means the most recent published claim rates or loss ratios based on the experience of all insurers in this State for a plan of insurance and class of business. However, if this State enters into agreements with other similar States, the use of the appropriate multi-State experience will be substituted for the experience in this State. If published experience is not available in this State or multi-State region, the claim rates assumed in this State's prima facie rates and the minimum loss ratio required by Section 5 will be used.

(g) "*Experience Period*" means the most recent period of time for which experience is reported, but not a period longer than three full years.

(i) If a case develops 100% credibility in less than three years, the experience period for that case will be the number of full years needed to develop credibility.

(ii) If a case develops the minimum credibility elected by the insurer in less than three years, the experience period for that case, at the option of the insurer, will be the number of full years needed to develop minimum credibility or three full years.

Experience incurred in the period immediately preceding the effective date of this regulation may be used to the extent necessary to fill out the experience periods, if it is available in proper form.

(iii) New Accounts with Experience.

If a new account of an insurer has experience in this State with a prior insurer, the new insurer must use the most recent experience of the account to the extent necessary to fill out an experience period.

(iv) Accounts with Multi-State Experience.

If an account has experience in more than this State, an insurer may use only the experience of the account in this State to rate the case or with the approval of the Commissioner may use the multi-State experience of the account for this purpose applied on an equitable basis.

(**Note**: The term "year," as used in this definition, for individual policies means a calendar year and for group policies means either a calendar year or a policy year at the option of the insurer.)

(h) "*Prima Facie Rates*" means those rates shown in Sections 7 and 8.

(i) "*Earned premiums at rates in use*" means actual earned premiums, that is, the premiums earned at the premium rates actually charged and in force during the experience period in accordance with the instructions and method of calculation for Reporting Form A.

(j) "*Earned premium at prima facie rate*" means the actual earned premiums adjusted to the amount which would have been earned had the premium rate during the experience period been equal to the current prima facie rate in accordance with instructions and method of calculation for Reporting Form A. Reasonable methods of approximations may be used.

(k) "*Incurred Claims*" means total claims paid during the experience period, adjusted for the change in the claim reserve.

(l) "*Credibility Factor*" means the extent to which the past experience of a case can be expected to recur in the future. For the Standard Case Rating Procedure, the credibility factor may be based on either the Number of Claims incurred or on the "Average Number of Life Years" for the case during the experience period using the Credibility Table.

The insurer shall notify the Commissioner in advance which method it will use to measure the credibility of all its cases in this State and may not change its method without the prior approval of the Commissioner. If "Claim Count" or "Life Year" data is not available, reasonable methods of approximation approved by the Commissioner may be used until such data is developed.

(m) "*Incurred Claim Count*" means the number of claims incurred for the case during the experience period. This means the total number of claims reported during the experience period, whether paid or in the process of payment plus any incurred but not reported (IBNR) at the end of the experience period less the number of claims incurred but not reported at the beginning of the experience period. If a debtor has been issued more than one certificate for the same plan of insurance, only one claim is counted. If a debtor receives disability benefits, only the initial claim payment for that period of disability is counted.

(n) "*Average Number of Life Years*" means the average number of group certificates or individual policies in force during the Experience Period (without regard to multiple coverage) times the number of years in the experience period, or some equivalent calculation.

(o) *Credibility Table for Purposes of the Standard Case Rating Procedure* means the following table:

CREDIBILITY TABLE

Credit Life	Average Number of Life Years Credit Accident and Health Plans Retroactive and Non-Retroactive Waiting Periods			Incurred Claim Count	Credibility Factor
	7 Day	14 Day	30 Day		
1	1	1	1	1	.00
1,800	95	141	209	9	.25
2,400	126	188	279	12	.30
3,000	158	234	349	15	.35
3,600	189	281	419	18	.40
4,600	242	359	535	23	.45
5,600	295	438	651	28	.50
6,600	347	516	767	33	.55
7,600	400	594	884	38	.60
9,600	505	750	1,116	48	.65
11,600	611	906	1,349	58	.70
14,600	768	1,141	1,698	73	.75
17,600	926	1,375	2,047	88	.80
20,600	1,084	1,609	2,395	103	.85
25,600	1,347	2,000	2,977	128	.90
30,600	1,611	2,391	3,558	153	.95
40,000	2,106	3,125	4,651	200	1.00

The above integral numbers represent the lower end of the bracket for each Z factor. The upper end is 1 less than the lower end for the next higher Z factor.

Section 11. Use of Rates—Direct Business Only (Alternative Short Form—Rating)

(See glossary of "terms and definitions" herein)

(1) *Minimum Loss Ratio Test.*

(a) *Loss Ratio Test.* Benefits will be considered reasonable in relation to the premium charged if the ratio of claims incurred to premium earned during the most recent experience period at the rates in use produces a loss ratio that equals or exceeds the Minimum Loss Ratio Standard specified in Section 5.

(b) *Broad Test.* This test will be made separately for:

(i) the total credit life insurance experience of the insurer in this state for all classes of business and plans of insurance combined, and for

(ii) the total credit accident and health insurance experiences of the insurer in this state for all classes of business and plans of insurance combined, provided, however,

(iii) a separate test is not required for each class of business or plan of insurance therein.

(c) *Scope of Test When Deviated Rates are in Use.* If an insurer has deviated rates approved under under (3)(a) or (3)(b), the test will exclude the experience of the accounts for which deviated rates are in use. The reasonableness of rates for those accounts will be determined by subsection (3).

(d) *Frequency of Test.* The test will be made each year when submitting the experience reports required in Section 10.

(2) *Use of Prima Facie Rates.*

An insurer that has rates on file which are equal to or lower than prima facie rates may retain on file and use those rates without further proof of their reasonableness while the experience of the insurer in this state for the accounts to which they are applied continues to satisfy the Minimum Loss Ratio Test specified in subsection (1). An insurer may at any time use a rate for an account that is lower than its filed rate without notice to the Commissioner.

(3) *Use of Deviated Rates.*

(a) *Loss Ratio Acceptance Range.*

Upward rate adjustments will not be considered nor will downward rate adjustments be required unless the loss ratio which results from the Loss Ratio Test is more than 5 percentage points higher or lower than the Minimum Loss Ratio Standard.

(b) *Use of Rates Higher Than Prima Facie Rates.*

If the Minimum Loss Ratio Test produces a loss ratio that is more than 5 percentage points higher than the Minimum Loss Ratio Standard, the insurer may file for approval and use rates that are higher than prima facie rates if it can be expected that the use of such higher rates will continue to produce a loss ratio for the accounts to which they are applied that will satisfy the Minimum Loss Ratio Test.

(c) *Use of Rates Lower Than Prima Facie Rates.*

If the Minimum Loss Ratio Test produces a loss ratio that is more than 5 percentage points lower than the Minimum Loss Standard, the insurer shall either file adjusted rates that can be expected to produce a loss ratio that will satisfy the Minimum Loss Ratio Test or submit reasons acceptable to the Commissioner why it should not be required to do so.

(d) *Determination of Deviated Rates.*

If deviated rates are to be filed under (a) or (b) above, the insurer may file rates for approval that will be:

(i) Applied uniformly to all accounts of the insurer.

(ii) applied on an equitable basis approved by the Commissioner to only one or more accounts of the insurer for which the experience has been more favorable or less favorable than expected, or

(iii) applied according to a case rating procedure on file with the Commissioner, subsection 3(a) notwithstanding.

The rate for each account which has been deviated must be redetermined on the same basis thereafter or until the rate for the account is no longer deviated.

(e) *Approval Period of Deviated Rates.*

A deviated rate will be in effect for a period of time not longer than the experience period used to establish the case rate (i.e. 1 year, 2 years, 3 years). An insurer may file for a new rate before the end of a rate period, but not more often than once during any 12 month period.

(f) *Change of Insurers.*

If a creditor changes insurers, the rate in effect for his account on the date of the change will continue to be in effect with the succeeding insurer for the remainder of the rate approval period or until a new rate is established, if sooner.

When submitting the Experience Reports required by Section 10, an insurer who has elected to file higher rates (3)(a) above or who is required to file reduced rates under (3)(b) above, or who has elected the Standard Case Rating Procedure shall also file a new schedule of rates as determined by those subsections. If the Commissioner does not disapprove the new schedule within 30 days after receipt of the filing, or July 1, whichever is later, rates not higher than the new rates shall be placed in effect on September 1 next following unless a different effective date has been approved by the Commissioner. In no event, however, may a rate increase be placed in effect earlier than the date rate decreases are required to be placed in effect.

(5) *Glossary of Terms and Definitions as Used in Section 11.*

(a) "*Plan of Insurance*" unless otherwise filed any approval means

(i) credit life insurance on a flat rated basis other than revolving accounts (i.e. including joint and single life coverage, decreasing and level insurance, outstanding balance and single premium),

(ii) credit life insurance on a revolving account basis,

(iii) credit life insurance on an age-graded basis,

(iv) credit accident and health insurance other than on revolving accounts combining outstanding balance and single premium but separately for each combination of waiting period and retroactive or non-retroactive.

(v) credit accident and health insurance on a revolving account basis separately for each combination of waiting period and retroactive or non-retroactive.

Note: For states which have a sufficient volume of business, the definition of the term "plan of insurance" may be more complex.)

(b) "*Class of business*" means a grouping of the classes of business in Section 10 having the same prima facie rate.

(c) "*Experience*" means "earned premiums" and incurred claims, during the experience period.

(d) "*Experience Period*" means the most recent period of time for which experience is reported, but not for a period longer than three full years.

(**Note:** The term "year" for individual policies means calendar year and for group policies means either a calendar year or a policy year at the option of the insurer.)

(e) "*Prima Facie Rates*" means those rates shown in Sections 7 and 8.

(f) "*Earned premiums at rates in use*" means actual earned premiums, that is, the premiums earned at the premium rates actually charged and in force during the experience period in accordance with the instructions and method of calculation for Reporting Form A.

(g) "*Earned premium at prima facie rate*" means the actual earned premiums adjusted to the amount which would have been earned had the premium rate during the experience period been equal to the current prima facie rate in accordance with instructions and method of calculation for Reporting Form A. Reasonable methods of approximations may be used.

(h) "*Incurred Claims*" means total claims paid during the experience period, adjusted for the change in the claim reserve.

Section 12. Supervision of Credit Insurance Operations.

(1) Each insurer transacting credit insurance in this state shall be responsible to conduct a thorough periodic review of creditors with respect to their credit insurance business with such creditors to assure compliance with the insurance laws of this state and the regulation promulgated by the Commissioner.

(2) Written records of such reviews shall be maintained by the insurer for review by the Insurance Commissioner.

Drafting note: The states may wish to specify the minimum time in accordance with their respective statutes.

Section 13. Prohibited Transactions.

The following practices, when engaged in by insurers in connection with the sale or placement of credit insurance, or as an inducement thereto, shall constitute unfair methods of competition and shall be subject to the Unfair Trade Practices Act of this State.

(1) The offer or grant by an insurer to a creditor of any special advantage or any service not set out in either the group insurance contract or in the agency contract, other than the payment of agents' commissions;

(2) Agreement by an insurer to deposit with a bank or financial institution money or securities of the insurer with the design or intent that the same shall affect or take the place of a deposit of money or securities which otherwise would be required of the creditor by such bank or financial institution as a compensating balance or offsetting deposit for a loan or other advancement; and

(3) Deposit by an insurer of money or securities without interest or at a lesser rate of interest than is currently being paid by the creditor, bank or financial institution to other depositors of like amounts. This paragraph shall not be construed to prohibit the maintenance by an insurer of such demand deposits or premium deposit accounts as are reasonably necessary for use in the ordinary course of the insurer's business.

Section 14. Disclosure and Readability.

A. Disclosure. When a premium or indentifiable charge is payable by a debtor for credit insurance coverage offered by a creditor, at the time such insurance is applied for, disclosures shall be made to the principal debtor and copies given and retained, in accordance with State and Federal law. The creditor shall also disclose the optional nature of the coverage, premium or identifiable charge separately by type of coverage, eligibility requirements, and policy limitations and exclusions. These disclosures shall be made prominently above the space for the signature indicating election to obtain such coverage. These disclosures may be made in conjunction with either (a) the Federal Truth-in-Lending disclosure, or (b) a Notice of Proposed Insurance, or insurance policy or certificate.

B. Readability. (This section is OPTIONAL.)

The commissioneer (Director or Superintendent) shall not approve any form unless the policy or certificate is written in non-technical, readily understandable language, using words of common every day usage:

(1) each insurer is required to test the readability of its policies or certificates by use of the Flesch Readability Formula, as set forth in Rudolf Flesch, *The Art of Readable Writing*, (1949, as revised 1974);

(2) a total readability score of forty (40) or more on the Flesch scale is required;

(3) all policies or certificates within the scope of this Section shall be filed with the Commissioner (Director or Superintendent) accompanied by a certification setting forth the Flesch score and certifying compliance with the guidelines set forth in this Section.

Drafting note: This optional section should be included only in those states which have not enacted the NAIC policy language simplification act.

Section 15. Severability.

If any provision or clause of this regulation or the application thereof to any person or situation is held invalid such invalidity shall not affect any other provision or application of the regulation which can be given effect without the invalid provision or application, and to this end the provisions of this regulation are declared severable.

Section 16. Effective Date

(1) This regulation shall take effect (insert date) as to premium rates.

(2) Approval of all forms not in compliance with this regulation are hereby withdrawn as of (insert date). No such form may be issued after date unless it has been submitted to and approved by the Commissioner subsequent to (30 days prior to effective date), or unless a rider approved subsequent to such date has been attached bringing such form into compliance with this regulation.

(3) Any deviations thought to be appropriate by an insurer as a result of promulgation of this regulation shall be filed in accordance with the provisions of Section 11 no later than (insert date).

(4) Certificates, notices of proposed insurance and premium rates in connection with existing group policies shall conform to the requirements of this regulation not later than the anniversary date of the group policy next following the effective date of this regulation.

(5) Any group policy issued to replace an existing group policy of credit insurance or an amendment to an existing group policy of credit insurance shall be ignored for the purposes of determining the anniversary date if such change is made (insert the date of publication of notice).

Drafting note: This Section should be drafted in accordance with the particular state's statutes regarding approval and disapproval of forms.

CREDIT INSURANCE EXPERIENCE REPORT
INSTRUCTIONS TO FORMS A, B AND C

FORM A

The purpose of this form is to provide state-wide experience data under various classifications which will permit the review and regulation of premium rates and loss ratios at both company and state level.

A. Class of business means any of the following:

1. Credit unions;
2. commercial & savings banks;
3. finance companies;
4. motor vehicle dealers;
5. other sales finance;
6. production credit associations; and bank agricultural loans;
7. all others.

B. Earned Premiums

1. Actual earned premiums (Line lf)-
The total of all premiums earned at the premium rate(s) actually charged and inforce during the experience period.

2. Earned premiums at prima facie rate (Line lg)-
Actual earned premiums adjusted (on Form B) to the amount which would have been earned had the premium rate during the experience period been equal to the current prima facie rate. Note that if premiums inforce differ from the current prima facie rate, Line lf will not equal Line lg.

C. Experience Period

1. The experience period will consist of a maximum of three calendar years, except that in the first and second years after implementation of this regulation, the experience period may, at the insurers option, include only one or two year's experience, respectively. Thereafter, three years experience will be required.

2. Data included in this report is to be the direct business of the current insurer, only, without adjustment for reinsurance assumed or ceded.

FORM B

The purpose of this form is to convert actual earned premiums (Form A, Line lf) to the amount of premiums which would have been earned had all business been written at the current prima facie rate.

Form B1 is applicable to Credit Life insurance and Form B2 is applicable to Credit Disability insurance

GENERAL

A. A Form B (Life or Disability Section) must be completed for each Form A where prima facie earned premium differs from actual earned premium. More than one Form B may be required when more than one year's data is presented, due to changes in prima facie rates or other factors.

B. Actual earned premiums are to be converted to prima facie earned premiums by the use of a conversion factor which is the ratio of the prima facie premium rate to the actual premium rate. This conversion must be performed for each premium rate with premiums inforce during the experience period.

C. The overall totals presented on Form B (either life or disability) must agree to the appropriate lines on the Form A to which they are attached.

D. Note that both Form B1 and Form B2 include actual earned premium at prima facie rate on Line A. This data is for balancing purposes, only, and in no way indicates that Form B must be completed if actual earned premium is equal to prima facie earned premium.

Form B1—Credit Life Insurance

A. Prima facie earned premium (Col. 5) is the product of actual earned premium (Col. 1) times the coversion factor (Col. 2 ÷ Col. 3).

B. See also General note C.

Form B2—Credit Disability Insurance

A. The conversion of actual earned premiums to prima facie earned premiums is accomplished in basically the same manner as described in Section IA, above. The conversion factor to be utilized, however, is the average of three ratios taken between prima facie and actual rates from 12, 24 and 36 month terms. The sum of these ratios, divided by three, becomes the conversion factor.

B. Prima facie premium rates are to be presented on Form B, Section II, Line A, Col. 2-4. All ratios (Line b) are to be calculated by dividing Line A by Line a.

C. This form should be reproduced as necessary to present the required conversion for all premium rates inforce during the experience period.

D. See also General note C.

Form C

The purpose of this form is to present a reconciliation between current year data presented on the various Forms A and the totals presented on Page 46 of the Annual Statement.

A. Due to the volume of Forms A which may be filed, each form will be listed by page number, only. All Forms A must be included on Form C to insure agreement to Page 46 of the Annual Statement.

B. Line references included in column headings refer to Form A.

C. This form should be reproduced as necessary to include all Forms A.

CREDIT LIFE & DISABILITY INSURANCE EXPERIENCE REPORT

STATE OF ____________________

CALENDAR YEAR OF 19_____

FORM A

CLASSES OF BUSINESS: Check one;

☐ (a) credit unions;
☐ (b) commercial & savings banks;
☐ (c) finance companies;
☐ (d) motor vehicle dealers;
☐ (e) other sales finance;
☐ (f) production credit associations; bank agricultural loans;
☐ (g) all others.

Mode of Premium Payment:

☐ Single Premium
☐ Revolving Account
☐ Outstanding Balance (Monthly Premium)

Plan of Benefits:

☐ Credit Life: ☐ Decreasing ☐ Single Life ☐ Gross
☐ Level ☐ Joint Life ☐ Net

☐ Credit Disability_____Days, ☐ Retro ☐ Non-Retro

1. Actual Earned Premiums	19____	19____	19____	**Total**
a. Gross premium written (before deduction for Dividends and Experience Rating Credits	_____	_____	_____	_______
b. Refunds on terminations	_____	_____	_____	_______
c. Net (a-b)	_____	_____	_____	_______
d. Premium reserve, beginning of period	_____	_____	_____	_______
e. Premium reserve, end of period	_____	_____	_____	_______
f. Actual earned premiums (c+d−e)	_____	_____	_____	_______
g. Earned premiums at prima facie rate (Form B)	_____	_____	_____	_______
2. Incurred Claims				
a. Claims paid	_____	_____	_____	_______
b. Unreported claims, beginning of period	_____	_____	_____	_______
c. Unreported claims, end of period	_____	_____	_____	_______
d. Claim reserve, beginning of period	_____	_____	_____	_______
e. Claim reserve, end of period	_____	_____	_____	_______
f. Incurred Claims (a−b+c−d+e)	_____	_____	_____	_______
3. Loss Ratio				
a. Actual loss ratio (2d÷1f)	_____	_____	_____	_______
b. Loss ratio at prima facie rate (2f÷1g)	_____	_____	_____	_______

____
(Company)

____
(Signature)

____
(Title)

CREDIT LIFE INSURANCE EXPERIENCE REPORT

STATE OF ____________________

PRIMA FACIE EARNED PREMIUM

FORM B1

Class of business____________ Calendar Year 19___

Premium Mode____________ Plan of Benefits____________

Credit Life Insurance

	Actual Earned Premiums Col. 1	Prima Facie Rate Col. 2	Actual Premium Rate Col. 3	Prima Facie Earned Premium Col. 4
A. Earned premiums at prima facie rate	______	XXX	XXX	______
B. Earned premiums at other than prima facie rates:				
1.__________	______	______	______	______
2.__________	______	______	______	______
3.__________	______	______	______	______
4.__________	______	______	______	______
5.__________	______	______	______	______
6.__________	______	______	______	______
	______	______	______	______
Totals	______ To Form A, Line 1f	XXX	XXX	______ To Form A, Line 1g

CREDIT DISABILITY INSURANCE EXPERIENCE REPORT

STATE OF______________________

PRIMA FACIE EARNED PREMIUM

FORM B2

Class of business ____________________ Calendar Year 19____

Premium Mode ______________________ Plan of Benefits ________________

Credit Disability Insurance

			Actual Earned Premium Col. 1	Premium Rates: 12 mo Col. 2	24 mo Col. 3	36 mo Col. 4	Prima Facie Earned Premium Col. 5
A.	Earned Premium at prima facie rate		____	____	____	____	____
B.	Earned Premium at other than prima facie rate:						
1.	a.	Actual Rate	XXX	____	____	____	XXX
	b.	Ratio	XXX	____	____	____	XXX
	c.	Earned Premium	____	__________			____
2.	a.	Actual Rate	XXX	____	____	____	XXX
	b.	Ratio	XXX	____	____	____	XXX
	c.	Earned Premium	____	__________			____
3.	a.	Actual Rate	XXX	____	____	____	XXX
	b.	Ratio	XXX	____	____	____	XXX
	c.	Earned Premium	____	__________			____
		Totals	____	XXX	XXX	XXX	____
			To Form A, Line 1f				To Form A, Line 1g

CREDIT LIFE INSURANCE EXPERIENCE

RECONCILIATION TO STATE PAGE

STATE OF ______________________

FOR THE CURRENT YEAR OF 19____

FORM C1

	Premiums		Claims	
	Written (Line 1c)	Earned (Line 1f)	Paid (Line 2a)	Incurred (Line 2f)
Credit Life:				
Page______of______	_______	_______	_______	_______
Page______of______	_______	_______	_______	_______
Page______of______	_______	_______	_______	_______
Page______of______	_______	_______	_______	_______
Page______of______	_______	_______	_______	_______
Page______of______	_______	_______	_______	_______
Page______of______	_______	_______	_______	_______
Page______of______	_______	_______	_______	_______
Page______of______	_______	_______	_______	_______
Page______of______	_______	_______	_______	_______
Page______of______	_______	_______	_______	_______
	_______	_______	_______	_______
Total Life	_______	_______	_______	_______
Annual Statement Page 46, Line 28	_______	_______	_______	_______

Explain any differences between "Total Life" and Page 46, Line 28.

CREDIT DISABILITY INSURANCE EXPERIENCE REPORT

RECONCILIATION TO STATE PAGE

STATE OF ______________________

FOR THE CURRENT YEAR OF 19___

FORM C2

	Premiums		Claims	
	Written (Line 1c)	Earned (Line 1f)	Paid (Line 2a)	Incurred (Line 2f)
Credit Life:				
Page_____of_____	______	______	______	______
Page_____of_____	______	______	______	______
Page_____of_____	______	______	______	______
Page_____of_____	______	______	______	______
Page_____of_____	______	______	______	______
Page_____of_____	______	______	______	______
Page_____of_____	______	______	______	______
Page_____of_____	______	______	______	______
Page_____of_____	______	______	______	______
Page_____of_____	______	______	______	______
Page_____of_____	______	______	______	______
	______	______	______	______
Total Life	______	______	______	______
Annual Statement Page 46, Line 31	______	______	______	______

Explain any differences between "Total Disability" and Page 46, Line 31.

____

Legislative History (all references are to the Proceedings of the NAIC*).*

1980 Proc. I
1980 Proc. II

Fig. 9.5 1979 Model Regulation (Reprinted by permission of the National Association of Insurance Commissioners.)

RICHMOND RESOLUTION

As Amended June, 1969

WHEREAS the NAIC has gone on record in favor of the application of a 50% minimum loss ratio benchmark in implementing the requirement of Section 7B of the Model Bill For the Regulation of Credit Life and Credit Accident and Health Insurance that there be a reasonable relationship between benefits and premiums; and

WHEREAS in adopting the Model Bill the NAIC rejected recommendations that compensation to creditors, in connection with credit life and credit accident and health insurance covering debtors of such creditors, be limited and instead adopted the requirement of Section 7B of the Model Bill that there be a reasonable relationship between benefits and premiums; and

WHEREAS questions have been recently raised concerning the propriety of implementing Section 7B of the Model Bill and the 50% minimum loss ratio benchmark by placing limits upon the amount of compensation to creditors and/or agents by way of commissions, dividends, retrospective rate credits, experience rating refunds and all other forms of compensation to creditors; and

WHEREAS such limitations may appear to have merit, but have been found to be ineffective in implementing Section 7B of the Model Bill and the 50% minimum loss ratio benchmark and therefore ineffective in protecting the public's interest and on the contrary have been found in practice to have unintended and undesirable consequences.

NOW THEREFORE the National Association of Insurance Commissioners recommends to the Commissioners of the individual states:

1. Enactment of the NAIC Model Bill to Provide for The Regulation of Credit Life and Credit

Accident and Health Insurance in all states where it has not been enacted.

2. The Implementation of Section 7B of the Model Bill by the adoption of the 50% minimum loss ratio benchmark and its enforcement.

3. As a simplified method of achieving and enforcing the 50% minimum loss ratio benchmark, concurrently and dependently, both,

    (a) the promulgation by the Commission of each state, after notice and hearing, of prima facie acceptable rates applicable to specified plans of benefits, terms of coverage is made available, which all insurers will be permitted to charge until such rates are changed, and

    (b) the adoption of a reasonable and simple procedure under which a deviation from such prima facie acceptable rates may be obtained, including a reasonable system for review of such deviations, *provided that a loss ratio of less than 60% shall not be considered for purposes of an upward deviation.* Such procedure shall take into consideration an insurer's own experience or its expected experience on a case, or a class of business, or assumptions based on the comparable experience of other insurers in supporting expected experience.

4. As a means of achieving control of the operation of the prima facie acceptable rates and the deviation procedure, the use of information now available in the Credit Life and Accident and Health Exhibit of each company and other relevant information. Insurers which produce loss ratios of less than *50% for any class of accounts* should be required to *make appropriate rate reduction or show cause why their premium rates should*

not be adjusted so as to produce loss ratios of at least 50%. If the premium rate for a particular account is as a consequence required to be reduced, the reduction shall continue, whether the account remains with the carrier or is transferred to another carrier, until a showing is made to and accepted by the Commissioner that the reduction is no longer appropriate.

5. The periodic review of credit insurance statistics becoming available in future NAIC studies and other relevant studies or statistics and of the information developed under 4 above. Based upon such reviews, the Commissioner, after notice and hearing, should adjust as necessary,

   (a) the level of prima facie acceptable rates and/or the plans of benefits, terms of coverage and conditions under which the coverage is made available to which such prima facie acceptable rates are applicable.

   (b) the procedure under which deviations from the prima facie rates may be obtained, so that loss ratios consistent with the 50% minimum loss ratio benchmark will be maintained.

IT IS URGED in view of the extreme importance of this matter that the foregoing recommendations be promptly implemented.

WHEREAS the Commissioners, have available the credit life insurance statistics from the NAIC 1964 study and other relevant studies or statistics it is urged that they be utilized as a basis for determining prima facie acceptable rates for credit life insurance.

WHEREAS The NAIC 1964 Study did not produce credible morbidity statistics for credit accident and health business,

IT IS URGED for credit accident and health insurance that:

(i) The NAIC Subcommittee to Study Mortality and Morbidity Experience of Credit Life and Credit Accident and Health Insurance continue its current efforts to obtain such statistics at the earliest possible date.

(ii) As an interim measure, pending the availability of such statistics, that the Commissioner of each state promulgate prima facie acceptable rates at levels consistent with the 50% minimum loss ratio benchmark, taking into consideration such relevant statistics as are available.

Fig. 9.6 1969 Version of Richmond Resolution (Reprinted by permisison of the National Association of Insurance Commissioners.)

LAS VEGAS RESOLUTION

WHEREAS it has been urged that there be a definitive interpretation of that part of the resolution known as the Richmond Resolution (ref. 1966 Proc. Vol. II pp. 402-403) dealing with the 50% minimum loss ratio benchmark for credit life and credit accident and health insurance adopted by the NAIC at the June, 1966 meeting in Richmond, Virginia; and WHEREAS it is also desirable to provided additional guidance regarding achievement of the benchmark.

NOW THEREFORE the National Association of Insurance Commissioners hereby takes the following action:

1. Reaffirms the Richmond Resolution and urges its prompt implementation by each and every state as the proper and appropriate means of protecting the public against abuses in the conduct of the credit insurance business.

2. Confirms that the promulgation by an individual state of a prima facie acceptable rate or system of rates which produces a loss ratio greater than 50% in the aggregate is not prohibited by the Richmond Resolution by the NAIC Resolution adopted at the December, 1959 meeting (ref. 1960 Proc. Vol. I p. 176), reading as follows:

"The Committee in Executive Session recommends to all insurance supervisors that a rate for Credit Life or Credit Accident and Health producing a loss ratio of under 50% should be considered to be excessive."

Fig. 9.7 Las Vegas Resolution (Reprinted by permission of the National Association of Insurance Commissioners.)

FEDERAL INVOLVEMENT IN CREDIT INSURANCE REGULATION

Before 1969, direct involvement by the federal government to regulate the insurance aspects of credit transactions could be characterized as "all talk and no action." During the period of 1954 to 1969, several congressional hearings addressed possible regulation by the federal government. Although no bill reached the point of being voted on by Congress, the specter of federal intervention may have spurred regulatory action at the NAIC and state level. Indirectly, federal regulations regarding financial institutions did influence the operation and development of credit insurance.

Under Public Law 15, known as the McCarran-Ferguson Act (1944), Congress left the regulation of insurance to the states, provided they did an adequate job of regulating the industry. The "business of insurance" was given a partial exemption from the Sherman Antitrust Act and the Fair Trade Practices Act. Several congressmen felt federal intervention was needed or justified relative to credit insurance because:

1. Alleged abuses and premium overcharges showed the states were not adequately regulating the product, and

2. The tie-in of the sale of credit insurance and extension of credit had possible antitrust implications.

In 1954, Senator Langer held hearings of the Senate Judiciary Subcommittee on Antitrust and Monopoly in several locations across the country. The hearings "uncovered" a variety of abuses concerning policy forms and marketing ploys. The Subcommittee's 1955 report was really a reiteration of the findings reported by the NAIC during this period. Comments raised the possibility that tie-in sales could have antitrust implications. No federal action was recommended, but the state regulators and the industry were admonished that federal regulation would come if appropriate state regulation did not develop. Several references to the Langer hearings were voiced during the NAIC discussion of the 1954 Model Rules and Regulations.

Several comments about credit insurance were made during the 1961 Celler hearings of the House Judiciary Antitrust Subcommittee. The Prudential-GMAC credit program was noted, again on the issue of tie-in sales. The thrust of the hearings did not involve insurance, and no action was recommended.

In 1967, Senator Hart held more hearings of the Senate Judiciary Subcommittee on Antitrust and Monopoly concerning credit insurance. Although a written record of the hearings was maintained, it is difficult to summarize the action. There was extensive industry and consumer group testimony. Several of the senators had strong negative opinions which were reflected in their questioning. Certain abuses were "found" concerning the marketing of the product, but those problems centered in states which had not adopted the NAIC Model Bill. In the opinion of the Subcommittee, states had failed to properly regulate the product, but no federal action was recommended.

The most serious intrusion into potential legislation occurred in 1969 when Senator Proxmire introduced Senate Bill 1754. Direct federal regulation of credit insurance rates was proposed. Rates were to be set by the Federal Reserve Board considering:

1. The loss ratios in other lines of group insurance,

2. The loss ratios in non-contributory group credit,

3. Actual losses and expenses of the insurer and out-of-pocket administrative expenses of the lenders, and

4. Such other factors as the Board found relevant to achieving the purposes of the bill.

During hearings of the Senate Subcommittee on Financial Institutions (of the Committee on Banking and Currency),

Senator Proxmire charged that state regulation was ineffective. Despite numerous industry presentations on state regulation, the strongly held opinions of several of the Senators were unaltered. However, no action was taken on the bill by the Senate.

Throughout the 1960s, Senator Douglas held hearings on proposed credit disclosure bills, which finally resulted in the Federal Consumer Credit Protection Act of 1968, commonly called the Truth-in-Lending Act. Central to the Act was the requirement that the borrower be provided a statement of all finance charges and the annual percentage rate (APR) of the loan. Under Regulation Z, which implemented portions of the Act, insurance charges were limited to the premiums for the loan obligations of the borrower and were to be included in the calculation of the finance charge unless:

1. The borrower was informed in writing of the cost of the insurance before credit was extended,

2. Insurance coverage was not required for the extension of credit,

3. The borrower was informed in writing that insurance was not required, and

4. The borrower agreed to the coverage in writing.

No disclosure was required if the benefits of another insurance policy were assigned to the lender in lieu of credit insurance, unless insurance coverage was required. If insurance was required, the premium for the full term of coverage had to be included in the calculation of the loan's finance charge. Subsequently, the Federal Reserve Board ruled that disclosure was not required if the financial institution paid for the insurance.

Most lenders chose to meet the four requirements, so credit documents were revised to provide a section on credit insurance. Premiums were displayed. Consumers were required to sign or initial a disclosure statement, indicating their awareness that the insurance was not required and that they accepted the purchase of the coverage. These practices continue today. A sample disclosure statement is shown in Figure 9.8. The Act has accomplished its purpose relative to insurance. Every consumer purchasing credit insurance acknowledges his awareness of the voluntary choice made and of the cost of the product.

Several rules, regulations, and positions by the Comptroller of the Currency, the Federal Reserve Board, and the Federal Credit Union Board have affected methods of compensation, availability of products, and captive reinsurance.

Sample Disclosure Statement

NAME	DATE OF LOAN	ACCOUNT NUMBER
STREET ADDRESS	DATE FUNDS DISBURSED	FINAL PAYMENT DUE DATE
APT. NUMBER OR P.O. BOX		NUMBER OF PAYMENTS
CITY, STATE, ZIP CODE	FINAL PAYMENT EQUAL IN ANY CASE TO UNPAID PRINCIPAL AND CHARGES	AMOUNT OF FIRST PAYMENT
ANNUAL PERCENTAGE RATE % / **FINANCE CHARGE** $ / AMOUNT FINANCED $ / TOTAL OF PAYMENTS $	OTHER PAYMENTS ARE DUE SAME DAY OF EACH SUCCEEDING MONTH	AMOUNT OF OTHER PAYMENTS
		FIRST PAYMENT DUE DATE / /

LATE CHARGE: If any payment is not paid in full within 10 days after the due date, you may collect a late charge which is the greater of $0.50 or 5% of the unpaid amount of the payment.

Prepayment: If I pay off early, I will not have to pay a penalty and I may be entitled to a refund of part of the finance charge.

See the contract documents for additional information about nonpayment, default, any required repayment in full before the scheduled date and prepayment refunds.

Security: I am giving a security interest in:

☐ Household Goods, Furniture & Appliances
☐ Motor Vehicles

YEAR MODEL	TRADE NAME	BODY TYPE & TRUCK TONNAGE	FACTORY SERIAL OR IDENTIFICATION NO.	STATE LICENSE NO.

☐ Other____________________

☐ Real estate located at the following address:____________________

ITEMIZATION OF AMOUNT FINANCED:

e means an estimate

PAID TO YOU OR ON YOUR BEHALF

Account Renewed $________
Less: Finance Charge Refund $________
Less: Other Credits $________ Equals net balance due to TFS on Acct. No.________ $________
To________ $________
To________ $________
To________ $________
To________ $________
To________ $________
To________ $________

Total Loan Renewals & Check Disbursements $________
Cash from this loan to Borrower $________
Total Loan Disbursement **(499)** $________ **(2)**

PAID TO OTHERS ON YOUR BEHALF

TO INSURANCE COMPANIES:

Credit Life Insurance for term of loan: months________ days________ ☐ single **(4065)** ☐ joint **(4069)** premium $________ **(3)**
Insured________ Insured________
Credit Disability Insurance, insuring________ Mo's________ Days________ Premium **(4067)** $________ **(4)**

(4037) Title Insurance $ | **(4040)** Auto Insurance $ Months | **(4030)** Household Effects Insurance $ Months — Premiums $________

TO PUBLIC OFFICIALS: R. E. Filing $ | Auto License $ | Auto Transfer $ | Financing Statement $ — Total Fees **(9682)** $________ **(11)**

AMOUNT FINANCED $________

Precomputed Finance Charges **(5660)** $________ **(5)**
Additional Day Charges, if any **(8260)** $________ **(6)**
Interest Surcharge **(8960)** $________ **(6)**

FINANCE CHARGE $________
TOTAL OF PAYMENTS **(460)** $________ **(1)**

INSURANCE:

CREDIT INSURANCE AUTHORIZATION: The Lender is authorized to arrange for the credit insurance indicated by the checkmarks in the boxes to the right, if any. The insurance is described in the NOTICE OF PROPOSED INSURANCE delivered herewith and is through the Lenders group policy(ies) with ________ LIFE INSURANCE COMPANY. The term of the insurance offered is the same as the term of the loan. With regard to Disability Insurance, NOTE that for loans with initial monthly payments of 60 months or less, the maximum amount of monthly benefit payable shall not exceed the lesser of (1) the amount of the monthly payment due or (2) $500. For loans with initial monthly payments of more than 60 months, the maximum amount of monthly benefit payable shall not exceed the lesser of (1) one-half the amount of the monthly payment due or (2) $500, and the premium for this coverage is based upon one-half of the initial amount of indebtedness.

I UNDERSTAND THAT CREDIT INSURANCE IS NOT REQUIRED IN ORDER TO OBTAIN THIS LOAN and that single or joint life coverage is available.

THE COST OF CREDIT INSURANCE WILL BE:

Decreasing Term Single Life Insurance $________ ☐ I want Credit Life Insurance for myself only.
Decreasing Term Joint Life Insurance $________ ☐ I want Credit Life Insurance for myself and my co-borrower.
Disability Insurance (14 day Retroactive) $________ ☐ I want Credit Disability Insurance.
☐ I DO NOT want Credit Insurance.

________ SIGNATURE ________ SIGNATURE

OPTION TO CANCEL CREDIT INSURANCE: Credit life and disability insurance may be cancelled at any time upon my written request. If notice of cancellation is received within 15 days of the date of this loan, or if I have completed an application for credit life insurance and the application 's rejected, the entire premium will be refunded in cash.

PROPERTY INSURANCE: The option has been extended to me to either retain any existing property insurance or to purchase property insurance from any insurance agent or broker of my selection. I elect to purchase property insurance coverage in the amount of $________ to cover the collateral securing my loan. I know that my loan obligation is $________, and I fix the value of the property to be insured at $________. I select ________ as agent or broker to procure such insurance. My selection of such insurance agent or broker was not made a condition precedent to obtaining this loan.

If I choose to buy property insurance from you the premium will be $________ for a term of________ months.

AUTOMOBILE INSURANCE: The option has been extended to me to either retain any existing Auto insurance or to purchase insurance from any insurance agent or broker of my selection. My selection of such insurance agent or broker was not made a condition precedent to obtaining this loan. If I choose to buy Automobile Insurance from you the premium will be $________ for a term of ________months.

Creditor:

THE UNDERSIGNED ACKNOWLEDGES RECEIPT OF A COPY OF THIS DISCLOSURE STATEMENT.

By________ X________ BORROWER (SEAL) X________ BORROWER (SEAL)

H.O. COPY

Fig. 9.8 Sample Disclosure statement.

BANK REGULATIONS

In 1950, the Comptroller of the Currency ruled that a national bank could not receive any compensation, including policyholder dividends, where an insurance premium was charged to the borrower. Service fees were permitted to cover the cost of furnishing the coverage, including administrative costs. Policyholder dividends were permitted where the bank paid for the insurance without making an identifiable charge. Banks in towns of less than 5,000 were exempt. The ruling did affirm the bank's insurable interest in the life of the borrower for an amount up to the unpaid loan balance. The ruling reduced the compensation to those banks receiving compensation at the prevailing commission levels.

This caused consternation. Insurers, on behalf of the banks, requested an opinion of the Comptroller about whether commissions could be paid directly to a bank officer or employee. The Comptroller ruled that an officer or employee could act as an agent, provided the bank directors approved of the situation. In many areas of the country, payment of commissions to lending officers became common practice. Lending officers had to receive the commissions directly and could not assign them to the bank. Lending officers were often paid low salaries because of their outside income.

In 1958, the Federal Reserve Board adopted Regulation "Y". This permitted a bank holding company to form subsidiaries which could earn income on activities that were closely related to banking, including the sale of credit insurance. Where state laws permitted, a subsidiary insurance agency could be formed, which could be named as agent and be permitted to receive commissions.

In 1972, the Federal Reserve Board expanded approved activities to include underwriting credit life and disability business produced by the banks in the bank holding company. A bank holding company was permitted to form a subsidiary insurance company to be a direct writer or a reinsurer. Risks underwritten by the subsidiary were strictly limited to credit insurance business produced within the bank holding company. The bank holding company, however, was required to show a *public benefit* to secure approval for the formation of the subsidiary. A public benefit was satisfied by appropriate reductions in the rates or increases in the benefits over the customary products available to the consumer. The requirement was generally met by reducing credit life rates by 5% under prima facie rates and by a 2% reduction in disability rates. A few bank holding companies chose to increase benefits by removing suicide exclusions, waiving preexisting conditions, or raising maximum age limits. In 1985, the Federal Reserve Board asked for comment on an amendment of Regulation Y to remove the public benefit requirement.

Some bank holding companies owned insurance companies prior to the Bank Holding Company Act. These insurance companies were forced to divest themselves of all non-credit insurance business. Other bank holding companies rapidly began to form direct-writing insurance companies or reinsurance companies. Most opted to form life reinsurance companies, but a few formed direct-writing companies. Others formed life companies for credit life and casualty companies for disability. Direct writers were formed in the domiciliary state of the bank holding company; reinsurers were primarily formed in Arizona, Texas, and Delaware. Practically all large bank holding companies own an insurance company subsidiary today.

The limitation requiring the underwriting of only the credit insurance produced by the bank holding company resulted in life status or Phase III tax problems for some of the captives. In order to expand their insurance operations and alleviate these tax problems, several bank holding companies petitioned the Federal Reserve Board in 1979 to expand the permitted range of products under certain conditions.

One proposal was to underwrite the decreasing term life insurance and disability insurance sold in connection with mortgage loans. The Federal Reserve Board denied this request. In 1986, the Federal Reserve Board revised its position and approved the underwriting of these products under certain limited conditions.

A second proposal was approved which permitted the insurance subsidiary to underwrite the employee benefit insurance programs of the bank holding company. The proposal was accepted under the provision of Regulation Y permitting a subsidiary to provide services to other members of the holding company.

Federal Reserve Board approval is not sufficient in most cases. Qualified employee benefit programs are regulated by the 1974 Employee Retirement and Insurance Standards Act, known as ERISA, generally regulated by the Department of Labor. The Department of Labor had already considered the underwriting of employee benefit programs by non-bank captives. Rules were established in 1975 permitting the activity provided:

1. Employee benefit premiums did not exceed unrelated party premiums,

2. No commissions were paid, and

3. Proper disclosure was made to employees.

Automatic exemptions were given permitting the activity for a direct writing captive. Reinsurance by a captive required approval from the Department of Labor. If the captive was domiciled in the United States, approval was routine, but might take eight to ten months.

A few bank holding companies have used the ruling to underwrite employee benefit programs in their captive. These programs have several distinct advantages:

1. The captive's insurance activities can be expanded in the expectation that future deregulation may permit a wide range of insurance activities,

2. The activity raises the visibility of the captive in the holding company organization, and

3. The cost of overhead is spread and the potential exists for underwriting gain (important since many captives are judged on the profit center concept).

Potential programs include group life insurance, group medical insurance, and pension programs. Pension programs may include the active life or the retired life portion of the corporate pension plan. As a result of acquisitions or incentive programs, bank holding companies may also have non-qualified pension programs for certain key, current, or former employees. Since these programs are not governed by ERISA, Department of Labor approval is not required.

CREDIT UNION REGULATION

Before 1971, federally-chartered credit unions were not permitted to charge borrowers for the cost of insurance. Traditionally, credit life insurance was provided as a part of the service. Disability insurance was prohibitively expensive to provide, except for a total and permanent, lump-sum benefit which was included by many credit unions. In 1971, the prohibition was lifted, and credit unions began to add life insurance and standard disability coverages as an option to their borrowers.

Compensation to the credit union was limited to reimbursement for actual expenses. Most insurers paid the credit union a percentage of premiums, ranging from 5% to 10%, to approximate the actual expenses. Growth of contributory coverages was slow but steady. In 1983, the regulations were changed, permitting the credit union to receive commission income. To do this, the credit union had to form a subsidiary, a Credit Union Service Organization (CUSO), which received the income, but very few CUSOs were formed. In 1984, the requirement of a CUSO to receive fee income was dropped. During this period, state-chartered credit unions did not have any restrictions other than those imposed on other financial institutions.

SAVINGS AND LOAN ASSOCIATIONS

In 1982, the Federal Savings and Loan Board permitted federally-chartered savings and loans to enter the consumer installment lending arena. The sale of credit insurance is a part of the expanded activities. Growth in consumer lending by savings and loans has been slow.

OTHER MARKET SEGMENTS

Aside from the Truth-in-Lending Act, federal regulations have not affected the sale of credit insurance by finance companies, automobile dealers, or retailers. State-chartered financial institutions operate under state laws which generally follow regulations for federally-chartered institutions. Substantial differences do arise. In the state of Washington, for example, state law permits a mutual savings bank. There are no state laws limiting insurance activity of these institutions, so they are permitted to own an insurer and to market any form of insurance.

CHAPTER TEN

STUDIES OF CONSUMER ATTITUDES AND CLAIM COSTS

Many studies have been commissioned over the years on the subject of credit insurance. Several studies addressed the attitude of the consumer toward the product and investigated the question of involuntary purchase. Regulatory and industry groups addressed the question of claim costs in credit insurance, and produced results which had a profound effect on product pricing. Finally, a few special studies were done to provide background information and to address specific issues. This chapter summarizes these studies, their scope and their findings. Each study is listed by its proper title, followed by the phrase used to refer to the report throughout this book. See the Bibliography for more specific information on these studies.

STUDIES OF CONSUMER ATTITUDES

Survey of Opinion Regarding Consumer Credit Insurance in the State of Colorado, **"The 1954 Colorado Study."**

A study was made in 1952-53 of borrowers' attitudes in Colorado. Commissioned by CCIA, the study was conducted by an independent market survey firm. The objective was to determine the attitudes of purchasers and of the general population toward the product. About 10,000 questionnaires were mailed to purchasers of credit insurance selected at random from the files of lenders. In addition, about 800 telephone interviews were conducted with a representative group of Colorado residents.

The primary findings were:

- 90% of the purchasers would purchase the insurance again,
- 70% of the purchasers would recommend the product to friends,
- 75% of the general population who had not purchased the product felt the availability of the product was a good thing, and
- 20% of the purchasers felt the insurance was required.

Consumer Credit Life and Disability Insurance, "The 1973 Ohio University Study."

The College of Business Administration staff of Ohio University conducted an independent study of credit insurance between 1967 and 1972. The final text was released in 1973. The work was supported by grants from the National Consumer Finance Association, the American Bankers Association, and CCIA. An industry advisory group assisted in the study.

The study was comprehensive and objective and included an excellent summary of the industry's history and its regulation. The researchers also surveyed consumers and state insurance regulators, and judged the marketplace using theoretical models. The product pricing structure was analyzed and recommendations made for a new pricing approach.

The survey of consumers was designed to determine their understanding about the purchase of credit insurance, the price of the product, and the coverage provided by the product. A separate section addressed the pressure felt by the consumer to purchase the product. The 1969-70 surveys used mailed questionnaires and personal interviews.

Loan customers of twenty-five commercial banks, thirty-nine personal finance companies, and three sales finance companies were surveyed. The customers were segregated into five groups:

1. Borrowers purchasing credit life insurance.
2. Borrowers not purchasing credit life insurance.
3. Borrowers purchasing credit disability insurance.
4. Borrowers not purchasing credit disability insurance, and
5. Borrowers who had filed disability claims.

Customers were selected who had obtained loans after the Truth-in-Lending and Regulation Z disclosure requirements were put into effect. Questionnaires were pretested. The authors went to great lengths to insure the objectivity of the study. A response rate of 23.2% produced 15,836 usable questionnaires representing all parts of the country and all age groups.

Summary of findings:

1. Consumers valued the insurance protection highly. Over 90% would purchase the coverage again.
2. Over 90% of those purchasing the insurance and 60% of those not purchasing the insurance would recommend the coverage to others.
3. High penetration rates were the result of strong consumer demand, not an inferior consumer bargaining position.
4. 20% of the purchasers of credit life felt the insurance was required.
5. Borrowers understood the product. The majority surveyed had heard about the insurance from prior loans.

6. Most of the borrowers declining coverage did so in the belief that their existing insurance was adequate, or that they had financial resources to handle their debts without insurance.

7. Consumers purchasing the insurance were aware of their purchase. A surprising number of those not purchasing the insurance thought they had purchased the coverage.

A separate questionnaire was also sent to each of the 51 state insurance Commissioners (including the District of Columbia). Thirty-nine responded. The questionnaire addressed the following areas:

- Department work load,
- Authority of the Commissioner,
- Enforcement of regulations,
- Use of submitted statistical data, and
- Proposals for new regulation.

Findings of the survey:

1. Thirty-three Commissioners felt existing staff was adequate to administer the credit insurance laws and regulations.

2. Most Commissioners had authority to establish maximum prima facie rates and minimum loss ratios.

3. The number of insurance department complaints was small. Complaints were primarily for non-payment of benefits or failure to make adequate refunds. About 45% of the complaints were deemed valid by the Com-

missioners. The Commissioners were almost unanimous in the opinion that only minimal or normal supervision was necessary to protect the public.

4. Insurers were providing accurate statistical data adequate to serve as a basis of regulation.

The remainder of the study addressed product pricing. Numerous tables compared the cost of credit insurance with other forms of life insurance, and compared the various levels of credit insurance premium rates. Claim costs were also measured and analyzed; however, most of this information is now dated and is of limited value.

A novel approach to the pricing of the product was presented. The approach included a component for each element of expense–claims, insurer expenses, and lender expenses. Premiums were a function of the size and term of the policy. Adoption of this approach would have introduced several new factors into the premium calculation, and the complexity of calculation would have increased significantly. The approach was discussed at the NAIC level, but support for this approach never developed.

In summary, the study was a major contribution to the knowledge of credit insurance. The surveys established that consumers were satisfied with the product. Regulation was adequate from the regulators' viewpoint. While the theoretical work on rating and the proposed approach to premium calculations were not used directly, new dimensions and considerations were added to discussions of the issues.

***A Background Study of the Regulation of Credit Life and Disability Insurance.* "The 1970 NAIC Background Study."**

In 1969, the NAIC directed its staff to prepare a study of credit insurance covering its development and the current regulatory environment, and to present and analyze the issues in credit insurance regulation. The report, released in June, 1970 presented a history of the industry, the scope of the products, and the development of the existing regulatory environment. Several new and unique proposals were espoused for the regulation of credit insurance.

Many industry personnel felt that the report was biased and that the proposed regulatory changes were totally unacceptable. A response was written by Paul Moo, "Credit Insurance Revisited, A Reply to the NAIC Staff Study," which criticized the NAIC Study for numerous inaccurate statements and for an unbalanced presentation reflecting a strong bias against the products by the authors of the study.

A Study of Tie-ins Between the Granting of Credit and Sales of Insurance by Bank Holding Companies and Other Lenders. **"The 1977 Federal Reserve Board Study."**

At the request of the Senate Committee on Banking, Housing and Urban Affairs, the staff of the Board of Governors of the Federal Reserve Board presented a study based on surveys conducted in 1977. The objective of the study was to determine the extent of any involuntary tie-in between the granting of credit and the sale of credit insurance. Emphasis was placed on bank holding companies. The basic question addressed whether consumers felt compelled to purchase insurance in order to secure a loan.

If involuntary tying exists, there would be a high proportion of joint purchases, buyer resentment, and coercive conduct by the lender. The buyer resentment should manifest itself by a low opinion of the tied product (the insurance) and by complaints about the product.

About 2,500 consumers were interviewed in 1977. The survey did find a high proportion of joint sales, but found very little evidence of buyer resentment or coercive lender conduct. Penetration rates (the percentage of borrowers purchasing insurance) varied by type of lender:

Banks	39.9%
Retailers	61.4%
Finance Companies	74.8%
Overall	62.2%

Only 16.4% of those interviewed felt the insurance was required, while another 8.8% felt it was strongly recommended. Over 90% felt credit insurance was a good thing. These findings were in line with other studies. Attitudes and practices of bank holding companies toward credit insurance were also surveyed. Nothing in their responses indicated evidence of coercive practices by the bank holding companies.

In summary, the report concluded that the explicit tying of credit insurance to lending was practically nonexistent, and implicit pressures were not significant. The high proportion of joint purchases were due to small premium costs as compared to inconvenience of shopping for alternative insurance. Purchasers valued the product and felt the price was reasonable.

STUDIES OF CLAIM COSTS

Various studies of the claim costs in credit insurance have been performed over the last thirty years, the most recent in 1982. Studies are listed as they are referenced elsewhere in the text.

1957 NAIC Mortality Study (NAIC Proceedings 1958, Vol. 1)

This study was sponsored by the NAIC. Claim costs were based on the loss experience reported by insurers in 1955 and 1956. Experience was based on the annual statement experience exhibit adopted by the NAIC in 1953. The annual statement exhibit provided only loss ratios. Claim costs were developed by multiplying the displayed loss ratios times an assumed average premium rate. The resulting claim costs in cents per $100 per year of coverage were:

1955	27.1¢/100/year
1956	28.5¢/100/year

The study presented demographic information which sheds some light on the structure of the industry at that time, including:

1. Insurance in force had increased from $365 million in 1945 to over $17 billion in 1956.

2. Weighted by premium, the distribution of business was about 70% written under group policies and 30% written under individual policies.

3. Loss ratios under group policies were higher than the loss ratios under individual policies. There was a wide variation in loss ratios by insurers. In general, specialty credit insurers had lower loss ratios than other insurers.

4. Data was gathered on disability insurance, but the study group was not able to derive credible experience. Only $32 million of disability premiums were written in 1956 compared with $180 million of life premiums. Two-thirds of the disability business was written under individual policies. Today, disability premiums often exceed life premiums and disability insurance is now written under group policies.

1960 New York Study **(NAIC Proceedings 1961, Vol. 1)**

The experience during 1956-59 of certain companies operating in New York was presented to the NAIC in 1960 by the New York Department of Insurance. Claim costs varied from 24.2¢/100/year to 28.7¢/100/year. Overall, the claim costs were 27.5¢/100/year. The study included a significant amount of non-contributory business.

1964 NAIC Mortality Study **(NAIC Proceedings 1964, Vol. 2)**

This study was released in 1964, covering experience in 1961-62. 289 of 391 insurers writing credit insurance submitted data on a special form developed for the study. Experience represented about 77% of all credit life insurance in force.

Life insurance claim costs were developed using the standard approach for ordinary life mortality studies. *Exposure* was reported. Exposure is the average amount of insurance in force during the study years. Actual claims were reported. Annual claim costs were calculated as the ratio of:

(Claims for the Year) / (Average Exposure in Thousands)

Experience was studied by class of business. The final report to the NAIC converted the annual claim costs to a (claim cost)/100/year using standard conversion formulas. The results were:

Automobile Dealers	35.9¢/100/year
Banks	30.1¢
Credit Unions	20.4¢
Sales Finance Companies	30.9¢
Small Loan Companies	33.2¢
Production Credit Associations	32.6¢
Other	28.0¢
Overall	29.5¢
	(30.6¢ excluding credit unions)

As with the 1955-56 study, the claim costs varied widely by insurer. Claim costs were higher on contributory coverages. Single premium plans also had higher costs when compared to monthly outstanding balance plans.

Credit insurance in force had increased 122% since 1956. A portion of the increase could be attributed to an increase in the percentage of loans covered by credit life insurance. About 79% of all loans were insured.

The studies were criticized by some industry groups primarily because the claim costs represented the average results from diverse experience. Policies contained a wide range of limitations and data from small insurers was not adequately represented. Claim costs were higher in the 29 states which had adopted a version of the Model Bill. Finally, the study found lower claim costs in the early durations. The growing volume of credit insurance during the study period included a disproportionate share of new business with lower claim costs.

The study was adopted by the NAIC in 1964 in spite of the criticisms. The overall result of a 30¢/100/year claim cost led several states with a 50% benchmark loss ratio to adopt a 60¢/100/year prima facie rate. The study also influenced several other states to adopt a 75¢/100/year prima facie rate. These states noted the wide variance by insurer. Another concern was that a 60¢/100/year prima facie rate would cause a flood of rate deviation requests.

Data was again gathered on disability insurance. The experience was not credible for most plans. Experience under the credible plans was inconsistent. Further study was urged.

1968 NAIC Disability Study (NAIC Proceedings 1968, Vol. 1)

The inability of the NAIC to determine disability claim costs was overcome by the publication of the 1968 study. Forty-five insurers provided data for 1965 and 1966. Although the insurers represented 75% of disability insurance premiums, the final study only contained about 10% of the total industry claims.

Tables of *claim frequency* (how many claims occur) and of *claim continuation* (how long a claimant remains disabled) were presented. These tables were used to derive *single claim costs* per $100 of initial indebtedness. The term single claim costs means the total claim cost for a policy with an initial term for the time shown in the months column. It is comparable to the single premium charged for the coverage. The raw data by amount was presented in December, 1967. The results indicated that even this study contained some serious inconsistencies.

SINGLE CLAIM COSTS PER $100 INITIAL INSURED INDEBTEDNESS

POLICY TERM	7 DAY RETROACTIVE	14 DAY RETROACTIVE	14 DAY NON-RETRO	30 DAY RETROACTIVE	30 DAY NON-RETRO
12	$ 1.25	$ 1.33	$ 1.17	$ 1.08	$. 57
24	1.76	1.78	1.73	1.44	.83
36	2.15	2.10	2.15	1.69	1.01
48	2.49	2.36	2.50	1.89	1.16
60	2.79	2.58	2.80	2.06	1.29

The results were smoothed and the irregularities eliminated. The final claim costs which were adopted as the 1968 Disability Table were:

POLICY TERM	7 DAY RETROACTIVE	14 DAY RETROACTIVE	14 DAY NON-RETRO	30 DAY RETROACTIVE	30 DAY NON-RETRO
12	$ 1.31	$ 1.31	$ 1.08	$ .86	$. 59
24	1.77	1.77	1.54	1.15	. 87
36	2.09	2.09	1.86	1.35	1.06
48	2.36	2.36	2.13	1.51	1.22
60	2.59	2.59	2.36	1.64	1.35

In 1969, claim costs were prepared for terms in excess of 60 months. These values were obtained by extrapolation from the 1968 Disability Table. In the words of the authors, "The claim costs may not reflect the true cost of insurance."

The extended claim costs were:

POLICY TERM	7 DAY RETROACTIVE	14 DAY RETROACTIVE	14 DAY NON-RETRO	30 DAY RETROACTIVE	30 DAY NON-RETRO
72	$ 2.82	$ 2.82	$ 2.57	$ 1.77	$ 1.47
84	3.02	3.02	2.77	1.89	1.59
96	3.20	3.20	2.95	1.99	1.69
108	3.37	3.37	3.12	2.09	1.79
120	3.53	3.53	3.28	2.18	1.88

In 1971, the NAIC adopted a resolution which recommended that disability prima facie rates be based on these claim costs. Gross single premiums were to be calculated using the formula:

$$1.25 \times (\text{Single Claim Cost}) + \$0.60$$

The resulting table of prima facie rates was adopted by many states. A review of Appendix D shows that these rates remain in effect today in some states.

A significant part of the problems credit insurers encountered with exceptionally high loss ratios in the 1970s can be traced to the table and the recommended loading formula. The study admits that the data was scarce for original terms in excess of 36 months. The table's values for 48-and 60-months proved to severly understate the actual experience of the 1970s. The use of a constant in the loading formula created an increasing loss ratio as the term of loan increased. The average term of a loan increased siginficantly during the 1970s. More business was written at the inadequate long-term rates as the decade progressed. The problem still exists. Many states have adequate rates for short-term loans, but the 48-month and 60-month rates are inadequate.

These criticisms should not be taken as harsh. The authors faced a difficult task compiling the study from data that was far from perfect. This is the first and only study ever accepted by the NAIC. The adopters of the loading formula did not foresee the dramatic increase in loan terms. No one expected the table to remain as the only recognized table for ten years. Changes in underlying experience, changes in required policy provisions, and changes in the legal environment also contributed to the high loss experience of the 1970s.

1969 NAIC Mortality Study (NAIC Proceedings 1971, Vol. 1)

A study was made of the life experience for 1969 based on the data supplied by 80 insurers. As a consequence of the growth of insurance in force, the one-year study had the same volume as the two-year 1964 NAIC Study. The results were comparable to prior studies:

Class of Business	Annual Claim Cost Per $100 Per Year
Banks	28.7¢/100/year
Credit Unions	22.2¢
Automobile Dealers	23.2¢
Sales Finance Companies	31.2¢
Small Loan Companies	37.4¢
Production Credit Associations	72.3¢
Other	32.2¢
Overall	30.0¢

Of particular interest was the finding that claim costs on policies with an initial in force over $15,000 were 47.0¢/100/year. Only minor differences were noted between group and individual experience. Policies without age restrictions had claim costs only 4%-7% above those with the standard age 65 limitation. Recent unpublished studies indicate that this differential has widened.

1974 NAIC Disability Study (NAIC Proceedings 1975, Vol. 1)

An update of the 1968 Disability Study was released in 1974. This new study covered the experience of 1971-72. While only 14 companies contributed data, the volume of data was more extensive than the 1968 Study. The single claim costs were:

POLICY TERM	7 DAY RETROACTIVE	14 DAY RETROACTIVE	14 DAY NON-RETRO	30 DAY RETROACTIVE	30 DAY NON-RETRO
12	$ 2.11	$ 2.03	$ 1.51	$ 1.58	$ .88
24	3.31	3.13	2.16	2.40	1.42
36	4.22	3.94	2.59	2.99	1.82
48	4.97	4.61	2.94	3.48	2.14
60	5.63	5.20	3.23	3.90	2.41

These claim costs were a shocking change from the 1968 NAIC Disability Study. The retroactive plans had claim costs which were almost double those of the previous study. The non-retroactive plans had costs of 40%-70% over the 1968 study.

The industry felt these costs accurately reflected current experience. Claim costs were rising because of regulatory restrictions on underwriting limitations. One trend was to limit the preexisting condition clause to the six-month provision which is now common. The study did have its technical problems. Again, the flaws arose from the quality of the underlying data rather than from the technical expertise applied to compile the table. The validity of the table was debated for several years. The table was never adopted by the NAIC.

CALIFORNIA STUDIES

The California Insurance Department studied the disability experience of California business for 1973-74. This study confirmed the results of the 1974 NAIC Disability Study for the retroactive plans, but found lower claim costs on the non-retroactive plans.

The California experience was updated to include the years 1975-76. This experience was combined with the 1974 Disability Study and graduation formulas to produce the 1978 Credit Morbidity Table. Although the NAIC Technical Task Force recommended the adoption of the table to replace the 1968 Disability Table, the NAIC only "received" the table. The primary objection was use of a national table heavily weighted by the experience of one state.

Claim costs were derived by class of business based on the California classifications. The claim costs for the bank and automobile dealer class (Class B) were:

POLICY TERM	14 DAY RETROACTIVE	14 DAY NON-RETRO	30 DAY RETROACTIVE	30 DAY NON-RETRO
12	$ 1.47	$ 1.15	$ 1.37	$ .88
24	2.07	1.70	1.93	1.45
36	2.60	2.18	2.42	1.94
48	3.06	2.58	2.85	2.36
60	3.45	2.93	3.22	2.73

Overall claim costs for life insurance for rolling three-year periods from 1973-80 have been calculated by the California Department. The claim costs included $40-$52 million of incurred claims for each three-year period on single life experience and $12-$24 million of joint life claims. The results per $100 per year were:

Period	Single Life Claim Costs	Joint Life Claim Costs	Ratio of Joint to Single Life
1973-75	24.0¢	35.3¢	1.471
1974-76	22.8¢	36.2¢	1.588
1975-77	21.6¢	35.9¢	1.662
1976-78	20.2¢	35.1¢	1.738
1977-79	19.7¢	35.4¢	1.797
1978-80	19.5¢	34.3¢	1.759

PILOT STUDY OF CREDIT INSURANCE

In 1978, the Society of Actuaries formed a special study committee on credit insurance, with the intent of performing a detailed study of credit life and disability insurance claim experience. The study was to evaluate all parameters potentially significant to claim costs. These parameters included:

- Age-rated experience
- Variation in claim costs by duration,
- Variation in claim costs by geographical area, and
- Variation by plan of benefit.

The finance company class was selected for study, since its data base contained the most complete information. Five companies submitted data for the years 1976-78. To date, efforts to process the data have not produced meaningful results.

1980 OHIO STUDY

In 1979, the Ohio Insurance Department convened a Credit Insurance Advisory Committee to assist in revising the Ohio credit insurance regulation. One aspect of the committee's work was to commission a study of the Ohio experience for the years 1977-79. The study was compiled by Booke and Company, an independent actuarial consulting firm. The study included almost $500 million of earned premiums for life and disability combined.

For life insurance, the results were presented for the four major classes of business. The single life claim costs were:

Credit Unions	21.7¢/100/year
Banks, Savings and Loans	22.9¢
Finance Companies	23.9¢
Automobile Dealers	20.3¢
Composite Average	22.0¢

The study found that a joint life multiple of 1.75 was representative of the claim cost differential between joint life coverage and single life coverage. The data did not show material differences in the claim costs of the various modes of payment (single premium versus MOB), plans of insurance (decreasing versus level) or types of coverage (gross versus net payoff). However, the loss experience varied significantly by insurer.

Disability claim costs were presented by class of lender. The following list is a comparison of the claim cost by class for a 48-month term on the 14-day retroactive plan:

Credit Unions	$3.67 per $100
Banks	$2.58
Finance Companies	$3.18
Automobile Dealers	$2.34
Other	$2.50

A comparison of claim costs for the Bank class, by plan and term, is shown in the following table:

POLICY TERM	14 DAY RETROACTIVE	14 DAY NON-RETRO	30 DAY RETROACTIVE	30 DAY NON-RETRO
12	$ 1.25	$ 1.07	$ .90	$ .65
24	1.76	1.58	1.27	1.05
36	2.19	2.02	1.60	1.42
48	2.58	2.38	1.87	1.72
60	2.94	2.70	2.13	1.99

The study found claim costs under monthly outstanding balance plans were higher than under single premium plans. A secondary study attempted to determine the difference in claim costs due to a policy provision which covered preexisting conditions. Ohio permits insurers to charge an additional 10% if preexisting conditions are covered. The loss ratio for the two variations indicated that the differential was reasonable; however, the results were not conclusive.

The discussions and recommendations of the Committee were interesting and indicative of the complex nature of the regulation of credit insurance. The Ohio Director of Insurance assembled a large, diverse committee. The Committee had participants representing trade associations, credit insurers, agents, legislators, and consumers. Lawyers, actuaries, and insurance executives debated the issues in credit insurance regulation over a period of eighteen months. A draft regulation was pieced together, but the final vote to recommend the draft regulation failed. The final tally was four in favor, five opposed, and six abstentions. The Director promptly dismissed the advisory committee. A new Director was appointed later who drafted a regulation without the assistance of an advisory committee.

1982 PENNSYLVANIA STUDY

In 1982, the Pennsylvania Insurance Department convened an industry advisory committee to assist in revising the Pennsylvania regulation. This committee fared better than the Ohio committee. The Committee did not recommend a regulation. Rather, it researched and made recommendations concerning 36 issues in credit insurance regulation.

The Pennsylvania experience for 1980 was studied. The data included about $70 million of earned life premium and $72.5 million of earned disability premiums. The claim costs were derived from the annual statistical filings. Incurred claim-earned premium loss ratios were calculated. Earned premiums in the calculations were based on prima facie rates. The loss ratios were multiplied times the prima facie rates to get the claim costs. Since the Pennsylvania rating structure includes an interest discount, the earned single premiums were undiscounted using interest factors for an assumed average term.

For life insurance, the claim costs were:

Credit Unions	19.8¢/100/year
Banks	23.6¢
Cash Loans	30.3¢
Automobile Dealers and Sales Finance	21.2¢

For disability insurance, the loss ratio approach produced a result by plan, but a breakdown by term was not available. Applying the study's loss ratios to the prima facie rates at thirty-six months produces the following claim costs by class:

CLASS OF BUSINESS	14 DAY RETROACTIVE	14 DAY NON-RETRO	30 DAY RETROACTIVE	30 DAY NON-RETRO
Credit Unions	NC	NC	$2.27	$2.40
Banks	$2.18	$2.04	1.97	1.54
Cash Loans	3.02	2.58	NC	NC
Automobile Dealers	2.11	NC	NC	NC

Cells with less than $500,000 of earned premium are shown as not credible (NC). The Committee found significant variation in claim costs in credit union business by the type of industry.

The Committee performed work on critical period disability rating. The use of the coverage was too recent for any credible volume of experience to have developed. However, the ratios of claim costs for certain critical period coverages to full benefit claim costs were developed.

A published table of disability experience was selected. Claim costs were calculated from the basic values for the critical period benefits and for the usual benefit which runs to the end of the loan term. The assumed tables and interest rates were:

Morbidity:	100% of the 1971 Modification of the 1964 Commissioners Disability Table for male lives using a twenty-year select period.
Mortality:	100% of the 1960 Basic Group Table
Interest:	4.5%

The morbidity table was not considered representative of the level of claim costs for credit disability insurance. The calculations only assume that the relationship between the two benefit coverages was applicable. The resulting ratios were applied to the prima facie credit disability rates to produce rates for critical period coverages. Since the intent in marketing critical period coverages is to reduce the total dollar outlay, ratios were developed only for the less expensive 30-day plans. The ratios demonstrate the premium reduction which can be achieved using critical period plans versus standard plans.

RATIOS OF CRITICAL PERIOD DISABILITY RATES TO CORRESPONDING RATES FOR STANDARD COVERAGE

	TERM OF LOAN IN MONTHS							
30 DAY RETROACTIVE	36	48	60	72	96	120	180	240
12 Month Benefit Period	.85	.79	.74	.70	.64	.60	.53	.48
24 Month Benefit Period	.97	.92	.88	.84	.77	.72	.64	.59
36 Month Benefit Period	—	.98	.95	.92	.86	.81	.73	.67
30 DAY NON-RETROACTIVE								
12 Month Benefit Period	.81	.73	.67	.63	.57	.52	.44	.40
24 Month Benefit Period	.96	.90	.85	.80	.72	.67	.58	.52
36 Month Benefit Period	—	.98	.94	.90	.83	.77	.68	.62

THE CREDIT LIFE INSURANCE COMPANY STUDY

The Credit Life Insurance Company studied its life claim costs for the years 1981-84 for the states requiring annual statistical filings on some version of the 1980 NAIC Form. This included the experience in 25 states and over $100 million of earned premiums.

The method used for the study was the same as the one used in the 1982 Pennsylvania Study for all states which required the conversion of earned premiums from actual premiums to prima facie premiums. Other states' data were used if most of the business was written at prima facie rates. The study is heavily weighted by experience in Ohio, New York, California, and Pennsylvania.

Single life claim costs for the four years were:

Automobile Dealers	21¢/100/year
Banks	24¢
Credit Unions	23¢
Finance Companies	30¢
Other	28¢

The joint life experience showed multiples from 1.57 to 1.83 for the different years, averaging 1.76 for the four-year period.

SUMMARY

These studies are included primarily to demonstrate average claim costs and their trend over time. The trend in life insurance claim costs is downward, paralleling the improvement in mortality rates in the general population. Credit life mortality costs have also been influenced by an increase in the proportion of female borrowers, both an increase in the percentage of females in the single life insureds and an increase in the percentage of loans covered by joint life protection.

The trend in disability insurance is more difficult to gauge because of the limitations of the available data. Claim costs rose significantly from the early 1960s to the late 1970s. Claim costs in the 1980s appear to have stabilized at the level of the late 1970s, but many insurers have experienced fluctuations from year to year. A factor in these trends has been the level of unemployment. The level of unemployment increased steadily until the mid-1970s. Although unemployment has remained high by historical levels, the rates have been fairly stable over the last few years. Another factor was the changes in policy provisions which occurred primarily from 1965 to 1975. The increase in the percentage of female insureds, with their higher disability claim costs, was a minor contributing factor.

Disability loss ratios have actually declined in the last ten years. The primary factor has been the use of rate deviations by insurers and the adoption of prima facie rates which were a more accurate reflection of the actual cost of disability insurance.

Every study of experience has shown a wide variation of claim costs by insurer. In addition, insurers find a wide range of experience by account. Claim costs definitely vary by the lender's class of business. The variation is more pronounced for disability insurance.

CHAPTER ELEVEN
THE CASE FOR CREDIT INSURANCE

Credit insurance has been sold for over 65 years and during that time the amount of credit life insurance in force has grown continuously, except for the World War II years. The post-war years, from 1945 to 1970, was a period of spectacular growth for the industry. Currently, over $189 billion of credit life insurance is in force, representing over 66 million policies and certificates. Credit disability insurance in force grew slowly until 1970, then experienced sixteen years of strong growth. The growth and size of credit insurance in force are clear evidence of the value of these consumer products.

Consumer acceptance can be traced to three properties of the products:

1. The products satisfy a real need,

2. The products are conveniently available, and

3. The cost of the products is reasonable.

Americans and Canadians have long recognized the need for insurance protection. Few people are without some form of life or health insurance. A natural time for considering additional insurance protection is when a consumer is assuming additional debt. Arthur Morris founded the first credit insurance company with the motto "No man's debt should live after him." The statement is as valid today as it was in 1917.

The death of a borrower or co-borrower can be a serious financial event. If the death is preceded by a prolonged or serious illness, the financial strain can be even more pronounced. Debt is usually incurred because a family's assets are not sufficient to meet the demands of a certain expenditure. Repayment depends on the continued earning power of the borrower. A prudent borrower makes a provision for the possibility that his earning power may be reduced or eliminated by death or disability.

Consumers are often underinsured because of:

1. Financial demands,

2. Lack of desire to discuss insurance, and

3. Promotion of whole life insurance.

Today's consumer faces a vast array of essentials and luxuries vying for a portion of the consumer's budget. The growth of two-income families demonstrates that financial demands strain available financial resources. Single parent families, which represent a growing percentage of the population, face difficult financial decisions. Purchase of insurance can easily be delayed or ignored when basic needs are not fully met. Consumers incurring debt for basic needs are more likely to be underinsured.

A major element of the success of credit insurance is people's dislike for discussing death or disability. Good insurance agents realize the problem, as the following personal experience of the author demonstrates.

> I was consulting with the president of a small ordinary life insurance company when his most successful agent dropped by for a chat. I said, "As an actuary, I have designed and priced many insurance products, but how do you sell them?"

> The agent took a long draw on his cigar and leaning forward said, "Are you ready to meet the Lord?"
>
> Slightly taken aback I finally uttered a flip answer to the effect, "If my time has come, I do not have much choice."
>
> He leaned back, looked intently at me, and said, "Well, are you in love?"
>
> I said, "Yes."
>
> "If I wanted to, I could get you to talk for hours about those you love, and your desires and goals for them. Let me tell you, if I have to talk to you about dying to sell you insurance, you will avoid me like the plague. But if I can show you what insurance can do for the ones you love, I will make a sale every time."

The varying success records of agents demonstrates that not all agents have learned this lesson. Even a successful agent is out of luck if the consumer anticipates discussing death and will not even let the agent in the door. Once inside, the ordinary life insurance agent has an array of products, often confusing to the consumer. Comparison shopping means talking to more agents. Even knowledgeable consumers have difficulty comparing ordinary life products and costs.

After the selection, the consumer is faced with completion of an application with some medical questions. A paramedical examination or a full medical examination may be required. Questions abound in the consumer's mind about how much to tell a stranger about his life. Few consumers would describe the purchase of insurance as an enjoyable experience, particularly if the alternative purchase is a new television or VCR.

A typical sales pitch for most credit insurance is simple and quick: "If you die, your loan is paid off. If you are under age 65, you qualify. Insurance on your spouse is available if your spouse is a co-borrower. Disability insurance is available to fulfill your monthly payments if you are disabled. You must remain disabled for fourteen days before you receive any benefits. The cost of the insurance is shown on this form. It will be added to the amount you borrow and will be financed. Your monthly payment including insurance is this amount. If you wish the insurance, just sign in the blocks marked."

No underwriting; no embarrassing health questions. The presentation is simple and easy to understand. The product meets the immediate need of the consumer in a convenient manner without the anticipation of a prolonged discussion of death or disability. Most consumers are aware of their underinsurance situation; they just do not want to do something about it. Faced with a convenient opportunity to quickly and simply fulfill part of their insurance needs, consumers opt for credit insurance. Since the cost is included in the monthly payment, the consumer does not have to make separate premium payments, unlike ordinary insurance which requires periodic payments which must be budgeted. Every premium due notice is an opportunity to discontinue the insurance for other needs or desires.

Most credit insurance purchasers perceive its cost as reasonable or inexpensive. The total dollars of premium involved are usually small. In obtaining loans, consumers are primarily concerned about their ability to meet the monthly payments. Credit life adds such a small amount to the monthly payment that many consumers, when offered the product, elect the coverage. Credit disability insurance is more costly, so fewer consumers elect the coverage, although the need is just as pressing.

Credit insurance is usually more expensive than ordinary term insurance. It can be compared to shopping at a convenience store for groceries. A loaf of bread costs more than at a warehouse grocery. Convenience outweighs the small cost involved. The time and aggravation involved with ordinary insurance outweigh the small savings. Older consumers and consumers with health problems often find credit insurance is less expensive than ordinary insurance products.

It is difficult to find comparable ordinary insurance products to cover only the approximate debt incurred. Consumer loans are generally under $10,000. Few ordinary life insurance agents want to take the time to write a policy of this size. Ordinary insurers do not pursue this market because of the fixed costs of issuing the policies. The unit cost of a $10,000 ordinary policy is not significantly different from that of credit insurance. Standard insurance policies require a policy fee which can be a high percentage of the premium on a $10,000 policy. Often a policy this size can only be obtained through monthly debit ordinary products–the modern day version of industrial insurance. Credit insurance compares favorably with the cost of monthly debit ordinary products.

Premium rates in credit life insurance have moved downward since 1950. In some states, the current rates are one-half of the 1950 rates. Credit insurance is an excellent buy in many states. For older consumers, the product is a real bargain anywhere, since one rate is charged for all ages. Credit insurance is actually less expensive than many of the alternatives available in the ordinary insurance marketplace. Consumers who would be classed as substandard by an ordinary insurer receive a very competitively priced product without the hassle of underwriting and the embarrassment of being rated or rejected by an insurer.

Finally, credit insurance is pure insurance protection–the life product is term insurance. One of the reasons consumers are underinsured is the propensity of insurers to sell whole life or universal life insurance. While these products have merit, a major portion of the premium dollar is really forced savings. In many cases, a consumer would be better off applying his entire insurance budget to purchase term insurance. Young families with children need all the insurance protection they can afford.

Purchase of credit insurance by the consumer offers advantages to the lender as well. Credit insurance is offered in practically all situations where consumer loans are extended. Lenders have found that the consumers want the service and will elect to purchase the insurance in great numbers. In addition, the lender:

- Has added security on repayment of the loan,
- Avoids collecting a debt from the spouse in a time of crisis, and
- May receive compensation for marketing and administration.

When credit insurance is elected by the consumer, his family is protected from the financial stress present at the time of disability or death. The coverage is particularly important for borrowers in lower socio-economic classes, because members of this group have few financial resources beyond their ability to earn an income. Finance companies stress this insurance coverage more than other financial institutions because the need is more pressing. This is one reason penetration rates are higher in finance companies.

Public relations plays an important role in encouraging the lender to offer an insurance program–no lending officer relishes the thought of collecting a debt or repossessing consumer goods from a widow or widower. Credit insurance provides a real social value by easing the financial burden on a surviving spouse.

Disability insurance is also valuable. A consumer may have only Social Security to provide disability protection. Some workers still face the situation of "no work, no pay." Others have only short-term sick pay with no provision for salary continuation after a few weeks of disability. All workers face the problem of medical costs which must be met in addition to regular living expenses. While most employees have some form of health insurance, deductibles and coinsurance payments can represent a major financial burden. Social Security benefits require a long waiting period.

Credit disability eases the stress. Its relatively short waiting period produces benefits during the critical period following a disability. If the lender knows the consumer is protected, it is not likely to press for payment at a time when the need for cash flow is critical. This prevents situations such as the repossession of a family car when the spouse may need it the most.

Lenders generally receive service fees, commissions, or other compensation for offering the product to the consumer. Some consumer advocates feel the lender should not receive compensation for offering a service which benefits the lender, but this position is counter to the whole fabric of American society. Lenders do incur expenses in offering the product–lending officers must take time to offer and explain the coverage; premiums and refunds must be processed; assistance given in filing of claim forms. Therefore, a lender must be satisfied that the return on the time and effort is satisfactory. The expense margins and profit objectives of the lenders vary, but the insurance industry must provide compensation to the lender sufficient to guarantee that this socially valuable product is available to the consumer.

Growth of credit insurance in force can also be traced to the responsiveness of the industry. New products have been introduced to meet the changing consumer loan environment. Net payoff life coverage and critical period disability coverage responded to the need for less costly alternatives on long-term loans. Benefit variations were developed to cope with variable interest rate loans. The monthly outstanding balance premium approach used in the 1950s was dusted off for use in credit card and line-of-credit lending. The industry has moved forward to offer products capable of meeting consumer needs, often overcoming regulatory constraints in the process. Regulations which were written in simpler times have not been updated to meet a rapidly changing financial world. In spite of these constraints, credit insurers have offered more new products in the last ten years than were introduced in the preceding fifty years.

Nothing is a better indicator of consumer satisfaction and acceptance than the prolonged growth of the amount of insurance in force. Studies of consumer attitudes reveal a strong desire for the product, further supporting the reasons for the in force growth. The details of these studies are in a separate chapter, but a summary of findings is relevant here.

From the 1954 Colorado Study:

"Those who have Credit Life Insurance think favorably of it as evidenced by these findings:

a. Better than 90% of the randomly selected owners, and better than 80% of the owners found in the random sample representative of Colorado voters would want Consumer Credit Insurance again if they were borrowing money or making a time payment.

b. Better than 70% of these same groups would recommend such policies to friends or relatives borrowing money or making time payment purchases, and an additional 8% to 20% would "in some cases." No more than 6.5% would definitely not recommend it.

c. 13% of the general Colorado public of voting age have had Credit Life Insurance policies.

d. Of the 87% with no experience with Credit Life Insurance in the Colorado public of voting age, three-fourths of them think having such insurance available is a good thing. Only 2.1% say definitely that it is not a good thing; the remainder having no opinion."

From the 1973 Ohio University Study:

"It is evident from the results of the consumer opinion survey that most borrowers value highly the protection afforded by consumer credit insurance, and that there is a strong demand for both credit life and credit disability (accident and health) coverages. Only a small percentage of the respondents would like to cancel their insurance and obtain a refund; and more than 90 per cent of the respondents would purchase the insurance again in connection with future loans or installment contract arrangements and would recommend the coverage to friends, relatives, and neighbors. Even among respondents whose own debts were not covered by credit insurance, over 60 per cent would recommend the coverage to others."

From the 1977 Federal Reserve Board Study:

"The theory (of tie-in sales) implies that the existence of tying, either explicit or involuntary, will be manifested in a high proportion of joint purchases, buyer resentment of being forced to make the purchase and supplier conduct conducive to tying. Analytically buyer resentment would be expected to show up either through a poor opinion of the tied good or, somewhat less directly, through complaints about its quality or cost.

In the belief that buyers' resentment would be strongest and most likely to generate complaints in those cases involving explicit formal tying, the complaint files of the Federal Reserve System were canvassed. No complaints had been filed since 1970 alleging violation of Section 106 of the Bank Holding Company Act by either businesses or consumers. This tends to support the findings of the 1970 study by the National Association of Insurance Commissioners in which the incidence of this type of alleged violation was also very low.

The special Federal Reserve survey of consumers focused on the most locally limited group of buyers who have the fewest alternatives for credit. It shows that, overall, 62.2 per cent of the borrowers had purchased credit insurance. Retailers and banks had the lowest penetration rates at 39.9 per cent and 61.4 per cent, respectively, while finance companies had the highest at 74.8 per cent.

These relatively high penetration rates do not, however, appear to have risen from either explicit coercion or involuntary tying. To a direct question about how much pressure consumers felt to purchase credit life insurance at the time they applied for credit, relatively few responded that the joint purchase was "required" (16.4 per cent) or even "strongly recommended (8.8 percent). Again, retailers and banks were the lender groups with the lowest proportion of customers who perceived that the purchase of credit insurance was either "required" or "strongly recommended." This finding confirms the finding of the 'Ohio Study' by Hubbard which is the most comprehensive study available dealing with the credit insurance industry. The absence of coercion is further supported by the very small proportion of customers viewing credit life and disability insurance as a 'bad' service. Most regard it as highly desirable and, more significantly, feel that its price is 'about right,' even 'inexpensive.'

. . . In particular, credit insurance is typically offered after the credit is approved and most respondents advise the customer that insurance is not required.

In conclusion, analysis of the surveys suggests that explicit tying between the granting of credit and the sale of credit related insurance is practically non-existent and that implicit pressures brought by lenders on the borrowers are neither very strong nor widespread in the industry. It does appear that a sizable minority of credit customers voluntarily prefer to place their property and casualty insurance with their lender, valuing their own convenience of doing so relatively highly, compared to searching for alternative sources of insurance services. The proportion of people opting for joint purchases of credit and insurance rises greatly among those purchasing credit life and disability insurance probably because of the small premium costs relative to search and shopping costs."

These findings show a historical acceptance of the product which has remained high since the product's creation.

Another source to measure consumer satisfaction is to review complaints received by insurance departments from consumers.

From the 1967 Kentucky "Report on Credit Insurance":

"From a review of 1966 Departmental complaint files it was found that very few complaints were lodged against credit life and accident and health insurers. In those complaints noted, which involved principally coverage questions, the issues were satisfactorily resolved without any degree of difficulty."

From the 1970 NAIC Study:

"In preparation of this paper the staff conducted a survey of the various state insurance departments to determine the number and nature of the complaints they received concerning credit insurance and the number of personnel involved in the regulation of credit insurance in each department. Replies to the questionnaire were received from 33 states. These states represent about 75% of the country's population and about 72% of the credit insurance premiums written.

The survey shows that the annual average number of complaints received by the responding insurance departments in all areas of insurance was 4,466. An average of 3% of these complaints involved credit insurance. Of this 3%, an average of: (1) 1.5% involved coverage in excess of the loan; (2) 7% involved failure to make proper refunds; (3) 0.7% involved coercion of debtors; (4) 8% involved failure to inform debtors of coverage; (5) 7% involved overcharging; (6) 0.8% involved pyramiding; (7) 3% involved excessive creditor compensation; (8) 48% involved refusal to pay benefits; (9) 3.5% involved compensating balances or interest-free deposits; and (10) 3.3% involved unlicensed persons selling credit insurance. Another 4% involved other assorted problems. Of all the complaints received on credit insurance, an average of 50% were deemed valid by the insurance department.

Generalizing from these figures, one could say first, that a very small percentage of the complaints received by departments involve credit insurance. It probably can be said that the average percentage is not significantly different from the percentage of premium involved in credit insurance and therefore does not seem to present problems greater than its premium significance. Second, refusal to pay benefits generates far more complaints than any other aspect of credit insurance. The other types of complaints are proportionately quite small. It should be noted, however, that on the average half of the complaints, which involve refusal to pay benefits as well as all other credit insurance complaints, turn out to be valid complaints and are dealt with by the departments on that basis. It would seem then that the complaint system serves a useful purpose as far as it applies to credit insurance. Third, it can be that the amount of personnel time expended on credit insurance does not vary greatly from the significance of credit insurance premiums in relation to all the premiums."

The following analysis is not exact, but it does place the importance of the NAIC findings in a general perspective.

Applying the data shown, 33 states averaged 4,466 complaints totaling 147,378 for all insurance. Total credit insurance complaints were 3% or 4,422. About 50% were deemed valid, so the final result is 2,211 valid complaints. The report does not state the time span involved in the receipt of the complaints.

In 1970, there was $96,455,000,000 of credit life insurance in force. Assuming a conservative average in force of $2,000, there were approximately 48 million consumers owning credit life policies. Many of this group also owned disability policies. Since the survey included only 72% of the country, one could estimate that about 36 million consumers generated 2,211 valid complaints. This is less than one-hundredth of one percent–a rather remarkable record.

In the 1973 Ohio University Study, a questionnaire was sent to each Commissioner of Insurance. The responses relative to Department complaints were:

> "Questions 3 & 4. The third and fourth questions in this section asked each commissioner to select from three statements the one which best described the complaints about credit life insurance or credit accident and health insurance received by his department, or to describe the nature of complaints in his own words. As can be seen in the following table, most commissioners reported a slightly higher incidence of complaint with credit disability insurance than with credit life insurance."

FREQUENCY OF COMPLAINTS
REGARDING CREDIT INSURANCE*

Statement Selected by Commissioners	Number for Credit Life	Number for Credit Disability
Complaints are numerous and suggest that the department must closely supervise the industry for the protection of the public	0	1
Complaints are average in frequency and suggest that normal supervision of the industry by the department is adequate for the protection of the public	13	18
Complaints are infrequent and suggest that only minimal supervision of the industry is required for the protection of the public	16	12

* From the 1973 Ohio University Study

Still, the social value of insurance proves itself at claim time, often having far-reaching benefits beyond the amount of money provided. No group has a greater appreciation of insurance than the actual beneficiaries of claim payments. Their loyalty to insurance is not surprising; the author's own experience is typical of the testimonials for insurance.

> "My parents worked at low-paying jobs in southern hosiery mills, an industry not known for its health benefits. After I left home to attend college, my parents purchased an automobile. My father borrowed about $1,500 to buy a 1964 Corvair. Shortly after, the furnace went out creating a $900 unexpected expense that could only be covered with another loan.
>
> Then disaster struck. He became seriously ill and his deteriorating condition left him unable to work again. He died after a difficult 24 months.
>
> My mother continued working as a clerk in the hosiery mill, struggling to support herself and my younger brother and cover the additional medical expenses. However, there were two monthly bills that she didn't have to worry about–the payments on the car loan and the furnace repairs.
>
> Whether my father purchased credit life and disability insurance on those two loans voluntarily or was 'coerced,' I will never know. But no one who knew us then could doubt the wisdom of the purchase. Without the cushion of the disability benefits and the subsequent death claim payment, the financial crisis would have been crippling.
>
> Without the insurance, my education would have been interrupted to help pay the bills. Without the credit insurance coverage to protect our family, it may have drastically altered the course of my life might have been drastically altered and this book on credit insurance may never have been written."

In summary, credit life and disability insurance products have a proven track record of providing essential benefits to borrowers. Consumers desire the products and elect the coverages in great numbers. The products are an essential component of the consumer borrowing process which has done so much to produce the highest standard of living in the world.

APPENDIX A

GLOSSARY

NOTE: The definitions in this glossary are the meaning of the words as they apply to credit insurance. Some words also have broader meanings.

ACCEPTANCE CORPORATION. A finance corporation formed by a manufacturer of consumer goods to provide financing which is available through the seller of its goods, typically automobiles and other expensive machinery or equipment.

ACCOUNT. A particular lender may be referred to by the insurer as an account.

ACCOUNTING DATE. The "as of" date on which an accounting statement is prepared. The last day of the accounting period.

ACTIVE LIFE RESERVES. A liability of an insurance company representing an estimate of benefit payments which will be paid after the accounting date on insureds who are in good health on the accounting date, but who will die or become disabled after the accounting date but before the insurance terminates.

ACTIVELY-AT-WORK CLAUSE. A policy requirement that the borrower must have worked thirty or more hours per week, for one to two months prior to the effective date of the insurance, in order to qualify for the insurance coverage.

ANNUAL PERCENTAGE RATE (APR). The effective annual rate of interest on a loan.

ANTI-SELECTION. The tendency of a borrower to select against the insurer, based on his knowledge of his health condition, when he is deciding whether to purchase insurance coverage.

ANY OCCUPATION DISABILITY. A disability which causes a claimant to be unable to perform the essential duties of any occupation for which he is reasonably qualified by training, education, or experience.

ASSET SHARES. Ordinary insurance profitability studies.

ASSIGNMENT OF COMMISSION. Where corporations cannot be licensed, the agent agrees to assign the commissions received from the sale of credit insurance to the corporation employing him. In this situation, he is acting in the same manner as the active agent under a corporation license.

ASSUME THE RISK. The acceptance of risk on an insurance policy by a reinsurer from the direct writer or another reinsurer.

ASSUMING REINSURER. A reinsurer accepting risk from a direct writer or another reinsurer, also called assuming company.

BALLOON LOAN. An installment loan which requires a final payment at maturity that is larger than the installment payments.

BENCHMARK LOSS RATIO. In state laws and regulations, the presumed loss ratio on which prima facie rates are based. Also, the loss ratio used to determine whether the benefits provided are reasonable in relation to the premium charged.

BORROWER. A consumer entering into a loan by receiving cash or purchasing a consumer product, also called the debtor.

CAPTIVE INSURANCE (OR REINSURANCE) COMPANY. An insurance company owned or controlled by a producer of credit insurance business for the purpose of insuring, or reinsuring, the credit insurance business sold by the producer.

CASE. The unit of experience for profitability studies or for rate deviation purposes. It may be a single account, or a group of accounts which are combined.

CASE RESERVE METHOD. Disability claim reserves set by a knowledgeable claims person who reviews each reported claim and estimates the remaining time of disability. The reserve is the product of the remaining months of disability times the claimant's monthly benefit.

CASH LOAN. A loan in which the borrower receives cash for the purchase of consumer goods or other expenditures.

CEDE. The transfer of risk on an insurance policy from the direct writer to a reinsurer.

CEDING FEE. The percentage of gross premiums minus refund premiums retained by the direct writer in a reinsurance transaction for general expenses, premium taxes, and profit.

CEDING INSURER. The direct writer who transfers a portion of its risk on an insurance policy to a reinsurer, also called a ceding company.

CEDING STATEMENT. A statement prepared by the direct writer in a reinsurance transaction showing the cash transactions for the accounting period, also called a cession statement or reinsurance cession.

CLAIM CLAUSES. Clauses in an insurance policy which define the process of filing a claim under the policy.

CLAIM COST. The dollar cost of the benefits provided by an insurance policy.

CLAIM FREQUENCY. The number of claims which occur.

CLAIM RESERVES. An estimate of the benefit payments which will be paid after the accounting date, on claims which have occurred prior to an accounting date. Categories of claim reserves are: incurred but not reported claims, claims in course of settlement, and continuing claims (disability only).

CLAIMANT. A borrower covered by a credit insurance policy who files a claim for a loss covered by the policy.

CLAIMS IN COURSE OF SETTLEMENT (CCS OR ICOS). Claims which have occurred and have been reported to the insurance company prior to the accounting date, but have not been paid on that date.

CLOSED-END LOAN. A loan for a specified amount and a fixed term. The amount borrowed cannot be increased.

COINSURANCE. A reinsurance arrangement by which the risk and all cash elements, except the direct writer's administrative fees, are shared proportionately by the direct writer and the reinsurer, also called quota share coinsurance.

COINSURANCE PERCENTAGE. The percentage of the total risk which is ceded to the reinsurer.

COLLATERAL. Security pledged by a borrower to protect the interest of the lender.

COMMISSION CAPS. State limitations on the maximum compensation paid by insurers to general agents and producers. See Appendix D for a list of states imposing limitations and the maximum percentage permitted in each state.

1958 COMMISSIONERS EXTENDED TERM (1958 CET). A mortality table based on a study of 1950-54 experience under an ordinary life insurance non-forfeiture option called extended term insurance. The table is often used to calculate mortality reserves for credit life insurance business.

1960 COMMISSIONERS STANDARD GROUP (1960 CSG). A mortality table based on a study of group mortality experience published in 1960. The table is occasionally used to calculate mortality reserves for credit life insurance.

1958 COMMISSIONERS STANDARD ORDINARY (1958 CSO). A mortality table based on a study of 1950-54 ordinary life insurance experience. The table is occasionally used to calculate mortality reserves for credit life insurance. For the ages applicable to most credit insurance business, the 1958 CET is equal to 130% of 1958 CSO.

COMPENSATING BALANCES. Deposits in a financial institution by an insurer where the interest paid on these deposits is less than market rates, usually in a non-interest-bearing checking account.

CONSUMER CREDIT INSURANCE. Insurance written in conjunction with consumer goods lending.

CONTESTABLE PERIOD. A period, usually two years, during which misrepresentations made by the insured in an application for insurance may be used as reason to deny a claim. After the contestable period, a valid claim may not be denied (i.e., it is incontestable) because of misrepresentations, except in cases of fraud.

CONTINGENT COMMISSIONS. Compensation paid to a general agent or producer which is paid only if his business is profitable, also called retroactive commissions or experience refunds.

CONTINUING CLAIMS. In disability insurance, claims which have occurred prior to the accounting date, and for which the claimants have received at least one disability payment.

CONTRIBUTORY PREMIUMS. The borrower has the option to purchase the credit insurance protection and pays an identifiable charge.

CONTROLLED FOREIGN CORPORATION. A non-U.S. corporation subject to U.S. taxation.

CREDIBILITY. In profitability studies, the degree of confidence that can be placed on the observed loss ratio as a predictor of the true experience of a case, usually determined by the amount of earned premiums, number of lives insured, or the number of claims.

CREDIT CARD LENDING. The purchaser may receive cash, or act as a purchaser of a consumer product, by agreeing to repay the amount charged to the account.

CREDIT DISABILITY INSURANCE. Disability insurance purchased in conjunction with a consumer credit transaction which provides a monthly benefit equal to the required monthly payment, during the continued disability of the insured, during the term of coverage.

CREDIT LIFE INSURANCE. Term life insurance purchased in conjunction with a consumer credit transaction, excluding first mortgage loans, which provides a death benefit sufficient to pay off the credit obligation in the event of an insured's death during the term of the coverage.

CREDITOR. The corporate entity making the loan and offering the insurance product to the consumer, also called financial institution or lending institution.

CRITICAL PERIOD DISABILITY COVERAGE. A coverage under which the maximum number of disability payments is limited to a specified number of months, or the number of remaining payments on the loan, whichever is less.

CRITICAL PERIOD LIFE COVERAGE. A coverage providing a death benefit equal to a specified number of monthly payments, or the remaining payments on the loan, whichever is less.

CROSS-CHECKS. The interrelationship of various lines within the statutory accounting financial statement.

CUSTODIAL TRUST. In a reinsurance transaction, a trust established by a reinsurer in a financial institution for the protection of the ceding company, also called a security fund. Establishment of the trust is usually required in order for the ceding insurer to take reserve credit in its statutory financial statement for business ceded to a non-admitted reinsurer.

CUSTODIAL TRUST AGREEMENT. An agreement between the ceding insurer, a reinsurer, and a bank which outlines the terms under which the reinsurer deposits "securities" in a bank trust as collateral for the reserves ceded under a reinsurance treaty.

DEBT. Any financial obligation entered into by a consumer who receives cash or purchases a consumer product under an installment sales contract.

DEBTOR. A consumer entering into a loan by receiving cash or purchasing a consumer product, also called the borrower.

DEEMER PROVISION. State law or regulation which specifies that a policy filing is approved unless the insurance department objects within a specified period of time.

DEFERRED ACQUISITION COSTS. Under GAAP accounting, the portion of expenses paid to acquire the business which may be expensed over the term of the policies. Only those expenses which "vary with and are directly related" to the amount of business produced may be deferred.

DEVIATED RATE. Any premium rate different from the state's prima facie rate.

DIRECT WRITER. The insurance company issuing an insurance policy.

DISABILITY INSURANCE. Accident and health protection that provides benefits if the insured is unable to work.

DISMEMBERMENT BENEFIT. Insurance which provides benefits if the insured suffers a loss of body parts, such as the loss of an arm or leg.

DOMESTIC INSURER. A direct writer is a domestic insurer in its state of domicile; i.e., its state of incorporation.

DOMICILE. Principal residence for legal purposes.

DOWNWARD DEVIATION. A rate lower than the state's prima facie rate. A mandatory downward deviation is one required by state law or regulation.

EARNED PREMIUM. The premiums collected (or written) for the accounting period, plus the unearned premiums at the beginning of the period, minus the unearned premiums at the end of the period.

EARNED REINSURANCE. A reinsurance arrangement under which the direct writer holds the money and accounts for the transaction on its statutory books as if the business were not reinsured until profits or losses emerge. Earned profits are paid to the reinsurer. If the result is a loss, the reinsurer must reimburse the direct writer.

EFFECTIVE DATE. The day insurance coverage begins, usually the effective date of the loan.

ELIGIBILITY CLAUSE. A clause in an insurance policy that specifies the requirements a borrower must meet to be eligible for coverage.

ELIMINATION PERIOD. In a disability policy, the specified period a claimant must remain disabled before any benefits are payable, also called the waiting period.

EVIDENCE OF INSURANCE. The individual policy or group certificate provided to the insured stating the amount of insurance, premium, term, description of coverage, exceptions, limitations and restrictions.

EXCESS OF LOSS REINSURANCE. A type of reinsurance under which the reinsurer is responsible for the losses exceeding a specific dollar amount which is level during the term of reinsurance coverage.

EXOTIC REINSURANCE COMPANY. A reinsurance company with more than one class of common or preferred stock. Each producer of credit insurance owns a class of stock. Profits on each producer's business inure to his class of stock.

EXPERIENCE REFUNDS. Compensation paid to a general agent or producer which is paid only if his business is profitable, also called contingent commissions or retroactive commissions.

EXPOSURE. In a mortality or morbidity study, the average amount of insurance in force during the period studied.

EXTRATERRITORIAL REGULATION. State regulations which require a company writing business in the state to abide by the regulations wherever it writes business.

FACTOR CARDS OR CHARTS. Charts used by a lending officer to calculate credit insurance premiums.

FACTOR RESERVE METHOD. Prior claim experience is studied to determine the actual experience during a time period in the past. A factor is developed from the prior experience which can be applied to a known quantity to estimate future claims.

FINANCE AND INSURANCE SPECIALISTS (F & I PEOPLE). Individuals employed in automobile dealerships who are trained to handle the financing and insurance matters of an automobile sale.

FINANCIAL INSTITUTION. The corporate entity making the loan and offering the insurance products to the consumer, also called the creditor or lending institution.

FIRST AND FINAL CLAIM. A disability claim in which the initial claim represents the total claim.

FIXED RATE LOAN. A loan which has an interest rate which is constant for the term of the loan.

FLESCH SCORING METHOD. An objective method for assessing readability of text material which judges the document's difficulty of comprehension by counting the syllables in the words and number of words in a sentence.

FRONT COMPENSATION (OR COMMISSIONS). Guaranteed compensation paid to a general agent or a producer based on net written premiums for the reporting period.

FULL LINE ORDINARY INSURANCE COMPANIES. Insurers offering the entire gamut of insurance products including ordinary life, annuities, accident and health, and group insurance.

GENERALLY ACCEPTED ACCOUNTING PRINCIPLES (GAAP). The principles of accounting which apply to most U.S. corporations.

GRACE PERIOD. A premium may be paid up to 30 or 31 days after the due date before the insurer will cancel the policy.

GROSS COVERAGE. Plans of credit insurance which insure the gross indebtedness of a loan.

GROSS INDEBTEDNESS. The sum of the remaining scheduled payments due under a debt obligation. This includes the net indebtedness plus the unearned interest charges.

GROSS MINUS REFUND PREMIUMS. Gross premiums collected by the direct writer minus premium refunds paid by the direct writer, also called G-R premiums and net written premiums.

GROSS WRITTEN PREMIUMS. Gross premiums collected from the insureds on new insurance issued during the reporting period.

GROUP MAXIMUM LIMITS. State laws and regulations which limit the maximum amount of insurance which can be provided by group insurance.

GROUP POLICY. In credit insurance, an insurance policy issued to a lender, where the group is defined as consumers obtaining loans from the lender. When a borrower is insured, he is enrolled in the group and receives a certificate of insurance as evidence of insurance.

GUARANTEED ISSUE LIMIT. The amount of insurance which will be accepted by the insurer without any medical questions or examination. It may be a "per life" limit or a "per policy" limit.

HIS OCCUPATION DISABILITY. A disability which causes a claimant to be unable to perform the essential duties of his usual occupation.

IN FORCE. The amount of insurance currently in effect.

INCURRED BUT NOT REPORTED (IBNR) CLAIMS. Claims which have occurred prior to the accounting date, but which have not been reported to the insurance company on that date.

INCURRED CLAIMS. The total cost of all claims which occur during the accounting period; equal to paid claims, minus the claim reserves at the beginning of the period, plus the claim reserves at the end of the period.

INCURRED LOSS RATIO. The ratio of incurred claims to earned premiums, normally expressed as a percentage.

INCURRED-EARNED LOSS RATIO. The ratio of the incurred claims to the earned premium, normally expressed as a percentage.

INDEBTEDNESS. The amount that is owed.

INDIVIDUAL INSURANCE. The insurance contract is directly between the insurance company and the person insured, who receives an individual policy as evidence of insurance.

INITIAL GROSS INDEBTEDNESS. Initial net indebtedness plus the scheduled interest charges.

INITIAL NET INDEBTEDNESS. The total amount advanced, which normally includes the principal of the loan plus the insurance premium.

INSOLVENCY CLAUSE. A clause in a reinsurance treaty which specifies what will happen in the event the direct writer becomes insolvent. It generally specifies that the reinsurer will continue to meet its obligations to the direct writer, or its statutory successor.

INSTALLMENT LOAN. A loan repayable in substantially equal monthly payments.

INSTALLMENT SALES CONTRACT. The purchaser of a consumer product receives the product in return for entering into a debt obligation which is to be repaid in monthly installment payments.

INSURABLE INTEREST. A party who may suffer financial or emotional loss if the insured is disabled or dies.

INVOLUNTARY TYING. The consumer feels compelled to purchase insurance or some other product in order to secure a loan.

IRREVOCABLE EVERGREEN LETTER OF CREDIT. A letter of credit which is an unqualified promise by the bank to pay the funds on demand.

JOINT LIFE INSURANCE. A credit life insurance policy that insures the borrower and a co-borrower.

LAG RESERVE METHOD. Prior experience is studied to estimate the average remaining period of disability after an accounting date, given the number of months of disability which have elapsed. Factors are developed which can be applied based on the time the insured has been disabled on the current accounting date.

LENDER. In this book, the corporate entity arranging or making the loan and offering the credit insurance product to the consumer. This encompasses lending institutions and corporations arranging installment sales contracts.

LENDING INSTITUTION. The corporate entity making the loan and offering the credit insurance product to the consumer, also called creditor or financial institution.

LEVEL LOAN. A single payment loan where the gross indebtedness remains level for the term of the loan. Only one payment is due from the borrower, which is paid at maturity.

LEVEL-DECREASING LIFE COVERAGE. A coverage providing a death benefit which is level for a portion of the term and then decreases once the remaining indebtedness drops below a specified dollar amount.

LINE-OF-CREDIT. A pre-approved borrowing limit.

LINE-OF-CREDIT COVERAGE. Credit insurance provided on credit card borrowing or other pre-authorized loans.

LOAN. In this book, a debt instrument entered into by a consumer who receives cash or purchases a consumer product under an installment sales contract.

LOSS RATIO. The ratio of claims to premiums, normally expressed as a percentage.

LUMP SUM COVERAGE. A disability benefit which is paid in a single sum once the definition of disability is satisfied, usually specified as total and permanent disability.

MANDATORY DOWNWARD DEVIATION. A reduction in premium rates required by state regulation when the loss ratio for a case is less than the benchmark loss ratio.

MISSTATEMENT OF AGE CLAUSE. A clause in a credit insurance policy stating the insurer's liability if a borrower misstates his age, and his true age is over the maximum age of eligibility. Usually, the premium is returned, and any claim is denied on the basis that the insurance was never in force.

MONTHLY BENEFIT GROSS COVERAGE. A disability benefit that pays a monthly benefit equal to the monthly loan payment on closed-end loans or the minimum payment due on open-end loans, during the continued disability of the insured.

MONTHLY CESSIONS. A ceding statement provided by the direct writer to a reinsurer showing the cash transactions of the month.

MONTHLY OUTSTANDING BALANCE (MOB) COVERAGE. A credit life benefit that covers the outstanding balance of the loan on the date of death. Monthly premiums are charged for the insurance provided during the month, commonly used for open-end loans.

MORRIS PLAN BANKS. Banks formed during the first half of this century under a franchise arrangement conceived by Arthur J. Morris. These banks first enabled borrowers to obtain bank loans using their earning power as collateral.

MORTALITY DISCOUNTS. A discount which may be applied in calculating credit life premiums if the insurer does not refund the unearned life insurance premium on the death of an insured.

MUTUAL LIFE INSURANCE COMPANY. A life insurance company that is owned by its policyholders. Profits from operations are returned to policyholders as policyholder dividends.

NET INDEBTEDNESS. The amount due under a debt obligation at any time. This normally includes the outstanding principal and insurance premium amounts, plus any accrued interest since the last payment.

NET PAYOFF COVERAGE. Life insurance protection where the death benefit is equal to the net indebtedness of the loan.

NET WRITTEN PREMIUMS. Gross premiums collected from the insureds on new insurance less the premium refunds paid to those who terminate their coverage prior to maturity.

NON-CONTRIBUTORY PREMIUMS. Protection is provided to all borrowers and the cost is absorbed by the lender.

NON-CONTROLLED FOREIGN CORPORATION. A non-U.S. corporation not subject to U.S. taxation.

NON-MEDICAL UNDERWRITING. The decision to accept or reject a risk is based only on the height, weight, and occupation of the borrower, and two or three general health questions; i.e., a medical examination is not required.

NON-RESIDENT AGENT LICENSE. Many states permit an out-of-state resident to solicit insurance in the state with a special license.

NON-RETROACTIVE BENEFITS. Under a disability policy, benefits are not payable for the period the insured is disabled during the elimination period.

OPEN-END LOAN. A loan which may be increased at any time by additional borrowing. The term of the loan is not fixed. The borrower makes monthly payments for any amount from the lender's required minimum payment up to the outstanding balance of the loan.

OVERRIDE COMMISSIONS. Compensation paid to the general agent on the business he produces. It is the difference between the total compensation paid by the insurer and the amount received by the lender, normally expressed as a percentage of net written premiums.

PAID LOSS RATIO. The ratio of paid claims to collected (or net written) premiums, normally expressed as a percentage.

PAID-EARNED LOSS RATIO. The ratio of paid claims to earned premiums, normally expressed as a percentage.

PENETRATION RATE. The percentage of eligible borrowers who purchase credit insurance protection.

PHASE III TAX. A federal income tax imposed when amounts are transferred out of the Policyholder Surplus Account.

POLICYHOLDER DIVIDENDS. Mutual insurance companies are owned by the policyholders and the profits of the company belong to them. Profits are returned to the policyholder by the payment of annual dividends.

POLICYHOLDER SURPLUS ACCOUNT (PSA). A memorandum account for federal income tax purposes representing the portion of prior taxable income which has yet to be taxed; applies only to 1983 and prior earnings of certain life insurance companies.

PREEXISTING CONDITION. An impairment for which the insured has been treated prior to the effective date of the insurance.

PREMIUM REFUND. When insurance on a loan is terminated prior to the scheduled maturity date, the unearned portion of the original insurance premium is paid to the borrower, also called refunded premiums.

PREMIUMS. The consideration paid for the insurance.

PRESUMPTIVE TEST OF DISABILITY. A disability is presumed "total and permanent" if it continues for a specified number of continuous days, normally 90 or 180 days.

PRIMA FACIE RATES. Maximum rates adopted by each state which may be used by an insurer without further justification. The rates are judged "on its face" to produce reasonable benefits in relationship to the premium charged.

PRINCIPAL (OF A LOAN). The cash advanced to the borrower or the portion of the product's purchase price which is financed.

PRO RATA. There are two meanings. The most common meaning is "in equal proportions." The second meaning is "in proportion to."

PRODUCER. The corporate entity offering the credit insurance product to the consumer.

PRODUCTION CREDIT ASSOCIATION (PCA). An organization which provides loans to farmers.

PUBLIC BENEFIT RATE. A bank holding company has to demonstrate a "public benefit" in order for the Federal Reserve Board to permit it to reinsure the credit insurance it produced into a wholly-owned subsidiary. The requirement is normally met by charging a premium rate less than prima facie rates.

PYRAMIDING. The sale of a new credit insurance policy on a refinanced loan without cancellation of the old policy.

QUOTA SHARE COINSURANCE. A reinsurance arrangement where the risk, and all cash elements except the direct writer's administrative fees, are shared proportionately by the direct writer and the reinsurer, also called coinsurance.

RATE CHARTS. Charts used by the lending officer to calculate the amount of the credit insurance premiums.

RECAPTURE. On business which has been reinsured, the risk assumed by the reinsurer is terminated and again becomes the responsibility of the ceding company.

RECOVERABILITY. Under GAAP accounting, an asset cannot be established for unamortized deferred acquisition costs unless the expenses can be recovered from the future earnings of the block of business.

REFINANCED LOAN. A loan which is terminated prior to maturity and replaced by a new loan.

REFUNDED PREMIUMS (OR REFUNDS). When insurance on a loan is terminated prior to the scheduled maturity date, the unearned portion of the original insurance premium is paid to the borrower, also called premium refunds.

REINSURANCE. The transfer of risk from one insurance company, the direct writer, to a second insurance company, the reinsurer.

REINSURER. An insurance company which accepts the risk on insurance policies written by another insurance company.

REPORT AND REMITTANCE. Monthly reports are received from each account concerning the business issued and refunds made. Remittance for the gross premium minus refund premium, less any deducted compensation, is sent to the insurer along with the supporting documentation.

RESERVES. An estimate of the future claim payments which will be paid to claimants after an accounting date on business in force on the accounting date.

RESIDENT AGENT. An agent must be licensed in his state of residency.

RETENTION. In standard insurance terminology, the maximum risk an insurer will accept and retain on one life. In credit insurance, it also refers to the administrative fee charged by a direct writer under captive reinsurance arrangements.

RETROACTIVE BENEFITS. Under a disability policy, benefits are payable from the first day of disability if the claimant remains disabled for the required elimination period.

RETROACTIVE COMMISSIONS. Compensation paid to a general agent or producer which is paid only if his business is profitable, also called contingent commissions or experience refunds.

RETROCEDE. The transfer of risk from one reinsurer to a second reinsurer.

RETROCESSIONAIRE. A reinsurer who accepts the risk on insurance policies from another reinsurer.

RETURN COMMISSION. A commission paid by the general agent or producer to the insurer on any premium refunds, equal to the front compensation percentage times the amount of refunds.

REVERSE COMPETITION. A marketplace phenomenon where the characteristics of a marketplace for a product cause prices to rise to the highest level.

RIDER. An addition to an insurance policy that changes some provision of the policy, or provides additional benefits.

RULE OF 78. A mathematical formula for calculating the sum of the digits from one to any specified number (n). The formula is:

$$\frac{n \times (n + 1)}{2}$$

The sum of the digits from 1 to 12 equals {12 x (13) / 2} or 78, also called the "sum of the digits."

RULE OF ANTICIPATION. Unearned premiums calculated as the gross single premium for a policy having the same benefits and term as the unexpired coverage, also called the single premium method.

SCHEDULED INTEREST CHARGES. The interest charges anticipated over the scheduled loan term calculated at the inception date of the loan.

SECOND MORTGAGE LENDING. Loans secured by placing a second mortgage lien on the borrower's home.

SECURITY FUND. In a reinsurance transaction, a trust established by a reinsurer in a financial institution for the protection of the ceding company, also called a custodial trust. Establishment of the trust is usually required in order for the ceding insurer to take reserve credit in its statutory financial statement for business ceded to a non-admitted reinsurer.

SERIATIM. Amounts calculated on a policy-by-policy basis.

SERVICE FEES. In states that do not permit payment of commissions to financial institutions, service fees are designed to allow reimbursement of the actual cost of offering credit insurance products.

SHAREHOLDER SURPLUS ACCOUNT. A memorandum account for tax purposes representing the portion of prior taxable income of an insurance company which has been taxed but not paid to the stockholders.

SINGLE PAYMENT LOAN. A loan where the only payment due is on the maturity date of the loan, also called a level loan.

SINGLE PREMIUM DECREASING GROSS COVERAGE. A credit life benefit that insures the gross indebtedness, paid for with one premium which is charged at the inception of the coverage. The amount of insurance decreases each month by the amount of one monthly payment, commonly used for closed-end installment loans.

SINGLE PREMIUM DECREASING NET (OR NET PAYOFF) COVERAGE. A credit life benefit that insures the net indebtedness, paid for with one premium which is charged at the inception of the coverage. The benefit is equal to the scheduled outstanding net indebtedness, commonly used for variable rate installment loans and long-term loans.

SINGLE PREMIUM LEVEL GROSS COVERAGE. A credit life benefit that insures the gross indebtedness on a single payment loan, paid for with one premium which is charged at the inception of the coverage.

SINGLE PREMIUM METHOD. An unearned premium calculated as the gross single premium for a policy having the same benefits and term as the unexpired coverage, also called the Rule of Anticipation.

SIX AND SIX EXCLUSION. A disability is not covered if the insured becomes disabled from a preexisting condition within six months after the effective date, if any treatment for that preexisting condition occurred within the six months prior to the effective date.

STATUTORY ACCOUNTING PRINCIPLES (SAP). Accounting principles, embodied in state statutes, which are the basis of the statutory financial statements filed annually with the state insurance departments by all insurers.

STOCK LIFE INSURANCE COMPANY. A life insurance company owned and controlled by stockholders.

STOP LOSS REINSURANCE. A reinsurance arrangement where the ceding insurer's loss is limited to a specified dollar amount or to a specified loss ratio.

SUM OF THE DIGITS. A mathematical formula for calculating the sum of the digits from one to any specified number (n). The formula is:

$$\frac{n \times (n + 1)}{2}$$

The sum of digits from 1 to 12 equals {12 x (13) / 2} or 78, also called Rule of 78.

TERM OF COVERAGE. The length of time the insurance will be in force, normally expressed in months.

TERMINATION DATE. The last day insurance coverage is in force.

THIRD PARTY PAPER. A loan obligation that has been sold from the originator of the loan to another financial institution.

TOTAL AMOUNT ADVANCED. The principal plus the insurance premium on a loan.

TOTAL AND PERMANENT DISABILITY. A disability meeting the "any occupation" disability test which is expected to continue for life.

TRUNCATED LIFE COVERAGE. A credit life benefit with a term of insurance coverage that is shorter than the term of the loan, usually insuring the net indebtedness.

TRUNCATED DISABILITY COVERAGE. A credit disability benefit with a term of insurance coverage which is shorter than the term of the loan. Disability benefits terminate when the insurance coverage terminates.

UNDERWRITING PROFIT. Pre-tax profit on insurance business before investment income–premium income less claims and expenses.

UNEARNED GROSS PREMIUM. The portion of the original gross premium representing the value of the unexpired insurance.

UNKNOWN ACCUMULATION COVER. Reinsurance which protects the insurer if losses exceed a specified limit on any one life, provided the excess insurance resulted from a claimant's having two or more policies with the insurer.

UPWARD DEVIATION. A rate in excess of the state's prima facie rate. To obtain an upward deviation, an insurer must demonstrate that actual experience produced a loss ratio in excess of the benchmark loss ratio.

VARIABLE RATE LOAN. A loan which has an interest rate that may change during the term of the loan based on periodic evaluations of the current interest rates.

VARIABLE REFERENCE. Items which are left blank when a policy is filed with a state insurance department. The variable items include maximum terms, amounts, and ages.

VOLUNTARY TERMINATION. Repayment of a loan prior to the scheduled maturity date.

WAITING PERIOD. In a disability policy, the specified period a claimant must remain disabled before any benefits are payable, also called an elimination period.

WRITTEN REINSURANCE. A reinsurance arrangement where the risk and the cash elements of the transaction pass from the direct writer directly and immediately to the reinsurer in proportion to the coinsurance percentage.

WRITTEN PREMIUMS. Gross premiums collected from the insureds on new insurance less the premium refunds paid to those who terminate their coverage prior to maturity.

ABBREVIATIONS

APR	Annual Percentage Rate (of a loan)
BOP	Beginning of Period
BOQ	Beginning of Quarter
BOY	Beginning of Year
CCS	Claims in Course of Settlement
CET	Commissioners Extended Term (Mortality Table)
CFC	Controlled Foreign Corporation
CPA	Certified Public Accountant
CSG	Commissioners Standard Group (Mortality Table)
CSO	Commissioners Standard Ordinary (Mortality Table)
DAC	Deferred Acquisition Costs
DEFRA	Deficit Recovery Act of 1984
EOP	End of Period
EOQ	End of Quarter
EOY	End of Year
ERISA	Employee Retirement and Insurance Security Act of 1974
FRB	Federal Reserve Board
G-R PREMIUMS	Gross premiums collected minus premium refunds

GAAP	Generally Accepted Accounting Principles
GFO	Gain From Operations
IBNR	Incurred But Not Reported
ICOS	Claims in Course of Settlement
IRS	Internal Revenue Service
ITD	Inception to Date
LICTI	Life Insurance Company Taxable Income
MOB	Monthly Outstanding Balance
MSVR	Mandatory Securities Valuation Reserve
PCA	Production Credit Association
PSA	Policyholder Surplus Account
SAP	Statutory Accounting Principles
SEC	Securities and Exchange Commission
TEFRA	Tax Equity and Fiscal Responsibility Act of 1982
TII	Taxable Investment Income
YTD	Year-to-Date
14 E	Fourteen-Day Elimination (Non-retroactive) Coverage
14 NR	Fourteen-Day Elimination (Non-Retroactive) Coverage
14 R	Fourteen-Day Retroactive Coverage
30 E	Thirty-Day Elimination (Non-retroactive) Coverage
30 R	Thirty-Day Retroactive Coverage

ASSOCIATIONS

ACLI	American Council of Life Insurance
AICPA	American Institute of Certified Public Accountants
ALC	American Life Convention
CCIA	Consumer Credit Insurance Association
HIAA	Health Insurance Association of America
LIAA	Life Insurance Association of America
NAIC	National Association of Insurance Commissioners
NALC	National Association of Life Companies
NALU	National Association of Life Underwriters

APPENDIX B

ISSUES IN CREDIT INSURANCE

The credit insurance industry has grown because of consumer acceptance and understanding of a valuable social product. The growth was aided by regulations which evolved to control or eliminate earlier abuses arising in the competitive marketplace. While regulations have generally served to improve the industry, they present certain obstacles to innovation for an industry coping with a rapidly changing financial services environment. At the same time, some insurance regulators, consumer advocates, and industry personnel feel more regulatory changes are needed.

DIVERSITY IN STATE REGULATION

A major problem facing credit insurers is the lack of uniformity among state insurance laws and regulations. Many states have regulations patterned after earlier NAIC model regulations. These states have a history of few regulatory changes except for occasional reevaluation of prima facie rates, but a sizable minority of the states have deviated from the NAIC models in widely scattered directions. These variations include:

1. Restriction or elimination of gross life coverage,

2. Variation in upper age limits,

3. Variation in suicide provisions,
4. Required downward deviations,
5. Method for upward deviations, if permitted,
6. Variation in refund formulas and reserve requirements,
7. Diverse statistical reporting requirements,
8. Various agent licensing requirements and limitations,
9. Compensation and reinsurance restrictions, and
10. Definition of preexisting conditions.

A national insurer faces an ever-increasing amount of administrative complexity for a product that was once considered simple to administer. Insurance regulations are developed state-by-state reflecting regional attitudes and the attitude of the individuals who influence each state's regulatory environment. Many of the variations are reasonable when considered by themselves; there are different yet valid approaches to any situation. But stepping back and looking at the fifty-state results, the observer discovers a dismaying complexity, serving neither the insurers nor the consuming public. The most recent NAIC model regulation is virtually unused. Regulation at the federal level does not have support within the industry. The industry and the state regulators need a concerted effort to find as much common ground as possible as regulations are revised. The adoption of the 1985 NAIC experience reporting form as a part of the statutory annual statement was a significant positive achievement.

REGULATION OF PREMIUM RATES

The focus of regulatory activity has changed in the last twenty years. Earlier regulations focused on the product design and marketing activities. For the most part, state insurance regulations and consumer lending laws eliminated prior abuses. Recent activity has been more concerned with premium rates and compensation to lenders.

Traditionally, insurance regulation has focused on the policy form, licensing of agents, and solvency of insurers. Few life insurance products are governed by any form of rate regulation. With over 1,800 life insurers, insurance is a competitive marketplace, and free market forces are deemed sufficient to guarantee rate competition. Even where the marketplace has anti-competitive forces, either real or imagined, state regulations do not impose direct rate regulation. However, in credit insurance, policy forms may be disapproved if the benefits provided are not reasonable in relation to the premium charged. The difference is subtle but important. Numerous discussions and debates produced this approach.

This indirect rate regulation is based on the perception that *reverse competition* exists in the marketplace. Reverse competition means that the marketplace operates to produce the highest cost to the consumer rather than the lowest cost. Producers of credit insurance present the consumer with an "accept or reject" proposal. Producers choose the insurer whose products are offered to the consumer. One element in their choice of the insurer is the compensation to the producer. The insurer charging the highest rates can pay the highest compensation.

Although there are facts which support the perception, equally valid facts refute the allegation. The truth is somewhere in between. Credit insurance premium rates do not reflect a true free market pricing mechanism. At the same time, the pricing is not free from competitive pressures. With over 400 insurers marketing the product, the marketplace is competitive. Direct rate regulation for this product would be unjustified in our free market society.

Commentators who believe that reverse competition exists purport that compensation is the only factor in the lender's choice of insurer–lenders find the insurer willing to charge the highest rate. In support of this opinion, they cite evidence that most credit insurance is sold at the prima facie rates. Supporters of this notion also have the vague conception that the consumer is a captive buyer, entirely at the lender's mercy. They often cite penetration percentages demonstrating that a majority of those eligible to purchase the product do so.

These arguments ignore the historical development and the realities of the marketplace. The single premium life product was originally sold for $1.00/100/year–1% of the gross note for each year of coverage. It was simple. This rate continued to be the standard for forty years. During this period a significant portion of the market was captured by insurers charging substantially less than the dollar rate. During the same time period few, if any, insurers charged more than the dollar rate. Clearly, the marketplace did not force all rates down to the level of low-rate companies, but neither did it allow rates to rise to exorbitant levels.

Penetration rates shown in the 1973 Ohio University Study and the 1977 Federal Reserve Board Study demonstrated that the consumer is not a captive buyer. Both studies concluded that the consumer exercises a freedom of choice. Penetration rates for disability insurance are lower than for life insurance. The lender usually receives the same percentage of premium as compensation for both products. The lender would not discourage the sale of disability insurance with its higher premium. One reason for this lower penetration is that it costs more, and the consumer is concerned about price. The higher cost of disability insurance sometimes crosses the barrier where a portion of the consumers reject the insurance. Consumers elect to purchase the products, and price is a factor in their decision.

BENCHMARK LOSS RATIOS

A concern of the industry and insurance regulators has been the benchmark loss ratios enacted in many states. For many years, credit life insurance experience has failed to produce the benchmark loss ratio in many states. Disability insurance experience has often exceeded the benchmark loss ratio. An example is the 1977-79 Ohio experience. Based on prima facie rates, credit life insurance had a 34.1% loss ratio and disability insurance had a 73% loss ratio. This produced a composite loss ratio slightly in excess of the state's 50% benchmark.

The result is acceptable to many industry personnel and some regulators. Whether the benchmark should apply to life and disability separately, or whether the benchmark should apply to the combined experience is a question of equity. If a state has a 50% benchmark, does the allocation between life and disability matter? When disability insurance was introduced, producers were paid the same compensation rate as was paid on life insurance. During the last fifteen years, the result has been profits on credit life and losses on credit disability for the insurers. Insurers judge their business on a case basis. The experience of a producer is evaluated, and a decision made whether to continue the arrangement with the producer. Life and disability results are combined in the evaluation process. Insurers often view the two separate products as one line of business. In 1975, one regulator said, "We know the disability rates are too low, but the life rates are too high. The combined experience is reasonable compared to the benchmark. There will not be any change until someone gets upset enough to push for a change."

By 1980, a lot of people were upset. Writers of trade articles focused on the credit insurance industry and its low loss ratios in life insurance. Often, the writers did not study the disability side of the product. Politicians and consumer advocates had a field day.

The upshot is that states are beginning to measure the loss experience and apply the benchmark loss ratio separately to life and disability. On the whole, the insurers do not care how the benchmark is achieved, whether separately by line or on a composite basis. One should note that the states with the lowest prima facie life rates have some of the highest prima facie disability rates in the country–New York and California are good examples.

Credit life claim costs have shown a steady decline for thirty years. Available data indicates that the claim costs were around 40¢/100/year in the late 1940s. By mid-1960s the cost had dropped to 30¢/100/year. Current experience for certain segments is now at 20¢/100/year, although 22-25¢ is more representative of the range. These reductions were caused by improved overall mortality rates. In addition, the percentage of female insureds has dramatically increased because of an increase in the number of single women borrowers and joint coverage on two-income households.

The strict benchmark loss ratio approach varies the premium directly with changes in the claim costs. A 50% benchmark and a 30¢ claim cost produces a 60¢ rate. If claim costs drop to 20¢, the rate goes to 40¢. In pennies, the claim cost element appropriately drops 10¢, but so does the expense element. A reduction in claims does reduce the insurer's expense somewhat, but it has little impact on the producer's expenses. A rise in disability claim costs produces rates with more expense loading. The drop in life rates improves life penetration rates, while higher disability rates cause disability penetration rates to drop.

Life claim costs have reached the point where some deviation from a strict benchmark approach should be considered. Fifty percent seems a reasonable benchmark loss ratio. When this produces a 40¢ rate, the number of pennies as well as the percentage must be considered. A typical automobile loan produces a premium of only $200 ($10,000 gross note for 48 months at 50¢/100/year). The fixed cost of processing the transaction becomes an element in the overall reasonableness test. The total expense dollars are small.

Several states have recognized the problem and provided some relief. At the time of some rate changes, the expense margin in the old prima facie rates was retained. This same approach has been used for deviated rates–the loading in the prima facie rate is frozen. The deviation reflects the variation in the actual claim costs from expected claim costs. Some regulations specifically require or permit the Commissioner to consider insurer and producer expenses in setting prima facie rates.

This leads us into the question of an acceptable benchmark loss ratio. Industry acceptance of the 50% benchmark is widespread. Many insurers accept a higher loss ratio on disability, based on the logic that the higher claim costs generate more expense dollars. Benchmark loss ratios of 60% or less would be acceptable to the industry except for the loading aspect of life insurance. A 50% life benchmark with a disability benchmark of 50%-60% represents the majority of regulations and an acceptable position. Insurers have concern over higher benchmarks. On life insurance, many believe the expense element needs to be at least 25¢. It is difficult to get much more than a 50% loss ratio without endangering the marketplace. On the disability side, the concern is more pressing from a risk standpoint. Disability experience is volatile; loss ratios vary more on a case basis. Economic conditions affect disability losses–when involuntary unemployment rises, disability claim costs rise. A period of losses must be sustained in order to qualify for deviations, and deviations only solve the problem prospectively. Insurer solvency must remain a consideration in evaluating reasonable benchmark positions.

The ultimate test of reasonableness is the subjective judgment of those individuals making the decision. Facts are important, but this area of rating really revolves on personal preferences and the power to promote those preferences when regulations are written or revised.

JOINT LIFE RATES

Another controversial aspect of premium rating is the multiple that states apply to the single life rate to produce the joint life rate. General population and insured population mortality studies indicate that female mortality is about 60% of male mortality for the ages insured by credit insurance. Recent studies of credit insurance mortality indicate that joint life claim costs are about 175% of single life claim costs.

The distribution of males and females in the single life insured population is unknown, because sex of the insured is rarely coded in credit insurance data processing systems. Since the single life premium is the same for both sexes, insurers have never pushed for a coding of the insured's sex.

Before 1970, the proportion of males in the single life insured population is estimated to have exceeded 90%. There is a definite trend towards a higher percentage of females in the single life insured population. Estimates range from 20%-30%. Note that the expected multiple would be 160% if the single life insured population were all male. The multiple would be 200% if the single life insured population were 50% male and 50% female. The measured multiple of 175% seems reasonable. Where joint life experience has been measured over time, the trend in the multiple is definitely upward.

Given a claim cost multiple of 175%, the question of the prima facie rate multiple must be addressed. Some consumer advocates and regulators feel the gross premium should not include an additional expense margin beyond the dollars provided by a single life policy. They argue that there are few additional expenses associated with the sale or processing of a joint life policy. This position contradicts the benchmark loss ratio approach by requiring a higher loss ratio on joint policies compared to single life policies. It makes little sense from the standpoint of the promotion of the product by the producer. If the producer sells more coverage and a higher priced product, many believe they are entitled to more dollars of compensation. If producers receive the same dollars of compensation under both plans, they may be prone to sell only single life coverage. Disability insurance or some other auxiliary service may be promoted instead of joint life insurance. Traditionally, producers have received the same percentage of premium compensation on joint and single life plans. This approach is reasonable and has resulted in a steady growth in joint life coverage. If the benchmark loss ratio approach is maintained, there is little justification for a prima facie rate multiple different from the claim cost multiple.

MORTALITY AND INTEREST DISCOUNTS

Several states include interest and/or mortality discounts in the formula for calculating life insurance single premiums. No one disagrees that the insurer receives the single premium up front and earns investment income on the funds. It is simply another source of income, no different from premium dollars. The inclusion of these discounts adds significant complexity to the rate calculation. Verification of the accuracy of a premium calculation requires a sophisticated calculator or computer. There is no reason to introduce this complexity, particularly for loans under 60 months–loans which constitute the preponderance of credit life policy terms. Much of the business for loans over 60 months is already written on net payoff coverage. Here the complexity is not a real burden since a computer is already required for the premium calculation. For short-term business, a state which feels that an adjustment is needed to reflect the investment income element should consider the income source when the benchmark loss ratio is set. A benchmark can be set that recognizes the insurers' investment income and leaves the premium calculation for gross coverage in its simplified form.

COMPENSATION

Producer compensation often becomes the topic of department hearings and other rating discussions. Far too much time and effort are involved in trying to regulate something that is difficult, if not impossible, to regulate. Arguments for commission caps purport that they eliminate excessive compensation and protect insurer solvency.

There is no need to regulate the commission to protect the public. If the benchmark loss ratio is reasonable and prima facie rates are acceptable, the compensation will take care of itself. Regulating the compensation will not change the price to the consumer. Why bother? Many consumer advocates agree.

Commission caps may help protect insurer solvency, but nothing replaces prudent management. Other lines of insurance use conservatism in the statutory reserves to protect solvency. Credit insurance reserves are just as conservative and accomplish the objective.

The basic problem is that caps are not enforced or even enforceable in most cases. State insurance departments are simply understaffed to cope with the problem, and several states have ignored reported violations. In 1982, Ohio eliminated the commission limitations on this basis alone. A regulation cannot be written that creative marketing personnel cannot circumvent. Where there is a will, there is a way; it does not take long to find a loophole.

As a practical matter, violations of caps are found only in a small portion of the automobile dealer segment. Banks, finance companies, and credit unions are too highly regulated and sensitive to adverse public relations to take a risk. Automobile dealers are smaller, less subject to regulation, and may even be unaware of the legal requirements. Some insurers exploit the situation. Caps tend to restrict the reputable insurers and open the market to less honorable insurers. Without effective enforcement, the reasons for caps become meaningless.

Along these lines, some have tried to portray captive reinsurance as compensation and a method of avoiding commission caps. However, captive reinsurance began long before commission caps were introduced, and producers in states without caps on compensation are just as likely to form captives as producers in states with caps. A U.S. reinsurer using the standard types of reinsurance arrangements places itself in a risk-taking position, and underwriting profits from true risk-taking are not commission income. Excessive losses can eliminate all expense and profit margins and even create an underwriting loss. While a producer may hope that underwriting profits exceed a straight commission arrangement, the element of risk changes the nature of the profits from compensation to insurance underwriting profits.

GROSS VERSUS NET PAYOFF LIFE COVERAGE

Gross coverage still generates controversy. Although few consumers have ever objected to the purchase of the small additional amount of coverage, as compared to net payoff coverage, consumer advocates have consistently objected to the coverage as overinsurance. Gross coverage was standard for about sixty years, because the cost of refined net payoff calculations was not feasible within the constraints of this mass-marketed product. Computers changed the situation; however, the power and efficiency of the computer has not been used to cut costs and improve productivity. Instead, the power has been used to justify the introduction of refinements and complexities which were not possible in earlier times.

Net payoff coverage is a sound product, as is gross coverage. Net payoff just costs more to administer and is more difficult to understand. On long-term loans, the industry has moved voluntarily to net payoff coverage in most cases, because the premium outlay for gross coverage becomes a barrier to the purchase for loans with terms exceeding five years. Net payoff offers less coverage for a reduced premium dollar outlay. Since the total premium is much larger on long-term loans, there are more expense dollars to cover the higher administrative costs.

A major drawback of net payoff coverage is the problem of delinquent payments. Most consumers are unconcerned about the details of the product. They have the basic expectation that the coverage purchased will pay off the loan. Gross coverage achieves this goal and often provides a welcome additional payment to the second beneficiary. Net payoff coverage has a higher likelihood of leaving a portion of the debt unpaid if the consumer has become delinquent in payments. When a death claim is paid, a second beneficiary does not complain about having purchased some additional coverage under gross coverage plans, but the consumer's needs have not been met if the insurance does not meet the basic expectations held at the time of purchase.

New York and Maine require net payoff coverage on all credit insurance, while several states require net payoff coverage for loans in excess of 60 months. The latter position is in keeping with industry trends. Loans in excess of 60 months involve second mortgage loans or large purchases (recreational vehicles, mobile homes) where the magnitude and term of the transaction dictate the use of the net payoff approach. The requirement of net payoff coverage for loans under 60 months has little merit from the standpoint of the consumer or the industry.

NEW PRODUCTS

Several new plans have been introduced which face restrictive regulations, although there is little regulatory concern about the products. The current regulations, written before the need for these coverages arose, just do not contain the flexibility to permit all of the insurance products necessary for today's marketplace.

The rapid and dramatic rise in interest rates in the 1978-82 period spawned the variable interest rate consumer loan. The radical departure from historical interest rate levels created the need for financial institutions to protect themselves. At the same time, terms for consumer loans were lengthening. To compensate for these trends, some institutions began to offer consumer loans with a variable interest rate provision. If interest rates rose during the loan term, the number of payments was extended. Less common variations were to adjust the monthly payment or to have a balloon payment at the time the loan matured.

Credit insurance products faced difficulties. If interest rates dropped, there was no problem, since the estate received the excess. A rise in interest rates meant more coverage was needed, yet collection of an additional premium was not feasible from a public relations or an administrative point of view. An extension of the loan term leaves the insurance expiring before the loan matures.

An acceptable solution is to assume two extra payments when calculating the premium. Insurance coverage then is an amount equal to the original scheduled net indebtedness plus a maximum of two monthly payments, if needed, to extinguish the debt. A consumer with no delinquent payments has a margin of two months if interest rates rise. This margin is sufficient for most interest rate scenarios. Insurers are permitted by existing regulations to extend the policy term up to two months. While this approach does not solve all problems, it meets the needs of most consumers and is equitable to the insurer. Several states have accepted this approach.

Critical period disability insurance has been introduced and accepted in the marketplace. The majority of states have approved the coverage, but a minority would not accept the plan due to constraining regulations. Although the product is unlikely to dominate the disability market, there is no reason to prohibit its use. Critical period coverage is used primarily for long-term loans where full benefit coverage is prohibitively expensive. Sales material and policy forms must clearly inform the consumer of its limited benefits. This approach is the basis of practically all ordinary disability coverages, so there is no reason to expect a problem with consumer acceptance.

REFUND BASIS

A final issue is the basis for calculating refunds. While the issue has been around for years, recent product innovations have added emphasis to the debate. Rule of 78 refunds on gross coverage decreasing life insurance are so close to theoretical values that they are accepted. On net payoff coverage, the refund is an understatement of the actuarial refund, particularly at early durations. For level term life insurance, pro rata refunds are appropriate and are used universally.

For disability insurance, the Rule of 78 understates the actuarial refund. The true actuarial refund is unknown since the pattern of claim costs has not been established. The accurate refund is greater than the Rule of 78 unearned premium and less than the pro rata unearned premium. For critical period disability, the same uncertainty exists, but the accurate refund is closer to pro rata than to the Rule of 78, especially on long-term loans.

Arguments for the Rule of 78 include the wide acceptance and common use of the method, as well as a recognition that some surrender charge is reasonable. The method has a long history and is widely understood in financial institutions. Calculations can be done by hand if necessary. Verification is quick and easy. Computers are not so prevalent that an acceptable manual procedure should be easily dismissed. Credit transactions take place in thousands of lending institutions, and not all of them have the sophistication of the large lenders.

When recognized, the understatement is generally justified as a surrender charge. This is neither unusual nor uncommon in financial transactions. Purchasers of certificates of deposit are familiar with "the substantial penalty for early withdrawal." Loans may have a prepayment penalty. In the insurance field, whole life cash values recognize the write-off of unamortized initial expenses. The calculations of premium rates for whole life and term insurance reflect lapse rates and their associated cost. The magnitude of the understatement in credit insurance refunds is generally considered a reasonable surrender charge. Since the understatement declines as the period in force lengthens, the charge reflects the recovery of acquisition expenses and the cost of processing the refund. An insured with a gross coverage life and disability policy has an understatement only on the disability portion. Since disability insurance is rarely sold without life coverage, the understatement is a small percentage of the total refund.

The understatement on net payoff life coverage is justified by the cost of processing this coverage, particularly refunds. If the

Single Premium Method is used for refunds, the insurer and the lender must maintain the ability to calculate the refund for all interest rates used during the period of in force loans. This may mean retaining the ability to reproduce rates for as long as ten years. Given the range of interest rates over the last ten years, it is easy to visualize the complexity involved.

Finally, the calculation of loss ratio statistics reflects the surrender charge, and results in a depression of the loss ratio. In time, the depression will reduce rates. While some inequity is introduced between generations of borrowers, some of the current borrowers will return to borrow in the future.

APPENDIX C

PROPERTY AND CASUALTY PRODUCTS

Several specialty property and casualty products are debt-related and have traditionally been marketed along with credit life and disability products. Since life insurance companies are not permitted to market these products, a separate property and casualty insurance company is required. Several credit life insurance companies have affiliated property and casualty companies to provide these loan-related products. The insurance is all credit-related and tied to specific loan agreements.

INVOLUNTARY UNEMPLOYMENT INSURANCE

This product was introduced in the early 1970s to the consumer credit market. Comparable stand-alone casualty products are not sold to the general public. Since credit is extended based on the earning power of the borrower, the contingencies of death or disability were addressed years ago by credit insurers. Now coverage is available from a few insurers to cover the contingency of involuntary unemployment.

The reluctance of the insurance industry to provide this product stems from several key concerns. To be affordable, the policy must contain a substantial number of restrictions and exclusions to offset the obvious potential for anti-selection. Statistical data regarding unemployment rates to use in setting premium rates is only available from broad studies of the general population. There may be substantial differences within a particular insured population. Experience may also vary by geographical region, even with local variations. For these reasons, insurers have proceeded with caution. Results from existing business and market tests are mixed. The product has been successful in the United Kingdom for more than a decade, but its success in this country is not assured.

The coverage provided is *involuntary* unemployment protection. Excluded forms of unemployment are: voluntary job termination, retirement, disability, and discharge for willful misconduct or criminal acts. A major consideration is whether to cover strikes, lockouts, or other labor disputes. Covering these contingencies raises the cost of the insurance considerably.

Eligibility requirements are also restrictive. Self-employed individuals, independent contractors, and seasonal workers are not eligible. Policies generally require the purchaser to be employed at least thirty hours per week for six (or twelve) months prior to the effective date.

The coverage is usually written on a group policy concept. Unemployment insurance is primary coverage–benefits are paid in addition to any other unemployment benefits received by the insured. Benefits are similar to critical period disability benefits, so any plan of disability coverage is viable. Thirty-day retroactive coverage is the most common plan.

The benefit is the payment of any monthly loan payment due during the period of involuntary unemployment, provided the elimination period has been met. A typical plan provides for the payment of up to four (or six) monthly payments in any twelve-month period, subject to a maximum of twelve payments during the term of the policy. Benefits may be limited during the first sixty days after issue to avoid anti-selection problems. A claimant must be available for work to receive benefits. One typical requirement is that the claimant must meet the requirements for state unemployment benefits. Receipt of state unemployment benefits constitutes proof of loss. Unearned premium refunds are paid on single premium policies if the loan is paid off early, or if the maximum number of benefit payments is made.

Premiums are expressed in the usual manner for credit insurance. For single premium plans, the rates vary from $1.00/100/year to $2.50/100/year depending on the exclusions and the number of possible benefit payments. Rates on a monthly outstanding balance basis are $2.50 to $3.00 per $1,000 per month. Only Pennsylvania has adopted prima facie rates.

Most business to date has been written in conjunction with credit card programs and revolving charge accounts. The Banking Holding Company Act of 1984 permits an insurance agency subsidiary of a bank holding company to receive compensation for the sale of the product. In theory, it could be reinsured by a captive of a bank holding company, but a captive formed as a casualty insurer would be required.

The lack of permissive regulations has hindered the product's development. Coverage is not permitted under most credit life and disability insurance statutes or regulations, but it can be written as an inland marine or a miscellaneous casualty coverage by casualty companies. The states of Ohio and Washington have definitions of credit disability insurance which may permit this coverage as a disability product. In these states, a life insurance company could write the product. Another problem is agent licensing–an agent generally must qualify for a full property and casualty license. A limited license, as used in credit insurance, does not exist.

CREDIT PROPERTY INSURANCE

Credit property insurance has been written for many years. It is also known as personal property insurance or household goods insurance. Loans are often made for the purchase of specific household goods–furniture, appliances, televisions, and stereos. The item purchased is pledged as collateral for the loan. Credit property insurance protects the lender and the borrower from damage or destruction to the pledged collateral for the perils covered by the policy.

Coverage is written by finance companies and banks where the loan is for a specific purchase. The insurance is also sold when an item of personal property is pledged as the collateral for a loan. Retail stores offer credit property for installment sales contracts and for their revolving charge accounts.

Most credit property insurance is written on a *dual interest basis*–the coverage protects the outstanding balance of the loan plus the borrower's equity in the property. Coverage is usually based on the replacement cost of the property or a stated amount, generally the purchase price. If the property is destroyed anytime during the term of the loan, the lender receives a payment for the outstanding loan balance, and the insured receives a check for the difference between the coverage amount and the loan balance. Coverage is comparable to level term life insurance. In some states, the coverage is sold on an *actual cash value* basis. This basis provides coverage equal to the purchase price minus depreciation, similar to the household goods protection in most homeowners policies.

Single interest policies are also sold. Coverage is provided only to the extent of the outstanding balance of the loan, so the borrower does not receive any benefit beyond the cancellation of the loan. Coverage is comparable to decreasing term life insurance.

As with credit life and disability insurance, the lender may require insurance, but cannot insist that insurance be purchased from the lender. A borrower's alternative to the purchase of this coverage is to add a loss payable endorsement to his existing homeowners insurance. While the endorsement is fairly simple, borrowers like the convenience of purchasing the insurance when the loan is closed. Several characteristics of the prevailing products make the coverage a reasonable alternative to the coverage provided by most homeowners insurance:

1. Coverage is primary. Benefits are paid in addition to any other coverage.

2. Coverage is first-dollar. No deductibles are applied except for theft. This is a distinct advantage over

homeowners insurance. Consumers have accepted higher deductibles for homeowners insurance in recent years to reduce homeowners premiums.

3. Many policies provide All Risk Coverage. Coverage is provided for any damage, destruction or theft, except for a few standard exclusions (wear and tear, mechanical breakdown). Flood protection is included, along with other catastrophes which are often excluded from homeowners insurance.

4. Replacement cost is covered in most states. Many homeowners policies only cover the depreciated cost of the damaged property. In the event of damage, credit property policies provide the insurer with the option to repair the property.

5. The product is available without geographical restrictions or rating. Renters and homeowners in high risk urban areas have difficulty finding renters or homeowners insurance. Credit property is available to anyone qualifying for a loan.

Lenders are more likely to require property insurance than to require credit life and disability insurance. The requirement is a carryover from automobile lending and home mortgage lending. Physical damage coverage is required on automobile loans, and homeowners insurance is required for mortgage loans. Credit property insurance is a logical coverage when the property is the collateral for a loan. Once the property is destroyed or stolen, the borrower loses interest in making the loan payments.

Credit property insurance must be sold by a property and casualty insurer. It is generally classified as *inland marine insurance*. This unusual classification stems from the separation in the early 1900s between fire insurers and casualty insurers. Marine insurers could cover both perils and were virtually unrestricted. They began to cover a variety of risks classified as inland marine. State regulations eventually recognized insurance on personal property risks as a valid inland marine coverage, but a few states classify the coverage as fire insurance.

Credit property insurance is subject to regulation in the same manner as other inland marine coverages. The significant distinction of inland marine coverages is that they are generally exempt from rate regulation and rate filing. In other respects, inland marine is subject to the same regulation as other property and casualty products. Since the insurance is sold in conjunction with consumer lending, it is subject to the federal Truth-in-Lending Act.

Where the coverage is classified as fire insurance, its rates are regulated as other fire insurance products. Even where the rates are not regulated by insurance regulations, lending laws may regulate the rate a finance company or a retail merchant may charge, producing an indirect rate regulation on the insurance company. Rates vary by the types of perils covered, and by insurer. A typical rate for dual interest, all-risk coverage is a single premium rate of $3.00/100/year.

NON-FILING INSURANCE

When a lender makes a loan on the basis of collateral owned by the borrower, a common practice is to register the lender's security interest with the state or local authorities. This assures that the lender's security interest is recognized by the government, and can be enforced if the loan is not repaid. A filing fee is required which is usually paid by the borrower.

Recording of the security interest is a cumbersome process, and the administrative cost to the lender is significantly higher than the filing fee. To avoid this administrative cost, some lenders prefer to buy *non-filing insurance* from a property and casualty insurer rather than actually filing their security interest.

Also known as *Non-Recording Insurance,* this coverage is generally classified as surety. A claim is paid when the lender is unable to recover the property under a defaulted loan, provided the loss occurs because the lender did not file its security interest.

The premium charged for this coverage is always less than or equal to the state filing fee, so the insurance purchase has no financial effect on the borrower. It greatly simplifies administration for the lender.

Non-filing insurance is generally sold where household goods are taken as collateral for a loan. It is not sold with automobile loans, since automobiles must be registered anyway.

BLANKET SINGLE INTEREST INSURANCE

This insurance is designed to protect lenders in the event there is physical damage to the collateral of an installment loan. This may occur when an item of property is purchased on an installment sales contract or pledged as collateral for a loan. Borrowers are required to carry physical damage insurance. Proof of existence of insurance should be presented at the time the loan is made. Lenders are unprotected if the insurance is not placed or is allowed subsequently to lapse.

Under a *blanket single interest* policy, a lender purchases coverage for all loans secured by property as collateral. A premium is paid monthly by the lender to the insurer. Rates are a flat premium per loan or a monthly outstanding balance premium per $1,000 of loan balances. Premiums are usually absorbed by the lender as a part of loan fees, although a charge may be passed on to the borrower in some states.

Coverage protects only the lender. For benefits to be payable, the loan must be in default and the property repossessed. The insurance covers only the difference between the value of the property at repossession and the loan balance at the time of repossession. A benefit is paid only if the loss is caused by damage to the property. Perils covered are similar to standard collision and comprehensive coverage. The lender must require the borrower to carry insurance.

COLLATERAL PROTECTION INSURANCE

Individual Non-repossession Policies are a recent development to overcome the two problems of blanket single interest policies:

1. An insurance premium is charged on all loans, although most borrowers have insurance, and

2. Repossession is required.

The underlying coverage is the same as blanket single interest, but only uninsured loans are covered by the issuance of an individual policy. A periodic audit is made of the lender's loan files by the insurer or agent. If a loan is uninsured, a policy is mailed to the borrower. The borrower must provide evidence of insurance or accept the collateral protection insurance. If evidence of insurance is not provided, the collateral protection premium is added to the loan balance and financed.

Repossession is not required for benefits to be payable. This permits the property to be repaired and the loan to continue. The borrower is charged a deductible for each non-repossession claim.

APPENDIX D

PRIMA FACIE CREDIT LIFE RATES

	Ala.*	Alaska	Ariz.	Ark.*	Calif.*	Colo.
MOB/1000/MO SINGLE	1.54	0.92	0.68	1.15	0.62	1.08
MOB/1000/MO JOINT	2.31	1.53	1.02	1.66	0.86	1.67
SP/100/YEAR SINGLE DECR	1.00	0.60	0.44	0.75	0.40	0.70
SP/100/YEAR JOINT DECR	1.50	1.00	0.66	1.20	0.56	1.08
	Conn.	**Del.**	**D.C.**	**Fla.**	**Ga.**	**Hawaii**
MOB/1000/MO SINGLE	0.80	1.00	0.75	0.93	1.15	0.92
MOB/1000/MO JOINT	1.20	1.51	1.13	1.61	1.77	1.61
SP/100/YEAR SINGLE DECR	0.50	0.65	0.49	0.60	0.75	0.60
SP/100/YEAR JOINT DECR	0.75	0.98	0.74	1.04	1.15	1.05
	Idaho	**Ill.**	**Ind.**	**Iowa**	**Kans.**	**Ky.***
MOB/1000/MO SINGLE	0.96	1.00	1.00	1.00	1.00	0.93
MOB/1000/MO JOINT	1.44	1.60	1.67	1.67	1.66	1.40
SP/100/YEAR SINGLE DECR	0.60	0.65	0.65	0.65	0.65	0.60
SP/100/YEAR JOINT DECR	0.90	1.08	1.08	1.08	1.08	0.90
	La.	**Maine***	**Md.***	**Mass.**	**Mich.***	**Minn.**
MOB/1000/MO SINGLE	1.54	0.67	0.87	0.77	0.93	0.92
MOB/1000/MO JOINT	2.31	1.08	1.45	0.77	1.32	1.54
SP/100/YEAR SINGLE DECR	1.00	0.43	0.56	0.50	0.60	0.60
SP/100/YEAR JOINT DECR	1.50	0.71	0.94	0.50	0.85	1.00
	Miss.	**Mo.**	**Mont.**	**Nebr.**	**Nev.**	**N.H***
MOB/1000/MO SINGLE	1.39	0.92	0.95	0.98	1.04	0.66
MOB/1000/MO JOINT	2.41	1.38	1.45	1.63	1.60	1.03
SP/100/YEAR SINGLE DECR	0.90	0.60	0.60	0.64	0.65	0.42
SP/100/YEAR JOINT DECR	1.57	0.90	0.90	1.07	1.00	0.65

PRIMA FACIE CREDIT LIFE RATES

	N.J.*	N.Mex.	N.Y.*	N.C.	N. Dak.	Ohio
MOB/1000/MO SINGLE	0.69	1.00	0.60	1.23	1.17	0.80
MOB/1000/MO JOINT	1.04	1.54	0.96	2.05	1.95	1.40
SP/100/YEAR SINGLE DECR	0.44	0.65	0.39	0.80	0.75	0.52
SP/100/YEAR JOINT DECR	0.66	1.00	0.62	1.35	1.25	0.91
	Okla.	**Oreg.**	**Penn.***	**R.I.**	**S.C.**	**S.Dak.**
MOB/1000/MO SINGLE	1.31	0.85	0.78	0.72	1.30	0.95
MOB/1000/MO JOINT	1.97	1.28	1.37	1.15	2.17	1.42
SP/100/YEAR SINGLE DECR	0.85	0.55	0.50	0.46	0.85	0.60
SP/100/YEAR JOINT DECR	1.28	0.83	0.88	0.74	1.42	0.90
	Tenn.	**Tex***	**Utah**	**Vt.***	**Va.***	**Wash.**
MOB/1000/MO SINGLE	1.02	0.80	0.75	0.69	0.85	0.96
MOB/1000/MO JOINT	1.54	1.20	1.28	1.04	1.39	1.60
SP/100/YEAR SINGLE DECR	0.66	0.50	0.49	0.44	0.55	0.60
SP/100/YEAR JOINT DECR	1.00	0.75	0.83	0.66	0.90	1.00
	W.Va.*	**Wis.**	**Wyo.**	**P. R.**		
MOB/1000/MO SINGLE	1.00	0.62	0.77	1.15		
MOB/1000/MO JOINT	1.54	0.92	1.23			
SP/100/YEAR SINGLE DECR	0.65	0.40	0.50	0.75		
SP/100/YEAR JOINT DECR	1.00	0.60	0.80			

* SEE NOTES FOR ADDITIONAL DETAILS
MAY, 1986

NOTES ON PRIMA FACIE CREDIT LIFE RATES

The following notes should be read in conjunction with the rate table. Amounts on the chart have been rounded so they may not exactly match rate charts. In some cases, MOB or single premiums have been calculated based on actuarial equivalency of SP = MOB * (13/20) from the general formula SP = MOB * (n+1)/20 at n equals 12 months. Particular care should be used for states requiring creditor size discounts and interest discounts.

ALABAMA	Does not apply to small loans less than $300.
ARKANSAS	Permits accidental death benefit at 13¢/100/year.
CALIFORNIA	All classes except Class A - personal property broker.
KENTUCKY	Terms less than 121 months; permits dismemberment benefit for 5¢/100/year.
MAINE	Single premium rates include interest discount; only net payoff coverage allowed.
MARYLAND	Rates shown are for gross coverage of 48 months or less.
MASSACHUSETTS	Joint coverage is not sold since the rates are the same as single life.

MICHIGAN	Different rates promulgated by Department - being litigated.
NEW HAMPSHIRE	MOB rates are for banks and automobile dealers; single premiums include an interest discount.
NEW JERSEY	Rates shown apply to largest creditor size - $5 million of in force.
NEW YORK	Requires case rerating every two years; interest discounts and average loan size discounts applied; rates apply to business with no age limits - 10% discount required for age 65 limit, 5% for age 70. Net payoff only.
PENNSYLVANIA	Requires annual case rerating; single premiums are discounted for interest.
TEXAS	Rates are for terms of 60 months or less.
VERMONT	Rates are for largest creditor size - $5,000,000 of in force; single premiums are discounted for interest and mortality.
VIRGINIA	Single premiums are discounted for interest.
WEST VIRGINIA	Single premiums discounted for interest; permits dismemberment benefit at 5¢/100/year.

PRIMA FACIE CREDIT DISABILITY RATES
RATES PER $100 OF INITIAL GROSS INDEBTEDNESS

PLAN	TERM	ALA	ALAS	ARIZ	ARK	CAL*	COLO	CONN
14R	12	2.20	2.20	1.82	2.39	2.43	2.20	2.49
14R	24	3.00	3.00	2.57	3.16	3.43	3.00	2.96
14R	36	3.80	3.80	3.23	3.69	4.30	3.80	3.31
14R	48	4.30	4.30	3.79	4.13	5.05	4.30	3.65
14R	60	4.70	4.70	4.28	4.52	5.70	4.70	3.97
14R	120	6.70	-0-	5.89	-0-	7.86	6.70	-0-
7R	12	3.00	2.30	-0-	2.79	-0-	2.30	-0-
7R	36	5.00	3.90	-0-	4.30	-0-	3.90	-0-
7R	48	5.70	4.40	-0-	4.81	-0-	4.40	-0-
14E	12	1.40	1.40	1.51	1.89	2.01	1.40	1.71
14E	36	3.00	3.00	2.85	3.18	3.80	3.00	2.51
14E	48	3.50	3.50	3.38	3.62	4.51	3.50	2.84
30R	12	1.70	1.70	1.68	2.23	2.24	1.70	1.94
30R	36	3.30	3.30	2.96	3.55	3.94	3.30	2.79
30R	48	3.90	3.80	3.47	4.00	4.63	3.80	3.14
30E	12	0.80	0.80	1.10	1.48	1.47	0.80	1.14
30E	36	2.40	2.40	2.41	2.75	3.21	2.40	1.95
30E	48	3.00	2.90	2.93	3.18	3.91	2.90	2.28

PLAN	TERM	DEL	D.C.	FLA	GA	HAW	IDAHO	ILL
14R	12	2.20		2.20	2.20	2.61	2.20	2.20
14R	24	3.00		3.00	3.00	3.53	3.00	2.80
14R	36	3.80		3.80	3.80	4.18	3.80	3.35
14R	48	4.30		4.30	4.60	4.72	4.30	3.90
14R	60	4.70		4.70	5.40	5.19	4.70	4.50
14R	120	-0-		6.70	9.40	6.78	6.70	6.85
7R	12	3.00		3.00	3.00	2.62	-0-	3.00
7R	36	5.00		5.00	5.00	4.18	-0-	5.00
7R	48	5.70		5.70	6.00	4.72	-0-	5.70
14E	12	1.40		1.40	1.40	2.17	1.40	1.60
14E	36	3.00		3.00	3.00	3.72	3.00	2.70
14E	48	3.50		3.50	3.50	4.26	3.50	3.20
30R	12	1.70		1.70	1.70	1.72	1.70	1.80
30R	36	3.30		3.30	3.30	2.70	3.30	2.90
30R	48	3.80		3.90	3.90	3.01	3.80	3.40
30E	12	0.80		0.80	0.80	1.18	0.80	1.50
30E	36	2.40		2.40	2.40	2.12	2.40	2.10
30E	48	2.90		3.00	3.00	2.43	2.90	2.50

PLAN	TERM	IND	IA	KAN	KY	LA*	ME	MD
14R	12	2.20	2.20	2.20	2.69	2.20	2.29	2.00
14R	24	3.00	3.00	3.00	3.91	3.00	2.98	2.73
14R	36	3.80	3.80	3.80	5.14	3.80	3.52	3.45
14R	48	4.15	4.30	4.30	6.36	4.60	3.87	3.91
14R	60	4.50	4.70	4.70	7.58	5.40	4.14	4.27
14R	120	5.85	6.70	6.70	-0-	9.40	-0-	-0-
7R	12	-0-	-0-	-0-	-0-	3.50	-0-	2.73
7R	36	-0-	-0-	-0-	-0-	5.10	-0-	4.55
7R	48	-0-	-0-	-0-	-0-	5.60	-0-	5.18
14E	12	1.50	1.40	1.40	2.02	-0-	1.86	1.27
14E	36	2.90	3.00	3.00	3.85	-0-	2.74	2.73
14E	48	3.25	3.50	3.50	4.77	-0-	3.03	3.18
30R	12	1.50	1.70	1.70	1.22	1.70	2.07	1.55
30R	36	2.85	3.30	3.30	3.70	3.30	2.97	3.00
30R	48	3.20	3.80	3.80	4.89	4.10	3.30	3.45
30E	12	1.15	0.80	0.80	0.91	-0-	1.27	0.73
30E	36	2.05	2.40	2.40	2.77	-0-	2.12	2.18
30E	48	2.35	2.90	2.90	3.67	-0-	2.48	2.64

PLAN	TERM	MASS*	MICH	MINN	MISS	MO	MONT	NEB
14R	12	0.50	2.20	2.61	2.20	2.20	2.20	2.00
14R	24	1.00	3.00	3.12	3.00	3.00	3.00	2.70
14R	36	1.50	3.80	3.52	3.80	3.80	3.80	3.40
14R	48	2.00	4.30	3.88	4.30	4.30	4.30	3.85
14R	60	2.50	4.70	4.24	4.70	4.70	4.70	4.20
14R	120	-0-	6.30	-0-	-0-	6.70	-0-	-0-
7R	12	-0-	-0-	3.56	-0-	3.00	-0-	-0-
7R	36	-0-	-0-	4.63	-0-	5.00	-0-	-0-
7R	48	-0-	-0-	5.41	-0-	6.00	-0-	-0-
14E	12	0.50	1.50	1.86	1.50	1.40	1.40	1.35
14E	36	1.50	2.90	2.75	2.50	3.00	3.00	2.35
14E	48	2.00	3.25	3.11	3.00	3.50	3.50	2.70
30R	12	0.50	1.50	2.01	1.50	1.70	1.70	1.35
30R	36	1.50	2.85	2.94	2.50	3.30	3.30	2.35
30R	48	2.00	3.20	3.30	3.00	3.80	3.80	2.70
30E	12	0.50	1.15	1.24	1.00	0.80	0.80	0.75
30E	36	1.50	2.05	2.13	3.00	2.40	2.40	1.30
30E	48	2.00	2.35	2.49	4.00	2.90	2.90	1.50

PLAN	TERM	NEV	NH	NJ*	NM	NY	NC	N DAK
14R	12	2.20	2.03	2.00	2.35	3.15	2.42	2.61
14R	24	3.00	2.51	2.40	3.25	4.44	3.30	3.53
14R	36	3.80	2.82	2.65	4.15	5.34	4.18	4.18
14R	48	4.30	3.06	2.85	4.60	6.06	5.06	4.72
14R	60	4.70	3.26	3.11	5.00	6.64	5.94	5.19
14R	120	-0-	3.89	4.11	6.60	8.77	10.34	6.21
7R	12	-0-	-0-	-0-	-0-	-0-	3.00	-0-
7R	36	-0-	-0-	-0-	-0-	-0-	5.00	-0-
7R	48	-0-	-0-	-0-	-0-	-0-	6.00	-0-
14E	12	1.40	1.77	1.49	1.50	2.43	1.65	2.17
14E	36	3.00	2.56	2.13	3.25	3.62	2.75	3.72
14E	48	3.50	2.81	2.38	3.85	3.96	3.30	4.26
30R	12	1.70	1.66	1.50	1.85	2.58	1.65	1.72
30R	36	3.30	2.19	2.24	3.60	4.19	2.75	2.70
30R	48	3.80	2.44	2.47	4.15	4.69	3.30	3.01
30E	12	0.80	1.20	0.99	0.75	1.59	1.10	1.18
30E	36	2.40	1.67	1.66	2.25	2.59	2.20	2.12
30E	48	2.90	1.81	1.89	3.00	2.90	2.75	2.43

PLAN	TERM	OHIO	OKLA	OREG	PENN*	RI	SC	S DAK
14R	12	2.47	2.20	2.65	2.13	2.74	1.90	1.98
14R	24	3.12	3.00	3.74	2.71	3.26	2.60	2.70
14R	36	3.56	3.80	4.69	3.11	3.64	3.20	3.42
14R	48	3.93	4.60	5.51	3.45	4.02	3.80	3.87
14R	60	4.26	5.40	6.22	3.74	4.37	4.40	4.23
14R	120	5.57	9.40	8.57	4.92	-0-	7.10	6.03
7R	12	-0-	3.00	-0-	-0-	-0-	-0-	-0-
7R	36	-0-	5.00	-0-	-0-	-0-	-0-	-0-
7R	48	-0-	6.00	-0-	-0-	-0-	-0-	-0-
14E	12	2.16	1.40	2.19	1.85	1.88	-0-	1.26
14E	36	3.25	3.00	4.15	2.83	2.76	-0-	2.70
14E	48	3.62	3.50	4.92	3.16	3.12	-0-	3.15
30R	12	1.86	1.70	2.44	1.58	2.13	1.60	1.53
30R	36	2.54	3.30	4.30	2.19	3.07	2.70	2.97
30R	48	2.75	3.80	5.05	2.38	3.45	3.10	3.42
30E	12	1.31	0.80	1.60	1.18	1.25	-0-	0.72
30E	36	2.14	2.40	3.50	1.83	2.15	-0-	2.16
30E	48	2.35	2.90	4.27	2.02	2.51	-0-	2.61

PLAN	TERM	TENN	TEX	UTAH	VT*	VA	WASH	W VA
14R	12	2.39	2.23	1.84	2.37	2.20	2.20	2.65
14R	24	3.16	2.81	2.50	2.84	3.00	3.00	3.35
14R	36	3.69	3.21	3.16	3.20	3.80	3.80	4.00
14R	48	4.13	3.55	3.58	3.53	4.30	4.30	4.30
14R	60	4.52	3.84	3.96	3.85	4.70	4.70	4.55
14R	120	6.85	-0-	5.22	5.45	6.70	5.80	5.75
7R	12	2.79	2.54	1.88	-0-	-0-	-0-	-0-
7R	36	4.30	3.52	3.20	-0-	-0-	-0-	-0-
7R	48	4.81	3.86	3.62	-0-	-0-	-0-	-0-
14E	12	1.89	1.95	1.63	1.69	1.50	1.40	1.95
14E	36	3.18	2.93	2.95	2.50	2.50	3.00	3.45
14E	48	3.62	3.26	3.37	2.83	3.00	3.50	3.75
30R	12	2.23	1.68	1.75	1.83	1.70	1.70	2.15
30R	36	3.55	2.29	3.07	2.67	3.30	3.30	3.50
30R	48	4.00	2.48	3.49	3.00	4.10	3.80	3.80
30E	12	1.48	1.18	1.41	1.13	1.00	0.80	1.40
30E	36	2.75	1.93	2.73	1.94	3.00	2.40	2.80
30E	48	3.18	2.12	3.15	2.26	4.00	2.90	3.05

PLAN	TERM	WIS	WYO
14R	12	2.23	2.20
14R	24	2.81	3.00
14R	36	3.21	3.80
14R	48	3.55	4.30
14R	60	3.84	4.70
14R	120	-0-	5.80
7R	12	-0-	3.00
7R	36	-0-	5.00
7R	48	-0-	5.70
14E	12	1.95	1.40
14E	36	2.93	3.00
14E	48	3.26	3.50
30R	12	1.68	1.70
30R	36	2.29	3.30
30R	48	2.48	3.80
30E	12	1.18	0.80
30E	36	1.93	2.40
30E	48	2.12	2.90

MAY, 1986

NOTES ON PRIMA FACIE CREDIT DISABILITY RATES

The following notes should be read in conjunction with the rate tables. Amounts in the tables have been rounded so they may not exactly match rate charts. Rates are for plans excluding preexisting conditions.

CALIFORNIA	Rates shown are for banks and auto dealers.
LOUISIANA	Elimination coverage no longer available in state.
MASSACHUSETTS	Rate of .50/100/year is same for all plans, only 30E sold.
NEW JERSEY	14R rates cover preexisting.
NEW YORK	Case rerating every two years.
PENNSYLVANIA	Annual case rerating.
VERMONT	Subject to creditor size discounts up to 35%.

Except for the following states, rates are promulgated for each monthly term or are calculated by interpolation. The following states have banded term rates:

Florida, Illinois, Indiana, Kentucky, Louisiana, Michigan, Massachusetts, Nevada, New Mexico, South Dakota, West Virginia

LIMITATIONS ON AGENT'S AND CREDITOR'S COMMISSIONS

ARKANSAS	None. Regulation pending.
CALIFORNIA	Life - 35%; includes general agent commission of 7.5%. Disability 30% includes general agent commission of 6.25%. (Note: Commissions are on sliding scale depending on creditor's size).
COLORADO (a)	40%
GEORGIA	40%
ILLINOIS (b)	40%
INDIANA (c)	42.5%: 35% to creditor, 7.5% to field agents.
MAINE	10%
MARYLAND	36%: 32% to creditor, 4% to agents.
MASSACHUSETTS	20% (state-chartered banks).
MICHIGAN	40%
MISSISSIPPI	50%
MISSOURI (d)	40%
MONTANA	40% (unofficial)

NEBRASKA	33.33%
NEVADA	40%
NEW YORK	No agent commission limitation. Creditor can receive compensation for fees "only in such amounts as would reflect the reasonable cost of performing . . . services." Fees and commission schedules must be filed.
OKLAHOMA	40%
PENNSYLVANIA (e)	30% Life: 27% plus 3% to general agent; Disability: 21% plus 4% to general agent.
SOUTH DAKOTA	40%
TENNESSEE	40%
UTAH	50% Life; 40% Disability
WASHINGTON	40%
WYOMING	37.5%: 30% to creditor, 7.5% to general agent.

(a) A schedule of varying commission levels is set forth in Reg 74-V1.

(b) Recently the Department's authority to enforce the 40% commission limit was challenged in court. In an out-of-court settlement between the parties, the Department agreed to a 50% limitation.

(c) Where salaried persons are used in the sale, no payment of compensation shall be paid to any agent except the creditor.

(d) An insurer may compensate independent general agents, not affiliated directly or indirectly with the creditor, by paying commissions or compensation, but no such commission or compensation shall exceed 10% of the rates specified in addition to the agent's commission or compensation. Such independent general agent may not pass on any portion of such compensation to creditors or other agents or brokers.

(e) The creditor is prohibited from receiving directly or indirectly all or any portion of the additional 3% commission for credit life or 4% for credit disability insurance.

NOTE: In Ohio, a bank is limited to a service fee of 10% of the net premiums. Any amount in excess of 10% is presumed excessive and an unlawful inducement, but can be justified by evidence that the excess is reasonable in relation to the services performed. However, there is no limitation on experience refunds.

SOURCE: Consumer Credit Insurance Association Information Bulletin, Vol. XXXV, Number 44, dated May 13, 1986.

BENCHMARK LOSS RATIOS

ALABAMA	None
ALASKA	50% (3 AAC 28.330)
ARIZONA	50% Life; 60% Disability (Rule R4-14-604)
ARKANSAS	50% (Rule 12,Section 4)
CALIFORNIA	55% Life; 60% Disability
COLORADO	Regulation requires a ratio of claims incurred to earned premiums of 66 2/3% after subtracting from earned premiums creditor compensation not to exceed 40%. This equates to a 40% required loss ratio. (Colorado Code Section 10-10-109(2))
CONNECTICUT	None
DELAWARE	50% (Department Regulation 5, Section 1)
DISTRICT OF COLUMBIA	None
FLORIDA	60% (Insurance Rules, Chapter 4-7.09)
GEORGIA	50% (Chapter 120-2-27-03 / Life) 50% (Chapter 120-2-27-07 / Disability)

HAWAII	50% (Title 24, Section 435-7)
IDAHO	50% (Department Regulation 19, Section 4)
ILLINOIS	50% (Rule 9.5.02)
INDIANA	50% (Department Rule 5)
IOWA	50% (Iowa Code Section 509.17-2)
KANSAS	50% (Department Regulation 40-5-107)
KENTUCKY	None
LOUISIANA	None
MAINE	60% to 80% (Department Regulations, Chapter 220)
MARYLAND	55% (Department Regulation Number 09.30.51.05)
MASSACHUSETTS	None
MICHIGAN*	60% (Insurance Department Bulletin 85-09)
MINNESOTA	50% (Department Regulation 2760.0300)
MISSISSIPPI	50% (Senate Bill Number 2482)
MISSOURI	50% (Statutes, Section 385.070 (3))

MONTANA	50% (Department Regulation 6.6.1110)
NEBRASKA	50% (Insurance Department Letter of 10-2-67)
NEVADA	50% (Department Regulation Number 690A.140)
NEW HAMPSHIRE	50% Life; 60% Disability (Department Regulation 1201.10)
NEW JERSEY	None
NEW MEXICO	50% (Insurance Department Ruling 1-20-1-4)
NEW YORK	70% to 80% Life; 65% to 78% Disability
NORTH CAROLINA	None
NORTH DAKOTA	None
OHIO	50% Life; 60% Disability (Department Regulation 3901-1-14 (C) (1) (2) (8))
OKLAHOMA	50% (Department Regulation 69-8, Section 3)
OREGON	55% (Department Regulation 836-60-021)

PENNSYLVANIA	60% Life; 60% Life with permanent disability; 65% Disability (14-day retroactive and non-retroactive); 60% Disability (30-day retroactive and non-retroactive); (Department Number 31 Pennsylvania Code, Chapter 73.22)
RHODE ISLAND	60% (Regulation IX, Section 5)
SOUTH CAROLINA	50% (Regulation 69-11.1)
SOUTH DAKOTA	50% Life (Administrative Rule Sections 20:06:06:01); 50% Disability (Rule 69-11.1-D)
TENNESSEE	50% Single Life; 66 2/3% Joint Life (Department Regulation Chapter 0780-1-4:06(1))
TEXAS	50% Life; 60% Disability (Board Order Number 37495)
UTAH	50% Life; 55% Disability (Section 31A-22-801)
VERMONT*	50% Disability (Section 38.1-482.7: ld)
VIRGINIA	50% Disability (Virginia Code Section 38.1-482.7:1D)
WASHINGTON	50% (WAC 284-48-010)
WEST VIRGINIA	50% (Department Regulation 6.07)

WISCONSIN	50% Life (WAC, Insurance Section 3.25 (12)); Disability Loss Ratio determined by rate level (WAC, Ins. 3.25 (13))
WYOMING	None

* States with proposed credit insurance regulations still under consideration which contain a different benchmark.

Source: Consumer Credit Insurance Association Information Bulletin, Volume XXXV, No. 61, dated July 16, 1986.

MAXIMUM LIMITS FOR GROUP CREDIT LIFE

1. $20,000 Limit - One State:	Hawaii	
2. $25,000 Limit - Five States:	District of Columbia (e)	
	Kansas	South Dakota
	Massachusetts	Vermont (a)
3. $30,000 Limit - One State:	Florida	
4. $40,000 Limit - Three States:	Kentucky	Georgia
	New Jersey (e)	
5. $50,000 Limit - Eight States:	California (c)	Ohio
	Iowa	Puerto Rico
	Louisiana	Texas (d)
	Maryland	Virginia (b)
6. $55,000 Limit - One State:	New York (f)	
7. $60,000 Limit - One State:	Pennsylvania	
8. $75,000 Limit - One State:	Idaho	
9. $100,000 Limit - One State:	Oklahoma	

10. No Maximum Limit - Thirty-one States:

Alabama	Minnesota	Oregon
Alaska	Mississippi	Rhode Island
Arizona	Missouri	South Carolina
Arkansas	Montana	Tennessee
Colorado	Nebraska	Utah
Connecticut	Nevada	Virgin Islands
Delaware	New Hampshire	Washington
Illinois	New Mexico	West Virginia
Indiana	North Carolina	Wisconsin
Maine	North Dakota	Wyoming
Michigan (g)		

NOTES

a. $50,000 on loans secured by a mortgage on real estate.

b. Limit imposed by credit regulations for loans up to 10 years.

c. $100,000 on loans for agricultural, or horticultural purposes not exceeding 18 months or payable in one lump sum.

d. $100,000 limit on agricultural, horticultural or educational loans.

e. $75,000 on loans secured by real estate.

f. $110,000 on loans secured by real estate.

g. Section 4416 of the Michigan Code, which imposes a $20,000 limit, ruled unconstitutional.

SOURCE: Consumer Credit Insurance Association Information Bulletin, Volume XXXIV, Number 83, dated November 25, 1985.

BIBLIOGRAPHY

Alinco Life Ins. Co. v. U.S., 373 F. 2d 336, 19 AFTR 2d. 745 (Ct.Cl. 1967) Par. No. 1.09; 1.22.

American Bankers Association, Insurance Tools for Bank Instalment Credit Insurance Coverages and Their Uses (1956), New York.

American Bar Association, 1952 Conference on Personal Finance Law, "Credit Life and Disability Insurance, Should It Be Sold in Connection with Small Loans? A Digest of Professional Opinions."

American Council of Life Insurance, Life Insurance Fact Book 1984, Washington, D.C.

American Council of Life Insurance, Life Insurance Fact Book 1985, Washington, D.C.

American Industrial Bankers Association, An Explanation of the Consumer Credit Protection Act of 1968 and Regulation Z (1969), Washington, D.C.

Best's Review, "Leading Writers of Credit Life Insurance in 1984," September, 1985, pp. 80-82.

Black, Robert P. and Harless, Doris E., Nonbank Financial Institutions, (1969), The Federal Reserve Bank of Richmond.

Board of Governors of the Federal Reserve System, "A Study of Tie-Ins Between the Granting of Credit and Sales of Insurance of Bank Holding Companies and Other Lenders," Oct., 1978.

Buck, Harold L., "Credit Life, Health and Accident Insurance: Functions and Operations." *Ins. Law J.*, June, 1953, p. 394.

Cade, Arthur J., "The Fundamental Issues of Consumer Credit Insurance." *Ins. Law J.*, Feb., 1955, p. 76.

Chapman, John M., and Shay, Robert P. (eds.) The Consumer Finance Industry: Its Costs and Regulation, (1967), Columbia University Press.

Christy, Robert H., "Credit Life, Health and Accident Insurance and the Small-Loan Industry in Indiana." *Ins. Law J.*, July, 1954, p. 465.

Comment–"Consumer Credit Insurance." (From the Consumer Credit Symposium: Developments in the Law.) 55 *N.W.L. Rev.* 301 (1960).

Consumer Credit Conference, Proceedings of the Third Annual Conference, "Credit Life Insurance and Small Loans: Pro and Con," Washington University, St. Louis, Missouri.

Consumer Credit Insurance Association, What About Consumer Credit Insurance (1952), Chicago.

Consumer Life Ins. Co. v. U.S. 725, 39 AFTR 2d 77-1261 (1977), Par. No 1.22; 8.17; 14.07; 14.10; 20.09; 25.24.

Darr, J. Reuben, "An Appraisal of Consumer Credit Insurance Policies." *Ins. Law J.*, June, 1957, p. 348.

Davee, Koehnlein, Keating, "Report of a Survey of Opinion on Consumer Credit Insurance in the State of Colorado," January, 1953.

Department of Insurance, Commonwealth of Kentucky, "Report on Credit Insurance," April, 1967. Frankfort, Kentucky.

Department of Insurance, State of California, File No. RH-116, Vol. II, April 17-20, 1967.

Department of Insurance, State of California Ruling No. 170, File No. RH-134, "In the Matter of Proposed Adoption of Rules and Regulations of the Insurance Commissioner Relating to Credit Life and Credit Disability Insurance," April 20, 1970.

Department of Insurance, State of Wisconsin, Hearings on Credit Life Insurance and Credit Accident and Sickness Insurance, Oct. 27, 1966.

Dineen, Robert E., Proctor, Clifford R., and Gardner, Daniel H., Insurance and Government, the Economics and Principles of Insurance Supervision (1960), Univ. of Wis. Insurance Series, Vol. II, No. 1.

Doss, Richard B., "Credit Life Insurance," Unlocking the Future, The Credit Insurance Women's Manual 1959-60, Credit Women's Breakfast Clubs of North America (1959).

Doss, Richard B., "Rate Regulation in Consumer Credit Insurance." *Ins. Law J.* Jan., 1967, p. 9.

Downey, F. Roger, "Insurance Installment Credit Transactions." *Ins. Law J.* April, 1958, p. 256.

Dunbar, Edward A., "Credit Insurance--Used by Licensed Lenders." *Ins. Law J.*, July, 1956, p. 443.

Fagg, Gary, Chm., et. al. "Report of the Credit Insurance Industry Advisory Committee to the Pennsylvania Insurance Department, Oct. 8, 1982.

Foster, Kenneth C., "Credit Life and Health Insurance." The Life and Health Insurance Handbook pp. 385-98.

Gardner, David M., "The Development of Companies Writing Consumer Credit Insurance." *Ins. Law J.*, June, 1957, p. 358.

Gerber, Joseph S., "Credit Insurance–Yesterday, Today and Tomorrow."

Best's Review (Life/Health Edition) Part I–Vol. 70, No. 10, p. 18; Part II--Vol. 70, No. 11, p. 28.

Ghee, William K., "Group Creditors Insurance." Ph.D. dissertation, (1964) Graduate School of Arts and Sciences, (1964), University of Pennsylvania.

Gingery, Stanley W., "Extensions of Creditor Group Coverages." The Group Insurance Handbook, pp. 667-81.

Gingery, Stanley W., and Bittle, W. Harold, "A Study of Credit Life Insurance Mortality," Transactions of the Society of Actuaries, October, 1965.

Goudzwaard, Maurice B., "The Economic Impact of Credit Insurance Charges." *J. of Risk and Ins.*, p. 515, 1969.

Gregg, David W., (ed.) Life and Health Insurance Handbook, (2nd Ed. 1964) pp. 385-98.

Greider, Janice E., and Beadles, William T., Principles of Life Insurance (1964) Vol. I, pp. 348-53.

Hopengarten, Fred, "National Consumer Act: A Model Act for Consumer Protection." Quarterly Report (Conference on Personal Finance Law), Spring, 1970, p. 52.

Hubbard, Charles L., (ed.) Consumer Credit Life and Disability Insurance (1973), College of Business Administration, Ohio University.

Huber, Joel, Monograph No. 13 "Consumer Perception of Credit Insurance on Retail Purchases" (1978), Krannert School of Management, Purdue University.

Huber, Joel, "If Credit Insurance Has So Many Friends, How Could It Have So Many Enemies?" an address to the 29th annual meeting of the Consumer Credit Association, June, 1980.

Hutchinson, Stanley P., "Credit Insurance and the Richmond Resolution." A paper presented to the Association of Life Insurance Counsel, Dec. 12, 1967, New York.

Jacobson, James B., "An Analysis of Group Creditors Insurance." (1955), Prudential Insurance Co.

Juster, F. Tomas, and Shay, Robert P., Consumer Sensitivity to Finance Rates: An Empirical and Analytical Investigation, National Bureau of Economic Research, Occasional Paper (1964), New York.

Kedzie, Daniel P., Consumer Credit Insurance (1957), Richard D. Irwin, Inc.

Kedzie, Daniel P., "Present Status, Characteristics and Trends." *Ins. Law J.* June, 1957, p. 334.

Kisselgoff, Avram, Factors Affecting the Demand for Consumer Installment Sales Credit, Technical Paper 7 (1952), New York.

Landon, Kirk A., "The Economic Viability of Life and Disability Insurance for Small Loan Borrowers," Miami, Florida.

Landon, Kirk A., "Finance Companies' Insurance" an address to the North Carolina Association of Independent Finance Companies Convention, Jan. 13, 1948.

Larson, J. Edwin, "Problems of State Regulation." *Ins. Law J.*, June, 1957, p. 327.

"The Loan Shark Problem Today." 19 Law and Contemporary Problems, 1 (1954), a symposium.

Long, John D., and Gregg, Davis W., (eds.), Property and Liability Insurance Handbook (1965), pp. 644-48.

MacKeen, W. Duncan, Odell, W. H., "Ohio Study Prepared for Ohio Credit Life and Credit A & H Task Force", December, 1980.

McCauley, J. L., "Credit Insurance." *Ins. Law J.*, Oct., 1956, p. 665.

McNulty, Fred H., "Credit Transactions in Which Insurance is Used and Why." *Ins. Law J.*, June, 1957, p. 342.

Minick, John B., "Consumer Credit In Nebraska," Ph.D. dissertation, (1959), Department of Economics, University of Southern California.

Minick, John B., "A Study of Insured and Uninsured Consumer Debts of Deceased Borrowers in the Kansas City Area," Essay on Consumer Credit Insurance No. 1, Feb., 1957, Consumer Credit Association.

Moo, Paul R., Credit Insurance Revisited, A Reply to the NAIC Staff Study. March, 1972, Professor of Law, University of Notre Dame.

Mooney, William E. Sr., "Procurement of Life Insurance in the Lending Company and the Question of Usury." *Ins. Law J.*, Aug., 1967, p. 453.

Morris, Arthur J., "The Development of Consumer Credit in the United States," an address to the School of Consumer Banking at the University of Virginia, Aug. 11, 1952.

Morris, Arthur J., "The Origin of Credit Life Insurance." *Ins. Law J.*, June, 1957, p. 329.

Mors, Wallace P., "Small-Loan Laws and Credit Insurance." *Ins. Law J.*, Dec., 1954, p. 778.

Mors, Wallace P., "Consumer Installment Credit Insurance." *Ins. Law J.*, May, 1956, p. 299.

National Association of Insurance Commissioners, "A Background Study of the Regulation of Credit Life and Disability Insurance," November, 1970.

NAIC Proceedings, 1948 p. 187.

NAIC Proceedings, 1949 pp.19, 40, 537.

NAIC Proceedings, 1950 pp. 136, 550.

NAIC Proceedings, 1951 pp. 189, 482.

NAIC Proceedings, 1952 p. 764.

NAIC Proceedings, 1953 I: 184, II: 611.

NAIC Proceedings, 1954 I: 114, 118, II: 299.

NAIC Proceedings, 1955 I: 125, II: 340.

NAIC Proceedings, 1956 I: 154, II: 370.

NAIC Proceedings, 1957 I: 119, II: 369.

NAIC Proceedings, 1958 I: 103, II: 342.

NAIC Proceedings, 1959 I: 126, II: 507.

NAIC Proceedings, 1960 I: 180, II: 478.

NAIC Proceedings, 1961 I: 294, II: 507

NAIC Proceedings, 1962 I: 132, II: 450.

NAIC Proceedings, 1963 I: 174, II: 585.

NAIC Proceedings, 1964 I: 154, II: 469.

NAIC Proceedings, 1965 I: 133, II: 465.

NAIC Proceedings, 1966 I: 145, II: 401.

NAIC Proceedings, 1967 I: 133, II: 395.

NAIC Proceedings, 1969 I: 143, II: 499, 573.

NAIC Proceedings, 1969 I: 281, 211.

NAIC Proceedings, 1969 II: 768.

NAIC Proceedings, 1970 I: 328, 331, 334; IIB: 1134, 1135.

NAIC Proceedings, 1971 I: 249, II: 422.

NAIC Proceedings, 1972 I: 580, II: 421.

NAIC Proceedings, 1973 I: 266, II: 480.

NAIC Proceedings, 1974 I: 427, II: 500.

NAIC Proceedings, 1975 I: 615, II: 393.

NAIC Proceedings, 1976 I: 512, II: 468.

NAIC Proceedings, 1977 I: 414, II: 468.

NAIC Proceedings, 1978 I: 376, II: 348.

NAIC Proceedings, 1979 I: 449, II: 408.

NAIC Proceedings, 1980 I: 472, II: 641

NAIC Proceedings, 1981 I: 488, II: 641.

NAIC Proceedings, 1983 II: 806.

NAIC Proceedings, 1984 I: 729, II: 824.

NAIC Proceedings, 1985 I: 808, II: 704

Peters, Philip H., "How Should Credit Life Insurance Be Regulated?" *Ins. Law J.* Aug., 1958, p. 529.

Public Law 15; The McCarran-Ferguson Act; U.S. Statutes at Large (79th Cong., 1st Sess.) Chap. 20.

Quackenbush, R. Donald, "Credit Insurance: Benefit or Burden?" Credit, National Consumer Finance Association, Washington, D.C.

Quackenbush, R. Donald, "Credit Insurance--Teapot on the Front Burner." *Best's Review*, (Life/Health Edition) April, 1969, p. 30.

Sanderson, R. Reid, "Legal Situations in Credit Insurance." *Ins. Law J.* June, 1957, p. 372.

Subcommittee on Antitrust and Monopoly of the Committee on the Judiciary of the United States Senate. The Consumer Credit Industry (Credit Insurance) (1967), (90th Cong. 1st Sess.), Vols. 1, 2, 3, and 3A.

Subcommittee on Banking and Currency, Senate on S. Res. S2755 of the Senate Committee on Banking and Currency, Consumer Credit Labeling Bill, U.S. Congress, (86th Cong. 2nd Sess).

Subcommittee on Financial Institutions of the Committee on Banking and Currency of the United States Senate, Hearings on S. 1754 (Consumer Credit Insurance Act.) (1969), (91st Cong., 1st Sess).

Subcommittee on General Credit Control and Debt Management of the Joint Economic Committee, U.S. Congress, (82nd Cong., 1st Sess). Part I, 1952.

Tucker, Keith A., Van Mieghem, Dennis P., Federal Taxation of Insurance Companies, (1982), Prentice Hall.

Vernon, David H., "Regulated Credit Life and Disability Insurance and the Small Loan." *29 N.Y. University Law Rev.* May, 1954, p. 1098.

Western Diversified Life Ins. Co. v. U.S., 49 AFTR 2d 82-353 (Ct. Cl. 1981 Par. No. 1.22; 2.23; 8.13.

Whittaker, Edmund B., "Group Creditors Life Insurance." *The J. of the Amer. Soc. of Chartered Life Underwriters,* June, 1953, p. 219.

Index

ABOUT THE AUTHOR

Gary T. Fagg is a Fellow in the Society of Actuaries and a member of the American Academy of Actuaries. He has been actively involved in the insurance industry for over 16 years. As Senior Vice President of The Credit Life Companies of Springfield, Ohio, he serves as an internal consultant relating to financial analysis, measurement of loss experience and profitability, captive and financial reinsurance transactions, and corporate strategy.

Mr. Fagg also provides actuarial consulting to captives and other credit insurers and reinsurers through Credit Life's subsidiary, CLICO Management, Inc. This includes: actuarial certification of financial statements, analysis of loss experience, pricing of excess reinsurance business, brokerage of credit reinsurance arrangements, and presentation of seminars on topics in credit insurance.

In addition, he serves as Director and General Manager of Sterling Life Insurance Company, an Arizona subsidiary of Credit Life, a director of Bankers Financial Life Insurance Company, and is president and owner of Dune Life Insurance Company, an Arizona reinsurance company.

Mr. Fagg currently serves on the CCIA Actuarial Subcommittee, the NAIC Industry Advisory Committee on Credit Insurance and the Society of Actuaries Special Study Committee on Credit Insurance. Previously, he served on the Ohio Credit Insurance Industry Advisory Committee and chaired the Pennsylvania Industry Advisory Committee on Credit Insurance.

Questions, inquiries, or comments about this book or credit insurance in general may be directed to the author at:

Sterling Life Insurance Company
11801 N. Tatum Blvd., Suite 140
Phoenix, AZ 85028
(602) 953-1564

